NON-LI FOOTBALL TABLES 1889-2020

EDITOR
Michael Robinson

British Library Cataloguing in Publication Data
A catalogue record for this book is available from the British Library

ISBN: 978-1-86223-425-3

Copyright © 2020   Soccer Books Limited, 72 St. Peters Avenue, Cleethorpes, DN35 8HU, United Kingdom   (01472 696226)

All rights are reserved. No part of this publication may be reproduced, stored into a retrieval system or transmitted, in any form or by any means, electronic, mechanical, photocopying, recording, or otherwise, without the prior written permission of Soccer Books Limited.

Printed in the UK by Severn

FOREWORD

Following the unprecedented impact of the Covid-19 pandemic, the 2019/2020 season in the Southern League, Northern Premier League and Isthmian League were suspended during mid-March 2020 when all sporting events across the country were postponed on public health grounds. It quickly became clear that it would be impossible to complete the season so all three Leagues were formally abandoned on 26th March 2020, with all results being expunged and no promotion or relegation taking place to, from, or within the competitions.

This decision was not universally supported and, on 30th March 2020, sixty-six non-league clubs sent an open letter to the Football Association requesting that this decision be reconsidered. However, a subsequent legal appeal was dismissed during June 2020 so the decision stood. In this book, although the season's results have been expunged, we include the final tables as they stood at the time play was abandoned.

We are once again publishing a separate book for the National League (formerly the Football Conference) from 1979-2020 which includes every result and final table together with promotion play-off results and comprehensive notes detailing changes in membership over the years.

This 19th edition of our Non-League Tables book includes the three Leagues which feed into the National League along with comprehensive explanatory notes for the Southern League (up to 1979 so far), in addition to those already included for the Northern Premier League and Isthmian League.

As usual, we have not used sponsored names other than in an indicative way on the cover and in the contents page.

In addition we have once more included the briefly-lived Football Alliance which became, effectively, the 2nd Division of the Football League in 1892 as well as its precursor, the Football Combination, which collapsed after less than one season. Also included for the first time are tables for the Staffordshire County Senior League from formation in 2005 to 2020.

We are indebted to Mick Blakeman for providing the tables for the Staffordshire County Senior League as well as the detailed information about historical changes to the membership of the various leagues. This includes some minor corrections discovered in the Southern League tables.

CONTENTS

FOOTBALL ALLIANCE 1889-1892
(including the Football Combination 1888-1889)

The formation of the Football League in 1888 caused a problem for those other leading clubs who had not been included. If the 12 top clubs had 22 fixed dates for Football League games, then they would have few free dates left to play the high-profile friendlies that before then, had been the best source of revenue for those other clubs.

The only logical response for those other clubs was to form their own competition and at a meeting held at the Royal Hotel, Crewe on 27th April 1888, the Football Combination was formed.

The Combination though did not adopt the same format as the League. Rather than have 12 clubs who all fielded their strongest side and played each other on a home and away basis on dates agreed before the start of the season, the Combination adopted a far more flexible approach.

There were 20 Combination clubs, who did not all play each other but instead, each of the 20 chose which others amongst the 20 they wanted to play, on dates to be arranged between the two clubs, with each playing a minimum of 8 games. This meant that some clubs played only a handful of games while others played considerably more.

Combination league tables were published very rarely and when two Combination members played each other, it was not always clear whether or not the game counted towards the Combination.

This all meant that Combination games were barely distinguishable from ordinary friendly games and so it was hardly surprising that the Football Combination collapsed in disarray and was formally abandoned on 5th April 1889.

The 20 clubs who formed the Football Combination were: Birmingham St. George, Blackburn Olympic, Bootle, Burslem Port Vale, Crewe Alexandra, Darwen, Derby Junction, Derby Midland, Gainsborough Trinity, Grimsby Town, Halliwell, Leek, Lincoln City, Long Eaton Rangers, Newton Heath, Northwich Victoria, Notts Rangers, Small Heath, South Shore and Walsall Town Swifts.

Given all the difficulties in establishing which were, and which were not, Combination games and the scarcity of published tables, the final positions of clubs cannot be absolutely certain but based on research carried out, it is believed that the table below shows the records of clubs when the Combination was disbanded:

FOOTBALL COMBINATION 1888-89

	P	W	D	L	F	A	P	Pts/game
Newton Heath	14	10	2	2	34	15	22	1.571
Northwich Victoria	9	6	1	2	19	11	13	1.444
Bootle	15	9	3	3	33	22	21	1.400
Grimsby Town	5	3	1	1	20	8	7	1.400
Small Heath	11	6	3	2	24	17	15	1.364
Notts Rangers	17	11	1	5	48	38	23	1.353
Walsall Town Swifts	17	10	2	5	38	35	22	1.294
Long Eaton Rangers	17	8	4	5	37	30	20	1.176
Birmingham St. George	14	5	5	4	32	22	15	1.071
Darwen	14	5	4	5	33	30	14	1.000
Halliwell	11	5	1	5	31	26	11	1.000
Crewe Alexandra	16	5	4	7	36	33	14	0.875
South Shore	14	5	2	7	26	34	12	0.857
Lincoln City	12	4	2	6	12	22	10	0.833
Derby Midland	16	4	5	7	20	29	13	0.813
Burslem Port Vale	25	6	4	15	38	56	16	0.640
Derby Junction	13	2	4	7	24	27	8	0.615
Gainsborough Trinity	10	1	3	6	14	30	5	0.500
Leek	15	3	1	11	19	43	7	0.467
Blackburn Olympic	5	0	2	3	3	13	2	0.400

FOOTBALL ALLIANCE 1889-1992

Following the collapse of the Football Combination, the committee summoned members to a meeting in Crewe in mid- April 1889 with the intention of forming a "second league". The meeting though was in two parts. Although several clubs were summoned to attend at 4.00 pm, a separate clique had met an hour earlier to settle everything and had decided to form an exact copy of the successful Football League. The 12 who had been self-selected were: – Birmingham St. George's, Bootle, Burslem Port Vale, Crewe Alexandra, Darwen, Derby Midland, Newton Heath, Notts Rangers, Sheffield Wednesday, Small Heath Alliance, South Shore and Walsall Town Swifts. Sheffield Wednesday were the only "second league" member not to have been playing in the Football Combination. Halliwell had been excluded principally because they had alienated some other clubs because of their refusal to play return games, particularly at Birmingham St. George's.

However, Burslem Port Vale and South Shore did not join the "second league" (titled the Football Alliance from late in May) and reverted to a programme of cup-ties and friendlies. Meanwhile, fragile finances convinced Derby Midland and Notts Rangers that their futures would be better served in the more localised Midland League and so applied to that competition instead.

That meant there were 4 vacancies to fill. Both Sunderland and Sunderland Albion were accepted for two of them, while Nottingham Forest withdrew from the Midland League to fill the third, followed soon afterwards by Grimsby Town. However, Sunderland withdrew at the end of June because they thought that their interests would clash with local rivals Sunderland Albion. Long Eaton Rangers were elected to replace them.

Of the remaining Combination members who were not selected for the Football Alliance, Derby Junction, Gainsborough Trinity, Leek and Lincoln City all became founder members of the Midland League while Halliwell and Northwich Victoria played just friendlies and cup-ties in 1889-90. Blackburn Olympic disbanded in the summer of 1889.

1889-90

Sheffield Wednesday	22	15	2	5	70	39	32
Bootle	22	13	2	7	66	39	28
Sunderland Albion	22	13	2	7	64	39	28
Grimsby Town	22	12	2	8	58	47	26
Crewe Alexandra	22	11	2	9	68	59	24
Darwen	22	10	2	10	70	75	22
Birmingham St. George	22	9	3	10	62	49	21
Newton Heath	22	9	2	11	40	44	20
Walsall Town Swifts	22	8	3	11	44	59	19
Small Heath	22	6	5	11	44	67	17
Nottingham Forest	22	6	5	11	31	62	17
Long Eaton Rangers	22	4	2	16	35	73	10

Birmingham St. George's 5-3 home win against Sunderland Albion 5-3 was declared void and Birmingham St. George refused to rearrange the game so it was awarded to Sunderland Albion. The clubs' records have been adjusted accordingly in the table above.

Stoke joined after losing their place in the Football League. Long Eaton Rangers were not re-elected and later joined the Midland League.

1890-91

Stoke	22	13	7	2	57	39	33
Sunderland Albion	22	12	6	4	69	28	30
Grimsby Town	22	11	5	6	43	27	27
Birmingham St. George	22	12	2	8	64	62	26
Nottingham Forest	22	9	7	6	66	39	23
Darwen	22	10	3	9	64	59	23
Walsall Town Swifts	22	9	3	10	34	61	21
Crewe Alexandra	22	8	4	10	59	67	20
Newton Heath	22	7	3	12	37	55	17
Small Heath	22	7	2	13	58	66	16
Bootle	22	3	7	12	40	61	13
Sheffield Wednesday	22	4	5	13	39	66	13

Nottingham Forest had 2 points deducted for fielding an unregistered player.

Stoke and Darwen were both elected to the Football League and Sunderland Albion left but continued in the Northern League. Burton Swifts joined from The Combination (a new league formed in 1890), Lincoln City joined from the Midland League and Ardwick joined, having not previously played in a league.

1891-92

Nottingham Forest	22	14	5	3	59	22	33
Newton Heath	22	12	7	3	69	33	31
Small Heath	22	12	5	5	53	36	29
Sheffield Wednesday	22	12	4	6	65	35	28
Burton Swifts	22	12	2	8	54	52	26
Crewe Alexandra	22	7	4	11	44	49	18
Ardwick	22	6	6	10	39	51	18
Bootle	22	8	2	12	42	64	18
Lincoln City	22	6	5	11	37	65	17
Grimsby Town	22	6	6	10	40	39	16
Walsall Town Swifts	22	6	3	13	33	59	15
Birmingham St. George	22	5	3	14	34	64	11

Grimsby Town and Birmingham St. George each had 2 points deducted for fielding ineligible players.

At the end of the season, the Football League expanded from one division to two. Newton Heath, Nottingham Forest and Sheffield Wednesday were elected to an expanded Division One and the remaining Football Alliance clubs became founder members of Division Two, with the exception of Birmingham St. George who disbanded. The Football Alliance then closed down.

SOUTHERN LEAGUE NOTES

FORMATION

The success of the Football League generated discussions all over the country about further leagues and London was no exception. The idea of a Southern League was first mooted in February 1889 and the pressure grew until the London F.A. convened a meeting to discuss it, held at the Salutation Tavern in Newgate Street on 13th March 1890. London Caledonians and Millwall Athletic backed the idea but the influential Old Boys clubs strongly opposed it and it was their view that prevailed.

The opposition of the London F.A. meant that the idea was not formally raised again until 24th February 1892 when another meeting was held at the instigation of Millwall Athletic and of Royal Arsenal, who in the summer of 1891 had become the first London club to turn professional. Around 30 clubs attended the meeting at Oliphant's Temperance Restaurant, St. Bride's Street, Ludgate Circus* and a ballot was held that resulted in 12 clubs being selected to form the new league – Chatham, Chiswick Park, Crouch End, Great Marlow, Ilford, Luton Town, Millwall Athletic, Old St. Marks', Reading, Royal Arsenal, Swindon Town and West Herts. A further 12 clubs were chosen to form a second tier Southern Alliance which did eventually go ahead, albeit after a number of membership changes, but it only lasted for one season.

Despite promises made on 24th February, Chatham, Chiswick Park, Crouch End, Great Marlow and Reading all soon withdrew because of the distances to be travelled and while Chesham had been added as a replacement, Royal Arsenal also later withdrew. They were comfortably the south's strongest club and wished to field their reserve side but this was unpopular with the other members. When Ilford and Old St. Marks' also withdrew, reducing membership to 5, the idea was again dropped.

It was another two years before Millwall Athletic again raised the subject. On 12th January 1894, they invited 6 other clubs – 2nd Scots Guards, Chatham, Clapton, Ilford, Luton Town and Reading – to a private meeting at the Billiter Coffee Rooms, Fishmonger Alley (now known as Cullum Street), just off Fenchurch Street, a venue that was at the time the head-quarters of Clapton F.C.. A further 7 clubs – Casuals, Crouch End, Crusaders, Old Carthusians, Old Westminsters, Royal Ordnance Factories and Swindon Town were invited to another meeting a week later but only the two last named accepted the invitation. The original seven, plus these two, thus formed a league of 9 clubs.

Arsenal, by then members of the Football League and known as Woolwich Arsenal, were also involved in discussions but these again foundered because they wished to field their reserve side which was not acceptable to the rest. When 2nd Scots Guards withdrew in late March, Southampton St. Mary's accepted an invitation to replace them, so finalising the 9-club membership.

Once fixtures had been agreed, some of those excluded considered the formation of a Second Division and a meeting was held at Billiter's on 23rd May to agree its composition. 15 clubs had been approached but St. Albans Town, Tottenham Hotspur, West Herts, Wolverton and Woodville were unable to enter. Of the remaining 10 – Chesham, Maidenhead, New Brompton, Old St. Luke's, Old St. Stephen's, Polytechnic, Sheppey United, Uxbridge, West Croydon and Woodford – 8 were chosen with Old St. Luke's and West Croydon being the two left out.

However, Polytechnic were forced to withdraw at the end of June when Woolwich Polytechnic itself was closed down because of financial losses and in early August, Woodford also withdrew, having lost their ground to building. That left the division with 6 members but Mr. Nat Whittaker, the newly appointed secretary of the league, was also a member of the Bromley F.C. committee and he arranged for Bromley to become the 7th founder member of the Second Division.

* Previous histories of the Southern League state that this meeting was held at nearby Anderton's Hotel in Fleet Street. Although Anderton's Hotel often hosted football meetings, all contemporary newspapers giving the precise location state that this particular meeting was held at Oliphant's Restaurant.

Southern League changes 1894-2020

1895 – Test matches (All played on 27th April)

Royal Ordnance Factories vs Old St. Stephen's   3-1   (played at Millwall Athletic)
Clapton vs Sheppey United   5-1   (played at Tottenham Hotspur)
Swindon Town vs New Brompton   1-5   (played at Reading)

As a result of the test matches, New Brompton were promoted to Division One but it was decided to increase the division to 10 clubs and so Swindon Town were not relegated.

Guildford joined Division Two while continuing to play in the West Surrey League. 1st Scots Guards, Windsor & Eton and Wolverton L&NWR also joined Division Two.

1895 – Test matches (All played on 25th April)

Clapton vs 1st Scots Guards   4-1   (played at Vicarage Ground, Barking Woodville)
Royal Ordnance Factories vs Sheppey United   2-4   (played at Overcliffe Ground, Gravesend)
Ilford vs Wolverton L&NWR   0-2   (played at West Herts Ground, Watford)

As a result of the test matches, Wolverton L&NWR and Sheppey United were promoted to Division One but it was decided to extend it to 12 clubs and so Royal Ordnance Factories were not relegated.

Division One   Ilford left to become founder members of the London League and Luton Town left to become founder members of the United League. Clapton also left the league and reverted to a programme of cup-ties and friendlies. Gravesend United and Northfleet both joined from the Kent League and also became founder members of the Thames & Medway Combination. Tottenham Hotspur also joined, having not played in a league since the closure of the Southern Alliance in 1893.

Division Two   Bromley left to become founder members of the London League and Guildford left to play solely in the West Surrey League. Dartford and Royal Engineers Training Battalion both joined from the Kent League and Warmley joined while continuing in the Western League. 1st Coldstream Guards, Freemantle, Southall, West Herts and Wycombe Wanderers also joined.

1897 – Test matches

24th April   Wolverton L&NWR vs Dartford   2-0   (played at West Herts Ground, Watford)
26th April   Northfleet vs Freemantle   0-3   (played at Millwall Athletic Ground)
(Freemantle fielded an ineligible player, so the game was subsequently awarded to Northfleet)
26th April   Sheppey United vs Royal Engineers T.B.   2-0   (played at Gravesend United Ground)

Division One   Bristol South End joined from the Western League and changed their name to Bristol City. Southampton St. Marys changed their name to Southampton.

Division Two   Freemantle moved to the Hampshire League and 1st Scots Guards and 1st Coldstream Guards both also left. Royal Artillery (Portsmouth) joined from the Hampshire League and St. Albans Town also joined.

1898 – Test matches

The Test match system was changed to a mini-league. The top two in Division Two each played the bottom two in Division One, home and away. Teams in the same division did not play each other so every team played 4 games. The top two in this mini-league qualified for Division One and the bottom two for Division Two.

Royal Artillery (Portsmouth)	4	3	1	0	8	4	7
Warmley (Bristol)	4	2	1	1	14	7	5
Northfleet	4	1	0	3	6	11	2
Wolverton L&NW Railway	4	0	2	2	5	11	2

As a result of the test matches, Royal Artillery (Portsmouth) and Warmley (Bristol) were promoted while Wolverton L&NWR and Northfleet were relegated. However, Northfleet decided to leave the Southern League and return to the Kent League.

Division One   Bedminster joined from the Western League and Brighton United also joined.

Division Two   Division expanded into two sections by the formation of a new South-West Section while the existing Division Two became the Metropolitan Section.

Metropolitan Section   Old St. Stephens changed their name to Shepherds Bush while West Herts merged with Watford St. Marys and continued in Division Two as Watford. Brentford, Fulham and Thames Ironworks all joined from the London League.

A South-West Section was formed with 8 clubs. Andover, Cowes, Eastleigh Athletic, Freemantle and Ryde Sports all joined from the Hampshire League. All of these except Andover also continued to play in the Hampshire League. Trowbridge Town joined from the Western League while the 1st East Lancashire Regiment and Sandown Bay also joined.

1899

Division Two championship decider

22nd April   Thames Ironworks vs Cowes   3-1   (played at Millwall)

Test matches reverted to single games played on a neutral ground:

29th April   Sheppey United vs Thames Ironworks   1-1   (played at Chatham)

29th April   Royal Artillery (Portsmouth) vs Cowes   1-4   (played at Southampton)

DIVISION ONE   As a result of the test matches, Cowes were promoted to Division One. Royal Artillery (Portsmouth) had been suspended after preparing too professionally for the F.A. Amateur Cup Final and were forced to field their reserve side for their test match. The club subsequently disbanded and was replaced by Portsmouth F.C. who were formed as a new professional club and allowed to join Division One. Both Sheppey United and Thames Ironworks were also allowed into Division One while Bristol Rovers joined from the Birmingham League and Queens Park Rangers joined from the West London League.

DIVISION TWO   Uxbridge moved to the Middlesex League and St. Albans Town disbanded. Dartford joined from the Kent League and Grays United also joined. Chesham changed their name to Chesham Town. The South-Western Section was disbanded and Andover, Eastleigh Athletic, Freemantle, Ryde Sports and Sandown Bay all reverted to the Hampshire League.

1900

Test matches

30th April   Thames Ironworks vs Fulham   5-1   (played at Tottenham)

30th April   Watford vs Sheppey United   2-1   (played at Watford)

DIVISION ONE   As a result of the test matches, Watford were promoted and Sheppey United were relegated. Bedminster merged into Bristol City while Thames Ironworks changed their name to West Ham United. Kettering joined from the Midland League and Luton Town joined from the Football League – Division Two. Chatham had resigned and disbanded in December 1900 but a new club called Chatham Amateurs was formed as a replacement and joined the Kent League.

DIVISION TWO   Dartford resigned and disbanded. A new club, called Dartford United, was formed as a replacement and joined the Kent League. Wolverton L&NWR also resigned and disbanded.

1901

Test matches

29th April   Swindon Town vs Brentford   0-0   (played at Elm Park, Reading)

29th April   Watford vs Grays United   0-0   (played at Watford)

DIVISION ONE   Bristol City were elected to the Football League – Division Two while Gravesend United moved to the Kent League. Northampton Town and Wellingborough Town both joined from the Midland League and Brentford were promoted.

DIVISION TWO   Sheppey United resigned but continued in the Kent League. West Hampstead joined from the Middlesex League and Brighton & Hove Albion joined as a newly formed club.

1902

Test matches

28th April   Brentford vs Grays United   1-1   (played at Memorial Ground, Canning Town)

30th April   Swindon Town vs Fulham   3-1   (played at Reading)

DIVISION ONE   There were no changes in membership.

DIVISION TWO   Shepherds Bush and West Hampstead both left to become founder members of the Metropolitan Amateur League. Maidenhead left and joined both the Berks & Bucks Senior League and also the West Berkshire League.

1903

Test matches

27th April   Watford vs Brighton & Hove Albion   3-5   (played at Memorial Ground, Canning Town)

28th April   Brentford vs Fulham   7-2   (played at Shepherds Bush)

As a result of the test matches and after a ballot, Watford were relegated while Brighton & Hove Albion and Fulham were both promoted. Test matches were abolished at the end of this season.

DIVISION ONE   Plymouth Argyle (formed in January 1903) joined the league. Millwall Athletic changed their name to Millwall.

DIVISION TWO   The reserve sides of 6 Division One clubs joined. Portsmouth and Southampton had been playing in the Hampshire League, Reading and Swindon Town had been playing in the Western League and Fulham and Millwall had been playing in the London League. All 6 also continued to play in their previous leagues.

1904

DIVISION ONE   Kettering moved to the Northamptonshire League. Watford were promoted from Division Two.

DIVISION TWO   Chesham Town moved to the Berks & Bucks League. Millwall withdrew their reserve team and West Ham United Reserves joined while continuing to play in the London League. Clapton Orient also joined from the London League while Brighton & Hove Albion Reserves and Watford Reserves both joined from the South-Eastern League.

1905

DIVISION ONE   Wellingborough Town resigned and disbanded. Norwich City joined from the Norfolk & Suffolk League.

DIVISION TWO   Clapton Orient left after being elected to the Football League – Division Two, Brighton & Hove Albion withdrew their reserve team and Southall disbanded. Leyton joined from the London League, Southern United joined from the South-Eastern League while both Crystal Palace and St. Leonards United joined as newly formed clubs.

1906

DIVISION ONE   Leyton and Crystal Palace were promoted from Division Two.

DIVISION TWO   Watford withdrew their reserve team who continued playing in the South-Eastern League. St. Leonards United merged with Hastings & St. Leonards of the South-Eastern League to form Hastings & St. Leonards United who continued in the Southern League, playing their matches at Hastings & St. Leonards' Central Ground. Grays United were expelled for not paying their subscription. They maintained their membership of the South-Eastern League but disbanded just before the start of the 1906-07 season. Tunbridge Wells Rangers joined from the Kent League and Salisbury City joined, leaving both the Hampshire League and the Western League. Royal Engineers (Aldershot) joined after the regiment moved their base from Chatham to Aldershot and Southend United joined as a newly formed club.

1907

DIVISION ONE   Fulham left after being elected to the Football League – Division Two and Bradford Park Avenue joined as a newly formed football club, having converted from the Northern Rugby Union game (known as Rugby League from 1922 onwards).

DIVISION TWO   Fulham and West Ham United both moved their reserves to the South-Eastern League while Royal Engineers (Aldershot) left the league and Reading Reserves also left. Croydon Common joined from the Southern Suburban League and Brighton & Hove Albion Reserves joined from the South-Eastern League.

1908

DIVISION ONE   Bradford Park Avenue and Tottenham Hotspur both left the league after being elected to the Football League – Division Two. Exeter City joined from the Plymouth & District League, Coventry City joined from the Birmingham & District League and Southend United were promoted from Division Two.

DIVISION TWO   Wycombe Wanderers moved to the Great Western Suburban League and Tunbridge Wells Rangers moved to the Kent League. Brighton & Hove Albion, Portsmouth and Swindon Town all moved their reserve sides to the South-Eastern League and Southampton Reserves also left. Depot Battalion Royal Engineers, 2nd Grenadier Guards and Chesham Town all joined from the South-Eastern League, South Farnborough Athletic joined from the Hampshire League and Gravesend Amateurs joined as a newly formed club.

1909

DIVISION ONE   Croydon Common were promoted from Division Two.

DIVISION TWO   Depot Battalion Royal Engineers moved to the Kent League and 2nd Grenadier Guards also left. Kettering and Peterborough City both joined from the Northamptonshire League, Burton United and Stoke both joined from the Birmingham & District League, Aberdare joined from the Western League, Merthyr Town joined from the Rhymney Valley League, Ton Pentre joined from the South Wales League and Romford joined from the South Essex League.

1910

Division Two championship decider

25th April   Stoke vs Hastings & St. Leonards   6-0   (at Stoke)

DIVISION ONE   Croydon Common and Reading were both relegated to Division Two.

DIVISION TWO   Peterborough City moved to the South-Eastern League, South Farnborough Athletic moved to the Hampshire League and Romford moved to the South Essex League. Both Burton United and Hastings & St. Leonards United disbanded. Cardiff City joined from the South Wales League, Treharris joined from the Western League and Walsall joined from the Birmingham & District League.

1911

DIVISION ONE   Portsmouth and Southend United were both relegated to Division Two from where Reading and Stoke were promoted.

DIVISION TWO   Salisbury City disbanded but a new amateur club with the same name was soon formed and joined the Hampshire League. Cwm Albion and Mardy both joined from the Glamorgan League while Pontypridd joined as a newly formed club.

1912

DIVISION ONE   Merthyr Town and Portsmouth were both promoted from Division Two and Luton Town were relegated. Leyton disbanded. New Brompton changed their name to Gillingham.

DIVISION TWO   Walsall moved to the Birmingham & District League, Kettering moved to the Central Alliance and Chesham Town left to become founder members of the Athenian League. Cwm Albion resigned and returned to local Welsh football but disbanded early in the 1912-13 season. Mid Rhondda, Newport County and Swansea Town joined as newly formed clubs and Llanelly joined from the Swansea & District League.

1913

DIVISION ONE   Brentford and Stoke were both relegated to Division Two. Cardiff City and Southend United were promoted.

DIVISION TWO   Abertillery Town and Caerphilly both joined as newly formed clubs and Barry joined from the Western League, having changed their name from Barry District.

1914

DIVISION ONE   Coventry City and Merthyr Town were both relegated to Division Two. Croydon Common and Luton Town were promoted.

DIVISION TWO   Aberdare and Treharris both disbanded. Stalybridge Celtic joined from the Central League, Ebbw Vale joined as a newly formed club and Leyton joined as a newly re-formed club.

1915-18

The Southern League closed down at the end of the 1914-15 season and was unable to resume until 1919 when the war ended.

1919

DIVISION ONE   Croydon Common did not re-form after the war and West Ham United were elected to the Football League – Division Two. Merthyr Town, Swansea Town, Brentford and Newport County were all promoted from Division Two.

DIVISION TWO   Leyton did not re-form after the war, Stoke and Coventry City were both elected to the Football League – Division Two and Stalybridge Celtic moved to the Central League. Aberaman Athletic joined, having been playing in the Welsh League before the war, and Porth Athletic joined as a newly formed club.

1920

DIVISION ONE   Cardiff City were elected to the Football League – Division Two. The Football League then decided to form a Third Division with two sections, North and South. The remaining 21 clubs in Division One of the Southern League became founder members of the new Division Three (South).

DIVISION TWO was renamed the Welsh Section. Caerphilly left the league but continued playing in the Welsh League and Aberdare Athletic joined as a newly formed club.

A new **ENGLISH SECTION** was formed with 13 members, 9 of which were the reserve sides of clubs whose first teams had become founder members of the new Football League – Division Three (South). They were: Brighton & Hove Albion, Gillingham, Luton Town, Millwall, Norwich City, Portsmouth, Reading, Southampton and Watford. Most of these reserve sides were also playing in either the South-Eastern League or the London Combination, which had been formed in 1915.

There were 4 new members. Boscombe and Thornycroft Athletic both joined from the Hampshire League and Charlton Athletic and Chatham both joined from the Kent League.

1920-21 Championship decider

22nd September 1921   Brighton & Hove Albion Reserves vs Barry 1-1   (after 80 minutes extra time)
Played at The Den, Millwall

19th October 1921   Brighton & Hove Albion Reserves vs Barry   2-1
Played at Ninian Park, Cardiff

1921

WELSH SECTION   Aberdare Athletic moved to the Football League – Division Three (South) and Llanelly also left but continued playing in the Welsh League. Swansea Town Reserves joined from the Western League while continuing to play in the Welsh League.

ENGLISH SECTION　Charlton Athletic joined the Football League – Division Three (South) and were replaced by their reserves who joined from the Kent League, Chatham moved to the Kent League and Thornycroft Athletic moved to the Hampshire League. Bath City, Bristol City Reserves, Bristol Rovers Reserves, Exeter City Reserves and Swindon Town Reserves all joined from the Western League, Plymouth Argyle Reserves joined from the Plymouth & District League, Guildford United joined as a newly formed club and Southend United Reserves also joined.

1921-22 Championship decider

11th September 1922　Plymouth Argyle Reserves vs Ebbw Vale　3-0
Played at Home Park, Plymouth.

1922

WELSH SECTION　Bridgend Town and Caerphilly Town both joined while continuing in the Welsh League.

ENGLISH SECTION　Gillingham Reserves moved to the Kent League and Charlton Athletic Reserves also resigned but continued in the London Combination. Torquay United and Yeovil & Petters United both joined from the Western League and Coventry City Reserves joined from the Birmingham & District League.

1922-23 Championship decider

3rd October 1923　Ebbw Vale vs Bristol Rovers Reserves　2-1　at Eastville (Bristol Rovers ground).

1923

WELSH SECTION / WESTERN SECTION　Porth Athletic disbanded, leaving just 6 members of the Welsh Section and so it was decided to re-organise the league into Western and Eastern Sections instead of Welsh and English.

The remaining 6 members of the Welsh Section – Aberaman Athletic, Barry, Bridgend Town, Ebbw Vale, Pontypridd and Swansea Town Reserves – all joined the new Western Section and were joined by 8 former members of the English Section – Bath City, Bristol City Reserves, Bristol Rovers Reserves, Exeter City Reserves, Plymouth Argyle Reserves, Swindon Town Reserves, Torquay United and Yeovil & Petters United.

The Section was made up to 18 clubs by the election of 4 new members – Cardiff City Reserves, Llanelly and Newport County Reserves all joined while continuing to play in the Welsh League and Weymouth joined while continuing to play in the Western League.

ENGLISH SECTION / EASTERN SECTION　8 former members of the English Section transferred to the new Western Section (see above) but Southend United Reserves moved to the London Combination while Boscombe changed name to Bournemouth & Boscombe Athletic and joined the Football League – Division Three (South). Their reserves replaced the first team in the new Eastern Section.

The remaining 10 former members of the English Section were Guildford United and 9 reserve sides – Brighton & Hove Albion, Coventry City, Luton Town, Millwall, Norwich City, Portsmouth, Reading, Southampton and Watford – and these 10 all joined the new Eastern Section which was made up to 16 clubs by the election of 5 new members.

Northampton Town Reserves joined from the Northamptonshire League and Fletton United also joined from the Northamptonshire League, having changed their name to Peterborough & Fletton United. Kettering and Leicester City Reserves both joined from the Central Alliance and Folkestone joined from the Kent League.

1923-24 Championship decider

18th September 1924　Peterborough & Fletton United vs Yeovil & Petters United　3-1
Played at London Road, Peterborough.

1924

WESTERN SECTION   Mid-Rhondda United joined while continuing in the Welsh League while Newton's & Taunton joined from the Somerset League having changed their name to Taunton United.

EASTERN SECTION   Nuneaton Town joined from the Birmingham & District League. Kettering officially changed their name to Kettering Town by which name they had been known for more than 30 years.

1924-25 Championship decider

7th September 1925   Southampton Reserves vs Swansea Town Reserves   2-1
Played at the Vetch Field, Swansea.

1925

WESTERN SECTION   Aberaman Athletic, Bridgend Town, Cardiff City Reserves, Newport County Reserves and Swansea Town Reserves all left but continued playing in the Welsh League. Llanelly disbanded.

EASTERN SECTION   Northampton Town Reserves moved to the Northamptonshire League. Grays Thurrock United joined from the Kent League and Fulham Reserves also joined while continuing to play in the London Combination.

1925-26 Championship decider

13th September 1926   Plymouth Argyle Reserves vs Millwall Reserves   1-0
Played at the Den, New Cross, London.

1926

WESTERN SECTION   Pontypridd disbanded. Newport County Reserves joined while continuing to play in the Welsh League.

EASTERN SECTION   Nuneaton Town moved to the Birmingham Combination, Coventry City Reserves moved to the London Combination and Fulham Reserves also left, continuing to play in the London Combination. Dartford joined from the Kent League and Poole joined while continuing to play in the Western League.

1926-27 Championship decider

5th October 1927   Brighton & Hove Albion Reserves vs Torquay United   4-0
Played at the Goldstone Ground, Brighton.

1927

WESTERN SECTION   Torquay United were elected to the Football League – Division Three (South) and were replaced by their reserves who joined from the Plymouth & District League. Aberdare Athletic failed to be re-elected to the Football League – Division Three (South) and so joined the Southern League – Western Section under the title of Aberdare & Aberaman. Aberdare had merged with Aberaman of the Welsh League a year earlier. Merthyr Town Reserves joined while continuing to play in the Welsh League and Taunton United changed their name to Taunton Town.

EASTERN SECTION   Leicester City Reserves, Luton Town Reserves, Portsmouth Reserves, Reading Reserves and Watford Reserves all left while continuing to play in the London Combination. Chatham, Gillingham Reserves, Northfleet United, Sheppey United and Sittingbourne all joined from the Kent League while Aldershot Town joined as a newly formed club. Guildford United changed their name to Guildford City following the creation of the Guildford Diocese. Construction of Guildford Cathedral began in 1936 and was completed in 1965 but the town has never been granted city status.

1927-28 Championship decider

6th September 1928   Kettering Town vs Bristol City Reserves   5-0   (at Rockingham Road, Kettering)

1928

WESTERN SECTION   Aberdare & Aberaman and Mid-Rhondda United both disbanded. Weymouth left while continuing to play in the Western League. Lovells Athletic joined from the Western League while continuing to play in the Welsh League.

EASTERN SECTION   Thames Association joined as a newly formed club.

1928-29 Championship decider

30th September 1929   Plymouth Argyle Reserves vs Kettering Town   4-2
Played at Rockingham Road, Kettering.

1929

WESTERN SECTION   Llanelly joined while continuing to play in the Welsh League.

EASTERN SECTION   Chatham and Gillingham Reserves both moved to the Kent League. Northampton Town Reserves joined from the Northamptonshire League.

1929-30 Championship decider

3rd September 1930   Aldershot Town vs Bath City   3-2   (at The Recreation Ground, Aldershot)

1930

WESTERN SECTION   Bristol City Reserves, Lovells Athletic and Yeovil & Petters United all moved to the newly formed Second Division of the London Combination. Merthyr Town joined after failing to be re-elected to the Football League – Division Three (South), replacing their reserves who were disbanded. Instead of a reserve side, Merthyr fielded an "A" side in the Welsh Amateur League.

EASTERN SECTION   Thames Association were elected to the Football League – Division Three (South) and were replaced in the Eastern Section by their newly-formed reserve side. Grays Thurrock United, Northfleet United and Sittingbourne all moved to the Kent League, Kettering Town moved to the Birmingham & District League, Bournemouth & Boscombe Athletic Reserves and Northampton Town Reserves both moved to the newly formed Second Division of the London Combination and Brighton & Hove Albion Reserves and Southampton Reserves also both left while continuing to play in the First Division of the London Combination.

1930-31 Championship decider

9th September 1931   Dartford vs Exeter City Reserves   7-2   (at St. James' Park, Exeter)

1931

WESTERN SECTION   Yeovil & Petters United joined while continuing to play in the Football Combination – Division Two and Newport County joined after failing to be re-elected to the Football League – Division Three (South). Newport's first team replaced their reserves who left the Southern League and were disbanded. Instead, Newport started an amateur side in the Newport & District League but this was withdrawn after losing its opening game at Liswerry as Newport said it would be unable to meet its commitments.

EASTERN SECTION   Thames Association disbanded their reserve side. Tunbridge Wells Rangers joined from the Kent League and Bournemouth & Boscombe Athletic Reserves joined while continuing to play in the Football Combination – Division Two.

1931-32 Championship decider

31st August 1932   Dartford vs Yeovil & Petters United   2-1   (at Watling Street, Dartford).

1932

WESTERN SECTION   Newport County were elected to the Football League - Division Three (South) and were replaced in the Southern League by their re-formed reserve side. Swindon Town Reserves moved to the Western League. Ebbw Vale also left but continued in the Welsh League.

EASTERN SECTION   Aldershot Town were elected to the Football League – Division Three (South) and changed their name to Aldershot. They were replaced by their newly formed reserve side who also replaced the first team in the London Combination. Sheppey United left but continued to play in the Kent League.

1932-33 Championship decider

31st August 1933   Norwich City Reserves vs Bath City 2-1   (played at Twerton Park, Bath)

1933

WESTERN SECTION   There were no changes in membership.

EASTERN SECTION   Aldershot Reserves left but continued to play in the London Combination. Clapton Orient Reserves joined from the London Combination and Margate joined while continuing to play in the Kent League.

CENTRAL SECTION   A third section of the league was formed to provide extra fixtures for clubs who were already members of the Western and Eastern Sections. The new section was called the Central Section and 10 existing members joined it. There were 4 from the Western Section: Bath City, Llanelly, Plymouth Argyle Reserves and Yeovil & Petters United, and 6 from the Eastern Section: Clapton Orient Reserves, Dartford, Folkestone, Guildford City, Norwich City Reserves and Tunbridge Wells Rangers.

1933-34 Championship decider

3rd September 1934   Norwich City Reserves vs Plymouth Argyle Reserves   2-2

Played at The Nest, Norwich.

26th September 1934   Plymouth Argyle Reserves vs Norwich City Reserves   3-0

Played at Home Park, Plymouth.

1934

WESTERN SECTION   Llanelly left but continued in the Welsh League and Merthyr Town disbanded.

EASTERN SECTION   Aldershot Reserves joined from the London Combination.

CENTRAL SECTION   Clapton Orient Reserves, Llanelly and Norwich City Reserves all left the league. Aldershot Reserves, Bristol Rovers Reserves, Margate and Torquay United Reserves all joined.

1934-35 Championship decider

9th September 1935   Yeovil & Petters United vs Norwich City Reserves   2-2

Played at The Huish Athletic Ground, Yeovil.

23rd September 1935   Norwich City Reserves vs Yeovil & Petters United 7-2

Played at Carrow Road, Norwich.

1935

WESTERN SECTION   Taunton Town disbanded. Cheltenham Town joined from the Birmingham Combination.

EASTERN SECTION   There were no changes in membership.

CENTRAL SECTION   Torquay United Reserves left the league and Cheltenham Town joined.

1935-36 Championship decider

17th September 1936   Margate vs Plymouth Argyle Reserves   3-1   (at Hartsdown Park, Margate)

1936

The league was restructured with the Western and Eastern Sections combined into one Saturday Section while the Central Section was replaced by a Midweek Section. Of the former Eastern Section clubs, Aldershot Reserves, Dartford, Folkestone, Guildford City, Margate, Norwich City Reserves and Tunbridge Wells Rangers all joined both the Saturday Section and the Midweek Section while Millwall Reserves joined just the Midweek Section. Bournemouth Reserves and Clapton Orient Reserves both left but continued in the London Combination.

Of the former Western Section clubs, Barry, Bath City, Cheltenham Town, Exeter City Reserves, Newport County Reserves, Plymouth Argyle Reserves, Torquay United Reserves and Yeovil & Petters United all joined the Saturday Section while Bath City also joined the Midweek Section. Bristol Rovers Reserves moved to the Birmingham & District League. Ipswich Town joined the Saturday Section from the Eastern Counties League and Portsmouth Reserves joined the Midweek Section while continuing to play in the London Combination.

1936-37 Championship decider

29th September 1937   Margate vs Ipswich Town   6-2   (at Portman Road, Ipswich)

1937

Margate resigned from both the Saturday and Midweek Sections and moved to the Kent League. Colchester United joined both the Saturday and Midweek Sections as a newly formed club. Bristol Rovers Reserves joined the Saturday Section from the Birmingham & District League and Swindon Town Reserves joined the Saturday Section from the Western League.

1937-38 Championship decider

17th October 1938   Guildford City vs Millwall Reserves   2-1   (at the Den, New Cross, London)

1938

Ipswich Town were elected to the Football League – Division Three (South) and were replaced in the Southern League by their reserves who joined from the Eastern Counties League. Gillingham joined after failing to be re-elected to the Football League – Division Three (South), Worcester City joined from the Birmingham & District League and Cardiff City Reserves also joined from the Birmingham & District League while continuing to play in the Welsh League. Arsenal Reserves joined while continuing to play in the London Combination and Chelmsford City joined as a newly formed club after the amateur Chelmsford club had been closed down. Bath City left the Midweek Section but continued to play in the Saturday Section.

1939

There was no Championship decider played for the 1938-39 season and, at the League's 1939 A.G.M., it was decided to scrap the Midweek Section. Folkestone moved to the Kent League. Hereford United and Kidderminster Harriers both joined from the Birmingham & District League. Millwall Reserves and Portsmouth Reserves both left but continued to play in the London Combination.

1940-1945

The 1940 A.G.M. was held in London on 30th July when it was decided to suspend all operations until further notice. There was then no further activity until 1st February 1945 when a special meeting was held in London. With the end of the war in sight, it was proposed to restart the league in the 1945-46 season. However, a final decision was deferred until it was certain that the war was over and that various ground difficulties – some had been requisitioned by the armed forces – could be overcome. At that meeting, Bedford Town who had been playing in the United Counties League before the war, were accepted into membership.

On 18th June 1945, it was agreed that there would be Western and Eastern Sections with 6 clubs in the Eastern Section – Aldershot Reserves, Bedford Town, Chelmsford City, Colchester United, Guildford City and Norwich City Reserves – and 7 in the Western Section – Barry Town (having changed their name from Barry), Bath City, Cardiff City Reserves, Cheltenham Town, Hereford United, Worcester City and Yeovil & Petters United. However, Norwich City Reserves and Aldershot Reserves later decided that they were unable to take part and, with the Eastern Section thus reduced to 4 clubs, it was decided that the league would run with just one section of 12 clubs, Swindon Town Reserves having re-joined after deciding that they would be able to participate. The number of members was reduced to 11 on 13th August when Guildford City decided that they would not be able to play as, after 4 years of Army occupation, their ground still needed considerable work doing on it to make it fit for play while many of their players still had military duties to perform. Thus the league resumed in the 1945-46 season with 11 clubs.

1946

Cardiff City Reserves and Swindon Town Reserves both moved to the Football Combination. Pre-war members Dartford, Exeter City Reserves and Guildford City all re-joined after not playing in 1945-46 and Gloucester City (pre-war members of the Birmingham Combination and members of the war-time Southern League in 1939-40) also joined after not playing in 1945-46. Pre-war members Gillingham re-joined after playing in the Kent League in 1945-46. Merthyr Tydfil joined from the Welsh League and Millwall Reserves joined while continuing to play in the Football Combination. Gravesend & Northfleet joined as a newly-formed club following a merger between Gravesend United of the Kent League and Northfleet United (pre-war members of the Kent League). Yeovil & Petters United changed their name to Yeovil Town.

There were 10 clubs who began the pre-war 1939-40 season who did not rejoin the league. Aldershot Reserves, Bristol Rovers Reserves, Ipswich Town Reserves, Norwich City Reserves and Plymouth Argyle Reserves all joined the Football Combination (previously called the London Combination) instead, while Arsenal Reserves continued to play solely in the Football Combination. Torquay United Reserves continued playing in the Plymouth & District League which they had joined in 1945 and Newport County Reserves continued in the Welsh League. Kidderminster Harriers continued to play in the Birmingham Combination which they had joined in 1945. Tunbridge Wells Rangers did not re-form after the war and there was no senior club in the town until 1947 when a newly formed amateur club called Tunbridge Wells joined the Kent Amateur League.

1947

Millwall Reserves left but continued to play in the Football Combination. Lovells Athletic joined from the Welsh League and Torquay United Reserves joined from the Plymouth & District League.

1948

Kidderminster Harriers joined from the Birmingham & District League. Chingford Town, Hastings United and Tonbridge all joined as newly formed clubs.

1949

Headington United joined from the Spartan League and Weymouth joined from the Western League.

1950

Colchester United and Gillingham both left the league after being elected to the Football League – Division Three (South). Llanelly joined from the Welsh League and Kettering Town joined from the Birmingham & District League.

1951

Torquay United Reserves moved to the newly formed South-Western League.

1952, 1953, 1954, 1955 and 1956

There were no changes in membership.

1957

Llanelly moved to the Welsh League – Division Two (West) and Poole Town joined from the Western League.

1958

The league expanded to two regional zones, North-Western and South-Eastern.

Barry Town, Bath City, Cheltenham Town, Gloucester City, Headington United, Hereford United, Kettering Town, Kidderminster Harriers, Lovells Athletic, Merthyr Tydfil and Worcester City were all placed in the North-Western Zone which was made up to 18 clubs by the election of Boston United, Corby Town and Wisbech Town from the Midland League, Burton Albion, Nuneaton Borough and Rugby Town from the Birmingham & District League and Wellington Town from the Cheshire League.

Bedford Town, Chelmsford City, Dartford, Exeter City Reserves, Gravesend & Northfleet, Guildford City, Hastings United, Poole Town, Tonbridge, Weymouth and Yeovil Town were all placed in the South-Eastern Zone which was made up to 17 clubs by the election of Cambridge City from the Athenian League, Cambridge United and Clacton Town from the Eastern Counties League, Kings Lynn from the Midland League, Trowbridge Town from the Western League and Yiewsley from the Corinthian League.

1958-59 Championship decider

9th May 1959   Hereford United vs Bedford Town   1-2   (at Edgar Street, Hereford)

1959

The league was re-organised into two divisions, Premier and First. The top 11 clubs in each of the previous season's two zones were placed in the Premier Division and the remainder were placed in Division One, with one exception – Lovells Athletic, who moved to the Welsh League.

The First Division was made up to 22 clubs by the election of Ashford Town, Bexleyheath & Welling, Dover, Folkestone Town, Margate, Ramsgate Athletic, Sittingbourne and Tunbridge Wells United, all from the Kent League, plus Hinckley Athletic from the Birmingham & District League and Romford from the Isthmian League.

1960

PREMIER DIVISION   Headington United changed their name to Oxford United.

FIRST DIVISION   Exeter City Reserves moved to the Western League and Kidderminster Harriers moved to the Birmingham & District League. Canterbury City joined from the Metropolitan League.

1961

PREMIER DIVISION   Boston United moved to the Central Alliance.

1962

PREMIER DIVISION   Oxford United left after being elected to the Football League – Division Four.

1963

PREMIER DIVISION   Bexleyheath & Welling changed their name to Bexley United.

FIRST DIVISION   Crawley Town joined from the Metropolitan League, Deal Town joined from the Aetolian League and Stevenage Town joined from the Delphian League. Tunbridge Wells United changed their name to Tunbridge Wells Rangers.

1964

FIRST DIVISION   Clacton Town moved to the Eastern Counties League and Wimbledon joined from the Isthmian League. Yiewsley changed their name to Hillingdon Borough.

1965

FIRST DIVISION   Barnet joined from the Athenian League and Dunstable Town joined from the Metropolitan League.

1966

FIRST DIVISION   Deal Town moved to the Greater London League and Banbury United joined from the West Midlands Regional League.

1967

FIRST DIVISION   Hinckley Athletic moved to the West Midlands Regional League, Sittingbourne moved to the Kent Premier League and Tunbridge Wells Rangers disbanded. They were replaced by a new club called Tunbridge Wells who replaced Tunbridge Wells Rangers Reserves in the Kent Premier League. Brentwood Town joined from the Metropolitan League.

1968

PREMIER DIVISION   Stevenage Town disbanded.

FIRST DIVISION   Salisbury joined from the Western League.

1969

PREMIER DIVISION   Wellington Town changed their name to Telford United.

1970

PREMIER DIVISION   Cambridge United left after being elected to the Football League – Division Four. Brentwood Town closed down as an independent club after being merged into Chelmsford City.

FIRST DIVISION   Wisbech Town moved to the Eastern Counties League and Stevenage Athletic joined from the Metropolitan League. Folkestone Town changed their name to Folkestone.

1971

The First Division was split into two divisions, (North) and (South).

First Division (North) consisted of 18 clubs: Gloucester City, Kettering Town and King's Lynn were relegated from the Premier Division while Banbury United, Barry Town, Burton Albion, Cheltenham Town, Corby Town, Dunstable Town, Rugby Town and Stevenage Athletic moved from the previous season's First Division. There were 7 new clubs: Bletchley and Bury Town both joined from the Metropolitan League, Ilkeston Town and Lockheed Leamington both joined from the Midland League, Stourbridge and Wellingborough Town both joined from the West Midlands Regional League and Wealdstone joined from the Isthmian League.

First Division (South) consisted of 16 clubs: Ashford Town were relegated from the Premier Division while Bexley United, Canterbury City, Crawley Town, Hastings United, Ramsgate Athletic, Salisbury, Tonbridge and Trowbridge Town moved from the previous season's First Division. There were 7 new clubs: Basingstoke Town, Waterlooville and Winchester City all joined from the Hampshire League, Metropolitan Police and Woodford Town both joined from the Metropolitan League, Andover joined from the Western League and Maidstone United joined from the Isthmian League.

1972

PREMIER DIVISION   Hereford United left after being elected to the Football League – Division Four.

FIRST DIVISION (NORTH)   Bletchley Town, Dunstable Town and Wealdstone all transferred to the First Division (South). Atherstone Town, Bedworth United, Bromsgrove Rovers, Kidderminster Harriers, Redditch United and Tamworth all joined from the West Midlands Regional League. Grantham joined from the Midland League and Enderby Town joined from the East Midlands Regional League.

FIRST DIVISION (SOUTH)   Woodford Town dropped into junior football. Bideford, Dorchester Town and Minehead all joined from the Western League and Bognor Regis Town joined from the Sussex County League. Ramsgate Athletic changed their name to Ramsgate.

1973

FIRST DIVISION (NORTH)   Ilkeston Town moved to the Midland League and Rugby Town resigned and ceased all playing activity while maintaining membership of the county F.A.. Witney Town joined from the Hellenic League. Lockheed Leamington changed their name to AP Leamington.

FIRST DIVISION (SOUTH)   Winchester City moved to the Hampshire League. Bletchley Town and Dunstable Town both transferred to First Division (North).

1974

PREMIER DIVISION   Guildford City merged with Dorking of the Athenian League and became Guildford & Dorking United. The merged club continued in the Southern League, playing at Dorking's former ground at Meadowbank Park. Folkestone changed their name to Folkestone & Shepway.

FIRST DIVISION (NORTH)   Bletchley Town changed their name to Milton Keynes City.

1975

FIRST DIVISION (NORTH)   Oswestry Town joined from the Cheshire League.

FIRST DIVISION (SOUTH)   Bideford moved to the Western League.

1976

FIRST DIVISION (NORTH)   Barnet transferred to First Division (South). Bury Town moved to the Eastern Counties League and Stevenage Athletic disbanded. A new club called Stevenage Borough was quickly formed and joined the Chiltern Youth League.

FIRST DIVISION (SOUTH)   Ramsgate moved to the Kent League and Bexley United disbanded. Aylesbury United joined from the Athenian League.

1977

PREMIER DIVISION   Wimbledon left after being elected to the Football League – Division Four.

FIRST DIVISION (NORTH)   Bridgend Town joined from the Welsh League.

FIRST DIVISION (SOUTH)   Metropolitan Police moved to the Isthmian League. Addlestone and Hounslow both joined from the Athenian League and Taunton Town joined from the Western League.

1978

FIRST DIVISION (NORTH)   Dunstable transferred to First Division (South). Alvechurch joined from the West Midlands Regional League.

FIRST DIVISION (SOUTH)   Romford disbanded. Gosport Borough joined from the Hampshire League.

1979

The Alliance Premier League (now called the National League) was formed as a national competition one level below the Football League. AP Leamington, Barnet, Bath City, Gravesend & Northfleet, Kettering Town, Maidstone United, Nuneaton Borough, Redditch United, Telford United, Wealdstone, Weymouth, Worcester City and Yeovil Town all left the Premier Division to become founder members of the new league. As a result, all of the remaining Southern League clubs were organised into two regional divisions. The Midland Division consisted of 22 clubs as follows: Bridgend Town, Cheltenham Town and Witney Town from the Premier Division; Alvechurch, Banbury United, Barry Town, Bedford Town, Bedworth United, Bromsgrove Rovers, Cambridge City, Corby Town, Enderby Town, Gloucester City, Kidderminster Harriers, King's Lynn, Merthyr Tydfil, Milton Keynes City, Stourbridge and Wellingborough Town, all from the First Division (North) and Minehead, Taunton Town and Trowbridge Town from the First Division (South).

The Southern Division consisted of 24 clubs as follows: Dartford, Dorchester Town, Hastings United, Hillingdon Borough and Margate from the Premier Division; Addlestone, Andover, Ashford Town, Aylesbury United, Basingstoke Town, Bognor Regis Town, Canterbury City, Chelmsford City, Crawley Town, Dover, Dunstable, Folkestone & Shepway, Gosport Borough, Hounslow, Poole Town, Salisbury, Tonbridge AFC, Waterlooville all from the First Division (South) and Fareham Town who joined from the Hampshire League.

Atherstone Town of the Premier Division disbanded and a replacement club called Atherstone United was quickly formed and joined the West Midlands Regional League.

Burton Albion, Grantham, Oswestry Town and Tamworth all left the First Division (North) and joined the Northern Premier League.

SOUTHERN LEAGUE

1894-95

First Division

Millwall Athletic	16	12	4	0	68	19	28
Luton Town	16	9	4	3	36	22	22
Southampton St Mary's	16	9	2	5	34	25	20
Ilford	16	6	3	7	26	40	15
Reading	16	6	2	8	33	38	14
Chatham	16	4	5	7	22	25	13
Royal Ordnance Factories	16	3	6	7	20	30	12
Clapton	16	5	1	10	22	38	11
Swindon Town	16	4	1	11	24	48	9

Second Division

New Brompton	12	11	0	1	57	10	22
Sheppey United	12	6	1	5	25	23	13
Old St Stephen's	12	6	0	6	26	26	12
Uxbridge	12	4	3	5	14	20	11
Bromley	12	4	1	7	23	30	9
Chesham	12	3	3	6	20	42	9
Maidenhead	12	2	4	6	19	33	8

1895-96

First Division

Millwall Athletic	18	16	1	1	75	16	33
Luton Town	18	13	1	4	68	14	27
Southampton St Mary's	18	12	0	6	44	23	24
Reading	18	11	1	6	45	38	23
Chatham	18	9	2	7	43	45	20
New Brompton	18	7	4	7	30	37	18
Swindon Town	18	6	4	8	38	41	16
Clapton	18	4	2	12	30	67	10
Royal Ordnance Factories	18	3	3	12	23	44	9
Ilford	18	0	0	18	10	81	0

Second Division

Wolverton L & NW Railway	16	13	1	2	43	10	27
Sheppey United	16	11	3	2	60	19	25
1st Scots Guards	16	8	5	3	37	22	21
Uxbridge	16	9	1	6	28	23	19
Old St Stephen's	16	6	3	7	34	21	15
Guildford	16	7	1	8	29	41	15
Maidenhead	16	4	1	11	20	49	9
Chesham	16	2	3	11	15	48	7
Bromley	16	2	2	12	16	49	6

Windsor & Eton resigned from the league in September 1895 after playing just one game, a 2-0 home defeat by Sheppey United, which was deleted from the table.

1896-97

First Division

Southampton St Mary's	20	15	5	0	63	18	35
Millwall Athletic	20	13	5	2	63	24	31
Chatham	20	13	1	6	54	29	27
Tottenham Hotspur	20	9	4	7	43	29	22
Gravesend United	20	9	4	7	35	34	22
Swindon Town	20	8	3	9	33	37	19
Reading	20	8	3	9	31	49	19
New Brompton	20	7	2	11	32	42	16
Northfleet	20	5	4	11	24	46	14
Sheppey United	20	5	1	14	34	47	11
Wolverton L & NW Railway	20	2	0	18	17	74	4

Royal Ordnance Factories resigned from the league and disbanded on 14th November 1896. Their record at the time was deleted:

	7	0	0	7	8	46	0

Second Division

Dartford	24	16	4	4	83	19	36
Royal Engineers Training Battalion	24	11	9	4	49	37	31
Uxbridge	24	11	5	8	62	37	27
Freemantle	24	12	4	8	58	40	26
Wycombe Wanderers	24	10	6	8	37	54	26
Chesham	24	11	3	10	41	55	25
Southall	24	9	6	9	55	52	24
1st Scot Guards	24	9	6	9	49	50	24
Warmley (Bristol)	24	10	3	11	44	43	23
West Herts	24	11	1	12	41	49	23
Old St Stephen's	24	5	7	12	36	52	17
Maidenhead	24	4	8	12	33	64	16
1st Coldstream Guards	24	3	6	15	30	66	12

Freemantle had originally finished in 3rd place but were found to have fielded an ineligible man in their promotion test match against Northfleet. They duly had 2 points deducted after the season had ended, moving them down from 3rd to 4th place.

1897-98

First Division

Southampton	22	18	1	3	53	18	37
Bristol City	22	13	7	2	67	33	33
Tottenham Hotspur	22	12	4	6	52	31	28
Chatham	22	12	4	6	50	34	28
Reading	22	8	7	7	39	31	23
New Brompton	22	9	4	9	37	37	22
Sheppey United	22	10	1	11	40	49	21
Gravesend United	22	7	6	9	28	39	20
Millwall Athletic	22	8	2	12	48	45	18
Swindon Town	22	7	2	13	36	48	16
Northfleet	22	4	3	15	29	60	11
Wolverton L & NW Railway	22	3	1	18	28	82	7

Second Division

Royal Artillery (Portsmouth)	22	19	1	2	75	22	39
Warmley (Bristol)	22	19	0	3	108	15	38
West Herts	22	11	6	5	50	48	28
Uxbridge	22	11	2	9	39	57	24
St Albans Town	22	9	5	8	47	41	23
Dartford	22	11	0	11	68	55	22
Southall	22	8	2	12	49	61	18
Chesham	22	8	2	12	38	48	18
Old St Stephen's	22	7	2	13	47	66	16
Wycombe Wanderers	22	7	2	13	37	55	16
Maidenhead	22	4	4	14	27	81	12
Royal Engineers Training Battalion	22	4	2	16	26	62	10

1898-99

First Division

Southampton	24	15	5	4	54	24	35
Bristol City	24	15	3	6	55	33	33
Millwall Athletic	24	12	6	6	59	35	30
Chatham	24	10	8	6	32	23	28
Reading	24	9	8	7	31	24	26
New Brompton	24	10	5	9	38	30	25
Tottenham Hotspur	24	10	4	10	40	36	24
Bedminster	24	10	4	10	35	39	24
Swindon Town	24	9	5	10	43	49	23
Brighton United	24	9	2	13	37	48	20
Gravesend United	24	7	5	12	42	52	19
Sheppey United	24	5	3	16	23	53	13
Royal Artillery (Portsmouth)	24	4	4	16	17	60	12

Warmley resigned and disbanded following their 2-1 home defeat by Royal Artillery (Portsmouth) on 21st January, 1899. Their record at the time was deleted when it stood as follows:

	17	2	2	13	25	68	6

Second Division – Metropolitan Section

Thames Ironworks	22	19	1	2	64	16	39
Wolverton L & NW Railway	22	13	4	5	88	43	30
Watford	22	14	2	6	62	35	30
Brentford	22	11	3	8	59	39	25
Wycombe Wanderers	22	10	2	10	55	57	22
Southall	22	11	0	11	44	55	22
Chesham	22	9	2	11	45	62	20
St Albans Town	22	8	3	11	45	59	19
Shepherds Bush	22	7	3	12	37	53	17
Fulham	22	6	4	12	36	44	16
Uxbridge	22	7	2	13	29	48	16
Maidenhead	22	3	2	17	33	86	8

Second Division – South West Section

Cowes	10	10	0	0	58	8	20
Ryde Sports	10	7	0	3	30	11	14
Freemantle	10	4	1	5	18	31	9
Sandown Bay	10	4	0	6	20	29	8
Eastleigh Athletic	10	2	1	7	17	37	5
Andover	10	2	0	8	14	41	4

Trowbridge Town resigned from the league and disbanded on 31st October 1898 and 1st East Lancashire Regiment also resigned during the season. The records of both clubs records were deleted.

1899-1900

First Division

Tottenham Hotspur	28	20	4	4	67	26	44
Portsmouth	28	20	1	7	58	27	41
Southampton	28	17	1	10	70	33	35
Reading	28	15	2	11	41	28	32
Swindon Town	28	15	2	11	50	42	32
Bedminster	28	13	2	13	44	45	28
Millwall Athletic	28	12	3	13	36	37	27
Queens Park Rangers	28	12	2	14	49	57	26
Bristol City	28	9	7	12	43	47	25
Bristol Rovers	28	11	3	14	46	55	25
New Brompton	28	9	6	13	39	49	24
Gravesend United	28	10	4	14	38	58	24
Chatham	28	10	3	15	38	58	23
Thames Ironworks	28	8	5	15	30	45	21
Sheppey United	28	3	7	18	24	66	13

Cowes resigned and disbanded in December 1899 and their record was deleted when it stood as: 13 3 1 9 17 43 7
Brighton United resigned and disbanded in February 1900 and their record at the time was deleted: 22 3 3 16 22 56 9

Second Division

Watford	20	14	2	4	56	25	30
Fulham	20	10	5	5	44	20	25
Chesham Town	20	9	6	5	46	34	24
Wolverton L&NWR	20	11	2	7	43	38	24
Grays United	20	7	7	6	57	29	21
Shepherds Bush	20	8	5	7	41	36	21
Wycombe Wanderers	20	8	3	9	35	50	19
Dartford	20	7	3	10	35	42	17
Brentford	20	5	7	8	31	48	17
Southall	20	6	3	11	20	42	15
Maidenhead	20	2	3	15	16	60	7

1900-01

First Division

Southampton	28	18	5	5	58	26	41
Bristol City	28	17	5	6	54	27	39
Portsmouth	28	17	4	7	56	32	38
Millwall Athletic	28	17	2	9	55	32	36
Tottenham Hotspur	28	16	4	8	55	33	36
West Ham United	28	14	5	9	40	28	33
Bristol Rovers	28	14	4	10	46	35	32
Queens Park Rangers	28	11	4	13	43	48	26
Reading	28	8	8	12	24	25	24
Luton Town	28	11	2	15	43	49	24
Kettering	28	7	9	12	33	46	23
New Brompton	28	7	5	16	34	51	19
Gravesend United	28	6	7	15	32	85	19
Watford	28	6	4	18	24	52	16
Swindon Town	28	3	8	17	19	47	14

Chatham resigned and disbanded in December 1900 and their record was deleted when it stood as: 10 1 2 7 6 32 4

Second Division

Brentford	16	14	2	0	63	11	30
Grays United	16	12	2	2	62	12	26
Sheppey United	16	8	1	7	44	26	17
Shepherds Bush	16	8	1	7	30	30	17
Fulham	16	8	0	8	38	26	16
Chesham Town	16	5	1	10	26	39	11
Maidenhead	16	4	1	11	21	49	9
Wycombe Wanderers	16	4	1	11	23	68	9
Southall	16	4	1	11	22	68	9

1901-02

First Division

Portsmouth	30	20	7	3	67	24	47
Tottenham Hotspur	30	18	6	6	61	22	42
Southampton	30	18	6	6	71	28	42
West Ham United	30	17	6	7	45	28	40
Reading	30	16	7	7	57	24	39
Millwall Athletic	30	13	6	11	48	31	32
Luton Town	30	11	10	9	31	35	32
Kettering	30	12	5	13	44	39	29
Bristol Rovers	30	12	5	13	43	39	29
New Brompton	30	10	7	13	39	38	27
Northampton Town	30	11	5	14	53	64	27
Queens Park Rangers	30	8	7	15	34	56	23
Watford	30	9	4	17	36	60	22
Wellingborough Town	30	9	4	17	34	75	22
Brentford	30	7	6	17	34	61	20
Swindon Town	30	2	3	25	17	93	7

Second Division

Fulham	16	13	0	3	51	19	26
Grays United	16	12	1	3	49	14	25
Brighton & Hove Albion	16	11	0	5	34	17	22
Wycombe Wanderers	16	7	3	6	36	30	17
West Hampstead	16	6	4	6	39	29	16
Shepherds Bush	16	6	1	9	31	31	13
Southall	16	5	2	9	28	52	12
Maidenhead	16	3	1	12	23	59	7
Chesham Town	16	2	2	12	24	64	6

1902-03

First Division

Southampton	30	20	8	2	83	20	48
Reading	30	19	7	4	72	30	45
Portsmouth	30	17	7	6	69	32	41
Tottenham Hotspur	30	14	7	9	47	31	35
Bristol Rovers	30	13	8	9	46	34	34
New Brompton	30	11	11	8	37	35	33
Millwall Athletic	30	14	3	13	52	37	31
Northampton Town	30	12	6	12	39	48	30
Queens Park Rangers	30	11	6	13	34	42	28
West Ham United	30	9	10	11	35	49	28
Luton Town	30	10	7	13	43	44	27
Swindon Town	30	10	7	13	38	46	27
Kettering	30	8	11	11	33	40	27
Wellingborough Town	30	11	3	16	36	56	25
Watford	30	6	4	20	35	87	16
Brentford	30	2	1	27	16	84	5

Second Division

Fulham	10	7	1	2	27	7	15
Brighton & Hove Albion	10	7	1	2	34	11	15
Grays United	10	7	0	3	28	12	14
Wycombe Wanderers	10	3	3	4	13	19	9
Chesham Town	10	2	1	7	9	37	5
Southall	10	1	0	9	10	35	2

1903-04

First Division

Southampton	34	22	6	6	75	30	50
Tottenham Hotspur	34	16	11	7	54	37	43
Bristol Rovers	34	17	8	9	66	42	42
Portsmouth	34	17	8	9	41	38	42
Queens Park Rangers	34	15	11	8	53	37	41
Reading	34	14	13	7	48	35	41
Millwall	34	16	8	10	64	42	40
Luton Town	34	14	12	8	38	33	40
Plymouth Argyle	34	13	10	11	44	34	36
Swindon Town	34	10	11	13	30	42	31
Fulham	34	9	12	13	33	34	30
West Ham United	34	10	7	17	38	43	27
Brentford	34	9	9	16	34	48	27
Wellingborough Town	34	11	5	18	44	63	27
Northampton Town	34	10	7	17	36	69	27
New Brompton	34	6	13	15	26	43	25
Brighton & Hove Albion	34	6	12	16	45	79	24
Kettering	34	6	7	21	30	78	19

Second Division

Watford	20	18	2	0	70	15	38
Portsmouth Reserves	20	15	2	3	85	25	32
Millwall Reserves	20	9	4	7	35	39	22
Southampton Reserves	20	9	3	8	59	35	21
Grays United	20	9	3	8	25	55	21
Fulham Reserves	20	8	4	8	40	34	20
Swindon Town Reserves	20	8	3	9	50	44	19
Reading Reserves	20	8	2	10	43	42	18
Wycombe Wanderers	20	5	5	10	29	64	15
Southall	20	4	2	14	25	62	10
Chesham Town	20	1	2	17	19	65	4

1904-05

First Division

Bristol Rovers	34	20	8	6	74	36	48
Reading	34	18	7	9	57	38	43
Southampton	34	18	7	9	54	40	43
Plymouth Argyle	34	18	5	11	57	39	41
Tottenham Hotspur	34	15	8	11	53	34	38
Fulham	34	14	10	10	46	34	38
Queens Park Rangers	34	14	8	12	51	46	36
Portsmouth	34	16	4	14	61	56	36
New Brompton	34	11	11	12	40	41	33
West Ham United	34	12	8	14	48	42	32
Brighton & Hove Albion	34	13	6	15	44	45	32
Northampton Town	34	12	8	14	43	54	32
Watford	34	14	3	17	41	44	31
Brentford	34	10	9	15	33	38	29
Millwall	34	11	7	16	38	47	29
Swindon Town	34	12	5	17	41	59	29
Luton Town	34	12	3	19	45	54	27
Wellingborough Town	34	5	3	26	25	104	13

Second Division

Fulham Reserves	22	16	4	2	78	25	36
Portsmouth Reserves	22	14	2	6	75	28	30
Swindon Town Reserves	22	12	3	7	54	47	27
Grays United	22	11	3	8	61	40	25
Southampton Reserves	22	10	5	7	52	35	25
Brighton & Hove Albion Reserves	22	9	3	10	48	49	21
West Ham United Reserves	22	8	5	9	45	47	21
Clapton Orient	22	7	7	8	47	56	21
Watford Reserves	22	5	6	11	30	62	16
Southall	22	7	2	13	31	66	16
Wycombe Wanderers	22	6	2	14	37	70	14
Reading Reserves	22	4	4	14	24	57	12

1905-06

First Division

Fulham	34	19	12	3	44	15	50
Southampton	34	19	7	8	58	39	45
Portsmouth	34	17	9	8	61	35	43
Luton Town	34	17	7	10	64	40	41
Tottenham Hotspur	34	16	7	11	46	29	39
Plymouth Argyle	34	16	7	11	52	33	39
Norwich City	34	13	10	11	46	38	36
Bristol Rovers	34	15	5	14	56	56	35
Brentford	34	14	7	13	43	52	35
Reading	34	12	9	13	53	46	33
West Ham United	34	14	5	15	42	39	33
Millwall	34	11	11	12	38	41	33
Queens Park Rangers	34	12	7	15	58	44	31
Watford	34	8	10	16	38	57	26
Swindon Town	34	8	9	17	31	52	25
Brighton & Hove Albion	34	9	7	18	30	55	25
New Brompton	34	7	8	19	20	62	22
Northampton Town	34	8	5	21	32	79	20

Second Division

Crystal Palace	24	19	4	1	66	14	42
Leyton	24	16	6	2	61	18	38
Portsmouth Reserves	24	12	8	4	52	24	32
Fulham Reserves	24	11	6	7	52	39	28
Southampton Reserves	24	7	9	8	39	41	23
Southern United	24	8	7	9	45	49	23
St Leonard's United	24	9	4	11	54	50	22
Watford Reserves	24	8	5	11	43	47	21
West Ham United Reserves	24	7	5	12	46	48	19
Grays United	24	8	3	13	24	77	19
Reading Reserves	24	6	5	13	36	49	15
Swindon Town Reserves	24	5	5	14	36	51	15
Wycombe Wanderers	24	5	3	16	36	83	13

1906-07

First Division

Fulham	38	20	13	5	58	32	53
Portsmouth	38	22	7	9	64	36	51
Brighton & Hove Albion	38	18	9	11	53	43	45
Luton Town	38	18	9	11	52	52	45
West Ham United	38	15	14	9	60	41	44
Tottenham Hotspur	38	17	9	12	63	45	43
Millwall	38	18	6	14	71	50	42
Norwich City	38	15	12	11	57	48	42
Watford	38	13	16	9	46	43	42
Brentford	38	17	8	13	57	56	42
Southampton	38	13	9	16	49	56	35
Reading	38	14	6	18	57	47	34
Leyton	38	11	12	15	38	60	34
Bristol Rovers	38	12	9	17	55	54	33
Plymouth Argyle	38	10	13	15	43	50	33
New Brompton	38	12	9	17	47	59	33
Swindon Town	38	11	11	16	43	54	33
Queens Park Rangers	38	11	10	17	47	55	32
Crystal Palace	38	8	9	21	46	66	25
Northampton Town	38	5	9	24	29	88	19

Second Division

Southend United	22	14	5	3	58	23	33
West Ham United Reserves	22	14	3	5	64	30	31
Portsmouth Reserves	22	11	6	5	53	34	28
Fulham Reserves	22	11	4	7	47	32	26
Hastings & St Leonards United	21	10	4	7	46	31	24
Tunbridge Wells Rangers	22	10	1	11	46	36	21
Salisbury City	22	9	2	11	40	42	20
Southampton Reserves	22	8	2	12	37	56	18
Swindon Town Reserves	22	7	3	12	25	46	17
Reading Reserves	22	6	4	12	32	47	16
Royal Engineers (Aldershot)	21	5	4	12	27	58	14
Wycombe Wanderers	22	4	6	12	28	68	14

The match between Tunbridge Wells Rangers and Royal Engineers (Aldershot) was not completed.
Southern United were disbanded by order of the F.A. on 25th February 1907 after they received a report which had been commissioned into the club's financial affairs. This recommended that the club not be allowed to continue to operate and their record was therefore deleted when it stood as follows:

	10	0	0	10	7	48	0

1907-08

First Division

Queens Park Rangers	38	21	9	8	82	57	51
Plymouth Argyle	38	19	11	8	50	31	49
Millwall	38	19	8	11	49	32	46
Crystal Palace	38	17	10	11	54	51	44
Swindon Town	38	16	10	12	55	40	42
Bristol Rovers	38	16	10	12	59	56	42
Tottenham Hotspur	38	17	7	14	59	48	41
Northampton Town	38	15	11	12	50	41	41
Portsmouth	38	17	6	15	63	52	40
West Ham United	38	15	10	13	47	48	40
Southampton	38	16	6	16	51	60	38
Reading	38	15	6	17	55	50	36
Bradford Park Avenue	38	12	12	14	53	54	36
Watford	38	12	10	16	47	49	34
Brentford	38	14	5	19	49	52	33
Norwich City	38	12	9	17	46	49	33
Brighton & Hove Albion	38	12	8	18	46	59	32
Luton Town	38	12	6	20	33	56	30
Leyton	38	8	11	19	51	73	27
New Brompton	38	9	7	22	44	75	25

Second Division

Southend United	18	13	3	2	47	16	29
Portsmouth Reserves	18	10	5	3	39	22	25
Croydon Common	18	10	3	5	35	25	23
Hastings & St Leonard's United	18	10	2	6	43	29	22
Southampton Reserves	18	7	4	7	54	46	18
Tunbridge Wells Rangers	18	7	3	8	42	38	17
Salisbury City	18	6	4	8	35	46	16
Swindon Town Reserves	18	5	5	8	36	40	15
Brighton & Hove Albion Reserves	18	4	4	10	34	47	12
Wycombe Wanderers	18	1	1	16	16	72	3

1908-09   First Division

Northampton Town	40	25	5	10	90	45	55
Swindon Town	40	22	5	13	96	55	49
Southampton	40	19	10	11	67	58	48
Portsmouth	40	18	10	12	68	60	46
Bristol Rovers	40	17	9	14	60	63	43
Exeter City	40	18	6	16	56	65	42
New Brompton	40	17	7	16	48	59	41
Reading	40	11	18	11	60	57	40
Luton Town	40	17	6	17	59	60	40
Plymouth Argyle	40	15	10	15	46	47	40
Millwall	40	16	6	18	59	61	38
Southend United	40	14	10	16	52	54	38
Leyton	40	15	8	17	52	55	38
Watford	40	14	9	17	51	64	37
Queens Park Rangers	40	12	12	16	52	50	36
Crystal Palace	40	12	12	16	62	62	36
West Ham United	40	16	4	20	56	60	36
Brighton & Hove Albion	40	14	7	19	60	61	35
Norwich City	40	12	11	17	59	75	35
Coventry City	40	15	4	21	64	91	34
Brentford	40	13	7	20	59	74	33

Second Division

Croydon Common	12	10	0	2	67	14	20
Hastings & St Leonard's United	12	8	1	3	42	18	17
Depot Battalion Royal Engineers	12	8	1	3	23	22	17
2nd Grenadier Guards	12	5	0	7	21	33	10
South Farnborough Athletic	12	2	4	6	20	39	8
Salisbury City	12	3	1	8	24	36	7
Chesham Town	12	2	1	9	17	52	5

Gravesend Amateurs adopted professionalism in November 1908 and changed their name to Gravesend Athletic. They resigned in December 1908 and their record was deleted:

	6	0	1	5	3	27	1

1909-10   First Division

Brighton & Hove Albion	42	23	13	6	69	28	59
Swindon Town	42	22	10	10	92	46	54
Queens Park Rangers	42	19	13	10	56	47	51
Northampton Town	42	22	4	16	90	44	48
Southampton	42	16	16	10	64	55	48
Portsmouth	42	20	7	15	70	63	47
Crystal Palace	42	20	6	16	69	50	46
Coventry City	42	19	8	15	71	60	46
West Ham United	42	15	15	12	69	56	45
Leyton	42	16	11	15	60	46	43
Plymouth Argyle	42	16	11	15	61	54	43
New Brompton	42	19	5	18	76	74	43
Bristol Rovers	42	16	10	16	37	48	42
Brentford	42	16	9	17	50	58	41
Luton Town	42	15	11	16	72	92	41
Millwall	42	15	7	20	45	59	37
Norwich City	42	13	9	20	59	78	35
Exeter City	42	14	6	22	60	69	34
Watford	42	10	13	19	51	76	33
Southend United	42	12	9	21	51	90	33
Croydon Common	42	13	5	24	52	96	31
Reading	42	7	10	25	38	73	24

Second Division – Section A

Stoke	10	10	0	0	48	9	20
Ton Pentre	10	4	2	4	17	21	10
Merthyr Town	9	4	1	4	16	21	9
Salisbury City	8	2	1	5	7	18	5
Burton United	6	2	0	4	8	21	4
Aberdare	7	1	0	6	6	11	2

Second Division – Section B

Hastings & St Leonard's	9	6	3	0	26	11	15
Kettering	10	6	0	4	34	19	12
Chesham Town	10	5	2	3	25	25	12
Peterborough City	10	4	2	4	16	23	10
South Farnborough Athletic	10	4	1	5	23	19	9
Romford	9	0	0	9	7	33	0

1910-11

First Divison

Swindon Town	38	24	5	9	80	31	53
Northampton Town	38	18	12	8	54	27	48
Brighton & Hove Albion	38	20	8	10	58	35	48
Crystal Palace	38	17	13	8	55	48	47
West Ham United	38	17	11	10	63	46	45
Queens Park Rangers	38	13	14	11	52	41	40
Leyton	38	16	8	14	57	52	40
Plymouth Argyle	38	15	9	14	54	55	39
Luton Town	38	15	8	15	67	63	38
Norwich City	38	15	8	15	46	48	38
Coventry City	38	16	6	16	65	68	38
Brentford	38	14	9	15	41	42	37
Exeter City	38	14	9	15	51	53	37
Watford	38	13	9	16	49	65	35
Millwall	38	11	9	18	42	54	31
Bristol Rovers	38	10	10	18	42	55	30
Southampton	38	11	8	19	42	67	30
New Brompton	38	11	8	19	34	65	30
Southend United	38	10	9	19	47	64	29
Portsmouth	38	8	11	19	34	53	27

Second Division

Reading	22	16	3	3	55	11	35
Stoke	22	17	1	4	72	21	35
Merthyr Town	22	15	3	4	52	22	33
Cardiff City	22	12	4	6	48	29	28
Croydon Common	22	11	3	8	61	26	25
Treharris	22	10	3	9	38	31	23
Aberdare	22	9	5	8	38	33	23
Ton Pentre	22	10	3	9	44	40	23
Walsall	22	7	4	11	37	41	18
Kettering	22	6	1	15	34	68	13
Chesham Town	22	1	3	18	16	93	5
Salisbury City	22	0	3	19	16	92	3

1911-12

First Division

Queens Park Rangers	38	21	11	6	59	35	53
Plymouth Argyle	38	23	6	9	63	31	52
Northampton Town	38	22	7	9	82	41	51
Swindon Town	38	21	6	11	82	50	48
Brighton & Hove Albion	38	19	9	10	73	35	47
Coventry City	38	17	8	13	66	54	42
Crystal Palace	38	15	10	13	70	46	40
Millwall	38	15	10	13	60	57	40
Watford	38	13	10	15	56	68	36
Stoke	38	13	10	15	51	63	36
Reading	38	11	14	13	43	69	36
Norwich City	38	10	14	14	40	60	34
West Ham United	38	13	7	18	64	69	33
Brentford	38	12	9	17	60	65	33
Exeter City	38	11	11	16	48	62	33
Southampton	38	10	11	17	46	63	31
Bristol Rovers	38	9	13	16	41	62	31
New Brompton	38	11	9	18	35	72	31
Luton Town	38	9	10	19	49	61	28
Leyton	38	7	11	20	27	62	25

Second Division

Merthyr Town	26	19	3	4	60	14	41
Portsmouth	26	19	3	4	73	20	41
Cardiff City	26	15	4	7	55	26	34
Southend United	26	16	1	9	73	24	33
Pontypridd	26	13	6	7	39	24	32
Ton Pentre	26	12	3	11	56	45	27
Walsall	25	13	1	11	44	41	27
Treharris	26	11	5	10	44	47	27
Aberdare	26	10	3	13	39	44	23
Kettering	26	11	0	15	37	62	22
Croydon Common	25	8	2	15	43	45	18
Mardy	24	6	6	12	37	51	18
Cwm Albion	22	5	1	16	27	70	11
Chesham Town	26	1	0	25	18	131	2

Cwm Albion were unable to complete their fixtures because of the National coal strike and 4 games remained unplayed.

1912-13

First Division

Plymouth Argyle	38	22	6	10	77	36	50
Swindon Town	38	20	8	10	66	41	48
West Ham United	38	18	12	8	66	46	48
Queens Park Rangers	38	18	10	10	46	36	46
Crystal Palace	38	17	11	10	55	36	45
Millwall	38	19	7	12	62	43	45
Exeter City	38	18	8	12	48	44	44
Reading	38	17	8	13	59	55	42
Brighton & Hove Albion	38	13	12	13	48	47	38
Northampton Town	38	12	12	14	61	48	36
Portsmouth	38	14	8	16	41	49	36
Merthyr Town	38	12	12	14	43	60	36
Coventry City	38	13	8	17	53	59	34
Watford	38	12	10	16	43	50	34
Gillingham	38	12	10	16	36	53	34
Bristol Rovers	38	12	9	17	55	64	33
Southampton	38	10	11	17	40	72	31
Norwich City	38	10	9	19	39	50	29
Brentford	38	11	5	22	42	55	27
Stoke	38	10	4	24	39	75	24

Second Division

Cardiff City	24	18	5	1	54	15	41
Southend United	24	14	6	4	43	23	34
Swansea Town	24	12	7	5	29	23	31
Croydon Common	24	13	4	7	51	29	30
Luton Town	24	13	4	7	52	39	30
Llanelly	24	9	6	9	33	39	24
Pontypridd	24	6	11	7	30	28	23
Mid Rhondda	24	9	4	11	33	31	22
Aberdare	24	8	6	10	38	40	22
Newport County	24	7	5	12	29	36	19
Mardy	24	6	3	15	38	38	15
Treharris	24	5	2	17	18	60	12
Ton Pentre	24	3	3	18	22	69	9

1913-14

First Division

Swindon Town	38	21	8	9	81	41	50
Crystal Palace	38	17	16	5	60	32	50
Northampton Town	38	14	19	5	50	37	47
Reading	38	17	10	11	43	36	44
Plymouth Argyle	38	15	13	10	46	42	43
West Ham United	38	15	12	11	61	60	42
Brighton & Hove Albion	38	15	12	11	43	45	42
Queens Park Rangers	38	16	9	13	45	43	41
Portsmouth	38	14	12	12	57	48	40
Cardiff City	38	13	12	13	46	42	38
Southampton	38	15	7	16	55	54	37
Exeter City	38	10	16	12	39	38	36
Gillingham	38	13	9	16	48	49	35
Norwich City	38	9	17	12	49	51	35
Millwall	38	11	12	15	51	56	34
Southend Unied	38	10	12	16	41	66	32
Bristol Rovers	38	10	11	17	46	67	31
Watford	38	10	9	19	50	56	29
Merthyr Town	38	9	10	19	38	61	28
Coventry City	38	6	14	18	43	68	26

Second Division

Croydon Common	30	23	5	2	76	14	51
Luton Town	30	24	3	3	92	22	51
Brentford	30	20	4	6	80	18	44
Swansea Town	30	20	4	6	66	23	44
Stoke	30	19	2	9	71	34	40
Newport County	30	14	8	8	49	38	36
Mid Rhondda	30	13	7	10	55	37	33
Pontypridd	30	14	5	11	43	38	33
Llanelly	30	12	4	14	45	39	28
Barry	30	9	8	13	44	70	26
Abertillery Town	30	8	4	18	44	57	20
Ton Pentre	30	8	4	18	33	61	20
Mardy	30	6	6	18	30	60	18
Caerphilly	30	4	7	19	21	103	15
Aberdare	30	4	5	21	33	87	13
Treharris	30	2	4	24	19	106	8

1914-15   First Division

Watford	38	22	8	8	68	46	52
Reading	38	21	7	10	68	43	49
Cardiff City	38	22	4	12	72	38	48
West Ham United	38	18	9	11	58	47	45
Northampton Town	38	16	11	11	56	52	43
Southampton	38	19	5	14	78	74	43
Portsmouth	38	16	10	12	54	42	42
Millwall	38	16	10	12	51	51	42
Swindon Town	38	15	11	12	77	59	41
Brighton & Hove Albion	38	16	7	15	46	47	39
Exeter City	38	15	8	15	50	41	38
Queens Park Rangers	38	13	12	13	55	56	38
Norwich City	38	11	14	13	53	56	36
Luton Town	38	13	8	17	61	73	34
Crystal Palace	38	13	8	17	47	61	34
Bristol Rovers	38	14	3	21	53	75	31
Plymouth Argyle	38	8	14	16	51	61	30
Southend United	38	10	8	20	44	64	28
Croydon Common	38	9	9	20	47	63	27
Gillingham	38	6	8	24	43	83	20

Second Division

Stoke	24	17	4	3	62	15	38
Stalybridge Celtic	24	17	3	4	47	22	37
Merthyr Town	24	15	5	4	46	20	35
Swansea Town	24	16	1	7	48	21	33
Coventry City	24	13	2	9	56	33	28
Ton Pentre	24	11	6	7	42	43	28
Brentford	24	8	7	9	35	45	23
Llanelly	24	10	1	13	39	32	21
Barry	24	6	5	13	30	35	17
Newport County	24	7	3	14	27	42	17
Pontypridd	24	5	6	13	31	58	16
Mid Rhondda	24	3	6	15	17	49	12
Ebbw Vale	24	3	1	20	23	88	7

Several clubs found it difficult to raise a team following the outbreak of war as many players joined the Army.

Caerphilly resigned from the league before playing a game.

Mardy resigned in November 1914 and their record was deleted when it stood as follows: 9   4   1   4   15   10   9

Leyton also resigned in November 1914 and their record was deleted when it stood as follows: 6   1   0   5   5   24   2

Abertillery Town resigned in February 1915 and their record was deleted when it stood as: 11   1   0   10   7   67   2

1919-20   First Division

Portsmouth	42	23	12	7	72	27	58
Watford	42	26	6	10	69	42	58
Crystal Palace	42	22	12	8	69	43	56
Cardiff City	42	18	17	7	70	43	53
Plymouth Argyle	42	20	10	12	56	29	50
Queens Park Rangers	42	18	10	14	62	50	46
Reading	42	16	13	13	51	43	45
Southampton	42	18	8	16	72	63	44
Swansea Town	42	16	11	15	53	45	43
Exeter City	42	17	9	16	57	52	43
Southend United	42	13	17	12	46	48	43
Norwich City	42	15	11	16	64	57	41
Swindon Town	42	17	7	18	65	67	41
Millwall	42	14	12	16	52	55	40
Brentford	42	15	10	17	53	59	40
Brighton & Hove Albion	42	14	8	20	60	72	36
Bristol Rovers	42	11	13	18	62	78	35
Newport County	42	13	7	22	45	70	33
Northampton Town	42	12	9	21	64	103	33
Luton Town	42	10	10	22	51	76	30
Merthyr Town	42	9	11	22	47	78	29
Gillingham	42	10	7	25	34	74	27

Second Division

Mid Rhondda	20	17	3	0	79	10	37
Ton Pentre	20	12	7	1	50	14	31
Llanelly	20	10	5	5	47	30	25
Pontypridd	20	10	3	7	33	29	23
Ebbw Vale	20	7	7	6	38	40	21
Barry	20	7	5	8	32	27	19
Mardy	20	7	5	8	29	30	19
Abertillery Town	20	6	5	9	29	40	17
Porth Athletic	20	4	4	12	30	74	12
Aberaman Athletic	20	4	3	13	28	48	11
Caerphilly	20	1	3	16	20	74	5
					415	416	

The record of goals for and goals against for the Second Division does not tally but it has not been possible to discover where the discrepancy lies.

1920-21

English Section

Brighton & Hove Albion Reserves	24	16	3	5	65	29	35
Portsmouth Reserves	24	13	7	4	44	20	33
Millwall Reserves	24	12	4	8	46	24	28
Southampton Reserves	24	10	7	7	53	35	27
Boscombe	24	10	6	8	25	40	26
Reading Reserves	24	11	3	10	41	34	25
Luton Town Reserves	24	8	8	8	38	35	24
Charlton Athletic	24	8	8	8	41	41	24
Watford Reserves	24	9	4	11	43	45	22
Norwich City Reserves	24	7	7	10	31	39	21
Gillingham Reserves	24	6	5	13	32	47	17
Chatham	24	5	6	13	24	47	16
Thornycrofts	24	4	6	14	29	74	14

Welsh Section

Barry	20	13	4	3	35	12	30
Aberdare Athletic	20	12	3	5	29	23	27
Ebbw Vale	20	10	5	5	34	23	25
Pontypridd	20	10	3	7	34	23	23
Mid Rhondda	20	10	3	7	26	18	23
Abertillery Town	20	8	5	7	35	24	21
Ton Pentre	20	7	5	8	32	34	19
Aberaman Athletic	20	5	7	8	30	33	17
Llanelly	20	7	2	11	28	46	16
Mardy	20	2	6	12	18	39	10
Porth Athletic	20	3	3	14	28	54	9

1921-22

English Section

Plymouth Argyle Reserves	36	22	5	9	91	38	49
Bristol City Reserves	36	18	8	10	73	50	44
Portsmouth Reserves	36	17	10	9	63	41	44
Southampton Reserves	36	19	5	12	70	47	43
Gillingham Reserves	36	17	9	10	65	47	43
Charlton Athletic Reserves	36	18	6	12	69	54	42
Boscombe	36	17	5	14	38	55	39
Luton Town Reserves	36	17	4	15	50	54	38
Watford Reserves	36	15	7	14	65	53	37
Brighton & Hove Albion Reserves	36	12	13	11	60	52	37
Bath City	36	16	5	15	55	53	37
Swindon Town Reserves	36	14	7	15	59	46	35
Bristol Rovers Reserves	36	13	7	16	50	82	33
Millwall Reserves	36	13	4	19	49	53	30
Reading Reserves	36	11	7	18	46	59	29
Exeter City Reserves	36	10	9	17	42	63	29
Guildford United	36	11	6	19	54	56	28
Norwich City Reserves	36	10	6	20	47	86	26
Southend United Reserves	36	9	3	24	47	92	21

Welsh Section

Ebbw Vale	16	11	3	2	33	11	25
Ton Pentre	16	9	4	3	35	14	22
Aberaman Athletic	16	7	5	4	25	19	19
Porth Athletic	16	6	6	4	31	20	18
Pontypridd	16	7	4	5	28	19	18
Swansea Town Reserves	16	7	4	5	24	17	18
Barry	16	3	3	10	14	35	9
Abertillery Town	16	3	2	11	21	45	8
Mardy	16	2	3	11	14	43	7

Mid-Rhondda were suspended by the Welsh F.A. on 3rd March 1922 for non-payment of debts owed to other clubs for transfers, gate money, etc. They were banned from playing any games until their liabilities had been met and the ban was not lifted until June 1923. Their record at the time of suspension was as follows: 11 6 3 2 16 8 15
This record was later deleted from the table.

1922-23

English Section

Bristol City Reserves	38	24	5	9	84	39	53
Boscombe	38	22	7	9	67	34	51
Portsmouth Reserves	38	23	3	12	93	51	49
Bristol Rovers Reserves	38	20	8	10	59	41	48
Plymouth Argyle Reserves	38	20	7	11	74	41	47
Torquay United	38	18	8	12	63	38	44
Brighton & Hove Albion Reserves	38	20	3	15	95	60	43
Luton Town Reserves	38	16	11	11	67	56	43
Southend United Reserves	38	18	6	14	69	68	42
Southampton Reserves	38	18	5	15	65	54	41
Millwall Reserves	38	15	10	13	61	55	40
Coventry City Reserves	38	15	8	15	56	61	38
Guildford United	38	15	7	16	65	59	37
Swindon Town Reserves	38	13	6	19	54	73	32
Bath City	38	10	8	20	44	71	28
Watford Reserves	38	11	6	21	34	79	28
Yeovil & Petters United	38	10	6	22	56	104	26
Norwich City Reserves	38	9	7	22	42	68	25
Exeter City Reserves	38	10	5	23	43	81	25
Reading Reserves	38	7	6	25	43	95	20

Welsh Section

Ebbw Vale	12	6	5	1	22	15	17
Aberaman Athletic	12	7	2	3	30	19	16
Swansea Town Reserves	12	6	2	4	25	14	14
Pontypridd	12	6	2	4	18	18	14
Barry	12	4	3	5	15	11	11
Bridgend Town	12	4	2	6	15	21	10
Porth Athletic	12	0	2	10	18	24	2

Four clubs left during the course of the season and their records were deleted from the table shown above but all four completed their fixtures in the Welsh League. The four who left were:
Caerphilly Town who resigned on 7th November 1922. Their record at the time of resignation was: 5 0 2 3 7 12 2
Abertillery Town who resigned in early April 1923. Their record at the time of resignation was 13 3 2 8 15 33 8
Ton Pentre were suspended by the league on 16th April for non-payment of membership fees and could not complete their fixtures. Their record at the time of suspension was: 15 4 3 8 19 27 11
Mardy did not complete their fixtures. Their record in the competition was as follows:
Caerphilly Town, Abertillery Town and Ton Pentre all disbanded at the end of the season. Mardy did not compete in the Southern League in 1923-24 but they continued playing in the Welsh League.

1923-24

Eastern Section

Peterborough & Fletton United	30	20	2	8	54	31	42
Leicester City Reserves	30	19	3	8	72	30	41
Southampton Reserves	30	18	5	7	60	36	41
Millwall Reserves	30	18	3	9	56	38	39
Portsmouth Reserves	30	16	2	12	66	37	34
Brighton & Hove Albion Reserves	30	13	7	10	55	42	33
Norwich City Reserves	30	13	6	11	46	34	32
Folkestone	30	12	5	13	61	51	29
Coventry City Reserves	30	10	8	12	39	4	28
Watford Reserves	30	11	6	13	36	48	28
Reading Reserves	30	11	6	13	32	43	28
Northampton Town Reserves	30	9	10	11	32	47	28
Luton Town Reserves	30	10	7	13	40	49	27
Guildford United	30	7	5	18	38	72	19
Kettering	30	5	8	17	30	67	18
Bournemouth Reserves	30	4	5	21	40	85	13

Western Section

Yeovil & Petters United	34	25	3	6	71	30	53
Plymouth Argyle Reserves	34	21	5	8	74	37	47
Pontypridd	34	19	8	7	81	44	46
Torquay United	34	19	7	8	59	25	45
Bristol City Reserves	34	17	9	8	63	39	43
Swansea Town Reserves	34	19	5	10	62	38	43
Bristol Rovers Reserves	34	17	6	11	69	43	40
Cardiff City Reserves	34	15	4	15	55	31	34
Exeter City Reserves	34	11	11	12	48	47	33
Weymouth	34	15	3	16	48	60	33
Llanelly	34	14	5	15	47	62	33
Swindon Town Reserves	34	11	6	17	36	60	28
Bridgend Town	34	11	5	18	57	72	27
Newport County Reserves	34	10	7	17	57	79	27
Ebbw Vale	34	8	8	18	38	62	24
Bath City	34	6	9	19	32	71	21
Barry	34	6	7	21	36	74	19
Aberaman Athletic	34	6	4	24	41	87	16

1924-25

Eastern Section

Southampton Reserves	32	17	10	5	65	30	44
Kettering Town	32	17	6	9	67	39	40
Brighton & Hove Albion Reserves	32	15	10	7	68	42	40
Millwall Reserves	32	15	10	7	65	48	40
Peterborough & Fletton United	32	15	9	8	56	29	39
Bournemouth Reserves	32	15	9	8	66	48	39
Leicester City Reserves	32	15	7	10	61	45	37
Portsmouth Reserves	32	15	7	10	51	40	37
Folkestone	32	13	11	8	55	46	37
Norwich City Reserves	32	13	8	11	65	58	34
Coventry City Reserves	32	12	9	11	51	41	33
Luton Town Reserves	32	15	2	15	48	63	32
Northampton Town Reserves	32	10	5	17	38	59	25
Watford Reserves	32	7	7	18	44	71	21
Nuneaton Town	32	8	2	22	37	62	18
Reading Reserves	32	8	1	23	38	87	17
Guildford United	32	4	3	25	40	107	11

Western Section

Swansea Town Reserves	38	25	4	9	73	26	54
Plymouth Argyle Reserves	38	22	10	6	97	35	54
Pontypridd	38	24	4	10	81	39	52
Bridgend Town	38	20	11	7	74	52	51
Mid Rhondda United	38	21	6	11	79	48	48
Weymouth	38	21	4	13	77	50	46
Cardiff City Reserves	38	18	6	14	56	44	42
Newport County Reserves	38	17	8	13	71	60	42
Swindon Town Reserves	38	17	8	13	48	46	42
Bristol City Reserves	38	18	5	15	51	43	41
Yeovil & Petters United	38	15	10	13	49	50	40
Exeter City Reserves	38	16	6	16	78	55	38
Taunton United	38	15	6	17	55	51	36
Bristol Rovers Reserves	38	13	6	19	45	50	32
Torquay United	38	9	11	18	41	73	29
Llanelly	38	6	12	20	49	94	24
Ebbw Vale	38	9	6	23	40	91	24
Bath City	38	8	8	22	28	85	24
Barry	38	8	6	24	38	82	22
Aberaman Athletic	38	6	7	25	39	95	19

1925-26

Eastern Section

Millwall Reserves	34	24	6	4	106	37	54
Leicester City Reserves	34	23	2	9	105	60	48
Brighton & Hove Albion Reserves	34	21	4	9	105	69	46
Kettering Town	34	19	5	10	98	68	43
Peterborough & Fletton United	34	19	3	12	76	62	41
Portsmouth Reserves	34	17	5	12	76	67	39
Norwich City Reserves	34	17	4	13	85	90	38
Bournemouth Reserves	34	15	7	12	76	67	37
Southampton Reserves	34	14	7	13	65	72	35
Fulham Reserves	34	13	6	15	86	77	32
Grays Thurrock United	34	13	5	16	63	77	31
Guildford United	34	11	8	15	71	87	30
Watford Reserves	34	12	2	20	62	94	26
Luton Town Reserves	34	11	3	20	70	78	25
Folkestone	34	9	6	19	67	93	24
Reading Reserves	34	10	3	21	58	84	23
Coventry City Reserves	34	9	5	20	54	93	23
Nuneaton Town	34	7	3	24	61	113	17

Western Section

Plymouth Argyle Reserves	26	20	1	5	67	31	41
Bristol City Reserves	26	16	4	6	48	28	36
Bristol Rovers Reserves	26	13	4	9	51	35	30
Swindon Town Reserves	26	13	4	9	57	40	30
Ebbw Vale	26	13	3	10	60	46	29
Torquay United	26	12	5	9	59	46	29
Yeovil & Petters United	26	9	8	9	43	48	26
Mid-Rhondda United	26	12	1	13	47	49	25
Weymouth	26	10	3	13	64	60	23
Exeter City Reserves	26	8	5	13	40	49	21
Barry	26	8	4	14	47	55	20
Taunton United	26	9	2	15	44	60	20
Pontypridd	26	7	5	14	44	77	19
Bath City	26	7	1	18	38	86	15

1926-27

Eastern Section

Brighton & Hove Albion Reserves	32	21	6	5	86	47	48
Peterborough & Fletton United	32	18	9	5	80	39	45
Portsmouth Reserves	32	19	6	7	95	65	44
Kettering Town	32	15	10	7	66	41	40
Millwall Reserves	32	16	5	11	67	56	37
Bournemouth Reserves	32	14	6	12	69	64	34
Norwich City Reserves	32	14	5	13	79	74	33
Dartford	32	13	7	12	60	71	33
Reading Reserves	32	12	8	12	75	79	32
Luton Town Reserves	32	10	11	11	75	70	1
Leicester City Reserves	32	12	5	15	94	72	29
Watford Reserves	32	10	8	14	74	84	28
Southampton Reserves	32	10	6	16	57	77	26
Poole	32	9	6	17	55	86	24
Grays Thurrock United	32	10	3	19	49	66	23
Guildford United	32	6	7	19	57	106	19
Folkestone	32	7	4	21	57	98	18

Western Section

Torquay United	26	17	4	5	63	30	38
Bristol City Reserves	26	14	10	2	77	37	38
Plymouth Argyle Reserves	26	15	4	7	56	38	34
Ebbw Vale	26	14	2	10	67	45	30
Bristol Rovers Reserves	26	12	4	10	51	43	28
Swindon Town Reserves	26	11	5	10	60	57	27
Barry	26	11	4	11	65	50	26
Exeter City Reserves	26	10	6	10	62	49	26
Weymouth	26	12	2	12	48	65	26
Newport County Reserves	26	9	6	11	57	53	24
Bath City	26	7	9	10	44	52	23
Yeovil & Petters United	26	9	5	12	49	66	23
Taunton United	26	4	4	18	36	83	12
Mid Rhondda United	26	2	5	19	22	89	9

1927-28

Eastern Section

Kettering Town	34	23	6	5	90	39	52
Peterborough & Fletton United	34	21	3	10	73	43	45
Northfleet United	34	17	7	10	83	54	41
Brighton & Hove Albion Reserves	34	20	0	14	90	63	40
Norwich City Reserves	34	17	6	11	69	69	40
Southampton Reserves	34	16	7	11	92	70	39
Aldershot Town	34	17	5	12	85	66	39
Sittingbourne	34	16	5	13	64	70	37
Millwall Reserves	34	15	6	13	66	59	36
Poole	34	15	5	14	69	84	35
Folkestone	34	12	6	16	71	91	30
Guildford City	34	12	5	17	65	89	29
Dartford	34	12	4	18	46	49	28
Gillingham Reserves	34	10	7	17	72	84	27
Sheppey United	34	11	3	20	57	87	25
Chatham	34	10	4	20	49	70	24
Grays Thurrock United	34	10	3	21	48	88	23
Bournemouth Reserves	34	9	4	21	48	62	22

Western Section

Bristol City Reserves	30	20	3	7	95	51	43
Exeter City Reserves	30	18	4	8	104	56	40
Bristol Rovers Reserves	30	16	3	11	80	64	35
Plymouth Argyle Reserves	30	16	2	12	88	53	34
Newport County Reserves	30	13	8	9	99	70	34
Ebbw Vale	30	15	3	12	67	74	33
Swindon Town Reserves	30	13	4	13	80	74	30
Aberdare & Aberaman	30	12	6	12	62	68	30
Yeovil & Petters United	30	11	7	12	64	57	29
Torquay United Reserves	30	11	6	13	51	67	28
Bath City	30	12	3	15	64	68	27
Taunton Town	30	11	5	14	60	65	27
Weymouth	30	10	6	14	50	83	26
Merthyr Town Reserves	30	9	4	17	50	77	22
Barry	30	8	6	16	45	87	22
Mid Rhondda United	30	7	6	17	36	81	20

1928-29

Eastern Section

Kettering Town	36	24	4	8	96	46	52
Peterborough & Fletton United	36	21	5	10	86	44	47
Brighton & Hove Albion Reserves	36	19	9	8	91	56	47
Millwall Reserves	36	21	4	11	90	67	46
Bournemouth Reserves	36	20	5	11	82	58	45
Aldershot Town	36	18	5	13	68	52	41
Sheppey United	36	17	7	12	58	58	41
Folkestone	36	17	6	13	83	80	40
Northfleet United	36	17	4	15	87	65	38
Gillingham Reserves	36	15	8	13	68	70	38
Guildford City	36	13	11	12	85	78	37
Southampton Reserves	36	14	6	16	86	79	34
Poole	36	13	8	15	62	66	34
Thames Association	36	13	5	18	67	74	31
Dartford	36	10	6	20	55	106	26
Chatham	36	8	8	20	47	81	24
Sittingbourne	36	11	1	24	59	98	23
Norwich City Reserves	36	8	6	22	48	96	22
Grays Thurrock United	36	6	6	24	47	91	18

Western Section

Plymouth Argyle Reserves	26	15	6	5	69	27	36
Newport County Reserves	26	15	2	9	64	58	32
Bristol Rovers Reserves	26	14	3	9	54	45	31
Bristol City Reserves	26	14	2	10	70	46	30
Torquay United Reserves	26	13	4	9	52	42	30
Bath City	26	13	4	9	43	59	30
Exeter City Reserves	26	11	6	9	69	53	28
Lovells Athletic	26	11	6	9	54	48	28
Swindon Town Reserves	26	11	5	10	68	74	27
Yeovil & Petters United	26	11	2	13	49	57	24
Taunton Town	26	9	5	12	58	66	23
Ebbw Vale	26	9	5	12	56	66	23
Barry	26	6	3	17	38	66	15
Merthyr Town Reserves	26	3	1	22	37	92	7

1929-30

Eastern Section

Aldershot Town	32	21	6	5	84	39	48
Millwall Reserves	32	21	3	8	75	56	45
Thames Association	32	17	6	9	80	60	40
Peterborough & Fletton United	32	18	3	11	66	39	39
Northampton Town Reserves	32	17	4	11	86	60	38
Southampton Reserves	32	14	7	11	73	62	35
Sheppey United	32	15	5	12	76	69	35
Kettering Town	32	13	7	12	70	69	33
Dartford	32	14	5	13	57	59	33
Norwich City Reserves	32	14	3	15	69	69	31
Guildford City	32	13	2	17	65	97	28
Bournemouth Reserves	32	10	7	15	59	63	27
Brighton & Hove Albion Reserves	32	12	2	18	56	79	26
Folkestone	32	13	0	19	56	82	26
Sittingbourne	32	10	5	17	55	59	25
Northfleet United	32	6	7	19	53	77	19
Grays Thurrock United	32	7	2	23	54	101	16

Poole found it impossible to continue and left 4 games unplayed. Their record was deleted when it was: 30 7 6 17 44 81 20
The club, which had been founded in 1887, was disbanded at the end of the season but a new club called Poole Town was formed at a meeting held at Poole Guild Hall on 12th June 1930. The new club could not afford the cost of the original club's ground in Fernside Road and played on a pitch at Ye Olde Farme in Wimborne Road, joining the Western League. The old Fernside Road ground was soon covered with housing.

Western Section

Bath City	28	16	6	6	85	52	38
Bristol Rovers Reserves	28	16	4	8	66	50	36
Taunton Town	28	14	7	7	50	40	35
Barry	28	15	3	10	65	55	33
Yeovil & Petters United	28	12	7	9	63	47	31
Plymouth Argyle Reserves	28	14	3	11	68	52	31
Newport County Reserves	28	13	4	11	68	76	30
Lovells Athletic	28	13	2	13	59	57	28
Exeter City Reserves	28	11	6	11	49	54	28
Bristol City Reserves	28	11	5	12	59	63	27
Swindon Town Reserves	28	10	6	12	69	67	26
Torquay United Reserves	28	10	6	12	76	77	26
Llanelly	28	10	4	14	55	52	24
Ebbw Vale	28	5	6	17	52	97	16
Merthyr Town Reserves	28	5	1	22	48	93	11

1930-31

Eastern Section

Dartford	16	9	5	2	39	18	23
Aldershot Town	16	10	3	3	50	28	23
Norwich City Reserves	16	9	1	6	47	38	19
Peterborough & Fletton United	16	6	5	5	35	29	17
Thames Association Reserves	16	7	2	7	38	31	16
Millwall Reserves	16	7	0	9	47	40	14
Folkestone	16	4	3	9	31	46	11
Guildford City	16	5	1	10	28	53	11
Sheppey United	16	4	2	10	31	63	10

Western Section

Exeter City Reserves	22	15	2	5	59	28	32
Llanelly	22	10	8	4	72	39	28
Merthyr Town	22	12	3	7	62	49	27
Plymouth Argyle Reserves	22	12	2	8	55	34	26
Bath City	22	10	6	6	47	39	26
Torquay United Reserves	22	9	5	8	66	49	23
Swindon Town Reserves	22	7	7	8	48	52	21
Bristol Rovers Reserves	22	7	6	9	58	64	20
Barry	22	7	5	10	29	39	19
Taunton Town	22	5	7	10	36	62	17
Newport County Reserves	22	6	2	14	36	66	14
Ebbw Vale	22	5	1	16	32	79	11

1931-32

Eastern Section

Dartford	18	12	3	3	53	18	27
Folkestone	18	12	2	4	58	27	26
Guildford City	18	11	1	6	33	24	23
Norwich City Reserves	18	9	2	7	46	33	20
Millwall Reserves	18	9	2	7	41	39	20
Tunbridge Wells Rangers	18	7	5	6	23	25	19
Bournemouth Reserves	18	6	4	8	43	61	16
Peterborough & Fletton United	18	4	5	9	28	29	13
Aldershot Town	18	3	5	10	17	30	11
Sheppey United	18	2	1	15	16	72	5

Western Section

Yeovil & Petters United	24	16	4	4	65	31	36
Plymouth Argyle Reserves	24	15	5	4	81	31	35
Bath City	24	12	7	5	50	33	31
Llanelly	24	12	4	8	65	46	28
Taunton Town	24	13	2	9	53	58	28
Newport County	24	10	6	8	70	51	26
Exeter City Reserves	24	9	7	8	59	43	25
Merthyr Town	24	9	4	11	66	73	22
Bristol Rovers Reserves	24	8	4	12	54	47	20
Swindon Town Reserves	24	8	4	12	54	95	20
Barry	24	7	3	14	58	76	17
Torquay United Reserves	24	5	6	13	43	66	16
Ebbw Vale	24	3	2	19	34	102	8

1932-33

Eastern Section

Norwich City Reserves	14	9	2	3	34	22	20
Dartford	14	8	2	4	26	23	18
Folkestone	14	7	1	6	35	32	15
Bournemouth Reserves	14	5	4	5	36	33	14
Tunbridge Wells Rangers	14	5	2	7	23	24	12
Guildford City	14	5	2	7	22	28	12
Millwall Reserves	14	5	1	8	27	31	11
Aldershot Reserves	14	3	4	7	24	34	10

Peterborough & Fletton United were suspended by the F.A. shortly before the start of the season for non-payment of some of the previous season's wages to their professional players. After making part payments, the suspension was lifted and the club was allowed to start the season but could only afford to field a team of local amateurs. It was decided to disband the club on 25th October 1932 and their record at the time was deleted. It stood as follows: 4 0 0 4 2 37 0

Western Section

Bath City	20	13	4	3	62	34	30
Exeter City Reserves	20	12	3	5	62	46	27
Torquay United Reserves	20	12	1	7	56	37	25
Plymouth Argyle Reserves	20	11	2	7	68	38	24
Yeovil & Petters United	20	11	2	7	59	44	24
Llanelly	20	10	2	8	53	33	22
Bristol Rovers Reserves	20	7	3	10	53	65	17
Newport County Reserves	20	6	4	10	42	55	16
Merthyr Town	20	7	1	12	39	58	15
Barry	20	3	4	13	30	72	10
Taunton Town	20	4	2	14	21	63	10

1933-34

Eastern Section

Norwich City Reserves	16	9	4	3	41	15	22
Margate	16	8	3	5	23	20	19
Millwall Reserves	16	7	4	5	28	28	18
Clapton Orient Reserves	16	8	1	7	33	34	17
Bournemouth Reserves	16	6	3	7	28	30	15
Tunbridge Wells Rangers	16	6	2	8	25	36	14
Folkestone	16	5	3	8	26	26	13
Guildford City	16	5	3	8	27	33	13
Dartford	16	4	5	7	15	24	13

Western Section

Plymouth Argyle Reserves	20	13	6	1	62	22	32
Bristol Rovers Reserves	20	14	3	3	56	27	31
Bath City	20	11	3	6	43	25	25
Torquay United Reserves	20	9	4	7	54	36	22
Yeovil & Petters United	20	10	1	9	35	39	21
Exeter City Reserves	20	8	3	9	54	47	19
Merthyr Town	20	8	2	10	39	50	18
Llanelly	20	8	1	11	25	39	17
Barry	20	4	5	11	37	64	13
Newport County Reserves	20	4	3	13	36	54	11
Taunton Town	20	5	1	14	27	65	11

Central Section

Plymouth Argyle Reserves	18	16	1	1	47	14	33
Clapton Orient Reserves	18	9	3	6	35	25	21
Norwich City Reserves	18	8	4	6	41	27	20
Yeovil & Petters United	18	7	4	7	34	38	18
Bath City	18	7	3	8	31	36	17
Dartford	18	6	4	8	28	26	16
Tunbridge Wells Rangers	18	7	1	10	26	37	15
Llanelly	18	6	2	10	28	39	14
Folkestone	18	6	1	11	30	41	13
Guildford City	18	6	1	11	28	45	13

1934-35

Eastern Section

Norwich City Reserves	18	12	1	5	52	21	25
Dartford	18	8	6	4	36	22	22
Margate	18	7	6	7	38	30	20
Bournemouth Reserves	18	8	3	8	34	26	19
Guildford City	18	7	5	6	41	34	19
Aldershot Reserves	18	7	3	8	29	43	17
Folkestone	18	5	6	7	30	39	16
Tunbridge Wells Rangers	18	6	4	8	32	56	16
Clapton Orient Reserves	18	5	4	9	33	35	14
Millwall Reserves	18	3	6	9	26	45	12

Western Section

Yeovil & Petters United	16	11	2	3	49	18	24
Newport County Reserves	16	8	5	3	45	29	21
Plymouth Argyle Reserves	16	7	5	4	40	24	19
Exeter City Reserves	16	7	2	7	38	32	16
Bath City	16	6	4	6	35	32	16
Bristol Rovers Reserves	16	5	5	6	33	37	15
Barry	16	6	3	7	30	40	15
Torquay United Reserves	16	5	3	8	24	29	13
Taunton Town	16	1	3	12	13	66	5

Central Section

Folkestone	20	11	4	5	43	31	26
Guildford City	20	11	4	5	43	39	26
Plymouth Argyle Reserves	20	6	9	5	40	28	21
Torquay United Reserves	20	7	6	7	34	35	20
Bristol Rovers Reserves	20	8	4	8	38	46	20
Margate	20	8	3	9	40	34	19
Dartford	20	8	3	9	43	38	19
Aldershot Reserves	20	8	3	9	33	44	19
Tunbridge Wells Rangers	20	8	2	10	33	37	18
Yeovil & Petters United	20	8	1	11	45	51	17
Bath City	20	6	3	11	34	43	15

1935-36

Eastern Section

Margate	18	13	2	3	49	16	28
Folkestone	18	11	3	4	46	23	25
Dartford	18	9	3	6	47	25	21
Tunbridge Wells Rangers	18	9	1	8	26	41	19
Clapton Orient Reserves	18	7	4	7	39	31	18
Millwall Reserves	18	7	3	8	42	39	17
Norwich City Reserves	18	8	0	10	39	38	16
Guildford City	18	6	3	9	32	52	15
Aldershot Reserves	18	6	1	11	24	45	13
Bournemouth Reserves	18	3	2	13	25	59	8

Western Section

Plymouth Argyle Reserves	16	12	3	1	51	18	27
Bristol Rovers Reserves	16	8	3	5	35	30	19
Newport County Reserves	16	8	3	5	29	30	19
Torquay United Reserves	16	7	1	8	25	28	15
Bath City	16	5	5	6	18	26	15
Cheltenham Town	16	6	2	8	32	28	14
Yeovil & Petters United	16	5	3	8	31	35	13
Barry	16	5	2	9	29	41	12
Exeter City Reserves	16	4	2	10	24	38	10

Central Section

Margate	20	14	3	3	57	18	31
Bristol Rovers Reserves	20	13	1	6	51	37	27
Plymouth Argyle Reserves	20	12	2	6	53	32	26
Aldershot Reserves	20	9	4	7	37	37	22
Folkestone	20	9	3	8	51	36	21
Tunbridge Wells Rangers	20	7	4	9	40	41	18
Dartford	20	7	3	10	34	42	17
Guildford City	20	7	3	10	33	47	17
Cheltenham Town	20	5	5	10	32	45	15
Bath City	20	5	5	10	34	52	15
Yeovil & Petters United	20	3	5	12	40	75	11

1936-37

Ipswich Town	30	19	8	3	68	35	46
Norwich City Reserves	30	18	5	7	70	35	41
Folkestone	30	17	4	9	71	62	38
Margate	30	15	4	11	64	49	34
Guildford City	30	15	4	11	54	60	34
Bath City	30	14	5	11	65	55	33
Yeovil & Petters United	30	15	3	12	77	69	33
Plymouth Argyle Reserves	30	11	8	11	64	58	30
Newport County Reserves	30	11	8	11	72	68	30
Barry	30	12	4	14	58	72	28
Cheltenham Town	30	10	4	16	61	70	24
Dartford	30	9	5	16	41	55	23
Exeter City Reserves	30	8	7	15	57	78	23
Tunbridge Wells Rangers	30	8	6	16	62	64	22
Torquay United Reserves	30	8	5	17	46	76	21
Aldershot Reserves	30	7	6	17	47	74	20

Midweek Section

Margate	18	12	1	5	48	24	25
Bath City	18	10	5	3	38	28	25
Norwich City Reserves	18	9	5	4	44	27	23
Folkestone	18	7	6	5	32	36	20
Millwall Reserves	18	8	3	7	44	47	19
Portsmouth Reserves	18	6	5	7	40	27	17
Tunbridge Wells Rangers	18	5	4	9	30	41	14
Aldershot Reserves	18	6	2	10	20	30	14
Guildford City	18	3	6	9	24	36	12
Dartford	18	4	3	11	19	43	11

1937-38

Guildford City	34	22	5	7	94	60	49
Plymouth Argyle Reserves	34	18	9	7	98	58	45
Ipswich Town	34	19	6	9	89	54	44
Yeovil & Petters United	34	14	14	6	72	45	42
Norwich City Reserves	34	15	11	8	77	55	41
Colchester United	34	15	8	11	90	58	38
Bristol Rovers Reserves	34	14	8	12	63	62	36
Swindon Town Reserves	34	14	7	13	70	76	35
Tunbridge Wells Rangers	34	14	6	14	68	74	34
Aldershot Reserves	34	10	12	12	42	55	32
Cheltenham Town	34	13	5	16	72	68	31
Exeter City Reserves	34	13	5	16	71	75	31
Dartford	34	9	11	14	51	70	29
Bath City	34	9	9	16	45	65	27
Folkestone	34	10	6	18	58	82	26
Newport County Reserves	34	10	6	18	56	86	26
Barry	34	8	7	19	50	88	23
Torquay United Reserves	34	8	7	19	46	81	23

Midweek Section

Millwall Reserves	18	13	3	2	59	21	29
Colchester United	18	13	1	4	42	23	27
Aldershot Reserves	18	11	3	4	38	29	25
Norwich City Reserves	18	9	1	8	45	39	19
Portsmouth Reserves	18	5	5	8	31	30	15
Dartford	18	6	3	9	32	35	15
Folkestone	18	6	3	9	34	38	15
Tunbridge Wells Rangers	18	5	4	9	28	36	14
Bath City	18	5	3	10	27	45	13
Guildford City	18	4	0	14	21	61	8

1938-39

Colchester United	44	31	5	8	110	37	67
Guildford City	44	30	6	8	126	52	66
Gillingham	44	29	6	9	104	57	64
Plymouth Argyle Reserves	44	26	5	13	128	63	57
Yeovil & Petters United	44	22	10	12	85	70	54
Arsenal Reserves	44	21	9	14	92	57	51
Cardiff City Reserves	44	24	3	17	105	73	51
Tunbridge Wells Rangers	44	22	6	16	93	76	50
Norwich City Reserves	44	23	4	17	86	76	50
Chelmsford City	44	18	8	18	74	73	44
Bath City	44	16	12	16	58	74	44
Barry	44	18	7	19	76	90	43
Cheltenham Town	44	16	9	19	76	105	41
Ipswich Town Reserves	44	14	12	18	64	76	40
Worcester City	44	13	14	17	72	90	40
Folkestone	44	16	6	22	74	85	38
Newport County Reserves	44	13	10	21	74	108	36
Exeter City Reserves	44	12	9	23	51	107	33
Torquay United Reserves	44	12	8	24	53	89	32
Swindon Town Reserves	44	11	9	24	66	101	31
Aldershot Reserves	44	12	6	26	69	92	30
Bristol Rovers Reserves	44	9	11	24	66	85	29
Dartford	44	8	5	31	53	119	21

Midweek Section

Tunbridge Wells Rangers	16	8	7	1	37	18	23
Colchester United	16	9	2	5	36	21	20
Norwich City Reserves	16	7	4	5	40	26	18
Millwall Reserves	16	7	4	5	33	23	18
Portsmouth Reserves	16	5	4	7	21	29	14
Guildford City	16	4	6	6	24	39	14
Aldershot Reserves	16	4	5	7	22	25	13
Folkestone	16	4	5	7	24	35	13
Dartford	16	4	3	9	24	45	11

1939-40

The league ceased operating when war was declared on 3rd September 1940 when the table was as below:

Guildford City	3	3	0	0	15	1	6
Yeovil & Petters United	3	3	0	0	5	2	6
Hereford United	4	2	2	0	6	4	6
Cheltenham Town	3	2	1	0	11	3	5
Swindon Town Reserves	3	2	1	0	11	3	5
Norwich City Reserves	2	2	0	0	2	0	4
Gillingham	3	2	0	1	6	4	4
Chelmsford City	4	2	0	2	5	9	4
Exeter City Reserves	2	1	1	0	2	1	3
Ipswich Town Reserves	3	1	1	1	4	2	3
Barry	3	1	1	1	7	4	3
Colchester United	3	1	1	1	4	3	3
Bristol Rovers Reserves	3	1	1	1	3	5	3
Arsenal "A"	1	1	0	0	3	1	2
Plymouth Argyle Reserves	2	1	0	1	5	4	2
Newport County Reserves	3	1	0	2	8	10	2
Kidderminster Harriers	3	1	0	2	2	3	2
Worcester City	3	1	0	2	2	4	2
Tunbridge Wells Rangers	3	0	1	2	2	5	1
Torquay United Reserves	3	0	1	2	2	6	1
Bath City	2	0	1	1	1	7	1
Cardiff City Reserves	3	0	0	3	3	6	0
Aldershot Reserves	3	0	0	3	3	9	0
Dartford	3	0	0	3	0	16	0

A war-time competition was set up for the 1939-40 season with Western and Eastern Sections.
There were 8 clubs who entered the Western Section: Barry, Bath City, Cheltenham Town, Gloucester City (pre-war members of the Birmingham Combination), Hereford United, Lovells Athletic (pre-war members of both the Welsh League and Western League), Worcester City and Yeovil & Petters United .
The 6 clubs who entered the Eastern Section were: Chelmsford City, Dartford, Gillingham, Guildford City, Norwich City Reserves and Tunbridge Wells Rangers. However, Gillingham withdrew before playing any games.

Neither section were able to complete their fixtures but the unplayed games could not alter the section winners.

Eastern Section

Chelmsford City	7	5	0	2	29	9	10
Guildford City	8	4	1	3	26	13	9
Tunbridge Wells Rangers	7	2	3	2	21	16	7
Dartford	7	2	1	4	17	30	5
Norwich City Reserves	7	2	1	4	9	34	5

Western Section

Lovells Athletic	14	11	1	2	53	22	23
Worcester City	14	9	2	3	55	30	20
Hereford United	14	8	0	6	45	31	16
Yeovil & Petters United	14	7	2	5	30	24	16
Gloucester City	14	5	0	9	35	49	10
Barry	14	4	1	9	31	56	9
Cheltenham Town	13	3	2	8	21	38	8
Bath City	13	3	2	8	21	41	8

War-time championship decider

18th May 1940   Chelmsford City vs Lovells Athletic 3-3
(Played at New Writtle Street, Chelmsford)

1945-46

Chelmsford City	18	15	1	2	66	23	34
Hereford United	20	13	3	4	59	31	29
Bath City	20	12	2	6	62	32	26
Cheltenham Town	18	9	1	8	35	54	22
Barry Town	20	8	4	8	42	42	20
Yeovil & Petters United	18	7	1	10	57	52	18
Worcester City	20	8	2	10	60	58	18
Colchester United	20	7	3	10	29	47	17
Bedford Town	16	4	1	11	30	49	15
Swindon Town Reserves	18	4	3	11	36	65	14
Cardiff City Reserves	20	4	5	11	39	60	13

Chelmsford City, Cheltenham Town, Yeovil & Petters United and Swindon Town Reserves all had 2 games unplayed and so were awarded an additional 3 points. Bedford Town had 4 games unplayed and so were awarded an additional 6 points.

1946-47

Gillingham	31	20	6	5	103	45	47
Guildford City	32	21	4	7	86	39	46
Merthyr Tydfil	31	21	2	8	104	37	45
Yeovil Town	32	19	6	7	100	49	44
Chelmsford City	31	17	3	11	90	60	38
Gravesend & Northfleet	32	17	4	11	82	58	38
Barry Town	30	14	6	10	89	61	36
Colchester United	31	15	4	12	65	60	35
Cheltenham Town	31	14	3	14	68	75	32
Millwall Reserves	24	8	5	11	59	57	29
Dartford	32	10	5	17	71	100	25
Bedford Town	32	8	8	16	63	98	24
Hereford United	32	8	7	17	37	85	23
Worcester City	31	8	5	18	55	90	22
Exeter City Reserves	32	10	2	20	69	126	22
Bath City	32	7	7	18	52	93	21
Gloucester City	32	8	1	23	57	120	17

Millwall Reserves left 8 games unplayed. It was decided that these would all be counted as drawn games and clubs were awarded an extra point for each unplayed game.

1947-48

Merthyr Tydfil	34	23	7	4	84	38	53
Gillingham	34	21	5	8	81	43	47
Worcester City	34	21	3	10	74	45	45
Colchester United	34	17	10	7	88	41	44
Hereford United	34	16	10	8	77	53	42
Lovells Athletic	34	17	6	11	74	50	40
Exeter City Reserves	34	15	7	12	65	57	37
Yeovil Town	34	12	11	11	56	50	35
Chelmsford City	34	14	7	13	62	58	35
Cheltenham Town	34	13	9	12	71	71	35
Bath City	34	12	8	14	55	62	32
Barry Town	34	10	9	15	60	70	29
Gravesend & Northfleet	34	11	6	17	52	81	28
Guildford City	34	11	4	19	69	74	26
Dartford	34	10	6	18	35	62	26
Gloucester City	34	8	6	20	45	78	22
Torquay United Reserves	34	6	9	19	43	95	21
Bedford Town	34	6	3	25	41	104	15

1948-49

Gillingham	42	26	10	6	104	48	62
Chelmsford City	42	27	7	8	115	64	61
Merthyr Tydfil	42	26	8	8	133	54	60
Colchester United	42	21	10	11	94	61	52
Worcester City	42	22	7	13	87	56	51
Dartford	42	21	9	12	73	53	51
Gravesend & Northfleet	42	20	9	13	60	46	49
Yeovil Town	42	19	9	14	90	53	47
Cheltenham Town	42	19	9	14	71	64	47
Kidderminster Harriers	42	19	6	17	77	96	44
Exeter City Reserves	42	18	7	17	83	73	43
Hereford United	42	17	6	19	83	84	40
Bath City	42	15	8	19	72	87	38
Hastings United	42	14	10	18	69	93	38
Torquay United Reserves	42	15	7	20	73	93	37
Lovells Athletic	42	14	8	20	73	74	36
Guildford City	42	12	12	18	58	85	36
Gloucester City	42	12	10	20	78	100	34
Barry Town	42	12	10	20	55	95	34
Tonbridge	42	9	7	26	54	105	25
Chingford Town	42	6	9	27	43	94	21
Bedford Town	42	5	8	29	32	101	18

1949-50

Merthyr Tydfil	46	34	3	9	143	62	71
Colchester United	46	31	9	6	109	51	71
Yeovil Town	46	29	7	10	104	45	65
Chelmsford City	46	26	9	11	121	64	61
Gillingham	46	23	9	14	93	61	55
Dartford	46	20	9	17	70	65	49
Worcester City	46	21	7	18	85	80	49
Guildford City	46	18	11	17	79	73	47
Weymouth	46	19	9	18	80	82	47
Barry Town	46	18	10	18	78	72	46
Exeter City Reserves	46	16	14	16	73	83	46
Lovells Athletic	46	17	10	19	86	78	44
Tonbridge	46	16	12	18	65	76	44
Hastings United	46	17	8	21	92	140	42
Gravesend & Northfleet	46	16	9	21	88	82	41
Torquay United Reserves	46	14	12	20	80	89	40
Bath City	46	16	7	23	61	78	39
Gloucester City	46	14	11	21	72	101	39
Hereford United	46	15	8	23	74	76	38
Cheltenham Town	46	13	11	22	75	96	37
Headington United	46	15	7	24	72	97	37
Bedford Town	46	12	11	23	63	79	35
Kidderminster Harriers	46	12	11	23	65	108	35
Chingford Town	46	10	6	30	61	151	26

1950-51

Merthyr Tydfil	44	29	8	7	156	66	66
Hereford United	44	27	7	10	110	69	61
Guildford City	44	23	8	13	88	60	54
Chelmsford City	44	21	12	11	84	58	54
Llanelly	44	19	13	12	89	73	51
Cheltenham Town	44	21	8	15	91	61	50
Headington United	44	18	11	15	84	83	47
Torquay United Reserves	44	20	6	18	93	79	46
Exeter City Reserves	44	16	12	16	90	94	44
Weymouth	44	16	12	16	82	88	44
Tonbridge	44	16	12	16	79	87	44
Gloucester City	44	16	11	17	81	76	43
Yeovil Town	44	13	15	16	72	72	41
Worcester City	44	15	11	18	69	78	41
Bath City	44	15	10	19	66	73	40
Dartford	44	14	11	19	61	70	39
Bedford Town	44	15	9	20	64	94	39
Gravesend & Northfleet	44	12	14	18	65	83	38
Kettering Town	44	13	11	20	87	87	37
Lovells Athletic	44	12	13	19	81	93	37
Kidderminster Harriers	44	13	9	22	58	103	35
Barry Town	44	13	7	24	54	104	33
Hastings United	44	11	6	27	91	143	28

Chingford Town resigned early in December 1950 and their record was
deleted when it stood as: 16   1   2   13   11   47   4
Their reserves, in effect, became the first team and completed their season
in the Metropolitan League but the club disbanded completely at the end
of the season.

1951-52

Merthyr Tydfil	42	27	6	9	128	60	60
Weymouth	42	22	13	7	81	42	57
Kidderminster Harriers	42	22	10	10	70	40	54
Guildford City	42	18	16	8	66	47	52
Hereford United	42	21	9	12	80	59	51
Worcester City	42	23	4	15	86	73	50
Kettering Town	42	18	10	14	83	56	46
Lovells Athletic	42	18	10	14	87	68	46
Gloucester City	42	19	8	15	68	55	46
Bath City	42	19	6	17	75	67	44
Headington United	42	16	11	15	55	53	43
Bedford Town	42	16	10	16	75	64	42
Barry Town	42	18	6	18	84	89	42
Chelmsford City	42	15	10	17	67	80	40
Dartford	42	15	9	18	63	65	39
Tonbridge	42	15	6	21	63	84	36
Yeovil Town	42	12	11	19	56	76	35
Cheltenham Town	42	15	4	23	59	85	34
Exeter City Reserves	42	13	7	22	76	106	33
Llanelly	42	13	6	23	70	111	32
Gravesend & Northfleet	42	12	7	23	68	88	31
Hastings United	42	3	5	34	41	131	11

1952-53

Headington United	42	23	12	7	93	50	58
Merthyr Tydfil	42	25	8	9	117	66	58
Bedford Town	42	24	8	10	91	61	56
Kettering Town	42	23	8	11	88	50	54
Bath City	42	22	10	10	71	46	54
Worcester City	42	20	11	11	100	66	51
Llanelly	42	21	9	12	95	72	51
Barry Town	42	22	3	17	89	69	47
Gravesend & Northfleet	42	19	7	16	83	76	45
Gloucester City	42	17	9	16	50	78	43
Guildford City	42	17	8	17	64	60	42
Hastings United	42	18	5	19	75	66	41
Cheltenham Town	42	15	11	16	70	89	41
Weymouth	42	15	10	17	70	75	40
Hereford United	42	17	5	20	76	73	39
Tonbridge	42	12	9	21	62	88	33
Lovells Athletic	42	12	8	22	68	81	32
Yeovil Town	42	11	10	21	75	99	32
Chelmsford City	42	12	7	23	58	92	31
Exeter City Reserves	42	13	4	25	71	94	30
Kidderminster Harriers	42	12	5	25	54	85	29
Dartford	42	6	5	31	40	121	17

1953-54

Merthyr Tydfil	42	27	8	7	97	55	62
Headington United	42	22	9	11	68	43	53
Yeovil Town	42	20	8	14	87	76	48
Bath City	42	17	12	13	73	67	46
Kidderminster Harriers	42	18	9	15	62	59	45
Weymouth	42	18	8	16	83	72	44
Barry Town	42	17	9	16	108	91	43
Bedford Town	42	19	5	18	80	84	43
Gloucester City	42	16	11	15	69	77	43
Hastings United	42	16	10	16	73	67	42
Kettering Town	42	15	12	15	65	63	42
Hereford United	42	16	9	17	66	62	41
Llanelly	42	16	9	17	80	85	41
Guildford City	42	15	11	16	56	60	41
Gravesend & Northfleet	42	16	8	18	76	77	40
Worcester City	42	17	6	19	66	71	40
Lovells Athletic	42	14	11	17	62	60	39
Tonbridge	42	15	9	18	85	91	39
Chelmsford City	42	14	10	18	67	71	38
Exeter City Reserves	42	11	13	18	61	72	35
Cheltenham Town	42	11	12	19	56	83	34
Dartford	42	6	13	23	42	89	25

1954-55

Yeovil Town	42	23	9	10	105	66	55
Weymouth	42	24	7	11	105	84	55
Hastings United	42	21	9	12	94	60	51
Cheltenham Town	42	21	8	13	85	72	50
Guildford City	42	20	8	14	72	59	48
Worcester City	42	19	10	13	80	73	48
Barry Town	42	16	15	11	82	87	47
Gloucester City	42	16	13	13	66	54	45
Bath City	42	18	9	15	73	80	45
Headington United	42	18	7	17	82	62	43
Kidderminster Harriers	42	18	7	17	84	86	43
Merthyr Tydfil	42	17	8	17	97	94	42
Exeter City Reserves	42	19	4	19	67	78	42
Lovells Athletic	42	15	11	16	71	68	41
Kettering Town	42	15	11	16	70	69	41
Hereford United	42	17	5	20	91	72	39
Llanelly	42	16	7	19	78	81	39
Bedford Town	42	16	3	23	75	103	35
Tonbridge	42	11	8	23	68	91	30
Dartford	42	9	12	21	55	76	30
Chelmsford City	42	11	6	25	73	111	28
Gravesend & Northfleet	42	9	9	24	62	97	27

1955-56

Guildford City	42	26	8	8	74	34	60
Cheltenham Town	42	25	6	11	82	53	56
Yeovil Town	42	23	9	10	98	55	55
Bedford Town	42	21	9	12	99	69	51
Dartford	42	20	9	13	78	62	49
Weymouth	42	19	10	13	83	63	48
Gloucester City	42	19	9	14	72	60	47
Lovells Athletic	42	19	9	14	91	78	47
Chelmsford City	42	18	10	14	67	55	46
Kettering Town	42	16	11	15	105	86	43
Exeter City Reserves	42	17	9	16	75	76	43
Gravesend & Northfleet	42	17	8	17	79	75	42
Hereford United	42	17	7	18	90	90	41
Hastings United	42	15	10	17	90	76	40
Headington United	42	17	6	19	82	86	40
Kidderminster Harriers	42	14	7	21	86	108	35
Llanelly	42	14	6	22	64	98	34
Barry Town	42	11	11	20	91	108	33
Worcester City	42	12	9	21	66	83	33
Tonbridge	42	11	11	20	53	74	33
Merthyr Tydfil	42	7	10	25	52	127	24
Bath City	42	7	10	25	43	107	24

1956-57

Kettering Town	42	28	10	4	106	47	66
Bedford Town	42	25	8	9	89	52	58
Weymouth	42	22	10	10	92	71	54
Cheltenham Town	42	19	15	8	73	46	53
Gravesend & Northfleet	42	21	11	10	74	58	53
Lovells Athletic	42	21	7	14	99	84	49
Guildford City	42	18	11	13	68	49	47
Hereford United	42	19	8	15	96	60	46
Headington United	42	19	7	16	64	61	45
Gloucester City	42	18	8	16	74	72	44
Hastings United	42	17	9	16	70	58	43
Worcester City	42	16	10	16	81	80	42
Dartford	42	16	10	16	79	88	42
Chelmsford City	42	16	9	17	73	85	41
Tonbridge	42	14	12	16	74	65	40
Yeovil Town	42	14	11	17	83	85	39
Bath City	42	15	8	19	56	78	38
Exeter City Reserves	42	10	10	22	52	89	30
Merthyr Tydfil	42	9	11	22	72	95	29
Barry Town	42	6	11	25	39	84	23
Kidderminster Harriers	42	7	10	25	60	83	20
Llanelly	42	5	8	29	39	123	18

Kidderminster Harriers had 4 points deducted for fielding an ineligible player†.

1957-58

Gravesend & Northfleet	42	27	5	10	109	71	59
Bedford Town	42	25	7	10	112	64	57
Chelmsford City	42	24	9	9	93	57	57
Weymouth	42	25	5	12	90	61	55
Worcester City	42	23	7	12	95	59	53
Cheltenham Town	42	21	10	11	115	66	52
Hereford United	42	21	6	15	79	56	48
Kettering Town	42	18	9	15	99	76	45
Headington United	42	18	7	17	90	83	43
Poole Town	42	17	9	16	82	81	43
Hastings United	42	13	15	14	78	77	41
Gloucester City	42	17	7	18	70	70	41
Yeovil Town	42	16	9	17	70	84	41
Dartford	42	14	9	19	66	92	37
Lovells Athletic	42	15	6	21	60	83	36
Bath City	42	13	9	20	65	64	35
Guildford City	42	12	10	20	58	92	34
Tonbridge	42	13	7	22	77	100	33
Exeter City Reserves	42	12	8	22	60	94	32
Barry Town	42	11	9	22	72	101	31
Kidderminster Harriers	42	10	10	22	60	101	30
Merthyr Tydfil	42	9	3	30	69	137	21

1958-59

North-Western Zone

Hereford United	34	22	5	7	80	37	49
Kettering Town	34	20	7	7	83	63	47
Boston United	34	18	8	8	73	47	44
Cheltenham Town	34	20	4	10	65	47	44
Worcester City	34	19	4	11	74	47	42
Bath City	34	17	5	12	89	62	39
Wellington Town	34	15	9	10	74	58	39
Nuneaton Borough	34	17	5	12	76	66	39
Wisbech Town	34	16	5	13	77	54	37
Headington United	34	16	3	15	76	61	35
Barry Town	34	15	5	14	64	67	35
Merthyr Tydfil	34	16	3	15	54	59	35
Gloucester City	34	12	6	16	50	65	30
Corby Town	34	10	8	16	59	79	28
Lovells Athletic	34	10	3	21	51	70	23
Rugby Town	34	7	6	21	45	93	20
Kidderminster Harriers	34	7	3	24	42	94	17
Burton Albion	34	3	3	28	41	104	9

South-Eastern Zone

Bedford Town	32	21	6	5	90	41	48
Gravesend & Northfleet	32	21	2	9	79	54	44
Dartford	32	20	3	9	77	41	43
Yeovil Town	32	17	8	7	60	41	42
Weymouth	32	13	11	8	61	43	37
Chelmsford City	32	12	12	8	74	53	36
King's Lynn	32	14	5	13	70	63	33
Poole Town	32	12	8	12	60	65	32
Cambridge City	32	12	7	13	61	54	31
Hastings United	32	13	5	14	60	59	31
Tonbridge	32	14	3	15	51	59	31
Cambridge United	32	11	8	13	55	77	30
Trowbridge Town	32	12	4	16	53	75	28
Exeter City Reserves	32	7	12	13	47	71	26
Guildford City	32	7	6	19	45	67	20
Clacton Town	32	6	7	19	44	81	19
Yiewsley	32	3	7	22	36	78	13

1959-60

Premier Division

Bath City	42	32	3	7	116	50	67
Headington United	42	23	8	11	78	61	54
Weymouth	42	22	9	11	93	69	53
Cheltenham Town	42	21	6	15	82	68	48
Cambridge City	42	18	11	13	81	72	47
Chelmsford Town	42	19	7	16	90	70	45
Bedford Town	42	21	3	18	97	85	45
King's Lynn	42	17	11	14	89	78	45
Boston United	42	17	10	15	83	80	44
Wisbech Town	42	17	10	15	81	84	44
Yeovil Town	42	17	8	17	81	73	42
Hereford United	42	15	12	15	70	74	42
Tonbridge	42	16	8	18	79	73	40
Hastings United	42	16	8	18	63	77	40
Wellington Town	42	13	11	18	63	78	37
Dartford	42	15	7	20	64	82	37
Gravesend & Northfleet	42	14	8	20	69	84	36
Worcester City	42	13	10	19	72	89	36
Nuneaton Borough	42	11	11	20	64	78	33
Barry Town	42	14	5	23	78	103	33
Poole Town	42	10	8	24	69	96	28
Kettering Town	42	9	10	23	60	90	28

First Division

Clacton Town	42	27	5	10	106	69	59
Romford	42	21	11	10	65	40	53
Folkestone Town	42	23	5	14	93	71	51
Exeter City Reserves	42	23	3	16	85	62	49
Guildford City	42	19	9	14	79	56	47
Sittingbourne	42	20	7	15	66	55	47
Margate	42	20	6	16	88	77	46
Trowbridge Town	42	18	9	15	90	78	45
Cambridge United	42	18	9	15	71	72	45
Yiewsley	42	17	10	15	83	69	44
Bexleyheath & Welling	42	16	11	15	85	77	43
Merthyr Tydfil	42	16	10	16	63	65	42
Ramsgate Athletic	42	16	8	18	83	84	40
Ashford Town	42	14	12	16	61	70	40
Tunbridge Wells United	42	17	5	20	77	73	39
Hinckley Athletic	42	14	8	20	62	75	36
Gloucester City	42	13	9	20	56	84	35
Dover	42	14	6	22	59	85	34
Kidderminster Harriers	42	14	6	22	59	97	34
Corby Town	42	15	3	24	75	91	33
Burton Albion	42	11	10	21	52	79	32
Rugby Town	42	10	11	21	67	91	31

1960-61   Premier Division

Oxford United	42	27	10	5	104	43	64
Chelmsford City	42	23	11	8	91	55	57
Yeovil Town	42	23	9	10	109	54	55
Hereford United	42	21	10	11	83	67	52
Weymouth	42	21	9	12	78	63	51
Bath City	42	18	14	10	74	52	50
Cambridge City	42	16	12	14	101	71	44
Wellington Town	42	17	9	16	66	68	43
Bedford Town	42	18	7	17	94	77	43
Folkestone Town	42	18	7	17	75	86	43
King's Lynn	42	13	16	13	68	66	42
Worcester City	42	15	11	16	69	69	41
Clacton Town	42	15	11	16	82	83	41
Romford	42	13	15	14	66	69	41
Guildford City	42	14	11	17	65	62	39
Tonbridge	42	16	6	20	79	85	38
Cheltenham Town	42	15	7	20	81	81	37
Gravesend & Northfleet	42	15	7	20	75	101	37
Dartford	42	13	11	18	57	90	37
Hastings United	42	8	9	25	60	100	25
Wisbech Town	42	9	6	27	58	112	24
Boston United	42	6	8	28	62	123	20

First Division

Kettering Town	40	26	7	7	100	55	59
Cambridge United	40	25	5	10	100	53	55
Bexleyheath & Welling	40	22	8	10	93	46	52
Merthyr Tydfil	40	23	6	11	88	65	52
Sittingbourne	40	21	10	9	77	63	52
Hinckley Athletic	40	17	13	10	74	59	47
Ramsgate Athletic	40	19	7	14	77	56	45
Rugby Town	40	18	9	13	89	71	45
Corby Town	40	16	10	14	82	73	42
Poole Town	40	18	5	17	71	65	41
Barry Town	40	16	9	15	65	74	41
Yiewsley	40	17	7	16	65	76	41
Trowbridge Town	40	14	10	16	71	73	38
Ashford Town	40	14	8	18	61	67	36
Margate	40	11	12	17	62	75	34
Dover	40	12	7	21	67	74	31
Canterbury City	40	10	10	20	52	75	30
Nuneaton Borough	40	11	7	22	60	91	29
Burton Albion	40	12	4	24	63	85	28
Tunbridge Wells United	40	8	5	27	56	115	21
Gloucester City	40	7	7	26	40	102	21

1961-62   Premier Division

Oxford United	42	28	5	9	118	46	61
Bath City	42	25	7	10	102	70	57
Guildford City	42	24	8	10	79	49	56
Yeovil Town	42	23	8	11	97	59	54
Chelmsford City	42	19	12	11	74	60	50
Weymouth	42	20	7	15	80	64	47
Kettering Town	42	21	5	16	90	84	47
Hereford United	42	21	2	19	81	68	44
Cambridge City	42	18	8	16	70	71	44
Bexleyheath & Welling	42	19	5	18	69	75	43
Romford	42	15	9	18	63	70	39
Cambridge United	42	13	12	17	76	78	38
Wellington Town	42	14	10	18	75	78	38
Gravesend & Northfleet	42	17	4	21	59	92	38
Bedford Town	42	16	5	21	73	79	37
Worcester City	42	15	7	20	51	64	37
Merthyr Tydfil	42	13	11	18	62	80	37
Clacton Town	42	13	10	19	74	91	36
Tonbridge	42	10	14	18	71	92	34
King's Lynn	42	12	8	22	59	74	32
Folkestone Town	42	12	6	24	64	103	30
Cheltenham Town	42	9	7	26	48	86	25

First Division

Wisbech Town	38	21	11	6	76	42	53
Poole Town	38	23	6	9	81	47	52
Dartford	38	21	8	9	89	50	50
Rugby Town	38	20	9	9	82	49	49
Margate	38	20	6	12	73	55	46
Corby Town	38	19	6	13	82	60	44
Sittingbourne	38	16	12	10	69	51	44
Dover	38	19	6	13	66	55	44
Yiewsley	38	18	6	14	64	51	42
Barry Town	38	14	11	13	55	51	39
Ashford Town	38	14	11	13	66	70	39
Hinckley Athletic	38	15	8	15	75	65	38
Burton Albion	38	16	5	17	70	79	37
Nuneaton Borough	38	12	12	14	63	69	36
Tunbridge Wells United	38	12	7	19	60	85	31
Canterbury City	38	11	8	19	60	82	30
Ramsgate Athletic	38	10	9	19	48	70	29
Trowbridge Town	38	9	9	20	45	69	27
Gloucester City	38	6	4	28	46	104	16
Hastings United	38	5	4	29	45	115	14

1962-63

Premier Division

Cambridge City	40	25	6	9	99	64	56
Cambridge United	40	23	7	10	74	50	53
Weymouth	40	20	11	9	82	43	51
Guildford City	40	20	11	9	70	50	51
Kettering Town	40	22	7	11	66	49	51
Wellington Town	40	19	9	12	71	49	47
Dartford	40	19	9	12	61	54	47
Chelmsford City	40	18	10	12	63	50	46
Bedford Town	40	18	8	14	61	45	44
Bath City	40	18	6	16	58	56	42
Yeovil Town	40	15	10	15	64	54	40
Romford	40	14	11	15	73	68	39
Bexleyheath & Welling	40	13	11	16	55	63	37
Hereford United	40	14	7	19	56	66	35
Merthyr Tydfil	40	15	4	21	54	71	34
Rugby Town	40	14	5	21	65	76	33
Wisbech Town	40	15	3	22	64	84	33
Worcester City	40	12	9	19	47	65	33
Poole Town	40	10	12	18	54	66	32
Gravesend & Northfleet	40	10	3	27	62	91	23
Clacton Town	40	3	7	30	50	135	13

First Division

Margate	38	21	13	4	86	47	55
Hinckley Athletic	38	22	9	7	66	38	53
Hastings United	38	22	8	8	86	36	52
Nuneaton Borough	38	21	10	7	82	41	52
Tonbridge	38	22	8	8	81	51	52
Dover	38	22	7	9	78	56	51
Corby Town	38	19	8	11	79	50	46
King's Lynn	38	19	7	15	76	66	45
Cheltenham Town	38	18	7	13	83	52	43
Folkestone Town	38	15	10	13	79	57	40
Canterbury City	38	14	8	16	42	56	36
Yiewsley	38	11	10	17	63	71	32
Ramsgate Athletic	38	12	7	19	58	82	31
Trowbridge Town	38	11	9	18	50	81	31
Burton Albion	38	10	10	18	48	76	30
Gloucester City	38	9	11	18	42	78	29
Sittingbourne	38	12	3	23	56	75	27
Ashford Town	38	9	6	23	58	76	24
Barry Town	38	6	5	27	35	75	17
Tunbridge Wells United	38	6	2	30	43	118	14

1963-64

Premier Division

Yeovil Town	42	29	5	8	93	36	63
Chelmsford City	42	26	7	9	99	55	59
Bath City	42	24	9	9	88	51	57
Guildford City	42	21	9	12	90	55	51
Romford	42	20	9	13	71	58	49
Hastings United	42	20	8	14	75	61	48
Weymouth	42	20	7	15	65	53	47
Bedford Town	42	19	9	14	71	68	47
Cambridge United	42	17	9	16	92	77	43
Cambridge City	42	17	9	16	76	70	43
Wisbech Town	42	17	8	17	64	68	42
Bexley United	42	16	10	16	70	77	42
Dartford	42	16	8	18	56	71	40
Worcester City	42	12	15	15	70	74	39
Nuneaton Borough	42	15	8	19	58	61	38
Rugby Town	42	15	8	19	68	86	38
Margate	42	12	13	17	68	81	37
Wellington Town	42	12	9	21	73	85	33
Merthyr Tydfil	42	12	8	22	69	108	32
Hereford United	42	12	7	23	58	86	31
Kettering Town	42	10	5	27	49	89	25
Hinckley Athletic	42	7	6	29	51	104	20

First Division

Folkstone Town	42	28	7	7	82	38	63
King's Lynn	42	28	5	9	94	44	61
Cheltenham Town	42	25	10	7	92	49	60
Tonbridge	42	24	11	7	98	54	59
Corby Town	42	24	7	11	114	56	55
Stevenage Town	42	21	6	15	70	59	48
Ashford Town	42	19	9	14	73	57	47
Burton Albion	42	19	8	15	76	70	46
Poole Town	42	17	11	14	75	61	45
Dover	42	18	9	15	86	75	45
Canterbury City	42	16	12	14	66	66	44
Crawley Town	42	20	2	20	81	71	42
Trowbridge Town	42	16	9	17	71	78	41
Clacton Town	42	19	1	22	76	88	39
Gloucester City	42	17	4	21	88	89	38
Yiewsley	42	15	8	19	63	77	38
Sittingbourne	42	15	8	19	52	70	38
Ramsgate Athletic	42	13	9	20	57	55	35
Tunbridge Wells Rangers	42	10	8	24	47	89	28
Gravesend & Northfleet	42	7	9	26	43	96	23
Deal Town	42	5	7	30	48	106	17
Barry Town	42	3	6	33	33	137	12

1964-65 Premier Division

Weymouth	42	24	8	10	99	50	56
Guildford City	42	21	12	9	73	49	54
Worcester City	42	22	6	14	100	62	50
Yeovil Town	42	18	14	10	76	55	50
Chelmsford City	42	21	8	13	86	77	50
Margate	42	20	9	13	88	79	49
Dartford	42	17	11	14	74	64	45
Nuneaton Borough	42	19	7	16	57	55	45
Cambridge United	42	16	11	15	78	66	43
Bedford Town	42	17	9	16	66	70	43
Cambridge City	42	16	9	17	72	69	41
Cheltenham Town	42	15	11	16	72	78	41
Folkestone Town	42	17	7	18	72	79	41
Romford	42	17	7	18	61	70	41
King's Lynn	42	13	13	16	56	79	39
Tonbridge	42	10	16	16	66	75	36
Wellington Town	42	13	10	19	63	78	36
Rugby Town	42	15	6	21	71	98	36
Wisbech Town	42	14	6	22	75	91	34
Bexley United	42	14	5	23	67	74	33
Hastings United	42	9	14	19	58	86	32
Bath City	42	13	3	26	60	86	29

First Division

Hereford United	42	34	4	4	124	39	72
Wimbledon	42	24	13	5	108	52	61
Poole Town	42	26	6	10	92	56	58
Corby Town	42	24	7	11	88	55	55
Stevenage Town	42	19	13	10	83	43	51
Hillingdon Borough	42	21	7	14	105	63	49
Crawley Town	42	22	5	15	83	52	49
Merthyr Tydfil	42	20	9	13	75	59	49
Gloucester City	42	19	10	13	68	65	48
Burton Albion	42	20	7	15	83	75	47
Canterbury City	42	13	16	13	73	53	42
Kettering Town	42	14	13	15	74	64	41
Ramsgate Athletic	42	16	8	18	51	59	40
Dover	42	14	10	18	54	59	38
Hinckley Athletic	42	13	9	20	56	81	35
Trowbridge Town	42	13	5	24	68	106	31
Ashford Town	42	11	8	23	60	98	30
Barry Town	42	11	7	24	47	103	29
Deal Town	42	7	13	22	61	127	27
Tunbridge Wells Rangers	42	10	6	26	51	107	26
Gravesend & Northfleet	42	9	7	26	57	101	25
Sittingbourne	42	8	5	29	58	103	21

1965-66 Premier Division

Weymouth	42	22	13	7	70	35	57
Chelmsford City	42	21	12	9	74	50	54
Hereford United	42	21	10	11	81	49	52
Bedford Town	42	23	6	13	80	57	52
Wimbledon	42	20	10	12	80	47	50
Cambridge City	42	19	11	12	67	52	49
Romford	42	21	7	14	87	72	49
Worcester City	42	20	8	14	69	54	48
Yeovil Town	42	17	11	14	90	70	45
Cambridge United	42	18	9	15	72	64	45
King's Lynn	42	18	7	17	75	72	43
Corby Town	42	16	9	17	66	73	41
Wellington Town	42	13	13	16	65	70	39
Nuneaton Borough	42	15	8	19	60	74	38
Folkestone Town	42	14	9	19	53	75	37
Guildford City	42	14	8	20	70	84	36
Poole Town	42	14	7	21	61	75	35
Cheltenham Town	42	13	9	20	69	99	35
Dartford	42	13	7	22	62	69	33
Rugby Town	42	11	10	21	67	95	32
Tonbridge	42	11	6	25	63	101	28
Margate	42	8	10	24	66	111	26

First Division

	P	W	D	L	F	A	Pts
Barnet	46	30	9	7	114	49	69
Hillingdon Borough	46	27	10	9	101	46	64
Burton Albion	46	28	8	10	121	60	64
Bath City	46	25	13	8	88	50	63
Hastings United	46	25	10	11	104	59	60
Wisbech Town	46	25	9	12	98	54	59
Canterbury City	46	25	8	13	89	66	58
Stevenage Town	46	23	9	14	86	49	55
Kettering Town	46	22	9	15	77	74	53
Merthyr Tydfil	46	22	6	18	95	68	50
Dunstable Town	46	15	14	17	76	72	44
Crawley Town	46	17	10	19	72	71	44
Bexley United	46	20	4	22	65	71	44
Trowbridge Town	46	16	11	19	79	81	43
Dover	46	17	8	21	59	62	42
Barry Town	46	16	10	20	72	94	42
Gravesend & Northfleet	46	16	9	21	84	86	41
Gloucester City	46	14	12	20	75	98	40
Sittingbourne	46	11	12	23	77	121	34
Ramsgate Athletic	46	9	15	22	35	76	33
Hinckley Athletic	46	10	12	24	59	93	32
Tunbridge Wells Rangers	46	12	8	26	47	88	32
Ashford Town	46	9	10	27	44	92	28
Deal Town	46	3	4	39	29	165	10

First Division

	P	W	D	L	F	A	Pts
Dover	46	29	12	5	92	35	70
Margate	46	31	7	8	127	54	69
Stevenage Town	46	29	8	9	90	32	66
Hastings United	46	25	16	5	89	45	66
Kettering Town	46	27	9	10	105	62	63
Crawley Town	46	26	8	12	81	48	60
Ramsgate Athletic	46	23	8	15	79	62	54
Dartford	46	19	15	12	92	67	53
Tonbridge	46	21	10	15	91	69	52
Trowbridge Town	46	20	12	14	73	60	52
Ashford Town	46	18	8	20	74	68	44
Merthyr Tydfil	46	17	9	20	81	71	43
Gloucester City	46	18	6	22	69	83	42
Canterbury City	46	17	8	21	57	75	42
Wisbech Town	46	16	9	21	87	93	41
Bexley United	46	13	15	18	53	69	41
Banbury United	46	13	14	19	88	100	40
Rugby Town	46	15	7	24	57	77	37
Dunstable Town	46	14	6	26	55	87	34
Barry Town	46	11	11	24	62	89	33
Gravesend & Northfleet	46	11	9	26	63	106	31
Hinckley Athletic	46	10	8	28	44	100	28
Tunbridge Wells Rangers	46	4	15	27	31	96	23
Sittingbourne	46	5	10	31	44	136	20

1966-67

Premier Division

	P	W	D	L	F	A	Pts
Romford	42	22	8	12	80	60	52
Nuneaton Borough	42	21	9	12	82	54	51
Weymouth	42	18	14	10	64	40	50
Wimbledon	42	19	11	12	88	60	49
Barnet	42	18	13	11	86	66	49
Guildford City	42	19	10	13	65	51	48
Wellington Town	42	20	7	15	70	67	47
Cambridge United	42	16	13	13	75	67	45
Chelmsford City	42	15	15	12	66	59	45
Hereford United	42	16	12	14	79	61	44
King's Lynn	42	15	14	13	78	72	44
Cambridge City	42	15	13	14	66	70	43
Cheltenham Town	42	16	11	15	60	71	43
Yeovil Town	42	14	14	14	66	72	42
Burton Albion	42	17	5	20	63	71	39
Corby Town	42	15	9	18	60	75	39
Poole Town	42	14	11	17	52	65	39
Hillingdon Borough	42	11	13	18	49	70	35
Bath City	42	11	12	19	51	74	34
Worcester City	42	11	8	23	59	79	30
Bedford Town	42	8	13	21	54	72	29
Folkestone Town	42	6	15	21	44	81	27

1967-68

Premier Division

	P	W	D	L	F	A	Pts
Chelmsford City	42	25	7	10	85	50	57
Wimbledon	42	24	7	11	85	47	55
Cambridge United	42	20	13	9	73	42	53
Cheltenham Town	42	23	7	12	97	67	53
Guildford City	42	18	13	11	56	43	49
Romford	42	20	8	14	72	60	48
Barnet	42	20	8	14	81	71	48
Margate	42	19	8	15	80	71	46
Wellington Town	42	16	13	13	70	66	45
Hillingdon Borough	42	18	9	15	53	54	45
King's Lynn	42	18	8	16	66	57	44
Yeovil Town	42	16	12	14	45	43	44
Weymouth	42	17	8	17	65	62	42
Hereford United	42	17	7	18	58	62	41
Nuneaton Borough	42	13	14	15	62	64	40
Dover	42	17	6	19	54	56	40
Poole Town	42	13	10	19	55	74	36
Stevenage Town	42	13	9	20	57	75	35
Burton Albion	42	14	6	22	51	73	34
Corby Town	42	7	13	22	40	77	27
Cambridge City	42	10	6	26	51	81	26
Hastings United	42	4	8	30	33	94	16

First Division

	P	W	D	L	F	A	Pts
Worcester City	42	23	14	5	92	35	60
Kettering Town	42	24	10	8	88	40	58
Bedford Town	42	24	7	11	101	40	55
Rugby Town	42	20	15	7	72	44	55
Dartford	42	23	9	10	70	48	55
Bath City	42	21	12	9	78	51	54
Banbury United	42	22	9	11	79	59	53
Ramsgate Athletic	42	17	7	8	70	37	51
Merthyr Tydfil	42	18	13	11	80	66	49
Tonbridge	42	18	9	15	76	71	45
Canterbury City	42	16	11	15	66	63	43
Ashford Town	42	18	6	18	73	78	42
Brentwood Town	42	16	9	17	63	73	41
Bexley United	42	12	13	17	56	64	37
Trowbridge Town	42	12	11	19	64	70	35
Gloucester City	42	12	9	21	54	68	33
Wisbech Town	42	11	10	21	43	78	32
Crawley Town	42	10	8	24	54	85	28
Folkestone Town	42	10	7	25	49	80	27
Dunstable Town	42	8	10	24	44	94	26
Barry Town	42	7	12	23	36	81	26
Gravesend & Northfleet	42	6	7	29	28	112	19

1968-69   Premier Division

	P	W	D	L	F	A	Pts
Cambridge United	42	27	5	10	72	39	59
Hillingdon Borough	42	24	10	8	68	47	58
Wimbledon	42	21	12	9	66	48	54
King's Lynn	42	20	9	13	68	60	49
Worcester City	42	19	11	12	53	47	49
Romford	42	18	12	12	58	52	48
Weymouth	42	16	15	11	52	41	47
Yeovil Town	42	16	13	13	52	50	45
Kettering Town	42	18	8	16	51	55	44
Dover	42	17	9	16	66	61	43
Nuneaton Borough	42	17	7	18	74	58	41
Barnet	42	15	10	17	72	66	40
Chelmsford City	42	17	6	19	56	58	40
Hereford United	42	15	9	18	66	62	39
Wellington Town	42	14	10	18	62	61	38
Poole Town	42	16	6	20	75	76	38
Burton Albion	42	16	5	21	55	71	37
Margate	42	14	7	21	79	90	35
Cheltenham Town	42	15	5	22	55	64	35
Bedford Town	42	11	12	19	46	63	34
Rugby Town	42	10	6	26	38	83	26
Guildford City	42	7	11	24	41	73	25

First Division

	P	W	D	L	F	A	Pts
Brentwood Town	42	26	12	4	44	37	64
Bath City	42	26	10	6	96	40	62
Gloucester City	42	25	9	8	100	53	59
Crawley Town	42	21	13	8	65	32	55
Corby Town	42	22	6	14	81	65	50
Dartford	42	20	8	14	79	51	48
Ramsgate Athletic	42	19	9	14	72	57	47
Salisbury	42	20	6	16	69	52	46
Cambridge City	42	18	10	14	73	63	46
Banbury United	42	16	12	14	67	72	44
Trowbridge Town	42	15	8	19	70	60	44
Folkestone Town	42	19	5	18	53	59	43
Canterbury City	42	17	7	18	67	63	41
Ashford Town	42	16	8	18	72	73	40
Bexley United	42	15	9	18	62	75	39
Hastings United	42	15	9	18	58	69	39
Wisbech Town	42	11	13	18	57	70	35
Dunstable Town	42	14	6	22	73	99	34
Merthyr Tydfil	42	10	7	25	49	101	27
Barry Town	42	8	10	24	39	78	26
Gravesend & Northfleet	42	8	9	25	51	79	25
Tonbridge	42	2	6	34	36	137	10

1969-70   Premier Division

	P	W	D	L	F	A	Pts
Cambridge United	42	26	6	10	86	49	58
Yeovil Town	42	25	7	10	78	48	57
Chelmsford City	42	20	11	11	76	58	51
Weymouth	42	18	14	10	59	37	50
Wimbledon	42	19	12	11	64	52	50
Hillingdon Borough	42	19	12	11	56	50	50
Barnet	42	16	15	11	71	54	47
Telford United	42	18	10	14	61	62	46
Brentwood Town	42	16	13	13	61	38	45
Hereford United	42	18	9	15	74	65	45
Bath City	42	18	8	16	63	55	44
King's Lynn	42	16	11	15	72	68	43
Margate	42	17	8	17	70	64	42
Dover	42	15	10	17	51	50	40
Kettering Town	42	18	3	21	64	75	39
Worcester City	42	14	10	18	35	44	38
Romford	42	13	11	18	50	62	37
Poole Town	42	8	19	15	48	57	35
Gloucester City	42	12	9	21	53	73	33
Nuneaton Borough	42	11	10	21	52	74	32
Crawley Town	42	6	15	21	53	101	27
Burton Albion	42	3	9	30	24	82	15

First Division

	P	W	D	L	F	A	Pts
Bedford Town	42	26	9	7	93	37	61
Cambridge City	42	26	8	8	104	43	60
Dartford	42	24	11	7	33	46	58
Ashford Town	42	19	15	8	71	43	53
Rugby Town	42	20	10	12	82	66	50
Trowbridge Town	42	20	8	14	72	65	48
Hastings United	42	18	11	13	67	51	47
Guildford City	42	19	9	14	68	58	47
Banbury United	42	19	8	15	86	72	46
Cheltenham Town	42	20	5	17	78	81	45
Canterbury City	42	15	13	14	61	57	43
Corby Town	42	14	15	13	58	53	43
Folkestone Town	42	19	5	18	57	55	43
Ramsgate Athletic	42	14	13	15	53	57	41
Salisbury	42	13	13	16	48	53	39
Gravesend & Northfleet	42	13	11	18	62	71	37
Bexley United	42	10	11	21	58	76	31
Dunstable Town	42	11	9	22	52	82	31
Merthyr Tydfil	42	9	11	22	40	80	29
Barry Town	42	11	6	25	39	76	28
Wisbech Town	42	8	9	25	58	116	25
Tonbridge	42	4	10	28	46	101	18

1970-71   Premier Division

	P	W	D	L	F	A	Pts
Yeovil Town	42	25	7	10	66	31	57
Cambridge City	42	22	11	9	67	38	55
Romford	42	23	9	10	63	42	55
Hereford United	42	23	8	11	71	53	54
Chelmsford City	42	20	11	11	61	32	51
Barnet	42	18	14	10	69	49	50
Bedford Town	42	20	10	12	62	46	50
Wimbledon	42	20	8	14	72	54	48
Worcester City	42	20	8	14	61	46	48
Weymouth	42	14	16	12	64	48	44
Dartford	42	15	12	15	53	51	42
Dover	42	16	9	17	64	63	41
Margate	42	15	10	17	64	70	40
Hillingdon Borough	42	17	6	19	61	68	40
Bath City	42	13	12	17	48	68	38
Nuneaton Borough	42	12	12	18	43	66	36
Telford United	42	13	8	21	64	70	34
Poole Town	42	14	6	22	57	75	34
King's Lynn	42	11	7	24	44	67	29
Ashford Town	42	13	3	21	52	86	29
Kettering Town	42	8	11	23	48	84	27
Gloucester City	42	6	10	26	34	81	21

First Division

Guildford City	38	22	10	6	76	36	54
Merthyr Tydfil	38	19	12	7	52	33	50
Gravesend & Northfleet	38	19	10	9	74	42	48
Folkestone	38	20	8	10	83	53	48
Burton Albion	38	19	10	9	56	37	48
Rugby Town	38	17	14	7	58	40	48
Ramsgate Athletic	38	20	5	13	83	54	45
Trowbridge Town	38	19	7	12	78	55	45
Bexley United	38	17	11	10	57	45	45
Crawley Town	38	15	11	12	84	68	41
Hastings United	38	13	12	13	51	50	38
Banbury United	38	13	11	14	58	53	37
Corby Town	38	14	8	16	57	60	36
Salisbury	38	13	7	18	56	60	33
Cheltenham Town	38	8	15	15	44	58	31
Stevenage Athletic	38	12	7	19	55	79	21
Tonbridge	38	8	8	22	48	83	24
Barry Town	38	9	6	23	35	82	24
Dunstable Town	38	8	4	26	32	81	20
Canterbury City	38	5	4	29	37	105	14

First Division (South)

Waterlooville	30	15	9	6	40	22	39
Ramsgate Athletic	30	14	11	5	42	27	39
Maidstone United	30	14	10	6	48	28	38
Crawley Town	30	15	5	10	67	55	35
Metropolitan Police	30	15	3	12	48	41	33
Tonbridge	30	12	9	9	37	34	33
Bexley United	30	14	4	12	52	46	32
Basingstoke Town	30	14	4	12	37	36	32
Andover	30	11	9	10	32	34	31
Ashford Town	30	12	4	14	43	48	28
Salisbury	30	10	7	13	45	44	27
Winchester City	30	10	7	13	40	47	27
Hastings United	30	10	7	13	28	42	27
Trowbridge Town	30	8	7	15	41	49	23
Canterbury City	30	7	8	15	39	56	22
Woodford Town	30	4	6	20	22	52	14

1972-73

Premier Division

Kettering Town	42	20	17	5	74	44	57
Yeovil Town	42	21	14	7	67	61	56
Dover	42	23	9	10	61	68	55
Chelmsford City	42	23	7	12	75	43	53
Worcester City	42	20	13	9	68	47	53
Weymouth	42	20	12	10	72	51	52
Margate	42	17	15	10	80	60	49
Bedford Town	42	16	15	11	43	36	47
Nuneaton Borough	42	16	14	12	51	41	46
Telford United	42	12	20	10	57	47	44
Cambridge City	42	14	15	13	64	53	43
Wimbledon	42	14	14	14	50	50	42
Barnet	42	15	11	16	60	59	41
Romford	42	17	5	20	51	65	39
Hillingdon Borough	42	16	6	20	52	58	38
Dartford	42	12	11	19	49	63	35
Folkestone	42	11	11	20	41	72	33
Guildford City	42	10	11	21	59	84	31
Ramsgate	42	9	13	20	35	61	31
Poole Town	42	10	10	22	50	88	30
Burton Albion	42	9	7	26	43	81	25
Waterlooville	42	4	16	22	33	63	24

1971-72

Premier Division

Chelmsford City	42	28	6	8	109	46	62
Hereford United	42	24	12	6	68	30	60
Dover	42	20	11	11	67	45	51
Barnet	42	21	7	14	80	57	49
Dartford	42	20	8	14	75	68	48
Weymouth	42	21	5	16	69	43	47
Yeovil Town	42	18	11	13	67	51	47
Hillingdon Borough	42	20	6	16	64	58	46
Margate	42	19	8	15	74	68	46
Wimbledon	42	19	7	16	75	64	45
Romford	42	16	13	13	54	49	45
Guildford City	42	20	5	17	71	65	45
Telford United	42	18	7	17	83	68	43
Nuneaton Borough	42	16	10	16	46	47	42
Bedford Town	42	16	9	17	59	66	41
Worcester City	42	17	7	18	46	57	41
Cambridge City	42	12	14	16	68	71	38
Folkestone	42	14	7	21	58	64	35
Poole Town	42	9	11	22	43	72	29
Bath City	42	11	4	27	45	86	26
Merthyr Tydfil	42	7	8	27	29	93	22
Gravesend & Northfleet	42	5	6	31	30	110	16

First Division (North)

Kettering Town	34	23	6	5	70	27	52
Burton Albion	34	18	13	3	58	27	49
Cheltenham Town	34	20	4	10	72	51	44
Rugby Town	34	18	7	9	52	36	43
Wellingborough Town	34	15	10	9	73	44	40
Stourbridge	34	13	14	7	59	42	40
King's Lynn	34	14	11	9	62	45	39
Corby Town	34	15	9	10	47	35	39
Ilkeston Town	34	14	11	9	44	38	39
Banbury United	34	14	5	15	54	46	33
Bury Town	34	14	5	15	47	44	33
Wealdstone	34	14	5	15	51	58	33
Lockheed Leamington	34	15	3	16	41	52	33
Gloucester City	34	8	8	18	46	61	24
Stevenage Athletic	34	8	8	18	41	69	24
Bletchley Town	34	7	7	20	36	70	21
Dunstable Town	34	5	7	22	29	75	17
Barry Town	34	1	7	26	22	84	9

First Division (North)

Grantham	42	29	8	5	113	41	66
Atherstone Town	42	23	11	8	82	48	57
Cheltenham Town	42	24	8	10	87	47	56
Rugby Town	42	20	10	12	60	47	50
Kidderminster Harriers	42	19	12	11	67	56	50
Merthyr Tydfil	42	17	12	13	51	40	46
Corby Town	42	14	16	12	62	56	44
Stourbridge	42	16	11	15	70	64	43
Gloucester City	42	18	7	17	55	64	43
Bromsgrove Rovers	42	17	8	17	63	54	42
Redditch United	42	18	6	18	58	59	42
Banbury United	42	18	5	19	60	53	41
Wellingborough Town	42	17	7	18	58	71	41
King's Lynn	42	14	12	16	45	49	40
Lockheed Leamington	42	13	12	17	51	58	38
Enderby Town	42	12	14	16	50	61	38
Stevenage Athletic	42	12	13	17	50	63	37
Tamworth	42	14	8	20	45	65	36
Bury Town	42	13	9	20	52	69	35
Barry Town	42	11	10	21	45	71	32
Ilkeston Town	42	9	6	27	35	68	24
Bedworth United	42	10	3	29	42	94	23

First Division (South)

	P	W	D	L	F	A	Pts
Maidstone United	42	25	12	5	90	38	62
Tonbridge	42	26	7	9	70	44	59
Ashford Town	42	24	7	11	90	40	55
Bideford	42	19	14	9	70	43	52
Minehead	42	20	12	10	65	47	52
Gravesend & Northfleet	42	22	7	13	81	55	51
Bath City	42	18	11	13	56	54	47
Wealdstone	42	16	12	14	81	61	44
Bletchley Town	42	14	13	15	54	51	41
Hastings United	42	14	13	15	53	53	41
Andover	42	15	11	16	62	70	41
Canterbury City	42	14	12	16	51	59	40
Basingstoke Town	42	14	12	16	48	57	40
Crawley Town	42	14	11	17	59	76	39
Metropolitan Police	42	15	8	19	82	75	38
Trowbridge Town	42	15	8	19	65	77	38
Bexley United	42	12	14	16	54	64	38
Salisbury	42	14	10	18	49	60	38
Bognor Regis Town	42	12	9	21	41	66	33
Dorchester Town	42	10	12	20	47	73	32
Winchester City	42	7	11	24	41	79	25
Dunstable Town	42	4	10	28	38	105	18

1973-74   Premier Division

	P	W	D	L	F	A	Pts
Dartford	42	22	13	7	67	37	57
Grantham	42	18	13	11	70	49	49
Chelmsford City	42	19	10	13	62	49	48
Kettering Town	42	16	16	10	62	51	48
Maidstone United	42	16	14	12	54	43	46
Yeovil Town	42	13	20	9	45	39	46
Weymouth	42	19	7	16	60	41	45
Barnet	42	18	9	15	55	46	45
Nuneaton Borough	42	13	19	10	54	47	45
Cambridge City	42	15	12	15	45	54	42
Atherstone Town	42	16	9	17	61	59	41
Wimbledon	42	15	11	16	50	56	41
Telford United	42	12	16	14	51	57	40
Dover	42	11	17	14	41	46	39
Tonbridge	42	12	15	15	38	45	39
Romford	42	11	17	14	39	52	39
Margate	42	15	8	19	56	63	38
Guildford City	42	13	11	18	48	67	37
Worcester City	42	11	14	17	53	67	36
Bedford Town	42	11	14	17	38	51	36
Folkestone	42	11	12	19	56	65	34
Hillingdon Borough	42	9	15	18	44	65	33

First Division (North)

	P	W	D	L	F	A	Pts
Stourbridge	42	29	11	2	103	36	69
Burton Albion	42	27	9	6	88	32	63
Cheltenham Town	42	24	8	10	75	51	56
AP Leamington	42	21	12	9	82	45	54
Enderby Town	42	19	14	9	60	36	52
Witney Town	42	20	10	12	69	55	50
Stevenage Athletic	42	19	11	12	65	46	49
Banbury United	42	19	11	12	69	57	49
King's Lynn	42	19	10	13	65	50	48
Kidderminster Harriers	42	15	14	13	67	53	44
Merthyr Tydfil	42	16	12	14	70	61	44
Redditch United	42	14	11	17	56	73	39
Bromsgrove Rovers	42	14	10	18	54	61	38
Bedworth United	42	14	10	18	50	77	38
Tamworth	42	13	11	18	42	51	37
Corby Town	42	12	11	19	40	57	35
Bletchley Town	42	10	15	17	47	71	35
Barry Town	42	10	8	24	53	85	29
Bury Town	42	10	6	26	57	84	26
Gloucester City	42	10	6	26	52	81	26
Wellingborough Town	42	7	9	26	42	87	23
Dunstable Town	42	5	11	26	26	83	21

First Division (South)

	P	W	D	L	F	A	Pts
Wealdstone	38	26	7	5	75	35	59
Bath City	38	20	8	10	55	34	48
Waterlooville	38	16	15	7	55	38	47
Minehead	38	16	15	7	69	52	47
Bideford	38	17	12	9	61	51	46
Poole Town	38	18	9	11	67	47	45
Bexley United	38	18	7	13	50	42	43
Hastings United	38	16	9	13	45	36	41
Basingstoke Town	38	14	11	13	55	44	39
Gravesend & Northfleet	38	13	13	12	58	52	39
Bognor Regis Town	38	13	12	13	48	54	38
Ashford Town	38	14	8	16	41	42	36
Ramsgate	38	13	9	16	46	44	35
Dorchester Town	38	10	13	15	40	48	33
Canterbury City	38	9	12	17	37	46	30
Trowbridge Town	38	8	14	16	44	61	30
Salisbury	38	10	9	19	40	60	29
Metropolitan Police	38	9	11	18	37	61	29
Andover	38	11	3	24	38	70	25
Crawley Town	38	6	9	23	35	79	21

1974-75   Premier Division

	P	W	D	L	F	A	Pts
Wimbledon	42	25	7	10	63	33	57
Nuneaton Borough	42	23	8	11	56	37	54
Yeovil Town	42	21	9	12	64	34	51
Kettering Town	42	20	10	12	73	41	50
Burton Albion	42	18	13	11	54	48	49
Bath City	42	20	8	14	63	50	48
Margate	42	17	12	13	64	44	46
Wealdstone	42	17	11	14	62	61	45
Telford United	42	16	13	13	55	56	45
Chelmsford City	42	16	12	14	62	51	44
Grantham	42	16	11	15	70	62	43
Dover	42	15	13	14	43	53	43
Maidstone United	42	15	12	15	52	52	42
Atherstone Town	42	14	14	14	48	53	42
Weymouth	42	13	13	16	66	58	39
Stourbridge	42	13	12	17	56	70	38
Cambridge City	42	11	14	17	51	56	36
Tonbridge	42	11	12	19	44	66	34
Romford	42	10	13	19	46	62	33
Dartford	42	9	13	20	52	70	31
Barnet	42	10	9	23	44	76	29
Guildford & Dorking United	42	10	5	27	45	82	25

First Division (North)

	P	W	D	L	F	A	Pts
Bedford Town	42	28	9	5	85	33	65
Dunstable Town	42	25	8	9	105	61	58
AP Leamington	42	25	7	10	68	48	57
Redditch United	42	22	12	8	76	40	56
Worcester City	42	24	8	10	84	50	56
Cheltenham Town	42	21	9	12	72	53	51
Tamworth	42	21	8	13	74	53	50
King's Lynn	42	19	10	13	71	64	48
Enderby Town	42	17	12	13	61	48	46
Banbury United	42	18	10	14	52	51	46
Stevenage Athletic	42	16	13	13	62	48	45
Bromsgrove Rovers	42	18	9	15	63	52	45
Merthyr Tydfil	42	11	15	16	53	64	37
Witney Town	42	16	4	22	57	76	36
Corby Town	42	11	13	18	60	57	35
Kidderminster Harriers	42	12	11	19	50	66	35
Gloucester City	42	13	8	21	55	75	34
Wellingborough Town	42	9	13	20	42	61	31
Barry Town	42	10	10	22	49	73	30
Bedworth United	42	9	9	24	40	70	27
Milton Keynes City	42	7	5	30	48	100	19
Bury Town	42	5	7	30	36	119	17

First Division (South)

Gravesend & Northfleet	38	24	12	2	70	30	60
Hillingdon Borough	38	22	8	8	87	45	52
Minehead	38	21	9	8	74	33	51
Ramsgate	38	19	11	8	70	37	49
Bexley United	38	19	7	12	61	44	45
Waterlooville	38	17	11	10	67	49	45
Ashford Town	38	16	12	10	64	55	44
Basingstoke Town	38	16	11	11	64	50	43
Canterbury City	38	16	9	13	54	43	41
Hastings United	38	13	14	11	54	45	40
Poole Town	38	11	13	14	50	60	35
Metropolitan Police	38	11	13	14	54	66	35
Folkestone & Shepway	38	10	14	14	53	57	34
Andover	38	12	8	18	52	71	32
Bognor Regis Town	38	10	11	17	49	64	31
Salisbury	38	9	11	18	45	66	29
Trowbridge Town	38	10	9	19	48	76	29
Bideford	38	10	8	20	40	71	28
Dorchester Town	38	8	10	20	40	63	26
Crawley Town	38	3	5	30	31	102	11

1975-76

Premier Division

Wimbledon	42	26	10	6	74	29	62
Yeovil Town	42	21	12	9	68	35	54
Atherstone Town	42	18	15	9	56	55	51
Maidstone United	42	17	16	9	52	39	50
Nuneaton Borough	42	16	18	8	41	33	50
Gravesend & Northfleet	42	16	18	8	49	47	50
Grantham	42	15	14	13	56	47	44
Dunstable Town	42	17	9	16	52	43	43
Bedford Town	42	13	17	12	55	51	43
Burton Albion	42	17	9	16	52	53	43
Margate	42	15	12	15	62	60	42
Hillingdon Borough	42	13	14	15	61	54	40
Telford United	42	14	12	16	54	51	40
Chelmsford City	42	13	14	15	52	57	40
Kettering Town	42	11	17	14	48	52	39
Bath City	42	11	16	15	62	57	38
Weymouth	42	13	9	20	51	67	35
Dover	42	8	18	16	51	60	34
Wealdstone	42	12	9	21	61	82	33
Tonbridge AFC	42	11	11	20	45	70	33
Cambridge City	42	8	15	19	41	67	31
Stourbridge	42	10	9	23	38	72	29

Tonbridge suffered financial problems and were re-formed during the
season as Tonbridge Angels. The re-formed club completed the fixture list
but were relegated to the First Division (South) at the end of the season.
Dunstable Town also suffered financial problems and were re-formed
during the season as Dunstable. They were allowed to complete their
fixtures as long as they accepted relegation at the end of the season. They
finished in 8th place.

First Division (North)

Redditch United	42	29	11	2	101	39	69
AP Leamington	42	27	10	5	85	31	64
Witney Town	42	24	9	9	66	40	57
Worcester City	42	24	8	10	90	49	56
Cheltenham Town	42	20	10	12	87	55	50
Barry Town	42	19	10	13	52	47	48
King's Lynn	42	17	14	11	52	48	48
Tamworth	42	18	11	13	65	43	47
Barnet	42	15	12	15	56	56	42
Oswestry Town	42	16	8	18	63	71	40
Enderby Town	42	16	6	20	48	51	38
Banbury United	42	15	8	19	58	67	38
Merthyr Tydfil	42	11	15	16	59	67	37
Bromsgrove Rovers	42	13	11	18	49	65	37
Milton Keynes City	42	15	6	21	51	63	36
Bury Town	42	12	11	19	52	72	35
Gloucester City	42	13	9	20	49	78	35
Kidderminster Harriers	42	13	8	21	54	70	34
Bedworth United	42	8	18	16	41	66	34
Corby Town	42	11	10	21	50	65	32
Wellingborough Town	42	9	11	22	42	68	29
Stevenage Athletic	42	6	6	30	46	105	18

First Division (South)

Minehead	38	27	8	3	102	35	62
Dartford	38	26	4	8	84	46	56
Romford	38	21	9	8	66	37	51
Salisbury	38	17	11	10	73	53	45
Hastings United	38	15	15	8	67	51	45
Poole Town	38	20	2	16	57	57	42
Bexley United	38	14	13	11	62	53	41
Waterlooville	38	13	13	12	62	54	39
Basingstoke Town	38	13	12	13	69	71	38
Ashford Town	38	14	8	16	67	73	36
Canterbury City	38	11	13	14	53	60	35
Folkestone & Shepway	38	10	14	14	36	51	34
Metropolitan Police	38	9	14	15	46	58	32
Trowbridge Town	38	11	10	17	48	75	32
Guildford & Dorking United	38	9	13	16	43	50	31
Bognor Regis Town	38	6	17	15	44	72	29
Ramsgate	38	9	10	19	57	76	28
Crawley Town	38	9	10	19	46	66	28
Andover	38	9	10	19	42	62	28
Dorchester Town	38	11	6	21	45	69	28

1976-77

Premier Division

Wimbledon	42	28	7	7	64	22	63
Minehead	42	23	12	7	73	39	58
Kettering Town	42	20	16	6	66	46	56
Bath City	42	20	15	7	51	30	55
Nuneaton Borough	42	20	11	11	52	35	51
Bedford Town	42	17	14	11	54	47	48
Yeovil Town	42	15	16	11	54	42	46
Dover	42	13	16	13	46	43	42
Grantham	42	14	12	16	55	50	40
Maidstone United	42	13	14	15	46	50	40
Gravesend & Northfleet	42	13	13	16	38	43	39
AP Leamington	42	12	15	15	44	53	39
Redditch United	42	12	14	16	45	54	38
Wealdstone	42	13	12	17	54	66	38
Hillingdon Borough	42	14	10	18	45	59	38
Atherstone Town	42	14	9	19	41	49	37
Weymouth	42	16	5	21	53	73	37
Dartford	42	13	10	19	52	57	36
Telford United	42	11	12	19	36	50	34
Chelmsford City	42	9	13	20	56	68	31
Burton Albion	42	10	10	22	41	52	30
Margate	42	9	10	23	47	85	28

First Division (North)

Worcester City	38	32	5	1	97	22	69
Cheltenham Town	38	23	8	7	85	35	54
Witney Town	38	21	8	9	48	31	50
Bromsgrove Rovers	38	20	8	10	61	37	48
Barry Town	38	19	8	11	62	45	46
Cambridge City	38	17	10	11	68	43	44
Stourbridge	38	17	9	12	48	35	43
Kidderminster Harriers	38	17	6	15	74	65	40
Banbury United	38	15	10	13	51	47	40
Gloucester City	38	18	4	16	70	81	40
Enderby Town	38	15	9	14	50	44	39
King's Lynn	38	13	11	14	47	53	37
Corby Town	38	11	13	14	56	64	35
Tamworth	38	11	13	14	49	58	35
Merthyr Tydfil	38	12	6	20	60	69	30
Oswestry Town	38	8	10	20	30	60	26
Wellingborough Town	38	8	7	23	37	73	23
Dunstable	38	7	7	24	38	84	21
Bedworth United	38	5	10	23	28	68	20
Milton Keynes City	38	7	6	25	31	76	20

First Division (North)

Witney Town	38	20	15	3	54	27	55
Bridgend Town	38	20	9	9	59	45	49
Burton Albion	38	17	11	10	48	32	45
Enderby Town	38	17	10	11	59	44	44
Bromsgrove Rovers	38	16	12	10	56	41	44
Banbury United	38	17	10	11	52	47	44
Kidderminster Harriers	38	16	11	11	58	41	43
Merthyr Tydfil	38	18	6	14	85	62	42
Cambridge City	38	14	12	12	56	45	40
Barry Town	38	14	11	13	58	48	39
Wellingborough Town	38	11	15	12	47	43	37
King's Lynn	38	12	13	13	55	55	37
Gloucester City	38	14	8	16	68	75	36
Corby Town	38	9	17	12	46	48	35
Dunstable	38	11	13	14	49	59	35
Stourbridge	38	9	15	14	52	53	33
Tamworth	38	10	11	17	37	48	31
Bedworth United	38	8	14	16	36	58	30
Milton Keynes City	38	5	11	22	26	74	21
Oswestry Town	38	6	8	24	29	85	20

First Division (South)

Barnet	34	23	8	3	65	25	54
Hastings United	34	18	11	5	47	18	47
Waterlooville	34	19	6	9	50	25	44
Dorchester Town	34	16	11	7	48	30	43
Salisbury	34	15	11	8	57	39	41
Romford	34	18	5	11	47	32	41
Poole Town	34	17	7	10	40	35	41
Trowbridge Town	34	15	8	11	47	39	38
Crawley Town	34	14	9	11	53	42	37
Folkestone & Shepway	34	12	11	11	39	42	35
Basingstoke Town	34	12	10	12	51	43	34
Canterbury City	34	6	16	12	36	46	28
Bognor Regis Town	34	9	9	16	33	50	27
Tonbridge AFC	34	9	9	16	33	50	27
Metropolitan Police	34	5	12	17	37	61	22
Andover	34	4	11	19	17	49	19
Ashford Town	34	5	8	21	32	65	18
Aylesbury United	34	5	6	23	27	68	16
Guildford & Dorking United disbanded during December 1976 and their record at the time was deleted:	15	2	2	11	11	34	6

First Division (South)

Margate	38	24	10	4	92	32	58
Dorchester Town	38	23	10	5	67	31	56
Salisbury	38	21	10	7	60	27	52
Waterlooville	38	19	13	6	66	36	51
Romford	38	17	15	6	58	37	49
Aylesbury United	38	20	7	11	56	42	47
Trowbridge Town	38	16	11	11	65	59	43
Chelmsford City	38	15	11	12	58	46	41
Folkestone & Shepway	38	16	9	13	64	56	41
Taunton Town	38	15	10	13	57	54	40
Addlestone	38	14	10	14	57	60	38
Crawley Town	38	14	9	15	61	60	37
Basingstoke Town	38	11	11	16	44	50	33
Tonbridge AFC	38	13	5	20	64	77	31
Ashford Town	38	9	13	16	39	60	31
Hounslow	38	10	10	18	43	62	30
Bognor Regis Town	38	9	8	21	52	69	26
Poole Town	38	8	10	20	43	68	26
Andover	38	4	12	22	30	68	20
Canterbury City	38	2	6	30	31	113	10

1977-78

Premier Division

Bath City	42	22	18	2	83	32	62
Weymouth	42	21	16	5	64	36	58
Maidstone United	42	20	11	11	59	41	51
Worcester City	42	20	11	11	67	50	51
Gravesend & Northfleet	42	19	11	12	57	42	49
Kettering Town	42	18	11	13	58	48	47
Barnet	42	18	11	13	63	58	47
Wealdstone	42	16	14	12	54	48	46
Telford United	42	17	11	14	52	45	45
Nuneaton Borough	42	15	14	13	38	36	44
Dartford	42	14	15	13	57	65	43
Yeovil Town	42	14	14	14	57	49	42
Hastings United	42	15	9	18	49	60	39
Cheltenham Town	42	12	14	16	43	52	38
Hillingdon Borough	42	13	9	20	45	54	35
Atherstone Town	42	10	15	17	41	56	35
Redditch United	42	15	5	22	40	55	35
AP Leamington	42	11	13	18	34	57	35
Minehead	42	11	12	19	43	48	34
Dover	42	9	13	20	41	63	31
Bedford Town	42	8	13	21	51	75	29
Grantham	42	11	6	25	40	66	28

1978-79

Premier Division

Worcester City	42	27	11	4	92	33	65
Kettering Town	42	27	7	8	109	43	61
Telford United	42	22	10	10	60	39	54
Maidstone United	42	18	18	6	55	35	54
Bath City	42	17	19	6	59	43	53
Weymouth	42	18	15	9	71	51	51
AP Leamington	42	19	11	12	65	53	49
Redditch United	42	19	10	13	70	57	48
Yeovil Town	42	15	16	11	59	49	46
Witney Town	42	17	10	15	53	52	44
Nuneaton Borough	42	13	17	12	59	50	43
Gravesend & Northfleet	42	15	12	15	56	55	42
Barnet	42	16	10	16	52	64	42
Hillingdon Borough	42	12	16	14	50	44	40
Wealdstone	42	12	12	18	51	59	36
Atherstone Town	42	9	17	16	46	65	35
Dartford	42	10	14	18	40	56	34
Cheltenham Town	42	11	10	21	38	72	32
Margate	42	10	9	23	44	75	29
Dorchester Town	42	7	11	24	46	86	25
Hastings United	42	5	13	24	37	85	23
Bridgend Town	42	6	6	30	39	90	18

First Division (North)

Grantham	38	21	10	7	70	45	52
Merthyr Tydfil	38	22	7	9	90	53	51
Alvechurch	38	20	10	8	70	42	50
Bedford Town	38	19	9	10	74	49	47
King's Lynn	38	17	11	10	57	46	45
Oswestry Town	38	18	8	12	63	43	44
Gloucester City	38	18	8	12	76	59	44
Burton Albion	38	16	10	12	51	40	42
Kidderminster Harriers	38	13	14	11	70	60	40
Bedworth United	38	13	14	11	41	34	40
Tamworth	38	15	8	15	47	45	38
Stourbridge	38	15	7	16	64	61	37
Barry Town	38	14	9	15	51	53	37
Enderby Town	38	14	8	16	46	55	36
Banbury United	38	10	13	15	42	58	33
Wellingborough Town	38	13	6	19	50	71	32
Cambridge City	38	9	9	20	37	62	27
Bromsgrove Rovers	38	6	14	18	33	61	26
Milton Keynes City	38	7	9	22	37	87	23
Corby Town	38	5	6	27	40	85	16

First Division (South)

Dover	40	28	9	3	88	20	65
Folkestone & Shepway	40	22	6	12	84	50	50
Gosport Borough	40	19	11	10	62	47	49
Chelmsfor d City	40	20	7	13	65	61	47
Minehead	40	16	13	11	58	39	45
Poole Town	40	15	15	10	48	44	45
Hounslow	40	16	12	12	56	45	44
Waterlooville	40	17	10	13	52	43	44
Trowbridge Town	40	15	12	13	65	61	42
Aylesbury United	40	16	9	15	54	52	41
Taunton Town	40	16	9	15	53	51	41
Bognor Regis Town	40	17	7	16	58	58	41
Dunstable	40	18	4	18	57	55	40
Tonbridge AFC	40	15	10	15	43	47	40
Salisbury	40	13	10	17	47	51	36
Basingstoke Town	40	12	11	17	49	62	35
Addlestone	40	12	9	19	56	64	33
Andover	40	12	6	22	47	69	30
Ashford Town	40	10	10	20	28	53	30
Crawley Town	40	9	9	22	44	75	27
Canterbury City	40	6	3	31	31	98	15

1979-80

Midland Division

Bridgend Town	42	28	6	8	85	39	62
Minehead	42	22	15	5	70	42	59
Bedford Town	42	20	12	10	71	42	52
Kidderminster Harriers	42	23	6	13	81	59	52
Merthyr Tydfil	42	20	11	11	70	47	51
Enderby Town	42	21	8	13	62	50	50
Stourbridge	42	19	11	12	67	49	49
Alvechurch	42	17	14	11	78	60	48
Trowbridge Town	42	19	9	14	62	61	47
Bromsgrove Rovers	42	18	10	14	67	56	46
Barry Town	42	15	12	15	64	58	42
King's Lynn	42	15	11	16	48	55	41
Banbury United	42	13	14	15	56	56	40
Taunton Town	42	16	8	18	55	62	40
Witney Town	42	10	19	13	43	45	39
Bedworth United	42	12	15	15	40	42	39
Milton Keynes City	42	15	7	20	46	59	37
Gloucester City	42	10	14	18	55	68	32
Cheltenham Town	42	13	5	24	49	70	31
Wellingborough Town	42	9	7	26	54	106	25
Cambridge City	42	6	9	27	30	73	21
Corby Town	42	5	9	28	40	94	19

Gloucester City had 2 points deducted

Southern Division

Dorchester Town	46	25	12	9	81	53	62
Aylesbury United	46	25	11	10	73	40	61
Dover	46	22	13	11	78	47	57
Gosport Borough	46	21	15	10	70	50	57
Dartford	46	21	14	11	66	45	56
Bognor Regis Town	46	20	15	11	66	38	55
Hillingdon Borough	46	19	16	11	64	41	54
Dunstable	46	17	19	10	93	64	53
Addlestone	46	20	13	13	72	57	53
Hastings United	46	19	15	12	74	65	53
Fareham Town	46	16	16	14	61	53	48
Waterlooville	46	17	12	17	67	64	46
Andover	46	16	13	17	65	65	45
Poole Town	46	16	13	17	49	64	45
Canterbury City	46	15	14	17	56	60	44
Hounslow	46	14	15	17	44	57	43
Margate	46	17	8	21	51	62	42
Folkestone & Shepway	46	14	11	21	54	63	39
Ashford Town	46	12	14	20	54	71	38
Crawley Town	46	13	11	22	55	72	37
Chelmsford City	46	9	18	19	47	69	36
Basingstoke Town	46	9	15	22	48	79	33
Salisbury	46	10	12	24	47	58	32
Tonbridge AFC	46	3	9	34	30	128	15

1980-81

Midland Division

Alvechurch	42	26	9	7	76	40	61
Bedford Town	42	25	11	6	63	32	61
Trowbridge Town	42	24	9	9	69	39	57
Kidderminster Harriers	42	23	9	10	67	41	55
Barry Town	42	21	9	12	60	40	51
Stourbridge	42	17	16	9	75	49	50
Enderby Town	42	21	8	13	71	47	50
Cheltenham Town	42	18	12	12	70	59	48
Bromsgrove Rovers	42	19	9	14	65	50	47
Corby Town	42	19	7	16	69	58	45
Bridgend Town	42	19	7	16	74	64	45
Minehead	42	19	7	16	54	60	45
Gloucester City	42	19	6	17	82	72	44
Merthyr Tydfil	42	15	12	15	60	50	42
Bedworth United	42	14	12	16	49	46	40
Banbury United	42	11	11	20	51	65	33
Taunton Town	42	10	9	23	48	68	29
Cambridge City	42	8	12	22	46	87	28
Witney Town	42	9	9	24	44	65	27
Wellingborough Town	42	10	7	25	43	91	27
Redditch United	42	11	4	27	54	92	26
Milton Keynes City	42	3	7	32	28	103	13

Southern Division

Dartford	46	26	14	6	76	39	66
Bognor Regis Town	46	25	13	8	95	43	63
Hastings United	46	24	14	8	87	43	62
Gosport Borough	46	24	12	10	84	52	60
Waterlooville	46	19	21	6	67	50	59
Dorchester Town	46	21	13	12	84	56	55
Dover	46	22	10	14	70	50	54
Poole Town	46	19	14	13	70	56	52
Addlestone & Weybridge	46	21	9	16	66	57	51
Dunstable	46	19	13	14	73	68	51
Aylesbury United	46	20	10	16	66	60	50
Hounslow	46	17	13	16	65	55	47
Hillingdon Borough	46	16	15	15	50	49	47
Basingstoke Town	46	16	14	16	69	58	46
Crawley Town	46	18	4	24	64	78	40
Ashford Town	46	12	15	19	55	76	39
Tonbridge AFC	46	12	15	19	44	68	39
Chelmsford City	46	13	12	21	54	78	38
Canterbury City	46	12	13	21	40	59	37
Salisbury	46	14	8	24	57	76	36
Folkestone	46	11	11	24	47	65	33
Margate	46	11	7	28	65	117	29
Fareham Town	46	5	18	23	31	73	28
Andover	46	6	10	30	41	94	22

1981-82

Midland Division

Nuneaton Borough	42	27	11	4	88	32	65
Alvechurch	42	26	10	6	79	34	62
Kidderminster Harriers	42	22	12	8	71	40	56
Stourbridge	42	21	10	11	69	47	52
Gloucester City	42	21	9	12	64	48	51
Bedworth United	42	20	10	12	59	40	50
Enderby Town	42	20	10	12	79	66	50
Witney Town	42	19	8	15	71	49	46
Barry Town	42	16	14	12	59	46	46
Corby Town	42	19	8	15	70	59	46
Merthyr Tydfil	42	16	12	14	63	54	44
Wellingborough Town	42	15	12	15	50	45	42
Bridgend Town	42	13	13	16	50	62	39
Bromsgrove Rovers	42	15	8	19	57	63	38
Bedford Town	42	12	13	17	45	54	37
Cheltenham Town	42	11	14	17	65	68	36
Taunton Town	42	12	8	22	46	76	32
Banbury United	42	11	8	23	63	91	30
Minehead	42	12	6	24	38	69	30
Cambridge City	42	10	8	24	38	80	28
Milton Keynes City	42	6	11	25	34	70	23
Redditch United	42	8	5	29	37	103	21

Southern Division

Wealdstone	46	32	8	6	100	32	72
Hastings United	46	31	9	6	79	34	71
Dorchester Town	46	21	18	7	76	41	60
Gosport Borough	46	26	8	12	76	45	60
Fareham Town	46	20	14	12	58	48	54
Poole Town	46	19	15	12	92	63	53
Waterlooville	46	22	9	15	75	53	53
Welling United	46	19	13	14	70	48	51
Addlestone & Weybridge	46	17	17	12	71	53	51
Chelmsford City	46	20	11	15	64	53	51
Aylesbury United	46	19	12	15	79	61	50
Basingstoke Town	46	18	12	16	74	61	48
Dover	46	19	8	19	61	63	46
Ashford Town	46	16	14	16	52	56	46
Tonbridge AFC	46	19	7	20	62	70	45
Dunstable	46	18	8	20	63	68	44
Salisbury	46	16	10	20	64	81	42
Hounslow	46	15	11	20	59	83	41
Hillingdon Borough	46	14	10	22	46	58	38
Canterbury City	46	10	16	20	49	78	36
Crawley Town	46	9	12	25	46	81	30
Folkestone	46	10	6	30	49	101	26
Andover	46	4	11	31	39	100	19
Thanet United	46	5	7	34	37	110	17

1982-83

Premier Division

AP Leamington	38	25	4	9	78	50	79
Kidderminster Harriers	38	23	7	8	69	40	76
Welling United	38	21	6	11	63	40	69
Chelmsford City	38	16	11	11	57	40	59
Bedworth United	38	16	11	11	47	39	59
Dartford	38	16	8	14	48	38	56
Gosport Borough	38	14	13	11	47	43	55
Fareham Town	38	16	7	15	73	82	55
Dorchester Town	38	14	12	12	52	50	54
Gravesend & Northfleet	38	14	12	12	49	50	54
Gloucester City	38	13	12	13	61	57	51
Witney Town	38	12	13	13	60	48	47
Alvechurch	38	13	8	17	60	66	47
Stourbridge	38	12	11	15	48	54	47
Corby Town	38	12	11	15	58	67	47
Hastings United	38	11	11	16	48	61	44
Enderby Town	38	11	9	18	44	62	42
Waterlooville	38	10	9	19	62	83	39
Poole Town	38	9	9	20	57	73	36
Addlestone & Weybridge	38	5	10	23	24	62	25

Witney Town had 2 points deducted for fielding an ineligible player

Midland Division

Cheltenham Town	32	22	5	5	65	29	71
Sutton Coldfield Town	32	21	7	4	62	24	70
Forest Green Rovers	32	21	3	8	68	32	66
Merthyr Tydfil	32	17	7	8	64	45	58
Willenhall Town	32	17	6	9	74	49	57
Oldbury United	32	16	6	10	52	49	54
Banbury United	32	15	3	14	59	55	48
Bridgend Town	32	12	11	9	46	37	47
Wellingborough Town	32	13	7	12	49	37	46
Bromsgrove Rovers	32	13	5	14	47	47	44
Dudley Town	32	12	7	13	40	45	43
Bridgwater Town	32	12	6	14	42	43	42
Aylesbury United	32	12	5	15	37	51	41
Redditch United	32	8	6	18	51	73	30
Taunton Town	32	5	7	20	30	64	22
Minehead	32	5	7	20	24	62	22
Milton Keynes City	32	0	4	28	22	90	4

Southern Division

Fisher Athletic	34	23	5	6	79	34	74
Folkestone	34	22	6	6	79	41	72
RS Southampton	34	21	7	6	66	30	70
Dunstable	34	19	5	10	57	39	62
Hillingdon Borough	34	14	11	9	41	30	53
Salisbury	34	14	10	10	58	49	52
Crawley Town	34	14	9	11	51	43	51
Ashford Town	34	13	10	11	51	41	49
Tonbridge AFC	34	14	5	15	57	57	47
Hounslow	34	11	12	11	46	47	45
Canterbury City	34	12	9	13	52	63	45
Cambridge City	34	12	5	17	56	63	41
Dover	34	11	7	16	35	52	40
Thanet United	34	10	5	19	30	61	35
Basingstoke Town	34	8	10	16	37	56	34
Woodford Town	34	6	9	19	29	57	27
Andover	34	6	8	20	28	53	26
Erith & Belvedere	34	5	9	20	26	62	24

Southern Division

RS Southampton	38	26	6	6	83	35	84
Crawley Town	38	22	9	7	68	28	75
Basingstoke Town	38	20	9	9	54	36	69
Tonbridge AFC	38	20	9	9	61	44	69
Addlestone & Weybridge	38	19	11	8	58	34	68
Poole Town	38	20	7	11	68	42	67
Hillingdon Borough	38	18	11	9	43	20	65
Ashford Town	38	19	5	14	65	47	62
Salisbury	38	17	8	13	61	48	59
Cambridge City	38	13	9	16	43	53	48
Canterbury City	38	12	9	17	44	52	45
Waterlooville	38	12	9	17	56	69	45
Dover Athletic	38	12	9	17	51	74	45
Chatham Town	38	11	10	17	46	56	43
Andover	38	12	6	20	35	54	42
Erith & Belvedere	38	11	9	18	43	68	42
Dunstable	38	10	8	20	38	65	38
Thanet United	38	9	8	21	40	65	35
Woodford Town	38	7	8	23	30	69	29
Hounslow	38	4	12	22	30	58	24

1983-84

Premier Division

Dartford	38	23	9	6	67	32	78
Fisher Athletic	38	22	9	7	80	42	75
Chelmsford City	38	19	9	10	67	45	66
Gravesend & Northfleet	38	18	9	11	50	38	63
Witney Town	38	18	6	14	75	50	60
King's Lynn	38	18	6	14	42	45	60
Folkestone	38	16	9	13	60	56	57
Cheltenham Town	38	16	7	15	63	56	55
Gloucester City	38	13	15	10	55	50	54
Hastings United	38	15	9	14	55	57	54
Bedworth United	38	15	9	14	51	55	54
Welling United	38	15	7	16	61	61	52
AP Leamington	38	14	9	15	73	83	51
Corby Town	38	12	14	12	55	54	50
Fareham Town	38	13	11	14	65	70	50
Alvechurch	38	12	12	14	56	62	48
Sutton Coldfield Town	38	10	14	14	49	53	44
Gosport Borough	38	6	15	17	31	64	33
Dorchester Town	38	4	8	26	40	69	20
Stourbridge	38	4	7	27	30	82	19

1984-85

Premier Division

Cheltenham Town	38	24	5	9	83	41	77
King's Lynn	38	23	6	9	73	48	75
Crawley Town	38	22	8	8	76	52	74
Willenhall Town	38	20	8	10	57	38	68
RS Southampton	38	21	4	13	76	52	67
Welling United	38	18	11	9	55	38	65
Folkestone	38	19	6	13	70	54	63
Fisher Athletic	38	19	5	14	67	57	62
Chelmsford City	38	17	10	11	52	50	61
Shepshed Charterhouse	38	18	5	15	67	50	59
Corby Town	38	15	6	17	56	54	51
Bedworth United	38	14	8	16	48	52	50
Gravesend & Northfleet	38	12	12	14	46	46	48
Fareham Town	38	13	8	17	52	55	47
Alvechurch	38	11	7	20	53	59	40
Hastings United	38	11	7	20	46	71	40
Witney Town	38	9	12	17	51	58	39
Gloucester City	38	10	6	22	49	74	36
Trowbridge Town	38	10	5	23	45	83	35
AP Leamington	38	2	5	31	22	112	11

Midland Division

Willenhall Town	38	27	4	7	100	44	85
Shepshed Charterhouse	38	25	5	8	88	37	80
Bromsgrove Rovers	38	20	8	10	73	43	68
Dudley Town	38	18	13	7	71	43	67
Aylesbury United	38	17	15	6	62	35	66
Moor Green	38	18	12	8	63	44	66
Rushden Town	38	17	12	9	68	42	63
Merthyr Tydfil	38	18	8	12	63	44	62
Redditch United	38	17	9	12	67	67	60
VS Rugby	38	15	12	11	68	51	57
Forest Green Rovers	38	15	12	11	67	51	57
Bridgnorth Town	38	16	9	13	64	52	57
Leicester United	38	12	9	17	58	58	45
Oldbury United	38	10	13	15	53	51	43
Coventry Sporting	38	11	7	20	40	67	40
Bridgwater Town	38	10	8	20	39	65	38
Wellingborough Town	38	7	9	22	43	80	30
Banbury United	38	6	11	21	37	78	29
Milton Keynes City	38	3	9	26	31	110	18
Tamworth	38	2	7	29	25	118	13

Midland Division

Dudley Town	34	21	8	5	70	36	71
Aylesbury United	34	20	7	7	62	30	67
Hednesford Town	34	18	7	9	58	42	61
Moor Green	34	17	9	8	63	43	60
VS Rugby	34	17	9	8	59	41	60
Bromsgrove Rovers	34	16	10	8	53	42	58
Stourbridge	34	15	11	8	52	45	56
Redditch United	34	12	11	11	68	57	47
Sutton Coldfield Town	34	13	6	15	50	56	45
Bridgnorth Town	34	13	5	16	67	65	44
Coventry Sporting	34	11	9	14	45	52	42
Merthyr Tydfil	34	10	11	13	43	46	41
Rushden Town	34	10	7	17	42	52	37
Forest Green Rovers	34	9	10	15	49	65	37
Wellingborough Town	34	10	7	17	39	63	37
Oldbury United	34	10	6	18	52	66	36
Banbury United	34	9	5	20	33	59	32
Leicester United	34	3	6	25	17	62	15

Southern Division

Basingstoke Town	38	24	9	5	61	22	81
Gosport Borough	38	22	6	10	78	41	72
Poole Town	38	20	12	6	69	38	72
Hillingdon	38	19	10	9	51	23	67
Thanet United	38	19	9	10	63	47	66
Salisbury	38	19	5	14	55	54	62
Sheppey United	38	18	6	14	49	45	60
Addlestone & Weybridge	38	16	9	13	68	54	57
Waterlooville	38	15	10	13	71	63	55
Canterbury City	38	15	7	16	61	64	52
Woodford Town	38	13	13	12	46	53	52
Tonbridge AFC	38	16	3	19	59	62	51
Andover	38	15	5	18	42	54	50
Dorchester Town	38	13	7	18	45	60	46
Cambridge City	38	11	11	16	59	71	44
Chatham Town	38	12	8	18	44	66	44
Ashford Town	38	10	9	19	54	69	39
Dunstable	38	8	10	20	35	56	34
Dover Athletic	38	7	7	24	39	78	28
Erith & Belvedere	38	6	8	24	36	65	26

Southern Division

Cambridge City	40	23	11	6	87	41	80
Salisbury	40	24	8	8	84	51	80
Hastings Town	40	23	9	8	83	51	78
Dover Athletic	40	23	6	11	89	53	75
Corinthian	40	20	9	11	78	45	69
Tonbridge AFC	40	17	13	10	65	51	64
Dunstable	40	17	11	12	70	61	62
Ruislip	40	17	6	17	67	66	57
Erith & Belvedere	40	14	12	14	35	40	54
Waterlooville	40	16	6	18	52	58	54
Burnham & Hillingdon	40	16	6	18	44	59	54
Canterbury City	40	13	13	14	58	58	52
Trowbridge Town	40	13	13	14	57	63	52
Sheppey United	40	14	10	16	43	53	52
Thanet United	40	13	7	20	58	63	46
Woodford Town	40	12	10	18	49	62	46
Poole Town	40	12	7	21	55	63	43
Ashford Town	40	10	12	18	45	65	42
Chatham Town	40	8	15	17	53	70	39
Andover	40	10	8	22	52	92	38
Dorchester Town	40	5	8	27	35	94	23

1985-86

Premier Division

Welling United	38	29	6	3	95	31	93
Chelmsford City	38	20	10	8	68	41	70
Fisher Athletic	38	20	7	11	67	45	67
Alvechurch	38	19	9	10	71	56	66
Worcester City	38	19	9	10	64	50	66
Crawley Town	38	18	5	15	76	59	59
Shepshed Charterhouse	38	19	1	18	51	52	58
Aylesbury United	38	14	10	14	52	49	52
Folkestone	38	14	10	14	56	56	52
Bedworth United	38	14	8	16	44	49	50
Willenhall Town	38	12	13	13	51	44	49
Dudley Town	38	15	4	19	58	62	49
Corby Town	38	14	7	17	61	67	49
King's Lynn	38	12	10	16	39	42	46
Basingstoke Town	38	13	4	21	36	67	43
RS Southampton	38	11	9	18	44	61	42
Witney Town	38	11	6	21	44	74	39
Gosport Borough	38	10	8	20	42	66	38
Fareham Town	38	8	13	17	40	62	37
Gravesend & Northfleet	38	9	9	20	29	55	36

Midland Division

Bromsgrove Rovers	40	29	5	6	95	45	92
Redditch United	40	23	6	11	70	42	75
Merthyr Tydfil	40	21	10	9	60	40	73
VS Rugby	40	17	14	9	41	31	65
Stourbridge	40	15	14	11	62	39	59
Rusden Town	40	17	7	16	69	74	58
Bilston Town	40	15	12	13	60	48	57
Bridgnorth Town	40	13	18	9	56	45	57
Gloucester City	40	15	12	13	61	57	57
Grantham	40	16	7	17	46	59	55
Wellingborough Town	40	15	9	16	56	56	54
Sutton Coldfield Town	40	13	14	13	60	45	53
Hednesford Town	40	14	9	17	67	70	51
Forest Green Rovers	40	14	9	17	52	56	51
Mile Oak Rovers	40	14	8	18	57	73	50
Leicester United	40	13	10	17	41	48	49
Banbury United	40	13	8	19	38	55	47
Coventry Sporting	40	10	15	15	42	48	45
Moor Green	40	12	6	22	63	91	42
Leamington	40	10	6	24	40	77	36
Oldbury United	40	8	7	25	50	87	31

1986-87

Premier Division

Fisher Athletic	42	25	11	6	72	29	86
Bromsgrove Rovers	42	24	11	7	82	41	83
Aylesbury United	42	24	11	7	72	40	83
Dartford	42	19	12	11	76	43	69
Chelmsford City	42	17	13	12	48	45	64
Cambridge City	42	14	20	8	68	52	62
Redditch United	42	16	14	12	59	54	62
Alvechurch	42	18	8	16	66	62	62
Corby Town	42	14	17	11	65	51	59
Worcester City	42	16	11	15	62	55	59
Shepshed Charterhouse	42	16	10	16	59	59	58
Bedworth United	42	15	12	15	55	51	57
Crawley Town	42	14	11	17	59	60	53
Fareham Town	42	11	17	14	58	49	50
Willenhall Town	42	13	11	18	48	57	50
Basingstoke Town	42	12	12	18	53	78	48
Witney Town	42	12	12	18	29	56	48
Gosport Borough	42	11	13	18	42	57	46
Salisbury	42	12	7	23	52	82	43
King's Lynn	42	9	13	20	48	72	40
Dudley Town	42	9	9	24	39	76	36
Folkestone	42	8	11	23	36	79	35

Midland Division

VS Rugby	38	25	5	8	81	43	80
Leicester United	38	26	1	11	89	49	79
Merthyr Tydfil	38	23	6	9	95	54	75
Moor Green	38	22	6	10	73	55	72
Halesowen Town	38	19	12	7	72	50	69
Hednesford Town	38	21	5	12	84	56	68
Gloucester City	38	19	5	14	77	59	62
Coventry Sporting	38	17	8	13	55	54	59
Forest Green Rovers	38	16	9	13	65	53	57
Stourbridge	38	16	7	15	56	56	55
Grantham	38	15	9	14	74	54	54
Banbury United	38	14	7	17	55	65	49
Buckingham Town	38	13	9	16	55	59	48
Bridgnorth Town	38	12	9	17	59	63	45
Wellingborough Town	38	13	6	19	55	76	45
Mile Oak Rovers	38	11	10	17	50	63	43
Sutton Coldfield Town	38	8	10	20	56	78	34
Bilston Town	38	8	7	23	37	76	31
Leamington	38	4	13	21	37	80	25
Rushden Town	38	1	10	27	42	124	13

Southern Division

	P	W	D	L	F	A	Pts
Dorchester Town	38	23	8	7	83	42	77
Ashford Town	38	23	7	8	63	32	76
Woodford Town	38	22	6	10	72	44	72
Hastings Town	38	20	10	8	74	54	70
Dover Athletic	38	20	6	12	66	43	66
Gravesend & Northfleet	38	18	7	13	67	46	61
Tonbridge AFC	38	16	10	12	73	67	58
Erith & Belvedere	38	15	12	11	57	50	57
Chatham Town	38	16	9	13	53	46	57
Thanet United	38	14	14	10	56	50	56
Waterlooville	38	16	8	14	66	65	56
Trowbridge Town	38	15	9	14	77	65	54
Dunstable	38	13	9	16	60	57	48
Corinthian	38	11	12	15	56	65	45
Sheppey United	38	9	12	17	43	65	39
Andover	38	9	9	20	51	80	36
Burnham & Hillingdon	38	7	11	20	32	62	32
Poole Town	38	8	6	24	50	90	30
Ruislip	38	6	12	20	35	75	30
Canterbury City	38	8	5	25	46	82	29

1987-88

Premier Division

	P	W	D	L	F	A	Pts
Aylesbury United	42	27	8	7	79	35	89
Dartford	42	27	8	7	79	39	89
Cambridge City	42	24	8	10	84	43	80
Bromsgrove Rovers	42	22	11	9	65	39	77
Worcester City	42	22	6	14	58	48	72
Crawley Town	42	17	14	11	73	63	65
Alvechurch	42	17	13	12	54	52	64
Leicester United	42	15	14	13	68	59	59
Fareham Town	42	16	11	15	51	59	59
Corby Town	42	16	8	18	61	64	56
Dorchester Town	42	14	14	14	51	57	56
Ashford Town	42	12	16	14	45	54	52
Shepshed Charterhouse	42	13	11	18	53	62	50
Bedworth United	42	12	14	16	49	64	50
Gosport Borough	42	10	17	15	39	49	47
Burton Albion	42	11	14	17	62	74	47
VS Rugby	42	10	16	16	52	57	46
Redditch United	42	10	13	19	55	63	43
Chelmsford City	42	11	10	21	60	75	43
Willenhall Town	42	9	12	21	39	76	39
Nuneaton Borough	42	8	13	21	58	77	37
Witney Town	42	8	11	23	45	71	35

Midland Division

	P	W	D	L	F	A	Pts
Merthyr Tydfil	42	30	4	8	102	40	94
Moor Green	42	26	8	8	91	49	86
Grantham Town	42	27	4	11	97	53	85
Atherstone United	42	22	10	10	93	56	76
Sutton Coldfield Town	42	22	6	14	71	47	72
Halesowen Town	42	18	15	9	75	59	69
Gloucester City	42	18	14	10	86	62	68
Dudley Town	42	20	5	17	64	55	65
Forest Green Rovers	42	14	16	12	67	54	58
Banbury United	42	17	7	18	48	46	58
Bridgnorth Town	42	16	7	19	59	75	55
Buckingham Town	42	15	9	18	74	75	54
King's Lynn	42	16	6	20	53	63	54
Wellingborough Town	42	14	10	18	67	70	52
Rushden Town	42	14	9	19	69	85	51
Trowbridge Town	42	14	3	25	53	82	45
Bilston Town	42	12	8	22	52	87	44
Hednesford Town	42	11	10	21	50	81	43
Mile Oak Rovers	42	9	14	19	43	65	41
Coventry Sporting	42	11	8	23	46	83	41
Stourbridge	42	10	10	22	46	79	40
Paget Rangers	42	10	9	23	49	89	39

Southern Division

	P	W	D	L	F	A	Pts
Dover Athletic	40	28	10	2	81	28	94
Waterlooville	40	27	10	3	88	33	91
Salisbury	40	24	11	5	71	33	83
Gravesend & Northfleet	40	20	12	8	60	32	72
Thanet United	40	17	13	10	60	38	64
Andover	40	17	13	10	64	58	64
Dunstable	40	17	12	11	78	56	63
Burnham	40	17	10	13	61	45	61
Bury Town	40	17	7	16	80	67	58
Erith & Belvedere	40	16	9	15	52	56	57
Sheppey United	40	14	10	16	58	52	52
Hastings Town	40	14	10	16	62	70	52
Tonbridge AFC	40	14	8	18	51	56	50
Poole Town	40	13	10	17	69	70	49
Baldock Town	40	12	12	16	44	53	48
Hounslow	40	11	8	21	41	76	41
Folkestone	40	9	11	20	47	76	38
Corinthian	40	9	10	21	49	67	37
Ruislip	40	5	13	22	33	80	28
Canterbury City	40	7	6	27	33	87	27
Chatham Town	40	7	5	28	39	88	26

1988-89

Premier Division

	P	W	D	L	F	A	Pts
Merthyr Tydfil	42	26	7	9	104	58	85
Dartford	42	25	7	10	79	33	82
VS Rugby	42	24	7	11	64	43	79
Worcester City	42	20	13	9	72	49	73
Cambridge City	42	20	10	12	72	51	70
Dover Athletic	42	19	12	11	65	47	69
Gosport Borough	42	18	12	12	73	57	66
Burton Albion	42	18	10	14	79	68	64
Bath City	42	15	13	14	66	51	58
Bromsgrove Rovers	42	14	16	12	68	56	58
Wealdstone	42	16	10	16	60	53	58
Crawley Town	42	14	16	12	61	56	58
Dorchester Town	42	14	16	12	56	61	58
Alvechurch	42	16	8	18	56	59	56
Moor Green	42	14	13	15	58	70	55
Corby Town	42	14	11	17	55	59	53
Waterlooville	42	13	13	16	61	63	52
Ashford Town	42	13	13	16	54	66	51
Fareham Town	42	15	6	21	43	68	51
Leicester United	42	6	11	25	46	84	29
Redditch United	42	5	7	30	36	105	22
Bedworth United	42	4	7	31	36	102	19

Midland Division

	P	W	D	L	F	A	Pts
Gloucester City	42	28	8	6	95	37	92
Atherstone United	42	26	9	7	85	38	87
Tamworth	42	26	9	7	85	45	87
Halesowen Town	42	25	10	7	85	42	85
Grantham Town	42	23	11	8	66	37	80
Nuneaton Borough	42	19	9	14	71	58	66
Rushden Town	42	19	8	15	71	50	65
Spalding United	42	17	13	12	72	64	64
Dudley Town	42	16	13	13	73	62	61
Sutton Coldfield Town	42	18	7	17	56	56	61
Willenhall Town	42	16	12	14	65	71	60
Forest Green Rovers	42	12	16	14	64	67	52
Bilston Town	42	15	7	20	63	71	52
Ashtree Highfield	42	12	15	15	57	62	51
Hednesford Town	42	12	15	15	49	57	51
Banbury United	42	10	14	18	53	74	44
Bridgnorth Town	42	12	7	23	59	77	43
Stourbridge	42	11	10	21	37	65	43
King's Lynn	42	7	13	22	31	67	34
Coventry Sporting	42	6	13	23	39	91	31
Wellingborough Town	42	5	15	22	39	72	30
Mile Oak Rovers	42	5	10	27	46	98	25

Southern Division

Team	P	W	D	L	F	A	Pts
Chelmsford City	42	30	5	7	106	38	95
Gravesend & Northfleet	42	27	6	9	70	40	87
Poole Town	42	24	11	7	98	48	83
Bury Town	42	25	7	10	75	34	82
Burnham	42	22	13	7	78	47	79
Baldock Town	42	23	5	14	69	40	74
Hastings Town	42	21	11	10	75	48	74
Hounslow	42	21	6	15	75	60	69
Salisbury	42	20	5	17	79	58	65
Trowbridge Town	42	19	7	16	59	52	64
Folkestone	42	17	8	17	62	65	59
Corinthian	42	13	13	16	59	69	52
Canterbury City	42	14	8	20	52	60	50
Witney Town	42	13	11	18	61	71	50
Dunstable	42	11	14	17	42	57	47
Buckingham Town	42	12	10	20	56	79	46
Erith & Belvedere	42	11	10	21	48	63	43
Andover	42	11	9	22	56	90	42
Sheppey United	42	10	8	24	50	90	38
Thanet United	42	7	15	20	47	95	36
Tonbridge AFC	42	7	6	29	50	98	27
Ruislip	42	6	0	20	47	112	26

Southern Division

Team	P	W	D	L	F	A	Pts
Bashley	42	25	7	10	80	47	82
Poole Town	42	23	8	11	85	60	77
Buckingham Town	42	22	10	10	67	46	76
Dunstable	42	20	14	8	56	38	74
Salisbury	42	21	9	12	72	50	72
Hythe Town	42	20	12	10	69	48	72
Trowbridge Town	42	20	9	13	79	64	69
Hastings Town	42	20	9	13	64	54	69
Bury Town	42	18	12	12	76	62	66
Baldock Town	42	18	11	13	69	52	65
Burnham	42	17	11	14	77	52	62
Fareham Town	42	14	14	14	49	53	56
Yate Town	42	16	6	20	53	52	54
Witney Town	42	16	6	20	54	56	54
Canterbury City	42	14	10	18	52	52	52
Margate	42	12	15	15	46	45	51
Folkestone	42	14	9	19	61	83	51
Andover	42	13	11	18	54	70	50
Hounslow	42	11	5	26	39	82	38
Erith & Belvedere	42	8	11	23	34	73	35
Corinthian	42	6	10	26	44	93	28
Sheppey United	42	6	7	29	35	83	25

1989-90   Premier Division

Team	P	W	D	L	F	A	Pts
Dover Athletic	42	32	6	4	87	27	102
Bath City	42	30	8	4	81	28	98
Dartford	42	26	9	7	80	35	87
Burton Albion	42	20	12	10	64	40	72
VS Rugby	42	19	12	11	51	35	69
Atherstone United	42	19	10	13	60	52	67
Gravesend & Northfleet	42	18	12	12	44	50	66
Cambridge City	42	17	11	14	76	56	62
Gloucester City	42	17	11	14	80	68	62
Bromsgrove Rovers	42	17	10	15	56	48	61
Moor Green	42	18	7	17	62	59	61
Wealdstone	42	16	9	17	55	54	57
Dorchester Town	42	16	7	19	52	67	55
Worcester City	42	15	10	17	62	63	54
Crawley Town	42	13	12	17	53	57	51
Waterlooville	42	13	10	19	63	81	49
Weymouth	42	11	13	18	50	70	46
Chelmsford City	42	11	10	21	52	72	43
Ashford Town	42	10	7	25	43	75	37
Corby Town	42	10	6	26	57	77	36
Alvechurch	42	7	5	30	46	95	26
Gosport Borough	42	6	5	31	28	93	23

Worcester City had 1 point deducted.

Midland Division

Team	P	W	D	L	F	A	Pts
Halesowen Town	42	28	8	6	100	49	92
Rushden Town	42	28	5	9	82	39	89
Nuneaton Borough	42	26	7	9	81	47	85
Tamworth	42	22	8	12	82	70	74
Barry Town	42	21	8	13	67	53	71
Spalding United	42	20	7	15	73	63	67
Sutton Coldfield Town	42	18	10	14	72	69	64
Stourbridge	42	17	12	13	73	61	63
Dudley Town	42	18	9	15	69	64	63
Stroud	42	16	13	13	75	62	61
Leicester United	42	17	5	20	66	77	56
Bridgnorth Town	42	13	14	15	68	73	53
King's Lynn	42	16	5	21	57	69	53
Grantham Town	42	14	10	18	57	63	52
Bedworth United	42	14	9	19	50	60	51
Hednesford Town	42	11	14	17	50	62	47
Bilston Town	42	11	14	17	40	54	47
Redditch United	42	11	13	18	57	64	46
Racing Club Warwick	42	11	11	20	45	66	44
Willenhall Town	42	9	9	24	37	66	36
Banbury United	42	9	9	24	46	83	34
Sandwell Borough	42	6	12	24	46	79	30

Banbury United had 2 points deducted.

1990-91   Premier Division

Team	P	W	D	L	F	A	Pts
Farnborough Town	42	26	7	9	79	43	85
Gloucester City	42	23	14	5	86	49	83
Cambridge City	42	21	14	7	63	43	77
Dover Athletic	42	21	11	10	56	37	74
Bromsgrove Rovers	42	20	11	11	68	49	71
Worcester City	42	18	12	12	55	42	66
Burton Albion	42	15	15	12	59	48	60
Halesowen Town	42	17	9	16	73	67	60
VS Rugby	42	16	11	15	56	46	59
Bashley	42	15	12	15	56	52	57
Dorchester Town	42	15	12	15	47	54	57
Wealdstone	42	16	8	18	57	58	56
Dartford	42	15	9	18	61	64	54
Rushden Town	42	14	11	17	64	66	53
Atherstone United	42	14	10	18	55	58	52
Moor Green	42	15	6	21	64	75	51
Poole Town	42	12	13	17	56	69	49
Chelmsford City	42	11	15	16	57	68	48
Crawley Town	42	12	12	18	45	67	48
Waterlooville	42	11	13	18	51	70	46
Gravesend & Northfleet	42	9	7	26	46	91	34
Weymouth	42	4	12	26	50	88	24

Midland Division

Team	P	W	D	L	F	A	Pts
Stourbridge	42	28	6	8	80	48	90
Corby Town	42	27	4	11	99	48	85
Hednesford Town	42	25	7	10	79	47	82
Tamworth	42	25	5	12	84	45	80
Nuneaton Borough	42	21	11	10	74	51	70
Barry Town	42	20	7	15	61	48	67
Newport AFC	42	19	6	17	54	46	63
King's Lynn	42	17	9	16	53	62	60
Grantham Town	42	17	7	18	62	56	58
Redditch United	42	16	10	16	66	75	58
Hinckley Town	42	16	9	17	72	68	57
Sutton Coldfield Town	42	15	11	16	56	56	56
Bedworth United	42	15	9	18	57	73	54
Bilston Town	42	14	9	19	69	79	51
Leicester United	42	14	10	18	65	67	51
Racing Club Warwick	42	12	13	17	56	65	49
Bridgnorth Town	42	13	9	20	62	74	48
Stroud	42	11	14	17	51	64	47
Dudley Town	42	11	13	18	48	73	46
Alvechurch	42	10	8	24	54	92	38
Willenhall Town	42	10	10	22	58	69	37
Spalding United	42	8	9	25	35	70	33

Nuneaton Borough had 4 points deducted. Willenhall Town had 3 points deducted. Leicester United had 1 point deducted.

Southern Division

Buckingham Town	40	25	8	7	73	38	83
Trowbridge Town	40	22	12	6	67	31	78
Salisbury	40	22	11	7	63	39	77
Baldock Town	40	21	9	10	66	52	72
Ashford Town	40	22	5	13	82	52	71
Yate Town	40	21	8	11	76	48	71
Hastings Town	40	18	11	11	66	46	65
Hythe Town	40	17	9	14	55	44	59
Andover	40	16	6	18	69	76	54
Margate	40	14	11	15	52	55	53
Burnham	40	12	16	12	57	49	52
Bury Town	40	15	5	20	58	74	50
Sudbury Town	40	13	10	17	60	68	49
Newport IOW	40	13	9	18	56	62	48
Gosport Borough	40	12	11	17	47	58	47
Witney Town	40	12	11	17	57	75	47
Dunstable	40	9	15	16	48	63	42
Canterbury City	40	12	6	22	60	83	42
Erith & Belvedere	40	10	6	24	46	73	36
Fareham Town	40	9	9	22	46	74	36
Corinthian	40	5	12	23	34	78	27

Hythe Town had 1 point deducted.

1991-92

Premier Division

Bromsgrove Rovers	42	27	9	6	78	34	90
Dover Athletic	42	23	15	4	66	30	84
VS Rugby	42	23	11	8	70	44	80
Bashley	42	22	8	12	70	44	74
Cambridge City	42	18	14	10	71	53	68
Dartford	42	17	15	10	62	45	66
Trowbridge Town	42	17	10	15	69	51	61
Halesowen Town	42	15	15	12	61	49	60
Moor Green	42	15	11	16	61	59	56
Burton Albion	42	15	10	17	59	61	55
Dorchester Town	42	14	13	15	66	73	55
Gloucester City	42	15	9	18	67	70	54
Atherstone United	42	15	8	19	54	66	53
Corby Town	42	13	12	17	66	81	51
Waterlooville	42	13	11	18	43	56	50
Worcester City	42	12	13	17	56	59	49
Crawley Town	42	12	12	18	62	67	48
Chelmsford City	42	12	12	18	49	56	48
Wealdstone	42	13	7	22	52	69	46
Poole Town	42	10	13	19	46	77	43
Fisher Athletic	42	9	11	22	53	89	38
Gravesend & Northfleet	42	8	9	25	39	87	33

Midland Division

Solihull Borough	42	29	10	3	92	40	97
Hednesford Town	42	26	13	3	81	37	91
Sutton Coldfield Town	42	21	11	10	71	51	74
Barry Town	42	21	6	15	88	56	69
Bedworth United	42	16	15	11	67	63	63
Nuneaton Borough	42	17	11	14	68	53	62
Tamworth	42	16	12	14	66	52	60
Rushden Town	42	16	12	14	69	63	60
Stourbridge	42	17	8	17	85	62	59
Newport AFC	42	15	13	14	72	60	58
Yate Town	42	14	15	13	65	64	57
Bilston Town	42	15	10	17	56	67	55
Grantham Town	42	11	17	14	59	55	50
King's Lynn	42	13	11	18	61	68	50
Hinckley Town	42	14	8	20	61	87	50
Leicester United	42	12	13	17	56	63	49
Bridgnorth Town	42	12	12	18	61	74	48
Racing Club Warwick	42	11	14	17	45	61	47
Stroud	42	14	4	24	66	88	46
Redditch United	42	12	8	22	52	92	44
Alvechurch	42	11	10	21	54	88	43
Dudley Town	42	8	9	25	41	92	33

Southern Division

Hastings Town	42	28	7	7	80	37	91
Weymouth	42	22	12	8	64	35	78
Havant Town	42	21	12	9	67	46	75
Braintree Town	42	21	8	13	77	58	71
Buckingham Town	42	19	15	8	57	26	69
Andover	42	18	10	14	73	68	64
Ashford Town	42	17	12	13	66	57	63
Sudbury Town	42	18	9	15	70	66	63
Sittingbourne	42	19	10	13	63	41	61
Burnham	42	15	14	13	57	55	59
Baldock Town	42	16	10	16	62	67	58
Salisbury	42	13	16	13	67	51	55
Hythe Town	42	15	10	17	61	62	55
Margate	42	13	16	13	49	56	55
Newport IOW	42	13	10	19	58	63	49
Dunstable	42	12	12	18	55	67	48
Bury Town	42	14	4	24	52	94	46
Witney Town	42	11	12	19	55	76	45
Fareham Town	42	12	8	22	45	71	44
Erith & Belvedere	42	11	10	21	44	67	43
Canterbury City	42	8	14	20	43	69	38
Gosport Borough	42	6	9	27	32	65	27

Buckingham Town had 3 points deducted.
Sittingbourne had 6 points deducted.

1992-93

Premier Division

Dover Athletic	40	25	11	4	65	23	86
Cheltenham Town	40	21	10	9	76	40	73
Corby Town	40	20	12	8	68	43	72
Hednesford Town	40	21	7	12	72	52	70
Trowbridge Town	40	18	8	14	70	66	62
Crawley Town	40	16	12	12	68	59	60
Solihull Borough	40	17	9	14	68	59	60
Burton Albion	40	16	11	13	53	50	59
Bashley	40	18	8	14	60	60	59
Halesowen Town	40	15	11	14	67	54	56
Waterlooville	40	15	9	16	59	62	54
Chelmsford City	40	15	9	16	59	69	54
Gloucester City	40	14	11	15	66	68	53
Cambridge City	40	14	10	16	62	73	52
Atherstone United	40	13	14	13	56	60	50
Hastings Town	40	13	11	16	50	55	50
Worcester City	40	12	9	19	45	62	45
Dorchester Town	40	12	6	22	52	74	42
Moor Green	40	10	6	24	58	79	36
VS Rugby	40	10	6	24	40	63	36
Weymouth	40	5	10	25	39	82	23

Bashley and Atherstone United both had 3 points deducted. Weymouth had 2 points deducted.

Midland Division

Nuneaton Borough	42	29	5	8	102	45	92
Gresley Rovers	42	27	6	9	94	55	87
Rushden & Diamonds	42	25	10	7	85	41	85
Barri	42	26	5	11	82	49	83
Newport AFC	42	23	8	11	73	58	77
Bedworth United	42	22	8	12	72	55	74
Stourbridge	42	17	9	16	93	79	60
Sutton Coldfield Town	42	17	9	16	82	78	60
Redditch United	42	18	6	18	75	79	60
Tamworth	42	16	11	15	65	51	59
Weston-super-Mare	42	17	7	18	79	86	58
Leicester United	42	16	9	17	67	67	57
Grantham Town	42	16	9	17	60	73	57
Bilston Town	42	15	10	17	74	69	55
Evesham United	42	15	8	19	67	83	53
Bridgnorth Town	42	15	7	20	61	68	52
Dudley Town	42	14	8	20	60	75	50
Yate Town	42	15	5	22	63	81	50
Forest Green Rovers	42	12	6	24	61	97	42
Hinckley Town	42	9	11	22	56	89	37
King's Lynn	42	10	6	26	45	90	36
Racing Club Warwick	42	3	7	32	40	88	16

Hinckley Town had 1 point deducted.

Midland Division

Rushden & Diamonds	42	29	11	2	109	37	98
VS Rugby	42	28	8	6	98	41	92
Weston-super-Mare	42	27	10	5	94	39	91
Newport AFC	42	26	9	7	84	37	87
Clevedon Town	42	24	10	8	75	46	82
Redditch United	42	19	11	12	79	62	68
Tamworth	42	19	7	16	82	68	64
Bilston Town	42	16	10	16	65	73	58
Stourbridge	42	17	6	19	71	75	57
Evesham United	42	16	8	18	50	60	56
Grantham Town	42	16	6	20	77	73	54
Bridgnorth Town	42	15	6	21	56	68	51
Racing Club Warwick	42	13	12	17	53	66	51
Dudley Town	42	13	10	19	64	61	49
Forest Green Rovers	42	12	12	18	61	84	48
Sutton Coldfield Town	42	12	8	22	53	75	44
Bedworth United	42	12	7	23	62	81	43
Hinckley Town	42	11	10	21	44	71	43
Leicester United	42	11	9	22	34	73	42
King's Lynn	42	9	11	22	47	72	38
Yate Town	42	10	6	26	48	86	36
Armitage	42	8	11	23	45	103	35

Southern Division

Sittingbourne	42	26	12	4	102	43	90
Salisbury City	42	27	7	8	87	50	88
Witney Town	42	25	9	8	77	37	84
Gravesend & Northfleet	42	25	4	13	99	63	79
Havant Town	42	23	6	13	78	55	75
Sudbury Town	42	20	11	11	89	54	71
Erith & Belvedere	42	22	5	15	73	66	71
Ashford Town	42	20	8	14	91	66	68
Braintree Town	42	20	6	16	95	65	66
Margate	42	19	7	16	65	58	64
Wealdstone	42	18	7	17	75	69	61
Buckingham Town	42	16	11	15	61	58	59
Baldock Town	42	15	9	18	59	63	54
Poole Town	42	15	7	20	61	69	52
Fareham Town	42	14	8	20	67	65	50
Burnham	42	14	8	20	53	77	50
Canterbury City	42	12	10	20	54	76	46
Newport IOW	42	9	16	17	44	56	43
Fisher Athletic	42	8	9	25	38	98	33
Andover	42	7	9	26	42	99	30
Dunstable	42	5	14	23	42	92	29
Bury Town	42	8	5	29	46	119	29

Southern Division

Gravesend & Northfleet	42	27	11	4	87	24	92
Sudbury Town	42	27	8	7	98	47	89
Witney Town	42	27	8	7	69	36	89
Salisbury City	42	26	10	6	90	39	88
Havant Town	42	27	4	11	101	41	85
Ashford Town	42	24	13	5	93	46	85
Baldock Town	42	26	7	9	76	40	85
Newport IOW	42	22	8	12	74	51	74
Margate	42	20	8	14	76	58	68
Weymouth	42	18	9	15	71	65	63
Tonbridge	42	19	5	18	59	62	62
Buckingham Town	42	14	14	14	43	42	56
Braintree Town	42	16	7	19	72	84	55
Fareham Town	42	12	12	18	54	75	48
Poole Town	42	13	6	23	54	86	45
Burnham	42	10	9	23	53	92	39
Fisher 93	42	9	10	23	52	81	37
Dunstable	42	9	7	26	50	91	34
Erith & Belvedere	42	9	5	28	40	72	32
Canterbury City	42	8	7	27	35	80	31
Wealdstone	42	6	7	29	45	95	25
Bury Town	42	3	5	34	36	121	14

1993-94   Premier Division

Farnborough Town	42	25	7	10	74	44	82
Cheltenham Town	42	21	12	9	67	38	75
Halesowen Town	42	21	11	10	69	46	74
Atherstone United	42	22	7	13	57	43	73
Crawley Town	42	21	10	11	56	42	73
Chelmsford City	42	21	7	14	74	59	70
Trowbridge Town	42	16	17	9	52	41	65
Sittingbourne	42	17	13	12	65	48	64
Corby Town	42	17	8	17	52	56	59
Gloucester City	42	17	6	19	55	60	57
Burton Albion	42	15	11	16	57	49	56
Hastings Town	42	16	7	19	51	60	55
Hednesford Town	42	15	9	18	67	66	54
Gresley Rovers	42	14	11	17	61	72	53
Worcester City	42	14	9	19	61	70	51
Solihull Borough	42	13	11	18	52	57	50
Cambridge City	42	13	11	18	50	60	50
Dorchester Town	42	12	11	19	38	51	47
Moor Green	42	11	10	21	49	66	43
Waterlooville	42	11	10	21	47	69	43
Bashley	42	11	10	21	47	80	43
Nuneaton Borough	42	11	8	23	42	66	41

1994-95   Premier Division

Hednesford Town	42	28	9	5	99	49	93
Cheltenham Town	42	25	11	6	87	39	86
Burton Albion	42	20	15	7	55	39	75
Gloucester City	42	22	8	12	76	48	74
Rushden & Diamonds	42	19	11	12	99	65	68
Dorchester Town	42	19	10	13	84	61	67
Leek Town	42	19	10	13	72	60	67
Gresley Rovers	42	17	12	13	70	63	63
Cambridge City	42	18	8	16	60	55	62
Worcester City	42	14	15	13	46	34	57
Crawley Town	42	15	10	17	64	71	55
Hastings Town	42	13	14	15	55	57	53
Halesowen Town	42	14	10	18	81	80	52
Gravesend & Northfleet	42	13	13	16	38	55	52
Chelmsford City	42	14	6	22	56	60	48
Atherstone United	42	12	12	18	51	64	48
VS Rugby	42	11	14	17	49	61	47
Sudbury Town	42	12	10	20	50	77	46
Solihull Borough	42	10	15	17	39	65	45
Sittingbourne	42	11	10	21	51	73	43
Trowbridge Town	42	9	13	20	43	69	40
Corby Town	42	4	10	28	36	113	21

Corby Town had 1 point deducted for fielding ineligible players

Midland Division

Newport AFC	42	29	8	5	106	39	95
Ilkeston Town	42	25	6	11	101	75	81
Tamworth	42	24	8	10	98	70	80
Moor Green	42	23	8	11	105	63	77
Bridgnorth Town	42	22	10	10	75	49	76
Buckingham Town	42	20	14	8	55	37	74
Nuneaton Borough	42	19	11	12	76	55	68
Rothwell Town	42	19	7	16	71	71	64
King's Lynn	42	18	8	16	76	64	62
Racing Club Warwick	42	17	11	14	68	63	62
Dudley Town	42	17	10	15	65	69	61
Bilston Town	42	17	8	17	73	64	59
Bedworth United	42	17	7	18	64	68	58
Evesham United	42	14	10	18	57	56	52
Hinckley Town	42	14	10	18	61	76	52
Stourbridge	42	15	7	20	59	77	52
Sutton Coldfield Town	42	12	10	20	62	72	46
Forest Green Rovers	42	11	13	18	56	76	46
Redditch United	42	8	14	20	47	64	38
Leicester United	42	10	8	24	51	99	38
Grantham Town	42	8	9	25	55	93	33
Armitage	42	2	5	35	35	116	11

Southern Division

Salisbury City	42	30	7	5	88	37	97
Baldock Town	42	28	10	4	92	44	94
Havant Town	42	25	10	7	81	34	85
Waterlooville	42	24	8	10	77	36	80
Ashford Town	42	21	12	9	106	72	75
Weston-super-Mare	42	18	13	11	82	54	67
Bashley	42	18	11	13	62	49	65
Weymouth	42	16	13	13	60	55	61
Newport IOW	42	17	10	15	67	67	61
Witney Town	42	14	14	14	57	57	56
Clevedon Town	42	14	13	15	73	64	55
Tonbridge Angels	42	14	12	16	74	87	54
Margate	42	15	7	20	60	72	52
Braintree Town	42	12	13	17	64	71	49
Wealdstone	42	13	8	21	76	94	47
Yate Town	42	11	13	18	57	75	46
Fisher 93	42	9	16	17	54	70	43
Bury Town	42	11	8	23	59	86	41
Erith & Belvedere	42	10	9	23	49	94	39
Poole Town	42	10	8	24	53	79	38
Fareham Town	42	10	8	24	46	91	38
Burnham	42	7	7	28	40	89	28

1995-96   Premier Division

Rushden & Diamonds	42	29	7	6	99	41	94
Halesowen Town	42	27	11	4	70	36	92
Cheltenham Town	42	21	11	10	76	57	74
Gloucester City	42	21	8	13	65	47	71
Gresley Rovers	42	20	10	12	70	58	70
Worcester City	42	19	12	11	61	43	69
Merthyr Tydfil	42	19	6	17	67	59	63
Hastings Town	42	16	13	13	68	56	61
Crawley Town	42	15	13	14	57	56	58
Sudbury Town	42	15	10	17	69	71	55
Gravesend & Northfleet	42	15	10	17	60	62	55
Chelmsford City	42	13	16	13	46	53	55
Dorchester Town	42	15	8	19	62	57	53
Newport AFC	42	13	13	16	53	59	52
Salisbury City	42	14	10	18	57	69	52
Burton Albion	42	13	12	17	55	56	51
Atherstone United	42	12	12	18	58	75	48
Baldock Town	42	11	14	17	51	56	47
Cambridge City	42	12	10	20	56	68	46
Ilkeston Town	42	11	10	21	53	87	43
Stafford Rangers	42	11	4	27	58	90	37
VS Rugby	42	5	10	27	37	92	25

Midland Division

Nuneaton Borough	42	30	5	7	82	35	95
King's Lynn	42	27	5	10	85	43	84
Bedworth United	42	24	10	8	76	42	81
Moor Green	42	22	8	12	81	47	74
Paget Rangers	42	21	9	12	70	45	72
Tamworth	42	22	3	17	97	64	69
Solihull Borough	42	19	9	14	77	64	66
Rothwell Town	42	17	14	11	79	62	65
Buckingham Town	42	18	9	15	74	62	63
Dudley Town	42	15	16	11	83	66	61
Stourbridge	42	17	8	17	60	63	59
Bilston Town	42	16	9	17	61	62	57
Sutton Coldfield Town	42	16	9	17	62	67	57
Grantham Town	42	17	5	20	71	83	56
Redditch United	42	14	11	17	57	77	53
Leicester United	42	13	13	16	58	72	52
Hinckley Town	42	14	7	21	62	83	49
Racing Club Warwick	42	10	13	19	67	90	43
Evesham United	42	11	6	25	59	94	39
Corby Town	42	9	7	26	52	95	34
Bury Town	42	8	8	26	57	95	32
Bridgnorth Town	42	7	6	29	53	112	27

Bedworth United 1 point deducted, King's Lynn had 2 points deducted

Southern Division

Sittingbourne	42	28	4	10	102	44	88
Ashford Town	42	25	9	8	75	44	84
Waterlooville	42	24	8	10	87	44	80
Newport IOW	42	24	6	12	75	58	78
Braintree Town	42	24	8	10	93	70	77
Weymouth	42	24	4	14	75	55	76
Havant Town	42	23	11	8	73	42	74
Forest Green Rovers	42	22	8	12	85	55	74
Trowbridge Town	42	18	8	16	86	51	62
Yate Town	42	17	8	17	85	71	59
Margate	42	18	5	19	68	62	59
Witney Town	42	16	11	15	60	54	59
Weston-super-Mare	42	16	9	17	78	68	57
Cinderford Town	42	16	8	18	74	77	56
Fisher 93	42	14	13	15	58	59	55
Bashley	42	14	11	17	63	61	53
Clevedon Town	42	15	6	21	70	80	51
Tonbridge Angels	42	13	10	19	58	79	49
Fleet Town	42	14	5	23	58	79	47
Fareham Town	42	12	5	25	71	97	41
Erith & Belvedere	42	4	4	34	38	111	16
Poole Town	42	0	1	41	17	188	1

Braintree Town 3 points deducted, Havant Town had 6 points deducted

1996-97   Premier Division

Gresley Rovers	42	25	10	7	75	40	85
Cheltenham Town	42	21	11	10	76	44	74
Gloucester City	42	21	10	11	81	56	73
Halesowen Town	42	21	10	11	77	54	73
King's Lynn	42	20	8	14	65	61	68
Burton Albion	42	18	12	12	70	53	66
Nuneaton Borough	42	19	9	14	61	52	66
Sittingbourne	42	19	7	16	76	65	64
Merthyr Tydfil	42	17	9	16	69	61	60
Worcester City	42	15	14	13	52	50	59
Atherstone United	42	15	13	14	46	47	58
Salisbury City	42	15	13	14	57	66	58
Sudbury Town	42	16	7	19	72	72	55
Gravesend & Northfleet	42	16	7	19	63	73	55
Dorchester Town	42	14	9	19	62	66	51
Hastings Town	42	12	15	15	49	60	51
Crawley Town	42	13	8	21	49	67	47
Cambridge City	42	11	13	18	57	65	46
Ashford Town	42	9	18	15	53	79	45
Baldock Town	42	11	8	23	52	90	41
Newport AFC	42	9	13	20	40	60	40
Chelmsford City	42	6	14	22	49	70	32

Midland Division

	P	W	D	L	F	A	Pts
Tamworth	40	30	7	3	90	28	97
Rothwell Town	40	20	11	9	82	54	71
Ilkeston Town	40	19	13	8	76	50	70
Grantham Town	40	22	4	14	65	46	70
Bedworth United	40	18	11	11	77	41	65
Solihull Borough	40	19	8	13	84	62	65
Bilston Town	40	18	10	12	74	57	64
Moor Green	40	18	7	15	88	68	61
Stafford Rangers	40	17	9	14	68	62	60
Raunds Town	40	16	11	13	61	66	59
Racing Club Warwick	40	16	10	14	70	72	58
Shepshed Dynamo	40	14	12	14	64	65	54
Redditch United	40	15	8	17	56	59	53
Paget Rangers	40	13	9	18	42	55	48
Dudley Town	40	12	10	18	70	89	46
Hinckley Town	40	11	11	18	39	63	44
Stourbridge	40	10	9	21	61	81	39
Evesham United	40	9	12	19	55	77	39
VS Rugby	40	9	9	22	49	81	36
Corby Town	40	8	8	24	49	88	32
Sutton Coldfield Town	40	7	9	24	29	85	30

Leicester United FC closed down and their record was expunged from the League table.

Southern Division

	P	W	D	L	F	A	Pts
Forest Green Rovers	42	27	10	5	87	40	91
St Leonards Stamcroft	42	26	9	7	95	48	87
Havant Town	42	23	10	9	81	49	79
Weston-super-Mare	42	21	13	8	82	43	76
Margate	42	21	9	12	70	47	72
Witney Town	42	20	11	11	71	42	71
Weymouth	42	20	10	12	82	51	70
Tonbridge Angels	42	17	15	10	56	44	66
Newport IOW	42	15	15	12	73	58	60
Fisher Athletic (London)	42	18	6	18	77	77	60
Clevedon Town	42	17	9	16	75	76	60
Fareham Town	42	14	12	16	53	70	54
Bashley	42	15	8	19	73	84	53
Dartford	42	14	10	18	59	64	52
Waterlooville	42	14	9	19	58	67	51
Cirencester Town	42	12	12	18	50	68	48
Cinderford Town	42	13	7	22	64	76	46
Trowbridge Town	42	11	11	20	50	61	44
Yate Town	42	12	8	22	55	87	44
Fleet Town	42	12	6	24	47	91	42
Erith & Belvedere	42	9	10	23	60	95	37
Buckingham Town	42	2	8	32	27	107	14

1997-98   Premier Division

	P	W	D	L	F	A	Pts
Forest Green Rovers	42	27	8	7	93	55	89
Merthyr Tydfil	42	24	12	6	80	42	84
Burton Albion	42	21	8	13	64	43	71
Dorchester Town	42	19	13	10	63	38	70
Halesowen Town	42	18	15	9	70	38	69
Bath City	42	19	12	11	72	51	69
Worcester City	42	19	12	11	54	44	69
King's Lynn	42	18	11	13	64	65	65
Atherstone United	42	17	12	13	55	49	63
Crawley Town	42	17	8	17	63	60	59
Gloucester City	42	16	11	15	57	57	59
Nuneaton Borough	42	17	6	19	68	61	57
Cambridge City	42	16	8	18	62	70	56
Hastings Town	42	14	12	16	67	70	54
Tamworth	42	14	11	17	68	65	53
Rothwell Town	42	11	16	15	55	73	49
Gresley Rovers	42	14	6	22	59	77	48
Salisbury City	42	12	12	18	53	72	48
Bromsgrove Rovers	42	13	6	23	67	85	45
Sittingbourne	42	12	8	22	47	66	44
Ashford Town	42	8	5	29	34	85	29
St Leonards Stamcroft	42	5	10	27	48	97	25

Midland Division

	P	W	D	L	F	A	Pts
Grantham Town	40	30	4	6	87	39	94
Ilkeston Town	40	29	6	5	123	39	93
Solihull Borough	40	22	9	9	81	48	75
Raunds Town	40	20	8	12	73	44	68
Wisbech Town	40	20	7	13	79	57	67
Moor Green	40	20	7	13	72	55	67
Bilston Town	40	20	5	15	69	57	65
Blakenall	40	17	13	10	66	55	64
Stafford Rangers	40	18	6	16	57	56	60
Redditch United	40	16	11	13	59	41	59
Stourbridge	40	16	9	15	57	55	57
Hinckley United	40	15	11	14	59	56	56
Brackley Town	40	15	7	18	45	57	52
Bedworth United	40	15	5	20	50	73	50
Racing Club Warwick	40	11	9	20	49	56	42
Shepshed Dynamo	40	9	14	17	55	74	41
Sutton Coldfield Town	40	9	12	19	42	68	39
Paget Rangers	40	9	12	19	40	75	39
VS Rugby	40	8	12	20	53	93	36
Evesham United	40	7	9	24	47	94	30
Corby Town	40	2	8	30	41	112	14

Southern Division

	P	W	D	L	F	A	Pts
Weymouth	42	32	2	8	107	48	98
Chelmsford City	42	29	8	5	86	39	95
Bashley	42	29	4	9	101	59	91
Newport IOW	42	25	9	8	72	34	84
Fisher Athletic (London)	42	25	5	12	87	50	80
Margate	42	23	8	11	71	42	77
Newport AFC	42	21	6	15	83	65	69
Witney Town	42	20	9	13	74	58	69
Clevedon Town	42	20	7	15	57	55	67
Waterlooville	42	17	7	18	69	64	58
Dartford	42	17	7	18	60	60	58
Havant Town	42	13	14	15	70	53	53
Fleet Town	42	16	5	21	63	83	53
Tonbridge Angels	42	14	10	18	49	55	52
Trowbridge Town	42	14	6	22	55	64	48
Erith & Belvedere	42	11	13	18	47	68	46
Fareham Town	42	12	9	21	75	87	45
Cirencester Town	42	12	7	23	63	88	43
Weston-super-Mare	42	12	5	25	49	86	41
Baldock Town	42	10	5	27	53	81	35
Cinderford Town	42	6	5	31	40	112	23
Yate Town	42	5	7	30	44	97	22

1998-99   Premier Division

	P	W	D	L	F	A	Pts
Nuneaton Borough	42	27	9	6	91	33	90
Boston United	42	17	16	9	69	51	67
Ilkeston Town	42	18	13	11	72	59	67
Bath City	42	18	11	13	70	44	65
Hastings Town	42	18	11	13	57	49	65
Gloucester City	42	18	11	13	57	52	65
Worcester City	42	18	9	15	58	54	63
Halesowen Town	42	17	11	14	72	60	62
Tamworth	42	19	5	18	62	67	62
King's Lynn	42	17	10	15	53	46	61
Crawley Town	42	17	10	15	57	58	61
Salisbury City	42	16	12	14	56	61	60
Burton Albion	42	17	7	18	58	52	58
Weymouth	42	14	14	14	56	55	56
Merthyr Tydfil	42	15	8	19	52	62	53
Atherstone United	42	12	14	16	47	52	50
Grantham Town	42	14	8	20	51	58	50
Dorchester Town	42	11	15	16	49	63	48
Rothwell Town	42	13	9	20	47	67	48
Cambridge City	42	11	12	19	47	68	45
Gresley Rovers	42	12	8	22	49	73	44
Bromsgrove Rovers	42	8	7	27	38	84	31

Hastings Town resigned from the League.

Midland Division

	P	W	D	L	F	A	Pts
Clevedon Town	42	28	8	6	83	35	92
Newport AFC	42	26	7	9	92	51	85
Redditch United	42	22	12	8	81	45	75
Hinckley United	42	20	12	10	58	40	72
Stafford Rangers	42	21	8	13	92	60	71
Bilston Town	42	20	11	11	79	69	71
Solihull Borough	42	19	12	11	76	53	69
Moor Green	42	20	7	15	71	61	67
Blakenall	42	17	14	11	65	54	65
Shepshed Dynamo	42	17	12	13	62	54	63
Sutton Coldfield Town	42	17	8	17	46	57	59
Stourbridge	42	16	10	16	60	55	58
Evesham United	42	16	9	17	63	63	57
Wisbech Town	42	16	9	17	59	66	57
Weston-super-Mare	42	15	10	17	59	56	55
Bedworth United	42	15	9	18	63	52	54
Cinderford Town	42	13	8	21	61	74	47
Stamford AFC	42	13	7	22	60	75	46
Paget Rangers	42	11	12	19	49	58	45
VS Rugby	42	12	9	21	53	74	45
Racing Club Warwick	42	5	8	29	38	93	23
Bloxwich Town	42	1	2	39	26	151	5

Southern Division

	P	W	D	L	F	A	Pts
Havant & Waterlooville	42	29	7	6	85	32	94
Margate	42	27	8	7	84	33	89
Folkestone Invicta	42	26	8	8	92	47	86
Newport IOW	42	23	7	12	68	40	76
Chelmsford City	42	20	12	10	91	51	72
Raunds Town	42	19	13	10	87	50	70
Ashford Town	42	17	12	13	59	54	63
Baldock Town	42	17	9	16	60	59	60
Fisher Athletic (London)	42	16	11	15	58	54	59
Bashley	42	17	7	18	74	77	58
Witney Town	42	15	12	15	56	48	57
Cirencester Town	42	16	8	18	61	66	56
Sittingbourne	42	12	18	12	53	56	54
Dartford	42	14	10	18	48	53	52
Erith & Belvedere	42	15	7	20	48	64	52
Tonbridge Angels	42	12	15	15	48	59	51
St Leonards	42	14	8	20	57	72	50
Fleet Town	42	12	11	19	54	72	47
Corby Town	42	10	10	22	48	73	40
Yate Town	42	10	7	25	37	79	37
Andover	42	6	10	26	50	115	28
Brackley Town	42	6	8	28	41	105	26

Eastern Division

	P	W	D	L	F	A	Pts
Fisher Athletic (London)	42	31	5	6	107	42	98
Folkestone Invicta	42	30	7	5	101	39	97
Newport IOW	42	25	7	10	74	40	82
Chelmsford City	42	24	8	10	74	38	80
Hastings Town	42	22	9	11	76	56	75
Ashford Town	42	21	9	12	70	49	72
Tonbridge Angels	42	20	10	12	82	60	70
Dartford	42	17	6	19	52	58	57
Burnham	42	15	9	18	55	64	54
Baldock Town	42	14	10	18	57	69	52
Erith & Belvedere	42	14	9	19	62	68	51
Witney Town	42	13	11	18	48	60	50
VS Rugby	42	13	11	18	58	79	50
Wisbech Town	42	14	7	21	58	66	49
Spalding United	42	14	6	22	52	71	48
Sittingbourne	42	13	7	22	48	75	46
Stamford	42	9	18	15	50	62	45
St Leonards	42	11	12	19	67	81	45
Raunds Town	42	11	12	19	44	63	45
Bashley	42	12	7	23	56	95	43
Corby Town	42	11	12	19	56	62	42
Fleet Town	42	8	8	26	54	104	32

Corby Town had 3 points deducted for fielding an ineligible player
Raunds Town gave notice to withdraw and take the place of the 2nd relegated Club. They then unsuccessfully sought re-election.

Western Division

	P	W	D	L	F	A	Pts
Stafford Rangers	42	29	6	7	107	47	93
Moor Green	42	26	12	4	85	33	90
Hinckley United	42	25	12	5	89	47	87
Tiverton Town	42	26	7	9	91	44	85
Solihull Borough	42	20	11	11	85	66	71
Blakenall	42	19	12	11	70	46	69
Cirencester Town	42	20	8	14	72	64	68
Bilston Town	42	16	18	8	66	52	66
Cinderford Town	42	17	11	14	62	64	62
Redditch United	42	17	10	15	73	65	61
Gresley Rovers	42	14	15	13	54	49	57
Weston-super-Mare	42	16	9	17	55	55	57
Sutton Coldfield Town	42	13	17	12	49	52	56
Evesham United	42	13	12	17	69	61	51
Bedworth United	42	13	10	19	52	71	49
Rocester	42	12	12	18	63	78	48
Bromsgrove Rovers	42	13	7	22	59	72	46
Shepshed Dynamo	42	12	7	23	46	66	43
Paget Rangers	42	11	4	27	44	82	37
Racing Club Warwick	42	7	14	21	41	82	35
Stourbridge	42	10	3	29	45	101	33
Yate Town	42	3	3	36	28	108	12

1999-2000 Premier Division

	P	W	D	L	F	A	Pts
Boston United	42	27	11	4	102	39	92
Burton Albion	42	23	9	10	73	43	78
Margate	42	23	8	11	64	43	77
Bath City	42	19	15	8	70	49	72
King's Lynn	42	19	14	9	59	43	71
Tamworth	42	20	10	12	80	51	70
Newport County	42	16	18	8	67	50	66
Clevedon Town	42	18	9	15	52	52	63
Ilkeston Town	42	16	12	14	77	69	60
Weymouth	42	14	16	12	60	51	58
Halesowen Town	42	14	14	14	52	54	56
Crawley Town	42	15	8	19	68	82	53
Havant & Waterlooville	42	13	13	16	63	68	52
Cambridge City	42	14	10	18	52	66	52
Worcester City	42	13	11	18	60	66	50
Salisbury City	42	14	8	20	70	84	50
Merthyr Tydfil	42	13	9	20	51	63	48
Dorchester Town	42	10	17	15	56	65	47
Grantham Town	42	14	5	23	63	76	47
Gloucester City	42	8	14	20	40	82	38
Rothwell Town	42	5	14	23	48	85	29
Atherstone United	42	5	13	24	30	76	28

2000-2001 Premier Division

Margate	42	28	7	7	75	27	91
Burton Albion	42	25	13	4	76	36	88
King's Lynn	42	18	11	13	67	58	65
Welling United	42	17	13	12	59	55	64
Weymouth	42	17	12	13	69	51	63
Havant & Waterlooville	42	18	9	15	65	53	63
Stafford Rangers	42	18	9	15	70	59	63
Worcester City	42	18	8	16	52	53	62
Moor Green	42	18	8	16	49	53	62
Newport County	42	17	10	15	70	61	61
Crawley Town	42	17	10	15	61	54	61
Tamworth	42	17	8	17	58	55	59
Salisbury City	42	17	8	17	64	69	59
Ilkeston Town	42	16	11	15	51	61	59
Bath City	42	15	13	14	67	68	55
Cambridge City	42	13	11	18	56	59	50
Folkestone Invicta	42	14	6	22	49	74	48
Merthyr Tydfil	42	11	13	18	49	62	46
Clevedon Town	42	11	7	24	61	74	40
Fisher Athletic (London)	42	12	6	24	51	85	39
Dorchester Town	42	10	8	24	40	70	38
Halesowen Town	42	8	13	21	47	69	37

Bath City and Fisher Athletic (London) both had 3 points deducted

Eastern Division

Newport IOW	42	28	10	4	91	30	94
Chelmsford City	42	27	9	6	102	45	90
Grantham Town	42	25	11	6	100	47	86
Histon	42	23	11	8	84	53	80
Baldock Town	42	23	10	9	81	44	79
Hastings Town	42	22	10	10	72	50	76
Stamford	42	20	11	11	69	59	71
Tonbridge Angels	42	18	11	13	79	58	65
Langney Sports	42	19	8	15	75	55	65
Rothwell Town	42	20	5	17	86	74	62
Corby Town	42	14	10	18	64	92	52
Ashford Town	42	15	4	23	53	83	49
Banbury United	42	12	11	19	57	54	47
Witney Town	42	12	11	19	55	71	47
Bashley	42	10	14	18	57	71	44
Dartford	42	11	11	20	49	67	44
Burnham	42	10	14	18	39	65	43
Wisbech Town	42	10	9	23	45	89	39
St Leonards	42	9	10	23	55	87	37
Erith & Belvedere	42	10	7	25	49	92	37
Sittingbourne	42	8	9	25	41	79	33
Spalding United	42	7	12	23	35	73	33

Burnham had 1 point deducted, Rothwell Town had 3 points deducted

Western Division

Hinckley United	42	30	8	4	102	38	98
Tiverton Town	42	28	7	7	97	36	91
Bilston Town	42	27	9	6	88	48	90
Evesham United	42	27	5	10	86	46	86
Mangotsfield United	42	25	9	8	91	45	84
Solihull Borough	42	22	12	8	73	43	78
Redditch United	42	17	13	12	76	69	64
Weston-super-Mare	42	17	10	15	68	58	61
Atherstone United	42	16	11	15	64	58	59
Rocester	42	18	5	19	57	77	59
Cirencester Town	42	14	15	13	65	74	57
Rugby United	42	13	10	19	51	68	49
Gloucester City	42	12	11	19	76	86	47
Blakenall	42	13	10	19	54	64	46
Shepshed Dynamo	42	12	9	21	56	73	45
Bedworth United	42	12	9	21	38	60	45
Racing Club Warwick	42	13	6	23	46	77	45
Gresley Rovers	42	11	8	23	46	65	41
Cinderford Town	42	11	8	23	56	84	41
Sutton Coldfield Town	42	7	14	21	45	66	35
Paget Rangers	42	9	4	29	38	93	31
Bromsgrove Rovers	42	7	9	26	47	92	30

Blakenall had 3 points deducted

2001-2002

Premier Division

Kettering Town	42	27	6	9	80	41	87
Tamworth	42	24	13	5	81	41	85
Havant & Waterlooville	42	22	9	11	74	50	75
Crawley Town	42	21	10	11	67	48	73
Newport County	42	19	9	14	61	48	66
Tiverton Town	42	17	10	15	70	63	61
Moor Green	42	18	7	17	64	62	61
Worcester City	42	16	12	14	65	54	60
Stafford Rangers	42	17	9	16	70	62	60
Ilkeston Town	42	14	16	12	58	61	58
Weymouth	42	15	11	16	59	67	56
Hinckley United	42	14	13	15	64	62	55
Folkestone Invicta	42	14	12	16	51	61	54
Cambridge City	42	12	16	14	60	70	52
Welling United	42	13	12	17	69	66	51
Hednesford Town	42	15	6	21	59	70	51
Bath City	42	13	11	18	56	65	50
Chelmsford City	42	13	11	18	63	75	50
Newport IOW	42	12	12	18	38	61	48
King's Lynn	42	11	13	18	44	57	46
Merthyr Tydfil	42	12	8	22	53	71	44
Salisbury City	42	6	8	28	36	87	26

Eastern Division

Hastings Town	42	29	8	5	85	38	95
Grantham Town	42	29	6	7	99	43	93
Dorchester Town	42	26	10	6	81	36	88
Histon	42	23	8	11	83	49	77
Stamford	42	24	4	14	76	61	76
Fisher Athletic (London)	42	20	10	12	83	56	70
Eastbourne Borough	42	21	6	15	63	46	69
Dartford	42	18	5	19	62	66	59
Erith & Belvedere	42	18	3	21	75	79	57
Bashley	42	15	11	16	71	64	56
Burnham	42	15	10	17	52	54	55
Rugby United	42	16	6	20	56	67	54
Rothwell Town	42	14	8	20	45	66	50
Ashford Town	42	14	6	22	58	78	48
Banbury United	42	13	9	20	53	66	47
Chatham Town	42	13	8	21	56	87	47
Sittingbourne	42	14	4	24	46	69	46
Spalding United	42	13	6	23	72	84	45
Tonbridge Angels	42	13	6	23	65	80	45
St Leonards	42	14	3	25	52	88	45
Corby Town	42	10	13	19	54	82	43
Wisbech Town	42	11	8	23	56	84	41

Banbury United had 1 point deducted.

Western Division

Halesowen Town	40	27	9	4	85	24	90
Chippenham Town	40	26	9	5	81	28	87
Weston-super-Mare	40	22	10	8	70	38	76
Solihull Borough	40	20	11	9	75	42	71
Gresley Rovers	40	19	9	12	59	50	66
Sutton Coldfield Town	40	17	11	12	53	46	62
Mangotsfield United	40	17	10	13	74	54	61
Stourport Swifts	40	18	6	16	59	59	60
Atherstone United	40	16	8	16	61	59	56
Clevedon Town	40	15	11	14	57	58	56
Bedworth United	40	16	7	17	59	63	55
Evesham United	40	16	7	17	54	70	55
Cirencester Town	40	17	3	20	64	69	54
Gloucester City	40	14	10	16	48	63	52
Cinderford Town	40	14	9	17	54	67	51
Shepshed Dynamo	40	10	10	20	64	84	40
Bilston Town	40	11	7	22	50	72	40
Redditch United	40	11	6	23	47	77	39
Swindon Supermarine	40	11	4	25	52	76	37
Racing Club Warwick	40	8	11	21	38	63	35
Rocester	40	5	12	23	33	75	27

2002-2003

Premier Division

Team	P	W	D	L	F	A	Pts
Tamworth	42	26	10	6	73	32	88
Stafford Rangers	42	21	12	9	76	40	75
Dover Athletic	42	19	14	9	42	35	71
Tiverton Town	42	19	12	11	60	43	69
Chippenham Town	42	17	17	8	59	37	68
Worcester City	42	18	13	11	60	39	67
Crawley Town	42	17	13	12	64	51	64
Havant & Waterlooville	42	15	15	12	67	64	60
Chelmsford City	42	15	12	15	65	63	57
Newport County	42	15	11	16	53	52	56
Hednesford Town	42	14	13	15	59	60	55
Moor Green	42	13	14	15	49	58	53
Hinckley United	42	12	16	14	61	64	52
Bath City	42	13	13	16	50	61	52
Welling United	42	13	12	17	55	58	51
Grantham Town	42	14	9	19	59	65	51
Weymouth	42	12	15	15	44	62	51
Cambridge City	42	13	10	19	54	56	49
Halesowen Town	42	12	13	17	52	63	49
Hastings United	42	10	13	19	44	57	43
Ilkeston Town	42	10	10	22	54	92	40
Folkestone Invicta	42	7	7	28	57	105	28

Eastern Division

Team	P	W	D	L	F	A	Pts
Dorchester Town	42	28	9	5	114	40	93
Eastbourne Borough	42	29	6	7	92	33	93
Stamford	42	27	6	9	80	39	87
Salisbury City	42	27	8	7	81	42	86
Bashley	42	23	12	7	90	44	81
King's Lynn	42	24	7	11	98	62	79
Rothwell Town	42	22	10	10	77	52	76
Banbury United	42	21	11	10	75	50	74
Tonbridge Angels	42	20	11	11	71	55	71
Histon	42	20	7	15	99	62	67
Ashford Town	42	18	9	15	63	57	63
Sittingbourne	42	15	8	19	57	69	53
Burnham	42	15	7	20	62	79	52
Fisher Athletic	42	15	5	22	57	80	50
Chatham Town	42	14	5	23	54	84	47
Newport IOW	42	12	6	24	53	87	42
Dartford	42	11	8	23	48	78	41
Erith & Belvedere	42	11	6	25	65	96	39
Corby Town	42	9	11	22	49	84	38
Fleet Town	42	8	8	26	34	80	32
Spalding United	42	4	6	32	40	108	18
St. Leonards	42	4	4	34	38	116	16

Salisbury City had 3 points deducted.

Western Division

Team	P	W	D	L	F	A	Pts
Merthyr Tydfil	42	28	8	6	78	32	92
Weston-super-Mare	42	26	7	9	77	42	85
Bromsgrove Rovers	42	23	7	12	73	41	76
Solihull Borough	42	21	13	8	77	48	76
Gloucester City	42	22	9	11	87	58	75
Mangotsfield United	42	21	10	11	106	53	73
Redditch United	42	22	6	14	76	42	72
Rugby United	42	20	9	13	58	43	69
Gresley Rovers	42	19	10	13	63	54	67
Taunton Town	42	20	7	15	76	78	67
Sutton Coldfield Town	42	18	10	14	63	53	64
Evesham United	42	19	6	17	76	72	63
Clevedon Town	42	14	13	15	54	60	55
Cirencester Town	42	15	7	20	62	82	52
Cinderford Town	42	13	12	17	50	67	51
Shepshed Dynamo	42	12	6	24	48	76	42
Stourport Swifts	42	10	11	21	48	66	41
Bedworth United	42	11	7	24	46	74	40
Swindon Supermarine	42	11	5	26	52	85	38
Atherstone United	42	9	10	23	45	78	37
Rocester	42	9	10	23	34	74	37
Racing Club Warwick	42	3	9	30	33	104	18

2003-2004

Premier Division

Team	P	W	D	L	F	A	Pts
Crawley Town	42	25	9	8	77	43	84
Weymouth	42	20	12	10	76	47	72
Stafford Rangers	42	19	11	12	55	43	68
Nuneaton Borough	42	17	15	10	65	49	66
Worcester City	42	18	9	15	71	50	63
Hinckley United	42	15	14	13	55	46	59
Newport County	42	15	14	13	52	50	59
Cambridge City	42	14	15	13	54	53	57
Welling United	42	16	8	18	56	58	56
Weston-super-Mare	42	14	13	15	52	52	55
Eastbourne Borough	42	14	13	15	48	56	55
Havant & Waterlooville	42	15	10	17	59	70	55
Moor Green	42	14	12	16	42	54	54
Merthyr Tydfil	42	13	14	15	60	66	53
Tiverton Town	42	12	15	15	63	64	51
Bath City	42	13	12	17	49	57	51
Dorchester Town	42	14	9	19	56	69	51
Chelmsford City	42	11	16	15	46	53	49
Dover Athletic	42	12	13	17	50	59	49
Hednesford Town	42	12	12	18	56	69	48
Chippenham Town	42	10	17	15	51	63	47
Grantham Town	42	10	15	17	45	67	45

Eastern Division

Team	P	W	D	L	F	A	Pts
King's Lynn	42	28	7	7	90	35	91
Histon	42	26	10	6	96	41	88
Tonbridge Angels	42	27	7	8	82	46	88
Eastleigh	42	27	4	11	88	40	82
Folkestone Invicta	42	20	15	7	91	45	75
Salisbury City	42	21	11	10	73	45	74
Stamford	42	20	11	11	63	45	71
Banbury United	42	19	10	13	65	57	67
Burgess Hill Town	42	19	7	16	67	54	64
Sittingbourne	42	18	8	16	61	55	62
Bashley	42	18	7	17	66	58	61
Ashford Town	42	15	9	18	51	53	54
Chatham Town	42	13	10	19	49	67	49
Fisher Athletic	42	13	10	19	61	81	49
Corby Town	42	12	9	21	44	75	45
Dartford	42	13	6	23	48	81	45
Burnham	42	12	11	19	52	76	44
Hastings United	42	12	7	23	60	91	43
Newport IOW	42	11	7	24	42	69	40
Rothwell Town	42	9	11	22	30	47	38
Erith & Belvedere	42	7	10	25	45	84	31
Fleet Town	42	5	7	30	35	114	22

Eastleigh and Burnham both had 3 points deducted.

Western Division

Team	P	W	D	L	F	A	Pts
Redditch United	40	25	9	6	75	30	84
Gloucester City	40	24	7	9	77	46	79
Cirencester Town	40	24	4	12	73	40	76
Halesowen Town	40	20	13	7	64	40	73
Rugby United	40	21	8	11	57	40	71
Team Bath	40	21	6	13	62	41	69
Solihull Borough	40	19	9	12	50	31	66
Sutton Coldfield Town	40	16	15	9	52	38	63
Bromsgrove Rovers	40	16	11	13	60	48	59
Ilkeston Town	40	16	10	14	58	59	58
Clevedon Town	40	16	5	19	55	59	53
Gresley Rovers	40	15	7	18	52	60	52
Mangotsfield United	40	14	8	18	70	70	50
Evesham United	40	15	5	20	56	57	50
Taunton Town	40	14	8	18	50	55	50
Yate Town	40	11	9	20	51	79	42
Swindon Supermarine	40	10	9	21	41	69	39
Stourport Swifts	40	9	11	20	43	62	38
Bedworth United	40	8	12	20	39	61	36
Cinderford Town	40	7	9	24	50	94	30
Shepshed Dynamo	40	5	13	22	31	87	28

2004-2005 Premier Division

Team	P	W	D	L	F	A	Pts
Histon	42	24	6	12	93	57	78
Chippenham Town	42	22	9	11	81	55	75
Merthyr Tydfil	42	19	14	9	62	47	71
Hednesford Town	42	20	10	12	68	40	70
Bedford Town	42	19	12	11	70	52	69
Bath City	42	19	12	11	57	43	69
Cirencester Town	42	19	11	12	63	52	68
Tiverton Town	42	18	13	11	70	55	67
Halesowen Town	42	19	9	14	64	52	66
Aylesbury United	42	20	3	19	67	66	63
King's Lynn	42	19	4	19	78	69	61
Chesham United	42	18	5	19	84	82	59
Grantham Town	42	17	7	18	57	55	58
Team Bath	42	14	12	16	54	68	54
Gloucester City	42	12	17	13	63	61	53
Rugby United	42	13	12	17	48	60	51
Banbury United	42	13	9	20	56	69	48
Hitchin Town	42	13	9	20	55	77	48
Hemel Hempstead Town	42	11	10	21	60	88	43
Dunstable Town	42	11	6	25	56	98	39
Stamford	42	6	18	18	40	60	36
Solihull Borough	42	10	4	28	45	85	34

Eastern Division

Team	P	W	D	L	F	A	Pts
Fisher Athletic	42	30	6	6	96	41	96
East Thurrock United	42	25	12	5	92	38	87
Maldon Town	42	27	6	9	92	51	87
Uxbridge	42	26	7	9	87	37	85
Wivenhoe Town	42	21	11	10	74	49	74
Barking & East Ham United	42	20	10	12	63	37	70
Boreham Wood	42	19	9	14	80	61	66
Barton Rovers	42	20	4	18	76	72	64
Waltham Forest	42	16	9	17	68	61	57
Leighton Town	42	13	15	14	57	59	54
Chatham Town	42	15	9	18	53	63	54
Wingate & Finchley	42	15	8	19	60	75	53
Arlesey Town	42	14	10	18	53	67	52
Beaconsfield SYCOB	42	12	12	18	54	65	48
Harlow Town	42	13	8	21	53	65	47
Dartford	42	11	13	18	58	75	46
Aveley	42	12	9	21	57	69	45
Berkhamsted Town	42	15	7	20	66	101	45
Sittingbourne	42	10	12	20	53	70	42
Great Wakering Rovers	42	9	11	22	45	78	38
Erith & Belvedere	42	11	7	24	56	92	37
Tilbury	42	6	9	27	41	108	27

Berkhamsted Town had 7 points deducted.
Erith & Belvedere had 3 points deducted.

Western Division

Team	P	W	D	L	F	A	Pts
Mangotsfield United	42	24	11	7	89	49	83
Yate Town	42	24	9	9	83	40	81
Evesham United	42	23	10	9	66	31	79
Clevedon Town	42	24	6	12	82	49	78
Bromsgrove Rovers	42	19	15	8	60	42	72
Ashford Town (Middlesex)	42	17	13	12	63	46	64
Brackley Town	42	18	10	14	69	53	64
Paulton Rovers	42	18	7	17	62	61	61
Burnham	42	17	7	18	64	64	58
Rothwell Town	42	16	10	16	57	57	58
Thame United	42	17	6	19	58	69	57
Corby Town	42	14	12	16	52	62	54
Marlow	42	13	14	15	58	67	53
Stourport Swifts	42	15	7	20	62	63	52
Bedworth United	42	15	7	20	51	60	52
Cinderford Town	42	13	12	17	50	64	51
Taunton Town	42	14	8	20	66	75	50
Sutton Coldfield Town	42	16	11	15	54	61	48
Swindon Supermarine	42	12	12	18	43	60	48
Bracknell Town	42	10	13	19	53	75	43
Oxford City	42	11	8	23	49	71	41
Egham Town	42	6	4	32	25	97	22

Sutton Coldfield Town had 11 points deducted.

2005-2006

Premier Division

Team	P	W	D	L	F	A	Pts
Salisbury City	42	30	5	7	83	27	95
Bath City	42	25	8	9	66	33	83
King's Lynn	42	25	7	10	73	41	82
Chippenham Town	42	22	11	9	69	45	77
Bedford Town	42	22	10	10	69	53	76
Yate Town	42	21	5	16	78	74	68
Banbury United	42	17	11	14	66	61	62
Halesowen Town	42	15	15	12	54	45	60
Merthyr Tydfil	42	17	9	16	62	58	60
Mangotsfield United	42	15	13	14	67	67	58
Grantham Town	42	15	11	16	49	49	56
Tiverton Town	42	14	10	18	69	65	52
Gloucester City	42	14	10	18	57	60	52
Hitchin Town	42	13	12	17	59	76	51
Rugby Town	42	13	11	18	58	66	50
Cheshunt	42	13	9	20	57	70	48
Team Bath	42	14	6	22	55	68	48
Cirencester Town	42	14	4	24	49	68	46
Northwood	42	12	6	24	53	88	42
Evesham United	42	9	14	19	46	58	41
Aylesbury United	42	9	12	21	43	69	39
Chesham United	42	9	9	24	43	84	36

Eastern Division

Team	P	W	D	L	F	A	Pts
Boreham Wood	42	24	12	6	84	41	84
Corby Town	42	25	9	8	63	33	84
Enfield Town	42	24	9	9	75	43	81
Stamford	42	20	10	12	73	53	70
Barking & East Ham United	42	20	10	12	63	47	70
Wivenhoe Town	42	17	11	14	56	54	62
Dartford	42	16	13	13	65	57	61
Waltham Forest	42	17	8	17	64	66	59
Harlow Town	42	14	16	12	57	56	58
Arlesey Town	42	15	11	16	58	65	56
Rothwell Town	42	13	14	15	48	53	53
Wingate & Finchley	42	13	14	15	57	64	53
Great Wakering Rovers	42	13	12	17	65	67	51
Uxbridge	42	13	11	18	62	64	50
Potters Bar Town	42	13	11	18	60	66	50
Enfield	42	13	11	18	52	64	50
Chatham Town	42	13	10	19	51	57	49
Sittingbourne	42	12	12	18	53	64	48
Barton Rovers	42	13	8	21	59	73	47
Aveley	42	11	13	18	51	70	46
Ilford	42	8	17	17	35	59	41
Berkhamsted Town	42	8	12	22	51	81	36

Western Division

Team	P	W	D	L	F	A	Pts
Clevedon Town	42	28	6	8	86	45	90
Ashford Town (Middlesex)	42	24	8	10	84	50	80
Brackley Town	42	23	9	10	71	34	78
Hemel Hempstead Town	42	22	9	11	86	47	75
Swindon Supermarine	42	22	9	11	70	47	75
Marlow	42	22	6	14	62	59	72
Sutton Coldfield Town	42	21	6	15	91	62	69
Leighton Town	42	19	8	15	55	48	65
Willenhall Town	42	17	12	13	78	61	63
Rushall Olympic	42	17	11	14	73	57	62
Bromsgrove Rovers	42	17	11	14	65	50	62
Solihull Borough	42	15	13	14	50	51	58
Beaconsfield SYCOB	42	14	13	15	60	66	55
Burnham	42	16	5	21	58	71	53
Cinderford Town	42	14	9	19	71	79	51
Bedworth United	42	14	9	19	46	57	51
Paulton Rovers	42	12	10	20	55	76	46
Taunton Town	42	12	9	21	67	81	45
Bracknell Town	42	12	6	24	53	77	42
Stourport Swifts	42	9	14	19	55	80	41
Dunstable Town	42	8	12	22	45	91	36
Thame United	42	4	5	33	30	122	17

2006-2007   Premier Division

	P	W	D	L	F	A	Pts
Bath City	42	27	10	5	84	29	91
Team Bath	42	23	9	10	66	42	78
King's Lynn	42	22	10	10	69	40	76
Maidenhead United	42	20	10	12	58	36	70
Hemel Hempstead Town	42	19	12	11	79	60	69
Halesowen Town	42	18	13	11	66	53	67
Chippenham Town	42	19	9	14	61	56	66
Stamford	42	16	11	15	65	62	59
Mangotsfield United	42	13	19	10	44	45	58
Gloucester City	42	15	13	14	67	70	58
Hitchin Town	42	16	9	17	55	68	57
Merthyr Tydfil	42	14	14	14	47	46	56
Banbury United	42	15	10	17	60	64	55
Yate Town	42	14	12	16	59	71	54
Tiverton Town	42	14	8	20	56	67	50
Cheshunt	42	14	7	21	56	71	49
Rugby Town	42	15	4	23	58	79	49
Clevedon Town	42	12	12	18	60	61	48
Wealdstone	42	13	9	20	69	82	48
Corby Town	42	10	9	23	52	69	39
Cirencester Town	42	9	12	21	46	76	39
Northwood	42	8	10	24	44	74	34

Division One Midlands

	P	W	D	L	F	A	Pts
Brackley Town	42	29	4	9	95	53	91
Bromsgrove Rovers	42	23	7	12	86	62	76
Chasetown	42	23	6	13	59	39	75
Willenhall Town	42	20	12	10	67	47	72
Evesham United	42	19	15	8	66	51	72
Aylesbury United	42	20	11	11	58	42	71
Stourbridge	42	17	15	10	70	53	66
Woodford United	42	18	11	13	71	54	65
Cinderford Town	42	18	10	14	70	60	64
Rothwell Town	42	18	7	17	72	61	61
Dunstable Town	42	16	12	14	64	53	60
Sutton Coldfield Town	42	16	9	17	62	63	57
Bishop's Cleeve	42	17	5	20	68	66	56
Solihull Borough	42	17	5	20	72	84	56
Rushall Olympic	42	15	9	18	56	55	54
Bedworth United	42	13	8	21	73	83	47
Malvern Town	42	12	11	19	46	66	47
Leighton Town	42	12	8	22	44	60	44
Spalding United	42	12	6	24	45	62	42
Barton Rovers	42	11	9	22	51	93	42
Berkhamsted Town	42	10	7	25	53	97	37
Stourport Swifts	42	9	7	26	43	87	34

Division One South & West

	P	W	D	L	F	A	Pts
Bashley	42	32	6	4	111	35	102
Paulton Rovers	42	20	14	8	66	42	74
Burnham	42	23	4	15	74	60	73
Swindon Supermarine	42	20	11	11	68	40	71
Taunton Town	42	19	14	9	68	50	71
Thatcham Town	42	21	7	14	70	60	70
Marlow	42	19	12	11	74	49	69
Uxbridge	42	20	8	14	68	58	68
Andover	42	19	9	14	70	59	66
Didcot Town	42	16	13	13	86	67	61
Abingdon United	42	16	11	15	68	67	59
Oxford City	42	17	8	17	62	75	59
Winchester City	42	16	10	16	67	65	58
Windsor & Eton	42	16	10	16	76	75	58
Chesham United	42	17	6	19	68	79	57
Hillingdon Borough	42	13	13	16	80	85	52
Lymington & New Milton	42	16	3	23	81	79	51
Brook House	42	14	6	22	71	92	48
Bracknell Town	42	11	13	18	51	62	46
Newport IOW	42	9	3	30	44	106	30
Hanwell Town	42	6	7	29	52	102	24
Beaconsfield SYCOB	42	5	6	31	36	104	21

Hanwell Town had one point deducted.

2007-2008   Premier Division

	P	W	D	L	F	A	Pts
King's Lynn	42	24	13	5	91	36	85
Team Bath	42	25	8	9	71	41	83
Halesowen Town	42	22	13	7	80	46	79
Chippenham Town	42	20	13	9	73	44	73
Bashley	42	19	12	11	60	46	69
Gloucester City	42	19	11	12	81	50	68
Hemel Hempstead Town	42	19	11	12	67	50	68
Brackley Town	42	16	12	14	57	53	60
Banbury United	42	14	16	12	55	57	58
Yate Town	42	16	10	16	71	76	58
Clevedon Town	42	13	18	11	49	46	57
Swindon Supermarine	42	14	12	16	51	67	54
Merthyr Tydfil	42	13	14	15	65	70	53
Mangotsfield United	42	12	16	14	38	42	52
Rugby Town	42	13	12	17	55	66	51
Corby Town	42	14	8	20	60	67	50
Tiverton Town	42	13	11	18	45	60	50
Hitchin Town	42	12	11	19	46	61	47
Bedford Town	42	12	9	21	54	73	45
Bromsgrove Rovers	42	10	12	20	46	67	42
Cirencester Town	42	8	8	26	44	80	32
Cheshunt	42	5	8	29	42	103	23

Division One Midlands

	P	W	D	L	F	A	Pts
Evesham United	40	28	7	5	68	24	91
Leamington	40	27	8	5	74	27	89
Stourbridge	40	25	3	12	97	48	78
Sutton Coldfield Town	40	23	8	9	93	52	77
Rushall Olympic	40	23	7	10	68	23	76
Chesham United	40	23	7	10	78	40	76
Chasetown	40	23	6	11	71	38	75
Aylesbury United	40	19	9	12	64	49	66
Leighton Town	40	17	12	11	59	42	63
Romulus	40	18	8	14	60	53	62
Barton Rovers	40	14	16	10	54	45	58
Bishop's Cleeve	40	17	7	16	63	61	58
Dunstable Town	40	14	5	21	63	65	47
Willenhall Town	40	12	13	15	53	58	46
Bedworth United	40	12	10	18	40	51	46
Cinderford Town	40	12	6	22	47	82	42
Stourport Swifts	40	10	8	22	40	81	38
Rothwell Town	40	9	5	26	34	69	32
Woodford United	40	7	6	27	30	88	27
Malvern Town	40	3	9	28	34	95	18
Berkhamsted Town	40	2	4	34	27	126	10

Willenhall Town had 3 points deducted.

Division One South & West

	P	W	D	L	F	A	Pts
Farnborough	42	27	8	7	120	48	89
Fleet Town	42	26	7	9	78	48	85
Didcot Town	42	24	11	7	99	42	83
Oxford City	42	24	9	9	82	41	81
Uxbridge	42	22	9	11	72	50	75
Bridgwater Town	42	19	13	10	74	45	70
Paulton Rovers	42	20	10	12	77	57	70
Windsor & Eton	42	20	9	13	75	66	69
Marlow	42	20	6	16	74	54	66
Burnham	42	18	9	15	67	55	63
Gosport Borough	42	18	8	16	69	67	62
Godalming Town	42	17	9	16	70	70	60
Hillingdon Borough	42	16	8	18	68	70	56
AFC Hayes	42	17	4	21	75	99	55
Thatcham Town	42	13	10	19	59	62	49
Abingdon United	42	13	9	20	64	75	48
Winchester City	42	13	9	20	58	71	48
Taunton Town	42	12	11	19	66	79	47
Andover	42	11	7	24	62	101	40
Bracknell Town	42	8	10	24	45	93	34
Slough Town	42	9	5	28	44	87	32
Newport IOW	42	2	5	35	25	143	11

2008-2009 Premier Division

Corby Town	42	25	9	8	85	38	84
Farnborough	42	23	14	5	67	36	83
Gloucester City	42	21	12	9	80	45	75
Cambridge City	42	21	10	11	62	40	73
Hemel Hempstead Town	42	21	7	14	71	48	70
Oxford City	42	19	10	13	76	55	67
Merthyr Tydfil	42	19	10	13	66	55	67
Chippenham Town	42	20	8	14	64	51	65
Evesham United	42	16	13	13	48	39	61
Halesowen Town	42	19	6	17	65	73	60
Brackley Town	42	15	12	15	69	62	57
Tiverton Town	42	16	9	17	51	50	57
Swindon Supermarine	42	15	12	15	59	61	57
Bashley	42	15	12	15	52	58	57
Bedford Town	42	14	8	20	44	55	50
Stourbridge	42	13	11	18	62	78	50
Rugby Town	42	11	10	21	63	71	43
Clevedon Town	42	11	10	21	51	80	43
Banbury United	42	11	8	23	43	83	41
Hitchin Town	42	10	10	22	57	79	40
Yate Town	42	9	9	24	54	91	36
Mangotsfield United	42	10	6	26	39	80	36

Chippenham Town and Halesowen town both had 3 points deducted.

Division One Midlands

Leamington	42	32	5	5	114	44	101
Nuneaton Town	42	28	8	6	85	31	92
Atherstone Town	42	24	13	5	82	45	85
Chasetown	42	25	9	8	67	31	84
Chesham United	42	22	10	10	70	38	76
Sutton Coldfield Town	42	24	4	14	79	62	76
Bury Town	42	22	9	11	88	41	75
Leighton Town	42	18	13	11	57	46	67
Marlow	42	19	9	14	65	53	66
Aylesbury United	42	19	7	16	65	58	64
Romulus	42	17	10	15	60	42	61
AFC Sudbury	42	17	10	15	66	65	61
Bromsgrove Rovers	42	15	8	19	58	53	53
Bedworth United	42	14	7	21	50	66	49
Soham Town Rangers	42	13	7	22	48	79	46
Stourport Swifts	42	10	10	22	46	74	40
Barton Rovers	42	12	4	26	50	79	40
Arlesey Town	42	11	5	26	40	70	38
Rothwell Town	42	8	12	22	35	79	36
Woodford United	42	9	7	26	38	80	34
Dunstable Town	42	11	3	28	54	89	23
Malvern Town	42	2	10	30	27	119	16

Dunstable Town had 13 points deducted.

Division One South & West

Truro City	42	29	8	5	120	49	95
Windsor & Eton	42	26	7	9	77	44	85
AFC Totton	42	23	13	6	89	39	82
Beaconsfield SYCOB	42	24	9	9	77	44	81
Didcot Town	42	21	10	11	91	52	73
Thatcham Town	42	20	8	14	74	58	68
Bridgwater Town	42	19	8	15	69	56	65
North Leigh	42	17	10	15	68	64	61
AFC Hayes	42	18	7	17	80	92	61
Paulton Rovers	42	16	10	16	65	62	58
Cinderford Town	42	15	11	16	71	75	56
Gosport Borough	42	15	10	17	64	67	55
Uxbridge	42	15	9	18	76	72	54
Cirencester Town	42	14	10	18	78	79	52
Abingdon United	42	15	7	20	63	77	52
Slough Town	42	11	12	19	62	91	45
Burnham	42	12	9	21	52	83	45
Bishop's Cleeve	42	10	13	19	51	71	43
Andover	42	10	12	20	58	102	42
Taunton Town	42	9	9	24	50	85	36
Bracknell Town	42	9	8	25	39	75	35
Winchester City	42	10	8	24	47	84	35

Winchester City had 3 points deducted.

2009-2010 Premier Division

Farnborough	42	28	9	5	100	44	93
Nuneaton Town	42	26	10	6	91	37	88
Chippenham Town	42	21	11	10	67	43	74
Hednesford Town	42	20	13	9	79	51	73
Brackley Town	42	21	9	12	83	61	72
Cambridge City	42	18	17	7	73	44	71
Bashley	42	20	11	11	79	61	71
Halesowen Town	42	21	17	4	84	53	70
Stourbridge	42	19	13	10	80	65	70
Leamington	42	19	8	15	84	75	65
Truro City	42	17	11	14	78	65	62
Banbury United	42	14	13	15	53	67	55
Oxford City	42	13	15	14	63	66	54
Swindon Supermarine	42	10	14	18	48	76	44
Didcot Town	42	10	11	21	56	70	41
Evesham United	42	9	14	19	35	52	41
Merthyr Tydfil	42	12	11	19	62	72	37
Bedford Town	42	9	10	23	50	88	37
Tiverton Town	42	8	12	22	35	61	36
Hemel Hempstead Town	42	8	10	24	50	81	34
Clevedon Town	42	6	11	25	48	92	29
Rugby Town	42	4	8	30	41	114	20

Halesowen Town and Merthyr Tydfil both had 10 points deducted.

Division One Midlands

Bury Town	42	32	6	4	115	40	102
Hitchin Town	42	31	7	4	91	36	100
Burnham	42	26	9	7	67	43	87
Chesham United	42	24	8	10	76	41	80
Slough Town	42	23	8	11	87	54	77
Sutton Coldfield Town	42	22	11	9	93	61	77
Woodford United	42	18	8	16	70	68	62
Romulus	42	16	13	13	66	48	61
Arlesey Town	42	17	10	15	58	48	61
Leighton Town	42	18	6	18	63	66	60
Soham Town Rangers	42	17	7	18	73	80	58
Biggleswade Town	42	14	13	15	56	63	55
Atherstone Town	42	15	9	18	65	82	54
AFC Sudbury	42	13	12	17	55	54	51
Marlow	42	12	14	16	64	65	50
Bedworth United	42	12	11	19	59	72	47
Stourport Swifts	42	11	10	21	63	69	43
Rothwell Town	42	11	8	23	53	80	41
Beaconsfield SYCOB	42	8	8	26	46	96	32
Bromsgrove Rovers	42	8	15	19	45	68	29
Barton Rovers	42	6	9	27	49	95	27
Aylesbury United	42	4	6	32	48	133	18

Bromsgrove Rovers had 10 points deducted.
Rothwell Town resigned from the League at the end of the season.

Division One South & West

Windsor & Eton	42	31	8	3	84	20	101
AFC Totton	42	32	4	6	105	36	100
Bridgwater Town	42	26	11	5	83	30	89
VT	42	25	7	10	90	52	82
Cirencester Town	42	23	9	10	91	46	78
Frome Town	42	20	15	7	68	44	75
Paulton Rovers	42	20	10	12	73	58	70
Gosport Borough	42	19	10	13	80	59	66
Mangotsfield United	42	19	5	18	77	66	62
North Leigh	42	18	7	17	83	72	61
Bishop's Cleeve	42	15	13	14	64	64	58
Thatcham Town	42	17	6	19	76	72	57
Yate Town	42	15	10	17	58	64	55
Abingdon United	42	15	7	20	65	84	52
Uxbridge	42	14	6	22	70	85	48
Cinderford Town	42	13	8	21	66	78	47
Hungerford Town	42	13	6	23	53	68	45
Bedfont Green	42	12	8	22	77	90	44
Taunton Town	42	11	7	24	50	85	40
Andover	42	9	11	22	54	85	38
AFC Hayes	42	7	4	31	55	105	25
Bracknell Town	42	2	0	40	29	187	6

Gosport Borough had 1 point deducted.

2010-2011

Premier Division

Truro City	40	27	6	7	91	35	87
Hednesford Town	40	26	5	9	82	38	83
Salisbury City	40	23	10	7	82	45	79
Cambridge City	40	24	7	9	74	40	79
Leamington	40	24	6	10	68	39	78
Chesham United	40	20	11	9	64	35	71
Chippenham Town	40	18	14	8	54	41	68
Stourbridge	40	18	8	14	72	61	62
Brackley Town	40	16	10	14	67	47	58
Swindon Supermarine	40	17	7	16	56	58	58
Bashley	40	14	10	16	55	63	52
Evesham United	40	14	9	17	54	49	51
Cirencester Town	40	13	8	19	59	67	47
Oxford City	40	11	12	17	48	54	45
Hemel Hempstead Town	40	13	6	21	50	59	45
Banbury United	40	11	8	21	44	67	40
Bedford Town	40	10	7	23	41	76	37
Weymouth	40	12	8	20	55	85	34
Didcot Town	40	7	11	22	39	69	32
Tiverton Town	40	7	8	25	33	77	29
Halesowen Town	40	5	9	26	24	107	24

Weymouth had 10 points deducted.
Banbury United had 1 point deducted.
Windsor & Eton was wound up in the High Court on 2nd February 2011,
due to unpaid taxes. Their record was expunged on 8th February 2011
when it stood as: 26   8   12   6   33   35   36

Division One South & West

AFC Totton	40	31	4	5	121	35	97
Sholing	40	30	5	5	90	27	95
Mangotsfield United	40	26	7	7	79	48	85
Frome Town	40	24	7	9	77	31	79
Thatcham Town	40	20	7	13	70	43	67
North Leigh	40	19	8	13	81	81	65
Hungerford Town	40	17	12	11	58	43	63
Almondsbury Town	40	17	12	11	62	54	63
Taunton Town	40	16	10	14	49	49	58
Bideford	40	17	7	16	68	73	58
Paulton Rovers	40	15	12	13	64	63	57
Cinderford Town	40	16	8	16	63	61	56
Gosport Borough	40	16	7	17	58	65	55
Yate Town	40	12	8	20	43	48	44
Bishop's Cleeve	40	10	12	18	47	59	42
Abingdon United	40	11	7	22	56	85	40
Stourport Swifts	40	10	10	20	52	81	40
Bridgwater Town	40	9	11	20	47	86	38
Wimborne Town	40	10	5	25	45	81	35
Clevedon Town	40	6	8	26	46	86	26
Andover	40	2	5	33	32	109	11

Almondsbury Town resigned from the League at the end of the season.

Division One Central

Arlesey Town	42	30	7	5	108	34	88
Hitchin Town	42	26	9	7	107	44	87
Daventry Town	42	26	9	7	95	47	81
Biggleswade Town	42	24	9	9	89	51	81
Slough Town	42	24	4	14	91	66	76
Rugby Town	42	20	11	11	74	56	71
Leighton Town	42	19	12	11	72	50	69
Aylesbury	42	19	11	12	73	62	68
Woodford United	42	18	9	15	61	59	63
Bedfont Town	42	17	12	13	66	66	63
Marlow	42	15	9	18	68	65	54
Barton Rovers	42	14	9	19	59	64	51
Uxbridge	42	14	8	20	76	87	50
Burnham	42	14	7	21	61	87	49
Bedworth United	42	12	12	18	49	62	48
Ashford Town	42	13	8	21	69	85	47
Soham Town Rangers	42	10	10	22	55	81	40
North Greenford United	42	10	10	22	51	86	40
AFC Hayes	42	11	6	25	54	96	39
Northwood	42	11	6	25	59	106	39
Atherstone Town	42	10	6	26	61	118	36
Beaconsfield SYCOB	42	7	12	23	49	75	33

Arlesey Town had 9 points deducted.
Daventry Town had 6 points deducted.
Atherstone Town resigned from the League at the end of the season.

2011-2012

Premier Division

Brackley Town	42	25	10	7	92	48	85
Oxford City	42	22	11	9	68	41	77
AFC Totton	42	21	11	10	81	43	74
Chesham United	42	21	10	11	76	53	73
Cambridge City	42	21	9	12	78	52	72
Stourbridge	42	20	12	10	67	45	72
Leamington	42	18	15	9	60	47	69
St Albans City	42	17	11	14	72	77	62
Barwell	42	17	10	15	70	61	61
Bedford Town	42	15	10	17	60	69	55
Chippenham Town	42	14	11	17	55	53	53
Frome Town	42	12	16	14	44	49	52
Bashley	42	13	13	16	58	74	52
Hitchin Town	42	13	12	17	54	57	51
Redditch United	42	14	9	19	45	50	51
Banbury United	42	13	10	19	54	61	49
Weymouth	42	13	9	20	54	75	48
Arlesey Town	42	12	11	19	48	60	47
Hemel Hempstead Town	42	10	14	18	46	66	44
Evesham United	42	12	8	22	49	71	44
Swindon Supermarine	42	11	11	20	50	86	44
Cirencester Town	42	7	9	26	40	78	30

2012-2013

Division One Central

St Neots Town	42	29	6	7	115	36	93
Slough Town	42	26	9	7	74	42	87
Bedworth United	42	23	9	10	90	57	78
Uxbridge	42	22	8	12	79	59	74
Beaconsfield SYCOB	42	20	9	13	65	55	69
Rugby Town	42	19	10	13	67	65	67
Northwood	42	19	9	14	74	62	66
Biggleswade Town	42	19	7	16	75	54	64
Ashford Town	42	16	11	15	62	61	59
AFC Hayes	42	14	16	12	58	59	58
Barton Rovers	42	16	8	18	64	63	56
Chalfont St Peter	42	14	14	14	65	68	56
Leighton Town	42	15	10	17	60	67	55
Bedfont Town	42	15	9	18	53	64	54
Burnham	42	13	13	16	64	67	52
Daventry Town	42	15	5	22	52	72	50
Chertsey Town	42	15	5	22	65	93	50
North Greenford United	42	13	10	19	56	72	49
Woodford United	42	12	8	22	56	70	44
Aylesbury	42	12	8	22	50	82	44
Fleet Town	42	8	8	26	43	83	32
Marlow	42	6	10	26	50	86	28

Bedfont Town resigned from the League at the end of the season.

Premier Division

Leamington	42	30	5	7	85	46	95
Stourbridge	42	25	8	9	94	42	83
Chesham United	42	21	12	9	69	48	75
Hemel Hempstead Town	42	22	6	14	95	71	72
Gosport Borough	42	19	13	10	78	43	70
Arlesey Town	42	21	6	15	70	51	69
Barwell	42	19	12	11	67	50	69
Cambridge City	42	20	6	16	63	57	66
Weymouth	42	18	8	16	59	71	62
Bedford Town	42	18	7	17	61	56	61
St Albans City	42	18	6	18	81	71	60
St Neots Town	42	15	7	20	77	77	52
Hitchin Town	42	15	7	20	62	68	52
AFC Totton	42	15	7	20	62	84	52
Chippenham Town	42	13	12	17	63	67	51
Banbury United	42	14	9	19	60	75	51
Bashley	42	13	10	19	47	63	49
Frome Town	42	11	12	19	40	55	45
Redditch United	42	12	7	23	32	65	43
Bideford	42	11	9	22	58	73	42
Bedworth United	42	11	9	22	39	73	42
Kettering Town	42	8	8	26	47	102	22

Kettering Town had 10 points deducted for financial irregularities.

Division One South & West

Bideford	40	28	8	4	77	41	92
Poole Town	40	25	6	9	78	39	81
Gosport Borough	40	22	14	4	73	44	80
Sholing	40	22	8	10	71	43	74
Hungerford Town	40	21	8	11	65	44	71
North Leigh	40	21	5	14	90	63	68
Paulton Rovers	40	18	10	12	60	39	64
Thatcham Town	40	16	14	10	51	42	62
Tiverton Town	40	16	11	13	52	42	59
Cinderford Town	40	17	8	15	49	39	59
Bishop's Cleeve	40	16	11	13	40	42	59
Halesowen Town	40	15	6	19	55	56	51
Yate Town	40	13	11	16	58	59	50
Mangotsfield United	40	14	7	19	62	66	49
Bridgwater Town	40	13	4	23	47	77	43
Didcot Town	40	11	9	20	39	68	42
Taunton Town	40	10	10	20	47	76	40
Abingdon United	40	9	10	21	35	69	37
Wimborne Town	40	8	11	21	50	77	35
Clevedon Town	40	9	6	25	51	75	33
Stourport Swifts	40	5	5	30	39	88	20

Andover resigned from the League and were wound up during July 2011.
Thatcham Town transferred to the Southern League Central Division at the end of the season.
Halesowen Town transferred to the Northern Premier League Division One South at the end of the season.

Division One Central

Burnham	42	31	6	5	108	39	99
Rugby Town	42	31	3	8	103	45	96
Godalming Town	42	28	8	6	94	39	92
Biggleswade Town	42	26	7	9	97	50	85
Beaconsfield SYCOB	42	26	6	10	81	47	84
Slough Town	42	26	5	11	103	50	83
Royston Town	42	24	10	8	86	49	82
Daventry Town	42	22	10	10	81	47	76
Guildford City	42	20	6	16	86	75	66
Ashford Town	42	17	10	15	85	79	61
Uxbridge	42	19	4	19	78	85	61
Aylesbury	42	16	10	16	76	73	58
Northwood	42	17	6	19	80	73	57
Barton Rovers	42	16	5	21	62	78	53
AFC Hayes	42	13	8	21	73	81	47
Chalfont St. Peter	42	18	7	17	76	74	46
Thatcham Town	42	10	5	27	59	86	35
Fleet Town	42	10	5	27	47	76	35
North Greenford United	42	9	6	27	56	95	33
Chertsey Town	42	9	4	29	50	98	31
Leighton Town	42	6	5	31	43	121	23
Woodford United	42	0	0	42	21	185	0

Chalfont St. Peter had 15 points deducted for fielding an ineligible player.

Division One South & West

Poole Town	42	30	8	4	82	36	98
Hungerford Town	42	26	6	10	71	44	84
Merthyr Town	42	24	11	7	84	38	83
Swindon Supermarine	42	25	6	11	79	51	81
Paulton Rovers	42	23	6	13	64	54	75
Yate Town	42	21	6	15	69	63	69
Sholing	42	20	8	14	87	56	68
Shortwood United	42	20	7	15	62	45	67
North Leigh	42	19	4	19	70	69	61
Cinderford Town	42	17	8	17	61	66	59
Cirencester Town	42	15	13	14	54	57	57
Wimborne Town	42	15	10	17	59	60	55
Mangotsfield United	42	15	10	17	53	61	55
Evesham United	42	14	9	19	49	58	51
Clevedon Town	42	12	13	17	61	67	49
Tiverton Town	42	11	14	17	51	58	47
Didcot Town	42	12	10	20	59	76	46
Taunton Town	42	12	8	22	59	85	44
Bridgwater Town	42	10	10	22	52	78	40
Abingdon United	42	10	8	24	42	66	38
Bishop's Cleeve	42	10	7	25	49	66	37
Winchester City	42	9	2	31	42	105	26

Winchester City had 3 points deducted for fielding an ineligible player.
Cirencester Town had 1 point deducted for fielding an ineligible player.
Sholing resigned from the League at the end of the season.

Division One Central

Dunstable Town	42	28	6	8	94	44	90
Rugby Town	42	27	8	7	100	45	89
Kettering Town	42	27	7	8	86	41	88
Daventry Town	42	27	5	10	82	40	86
Slough Town	42	26	5	11	101	51	83
Barton Rovers	42	24	8	10	79	48	80
Royston Town	42	21	10	11	80	58	73
Beaconsfield SYCOB	42	22	7	13	79	60	73
Northwood	42	21	6	15	72	62	69
Uxbridge	42	18	7	17	84	70	61
Egham Town	42	17	9	16	80	58	60
Aylesbury United	42	16	9	17	64	72	57
St. Ives Town	42	16	8	18	68	77	56
Chalfont St. Peter	42	14	8	20	49	60	50
Potters Bar Town	42	13	10	19	61	86	49
Aylesbury	42	14	6	22	56	73	48
Marlow	42	12	11	19	73	84	47
AFC Hayes	42	12	8	22	51	74	44
Leighton Town	42	6	13	23	45	85	31
North Greenford United	42	7	5	30	52	114	26
Chertsey Town	42	6	4	32	38	117	22
Ashford Town	42	5	6	31	32	107	21

2013-2014

Premier Division

Hemel Hempstead Town	44	32	6	6	128	38	102
Chesham United	44	29	5	10	102	47	92
Cambridge City	44	27	7	10	95	49	88
St. Albans City	44	25	10	9	89	49	85
Stourbridge	44	26	6	12	114	54	84
Hungerford Town	44	26	6	12	83	45	84
Poole Town	44	25	10	9	82	48	82
Bideford	44	18	13	13	75	64	67
Biggleswade Town	44	16	16	12	85	61	64
Redditch United	44	20	3	21	68	85	63
Corby Town	44	18	6	20	65	68	60
Weymouth	44	18	6	20	69	80	60
Hitchin Town	44	16	11	17	63	52	59
Frome Town	44	16	9	19	63	74	57
Arlesey Town	44	15	10	19	68	79	55
St Neots Town	44	15	9	20	74	76	54
Truro City	44	15	9	20	68	84	54
Chippenham Town	44	14	6	24	59	87	48
Banbury United	44	14	5	25	64	116	47
Burnham	44	12	8	24	60	91	44
AFC Totton	44	10	7	27	58	119	37
Bedford Town	44	6	6	32	46	114	24
Bashley	44	4	4	36	33	131	16

Poole Town had 3 points deducted for fielding an ineligible player.
Hinckley United folded on 7th October 2013 and their record was officially
expunged from the league table on 21st October 2013 when it stood as:

10	1	3	6	9	20	6

Division One South & West

Cirencester Town	42	29	5	8	95	45	92
Merthyr Town	42	28	5	9	111	58	89
Tiverton Town	42	26	8	8	80	51	86
Paulton Rovers	42	24	9	9	102	54	81
Swindon Supermarine	42	24	7	11	91	52	79
Shortwood United	42	23	9	10	91	44	78
North Leigh	42	22	6	14	83	46	72
Taunton Town	42	21	7	14	71	58	69
Yate Town	42	20	8	14	81	69	68
Stratford Town	42	19	5	18	103	85	62
Mangotsfield United	42	18	7	17	65	62	61
Didcot Town	42	17	6	19	70	85	57
Wimborne Town	42	16	7	19	78	70	55
Bridgwater Town	42	14	11	17	62	64	53
Cinderford Town	42	13	10	19	69	79	49
Evesham United	42	12	11	19	66	80	47
Clevedon Town	42	12	5	25	48	96	41
Godalming Town	42	10	9	23	47	79	39
Thatcham Town	42	11	6	25	41	99	39
Bishop's Cleeve	42	11	1	30	52	93	34
Fleet Town	42	7	8	27	43	90	29
Guildford City	42	7	6	29	45	134	27

Taunton Town had 1 point deducted for fielding an ineligible player.
Thatcham Town resigned from the League at the end of the season.

2014-2015

Premier Division

Corby Town	44	29	7	8	86	47	94
Poole Town	44	28	7	9	84	35	91
Truro City	44	27	5	12	83	58	86
Hungerford Town	44	22	13	9	64	36	79
St. Neots Town	44	20	16	8	82	58	76
Redditch United	44	21	12	11	73	44	75
Weymouth	44	22	7	15	71	71	73
Cirencester Town	44	20	12	12	77	54	72
Hitchin Town	44	20	10	14	78	63	70
Paulton Rovers	44	18	10	16	65	62	64
Chippenham Town	44	16	13	15	54	54	61
Chesham United	44	16	12	16	79	72	60
Cambridge City	44	14	15	15	71	62	57
Dunstable Town	44	16	9	19	71	78	57
Bideford	44	16	7	21	66	85	55
Slough Town	44	13	12	19	66	88	51
Dorchester Town	44	14	8	22	63	74	50
Histon	44	13	10	21	53	74	49
Biggleswade Town	44	11	12	21	57	75	45
Frome Town	44	10	11	23	49	80	41
Banbury United	44	9	10	25	53	86	37
Arlesey Town	44	10	6	28	43	84	36
Burnham	44	5	8	31	41	89	20

Burnham had 3 points deducted for fielding an ineligible player.
Hereford United FC was liquidated on 19th December 2014 and the club's record was expunged on 5th January 2015 when it stood as:

	25	8	6	11	35	42	30

Division One South & West

Merthyr Town	42	32	6	4	122	34	102
Evesham United	42	27	10	5	94	36	91
Stratford Town	42	28	5	9	82	40	89
Taunton Town	42	24	8	10	71	42	80
Larkhall Athletic	42	23	8	11	82	50	77
Yate Town	42	21	9	12	79	52	72
Didcot Town	42	20	11	11	95	66	71
North Leigh	42	18	13	11	99	58	67
Cinderford Town	42	19	10	13	79	48	67
Mangotsfield United	42	20	7	15	73	58	67
Shortwood United	42	17	14	11	77	55	65
Bridgwater Town	42	17	11	14	67	59	62
Wimborne Town	42	18	7	17	71	68	61
Swindon Supermarine	42	17	5	20	81	79	56
AFC Totton	42	16	5	21	65	75	53
Tiverton Town	42	13	10	19	60	69	49
Sholing	42	11	10	21	48	75	43
Clevedon Town	42	10	6	26	54	111	36
Fleet Town	42	8	8	26	49	97	32
Wantage Town	42	8	4	30	43	100	28
Bishop's Cleeve	42	6	4	32	52	143	22
Bashley	42	1	5	36	20	148	8

Division One Central

Kettering Town	42	30	5	7	90	36	95
Royston Town	42	27	3	12	74	50	84
Aylesbury	42	25	7	10	81	46	82
Bedworth United	42	25	4	13	85	55	79
Barton Rovers	42	23	9	10	83	53	78
Rugby Town	42	22	7	13	78	51	73
Hanwell Town	42	21	5	16	71	60	68
Godalming Town	42	18	10	14	67	62	64
St Ives Town	42	16	12	14	70	77	60
Northwood	42	15	12	15	60	61	57
Marlow	42	15	12	15	58	59	57
Uxbridge	42	15	10	17	71	69	55
Aylesbury United	42	15	8	19	66	80	53
Potters Bar Town	42	16	2	24	68	77	50
Egham Town	42	14	8	20	64	81	50
Chalfont St Peter	42	11	15	16	60	66	48
Bedford Town	42	13	8	21	62	72	47
Leighton Town	42	10	13	19	52	71	43
Daventry Town	42	12	6	24	47	77	42
Beaconsfield SYCOB	42	8	16	18	62	75	40
North Greenford United	42	8	11	23	55	97	35
AFC Hayes	42	8	7	27	39	88	31

2015-2016

Premier Division

Poole Town	46	27	12	7	86	35	93
Redditch United	46	24	15	7	82	37	84
Hitchin Town	46	24	12	10	78	50	84
Hungerford Town	46	24	11	11	73	43	83
Leamington	46	23	12	11	59	38	81
Kettering Town	46	24	8	14	83	53	80
Weymouth	46	21	14	11	63	39	77
Chippenham Town	46	21	13	12	76	53	76
King's Lynn Town	46	21	7	18	58	54	70
Merthyr Town	46	19	9	18	69	58	66
Chesham United	46	18	10	18	72	70	64
Dunstable Town	46	17	11	18	68	68	62
Dorchester Town	46	18	8	20	67	69	62
Biggleswade Town	46	17	9	20	76	82	60
Cirencester Town	46	18	6	22	67	76	60
Frome Town	46	14	16	16	51	73	58
Slough Town	46	16	9	21	67	77	57
Cambridge City	46	15	7	24	63	80	52
Stratford Town	46	13	11	22	59	68	50
St Neots Town	46	10	18	18	69	78	48
Bedworth United	46	12	8	26	58	107	44
Histon	46	11	7	28	63	98	40
Bideford	46	8	13	25	38	88	37
Paulton Rovers	46	8	12	26	38	89	36

Redditch United had 3 points deducted for fielding ineligible players

2016-2017

Division One Central

	P	W	D	L	F	A	Pts
Kings Langley	42	27	6	9	83	44	87
Royston Town	42	25	8	9	99	46	83
Egham Town	42	26	5	11	80	39	83
St Ives Town	42	22	12	8	72	38	78
AFC Rushden & Diamonds	42	23	8	11	81	44	77
Chalfont St Peter	42	23	2	17	76	71	71
Northwood	42	20	9	13	62	49	69
Aylesbury	42	20	8	14	72	52	68
Beaconsfield SYCOB	42	19	10	13	77	54	67
Godalming Town	42	19	10	13	51	45	67
Ware	42	19	6	17	67	69	63
Potters Bar Town	42	16	10	16	62	64	58
Petersfield Town	42	16	7	19	71	80	55
Bedford Town	42	12	13	17	57	60	49
Uxbridge	42	13	9	20	59	71	48
Arlesey Town	42	14	5	23	48	87	47
Fleet Town	42	12	9	21	55	78	45
Barton Rovers	42	9	15	18	51	75	42
Aylesbury United	42	11	7	24	45	81	40
Hanwell Town	42	10	9	23	38	64	39
Leighton Town	42	9	8	25	47	86	35
North Greenford United	42	6	6	30	51	107	24

Premier Division

	P	W	D	L	F	A	Pts
Chippenham Town	46	31	10	5	94	47	103
Leamington	46	27	11	8	74	32	92
Merthyr Town	46	25	14	7	92	42	89
Hitchin Town	46	24	14	8	79	45	86
Slough Town	46	26	7	13	84	56	85
Banbury United	46	24	8	14	67	40	80
Biggleswade Town	46	21	11	14	85	59	74
Frome Town	46	20	14	12	80	67	74
Kettering Town	46	21	10	15	84	66	73
Weymouth	46	16	18	12	79	58	66
Chesham United	46	18	10	18	67	62	64
Basingstoke Town	46	18	8	20	65	72	62
King's Lynn Town	46	14	18	14	60	69	60
Stratford Town	46	13	17	16	64	66	56
St. Ives Town	46	15	11	20	49	70	56
Dunstable Town	46	16	6	24	46	65	54
Redditch United	46	13	11	22	54	75	50
Dorchester Town	46	12	12	22	52	80	48
St. Neots Town	46	14	6	26	66	101	48
Kings Langley	46	11	14	21	57	72	47
Cambridge City	46	12	11	23	46	72	47
Cirencester Town	46	11	9	26	54	92	42
Hayes & Yeading United	46	10	11	25	48	81	41
Cinderford Town	46	8	3	35	49	106	27

Division One South & West

	P	W	D	L	F	A	Pts
Cinderford Town	42	29	9	4	80	29	96
Banbury United	42	28	10	4	97	38	94
Taunton Town	42	27	8	7	94	34	89
Swindon Supermarine	42	27	6	9	81	42	87
Winchester City	42	24	11	7	97	49	83
Evesham United	42	24	9	9	92	38	81
Shortwood United	42	24	6	12	88	59	78
Tiverton Town	42	20	13	9	76	44	73
North Leigh	42	21	5	16	79	53	68
Didcot Town	42	18	10	14	82	57	64
Larkhall Athletic	42	15	10	17	62	65	55
Bishop's Cleeve	42	14	13	15	55	66	55
Marlow	42	15	7	20	68	79	52
Mangotsfield United	42	12	12	18	59	65	48
AFC Totton	42	14	6	22	73	81	48
Yate Town	42	12	11	19	48	62	47
Wimborne Town	42	12	8	22	65	80	44
Slimbridge	42	10	12	20	46	57	42
Bridgwater Town	42	9	7	26	42	83	34
Wantage Town	42	8	5	29	45	100	29
Burnham	42	6	6	30	39	99	24
Bashley	42	0	2	40	13	201	2

Division One Central

	P	W	D	L	F	A	Pts
Royston Town	42	32	6	4	121	48	102
Farnborough	42	28	6	8	96	51	90
Barton Rovers	42	23	8	11	91	66	77
Marlow	42	23	8	11	65	43	77
Egham Town	42	20	14	8	79	51	74
AFC Kempston Rovers	42	21	10	11	82	61	73
AFC Dunstable	42	21	8	13	85	53	71
Bedford Town	42	18	13	11	76	58	67
Potters Bar Town	42	16	14	12	71	61	62
Ashford Town	42	17	8	17	73	71	59
Kidlington	42	18	5	19	70	79	59
Hanwell Town	42	16	10	16	64	67	57
Aylesbury United	42	16	7	19	58	68	55
Fleet Town	42	13	11	18	72	81	50
Arlesey Town	42	14	8	20	55	69	50
Beaconsfield SYCOB	42	13	9	20	81	85	48
Uxbridge	42	13	8	21	67	80	47
Chalfont St. Peter	42	14	5	23	49	77	47
Aylesbury	42	12	8	22	54	75	44
Northwood	42	9	12	21	57	88	39
Histon	42	9	7	26	54	93	34
Petersfield Town	42	2	3	37	32	127	9

At the end of the season, the Southern Football League Division One Central was renamed the East Division.

Division One South & West

Hereford	42	33	8	1	108	32	107
Salisbury	42	29	2	11	118	52	89
Tiverton Town	42	27	7	8	92	50	88
Taunton Town	42	27	7	8	114	42	85
Evesham United	42	24	8	10	88	50	80
North Leigh	42	22	9	11	84	65	75
Swindon Supermarine	42	21	9	12	85	57	72
Mangotsfield United	42	21	7	14	73	69	70
Shortwood United	42	19	5	18	65	77	62
Bideford	42	15	12	15	61	58	57
Wimborne Town	42	17	6	19	67	68	57
Didcot Town	42	14	12	16	70	71	54
Larkhall Athletic	42	13	14	15	69	69	53
Winchester City	42	16	5	21	62	70	53
Paulton Rovers	42	15	6	21	62	69	51
Bishop's Cleeve	42	14	8	20	66	86	50
Barnstaple Town	42	13	6	23	52	68	45
Yate Town	42	12	8	22	49	77	44
AFC Totton	42	10	9	23	49	86	39
Slimbridge	42	10	7	25	47	90	37
Wantage Town	42	4	9	29	29	110	21
Bridgwater Town	42	2	4	36	23	117	10

Taunton Town had 3 points deducted for fielding an ineligible player.

At the end of the season, the Southern Football League Division One South & West was renamed the West Division.

2017-2018

Premier Division

Hereford	46	36	5	5	111	33	113
King's Lynn Town	46	30	10	6	99	39	100
Slough Town	46	30	9	7	111	49	99
Kettering Town	46	30	7	9	122	56	97
Weymouth	46	30	7	9	103	48	97
Tiverton Town	46	24	6	16	78	69	78
Royston Town	46	24	5	17	84	65	77
Chesham United	46	21	11	14	85	61	74
Banbury United	46	19	15	12	90	59	72
Basingstoke Town	46	21	8	17	92	72	71
Hitchin Town	46	19	9	18	67	66	66
St. Neots Town	46	17	13	16	79	79	64
Frome Town	46	18	7	21	78	96	61
Redditch United	46	15	10	21	73	73	55
Stratford Town	46	15	10	21	68	81	55
Biggleswade Town	46	14	11	21	52	63	53
Merthyr Town	46	13	14	19	76	98	53
Bishop's Stortford	46	14	10	22	74	79	52
Dorchester Town	46	13	12	21	62	83	51
Farnborough	46	15	6	25	82	120	51
Kings Langley	46	8	14	24	63	98	38
St. Ives Town	46	8	9	29	54	105	33
Gosport Borough	46	5	5	36	41	142	20
Dunstable Town	46	4	5	37	27	137	17

East Division

Beaconsfield Town	42	29	5	8	99	46	92
AFC Rushden & Diamonds	42	27	10	5	92	25	91
Hayes & Yeading United	42	26	5	11	103	49	83
Hartley Wintney	42	26	4	12	96	53	82
AFC Dunstable	42	23	10	9	80	37	79
Cambridge City	42	23	8	11	99	53	77
Kempston Rovers	42	21	10	11	80	68	73
Bedford Town	42	22	6	14	70	48	72
Chalfont St. Peter	42	20	12	10	56	39	72
Moneyfields	42	19	12	11	79	63	69
Thame United	42	20	4	18	84	78	64
Ashford Town	42	16	8	18	81	68	56
Aylesbury United	42	17	4	21	52	73	55
Marlow	42	13	10	19	54	75	49
Uxbridge	42	14	7	21	58	87	49
Egham Town	42	13	9	20	54	88	48
Northwood	42	10	11	21	54	71	41
Hanwell Town	42	9	7	26	48	88	34
Fleet Town	42	8	10	24	38	86	34
Barton Rovers	42	8	9	25	39	86	33
Aylesbury	42	9	6	27	40	88	33
Arlesey Town	42	3	5	34	36	123	14

West Division

Taunton Town	42	31	10	1	107	41	103
Salisbury	42	25	9	8	108	55	84
Wimborne Town	42	23	8	11	104	57	77
Evesham United	42	23	7	12	73	53	76
Swindon Supermarine	42	21	11	10	86	54	74
Didcot Town	42	21	10	11	89	63	73
Cirencester Town	42	22	7	13	93	74	73
Bideford	42	21	9	12	79	58	72
Bristol Manor Farm	42	20	9	13	83	61	69
AFC Totton	42	19	9	14	65	49	66
Winchester City	42	17	10	15	73	66	61
Kidlington	42	15	12	15	80	64	57
Cinderford Town	42	14	12	16	81	71	54
Yate Town	42	14	14	14	72	74	53
Larkhall Athletic	42	13	6	23	66	78	45
Mangotsfield United	42	10	11	21	53	86	41
Shortwood United	42	10	10	22	63	124	40
North Leigh	42	10	8	24	53	84	38
Paulton Rovers	42	10	7	25	57	81	37
Slimbridge	42	9	8	25	54	130	35
Barnstaple Town	42	7	8	27	53	105	29
Bishop's Cleeve	42	8	3	31	43	107	27

Yate Town had 3 points deducted for fielding ineligible players.
Shortwood United resigned from the league at the end of the season

At the end of the season, a new Division at Step 3 of the Non-League Pyramid was created under the control of the Southern Football League.

The Premier Division was split into two divisions, named the Central Division and the South Division with clubs transferring across from the Northern Premier League and Isthmian League to fill up thes new places.

The Southern Football League East and West Divisions remained at Step 4 though a number of the clubs from the East Division transferred to the Isthmian League following the creation of a new Step 4 division under their control.

2018-2019

Premier Division Central

Kettering Town	42	30	4	8	84	41	94
King's Lynn Town	42	23	11	8	80	41	80
Stourbridge	42	22	12	8	79	40	78
Alvechurch	42	21	10	11	66	53	73
Stratford Town	42	21	9	12	55	49	72
Coalville Town	42	20	7	15	78	66	67
Biggleswade Town	42	18	12	12	67	54	66
Rushall Olympic	42	17	11	14	56	49	62
AFC Rushden & Diamonds	42	15	16	11	60	49	61
Royston Town	42	18	7	17	59	53	60
Needham Market	42	17	9	16	68	65	60
Tamworth	42	15	13	14	64	46	58
St. Ives Town	42	14	13	15	36	43	55
Lowestoft Town	42	14	9	19	55	60	51
Redditch United	42	14	8	20	63	79	50
Barwell	42	12	13	17	55	55	49
Banbury United	42	13	14	15	53	55	49
Hitchin Town	42	14	6	22	50	71	48
Leiston	42	12	11	19	54	73	47
St. Neots Town	42	9	9	24	32	73	36
Halesowen Town	42	6	14	22	26	66	32
Bedworth United	42	3	10	29	32	91	19

Royston United had one point deducted for fielding an ineligible player. Banbury United had 4 points deducted for an infringement of the league's rules.

Premier Division South

Weymouth	42	25	11	6	96	51	86
Taunton Town	42	26	7	9	89	56	85
Metropolitan Police	42	22	12	8	91	64	78
Salisbury	42	22	11	9	97	69	77
Poole Town	42	20	10	12	84	59	70
Kings Langley	42	21	6	15	65	61	69
Harrow Borough	42	18	9	15	97	77	63
Hartley Wintney	42	17	12	13	82	70	63
Farnborough	42	18	8	16	72	72	62
Chesham United	42	15	14	13	54	55	59
Swindon Supermarine	42	16	10	16	70	59	58
Beaconsfield Town	42	15	13	14	65	65	58
Merthyr Town	42	15	9	18	68	67	54
Wimborne Town	42	15	7	20	72	75	52
Dorchester Town	42	14	10	18	67	75	52
Hendon	42	14	10	18	64	74	52
Walton Casuals	42	14	9	19	69	78	51
Tiverton Town	42	13	12	17	65	75	51
Gosport Borough	42	15	5	22	63	70	50
Basingstoke Town	42	14	7	21	81	82	49
Frome Town	42	11	4	27	45	74	37
Staines Town	42	4	0	38	40	168	12

Division One Central

Peterborough Sports	38	30	5	3	109	28	95
Bromsgrove Sporting	38	27	6	5	108	44	87
Corby Town	38	24	5	9	106	60	77
Bedford Town	38	21	2	15	84	52	65
Sutton Coldfield Town	38	17	11	10	65	49	62
Berkhamsted	38	17	8	13	68	53	59
Didcot Town	38	16	10	12	69	61	58
Thame United	38	17	6	15	60	61	57
Coleshill Town	38	16	8	14	60	58	56
AFC Dunstable	38	16	7	15	58	71	55
Yaxley	38	15	4	19	72	92	49
Cambridge City	38	12	11	15	58	54	47
Kempston Rovers	38	11	10	17	58	75	43
Welwyn Garden City	38	11	10	17	52	64	42
Aylesbury United	38	12	6	20	62	86	42
Barton Rovers	38	10	11	17	45	68	41
North Leigh	38	9	7	22	67	106	34
Kidlington	38	9	7	22	43	82	34
Aylesbury	38	8	7	23	42	79	31
Dunstable Town	38	8	7	23	49	92	31

Welwyn Garden City had one point deducted for fielding an ineligible player.

Division One South

Blackfield & Langley	38	26	4	8	75	34	82
Cirencester Town	38	23	6	9	110	52	75
Yate Town	38	23	6	9	74	51	75
Moneyfields	38	21	8	9	73	43	71
Cinderford Town	38	21	8	9	64	39	71
Winchester City	38	21	7	10	84	46	70
Evesham United	38	19	6	13	66	53	63
Street	38	17	10	11	58	51	61
Bideford	38	18	4	16	66	68	58
AFC Totton	38	17	5	16	72	55	56
Thatcham Town	38	17	5	16	57	58	56
Melksham Town	38	17	5	16	59	70	56
Larkhall Athletic	38	16	7	15	52	51	55
Highworth Town	38	13	9	16	63	71	48
Bristol Manor Farm	38	13	7	18	65	77	46
Mangotsfield United	38	11	4	23	64	78	37
Paulton Rovers	38	10	3	25	49	79	33
Slimbridge	38	8	6	24	43	87	30
Barnstaple Town	38	6	5	27	42	100	23
Fleet Town	38	5	1	32	48	121	16

Street resigned from the league at the end of the season.

2019-2020

Premier Division Central

Peterborough Sports	33	19	8	6	90	46	65
Tamworth	30	21	2	7	63	27	65
Royston Town	30	19	6	5	62	28	63
Bromsgrove Sporting	32	17	6	9	80	43	57
Rushall Olympic	33	15	8	10	58	43	53
Stourbridge	32	16	5	11	53	52	53
Banbury United	32	14	10	8	48	31	52
Coalville Town	30	14	9	7	51	32	51
Nuneaton Borough	33	14	8	11	57	46	50
Kings Langley	30	15	5	10	51	41	50
AFC Rushden & Diamonds	30	14	7	9	50	45	49
Barwell	32	14	6	12	58	54	48
Needham Market	33	13	9	11	43	40	48
Hednesford Town	32	14	5	13	50	44	47
Biggleswade Town	30	13	4	13	44	45	43
Lowestoft Town	33	13	2	18	48	62	41
Hitchin Town	32	10	9	13	43	49	39
Stratford Town	33	8	4	21	42	74	28
Leiston	32	6	8	18	39	87	26
St. Ives Town	33	6	5	22	33	76	23
Alvechurch	30	4	5	21	25	58	17
Redditch United	33	3	3	27	24	89	12

Division One Central

Berkhamsted	28	20	4	4	69	24	64
Halesowen Town	27	20	3	4	72	19	63
Corby Town	28	18	5	5	64	26	59
Welwyn Garden City	29	15	6	8	59	36	51
Aylesbury United	29	13	10	6	49	30	49
Biggleswade	27	13	5	9	44	33	44
Barton Rovers	29	13	5	11	65	55	44
Yaxley	29	13	5	11	55	52	44
Bedworth United	27	13	5	9	46	43	44
North Leigh	27	13	3	11	50	50	42
Thame United	27	12	4	11	51	35	40
Bedford Town	29	11	7	11	49	54	40
Daventry Town	28	12	4	12	42	48	40
Coleshill Town	28	10	6	12	50	47	36
AFC Dunstable	29	10	4	15	51	54	34
Kidlington	28	9	6	13	32	48	33
Didcot Town	27	7	4	16	20	44	25
St. Neots Town	28	6	3	19	33	59	21
Kempston Rovers	28	5	2	21	29	68	17
Wantage Town	28	1	1	26	16	121	4

Premier Division South

Truro City	31	21	4	6	65	30	67
Chesham United	33	21	3	9	70	44	66
Hayes & Yeading United	32	17	6	9	65	42	57
Swindon Supermarine	32	17	6	9	50	41	57
Tiverton Town	29	16	7	6	69	41	55
Taunton Town	31	15	8	8	63	53	53
Salisbury	30	14	9	7	57	42	51
Gosport Borough	33	13	10	10	35	32	49
Poole Town	27	14	6	7	46	28	48
Weston-super-Mare	29	13	6	10	54	45	45
Metropolitan Police	30	13	4	13	46	48	43
Farnborough	30	13	3	14	41	43	42
Merthyr Town	31	9	11	11	37	37	38
Hendon	31	10	8	13	47	51	38
Wimborne Town	33	10	7	16	39	52	37
Hartley Wintney	27	10	6	11	38	39	36
Harrow Borough	34	9	9	16	44	62	36
Blackfield & Langley	31	8	9	14	33	50	33
Yate Town	31	8	5	18	38	56	29
Walton Casuals	33	7	6	20	40	71	27
Beaconsfield Town	32	6	7	19	29	54	25
Dorchester Town	32	4	6	22	36	81	18

Division One South

Thatcham Town	27	18	4	5	66	28	58
Frome Town	28	17	7	4	57	27	58
Larkhall Athletic	27	14	7	6	45	37	49
Winchester City	27	14	6	7	53	37	48
Melksham Town	28	14	5	9	58	51	47
Cirencester Town	27	14	3	10	58	38	45
Paulton Rovers	27	13	6	8	61	43	45
Cinderford Town	26	13	4	9	59	45	43
Evesham United	28	11	8	9	52	50	41
Sholing	25	12	2	11	39	33	38
Bideford	28	10	7	11	49	50	37
Slimbridge	26	11	2	13	54	53	35
Highworth Town	28	8	8	12	36	41	32
Willand Rovers	24	10	2	12	32	37	32
Bristol Manor Farm	27	8	6	13	31	44	30
AFC Totton	27	7	8	12	39	53	29
Mangotsfield United	29	8	4	17	46	65	28
Moneyfields	25	7	6	12	37	50	27
Basingstoke Town	27	5	4	18	34	76	18
Barnstaple Town	27	5	1	21	26	74	16

Basingstoke Town had 1 point deducted for fielding an ineligible player.

Play was suspended during mid-March 2020 due to the effects of the Covid-19 pandemic and the season was subsequently abandoned.

The tables shown are correct to the final match played in each division.

ISTHMIAN LEAGUE NOTES

FORMATION

Although professionalism in football was sanctioned by the Football Association in 1885, it took many years for it to be fully accepted in London and the Home Counties. While the Southern League was formed in 1894 and accepted both professional and amateur clubs, many of the leading amateur clubs stood aloof from it, preferring to compete only against other amateur clubs. This meant that their fixture list consisted solely of cup-ties and friendly games.

This situation was finally changed on 8th March 1905 when, following a number of preliminary meetings, representatives of 6 leading amateur clubs met at Winchester House, Old Broad Street and formed the Isthmian League. The 6 founder members were Casuals, Civil Service, Clapton, Ealing Association, Ilford and London Caledonians. Winchester House was to remain the venue for Isthmian League meetings for 60 years.

Isthmian League changes 1906-2020

1906   There were no changes to the league's constitution.

1907   At the Football Association's Annual General Meeting on 31st May, a resolution was passed requiring all county associations to admit professional, as well as amateur, clubs into membership. Neither the Surrey nor the Middlesex County F.A.s were prepared to do so and they disaffiliated from the F.A.. The F.A. then passed another resolution banning its clubs and players from playing against other clubs and players that were not under the F.A.'s jurisdiction.

As a result, there was a meeting on 8th July 1907 at which the Amateur Football Association was formed as a completely separate organisation to the Football Association. It formed its own county associations and cup and league competitions and its members did not play competitive or even friendly games against F.A. affiliated clubs.

Amateur clubs then had to choose whether to stay in the F.A. or join the A.F.A.. The Isthmian League had been operating under F.A. jurisdiction and so clubs that wished to join the A.F.A. had to resign from the league. Casuals, Civil Service and Ealing Association chose to do that and joined the new A.F.A. competition, the Southern Amateur League. Clapton, Ilford and London Caledonians remained in the Isthmian League.

The three clubs who resigned were replaced by Dulwich Hamlet and West Norwood who both joined from the Southern Suburban League, and Oxford City who were not playing in a league.

1908   Bromley, Leytonstone, Nunhead and Shepherd's Bush all joined from the Spartan League.

1909-10   There were no changes to the league's constitution.

1911   Bromley moved to the Kent League. Tunbridge Wells joined from the Southern Amateur League and Woking joined from the West Surrey League.

1912   There were no changes to the league's constitution.

1913   Tunbridge Wells moved to the Spartan League. New Crusaders joined from the Southern Amateur League.

1914   The league was suspended upon the outbreak of war.

1919   Shepherd's Bush disbanded in 1915 and New Crusaders did not resume in competitive football after the war and also subsequently disbanded.

The F.A. and A.F.A. had resolved their dispute in 1914 and Civil Service and Casuals rejoined from the Southern Amateur League. Tufnell Park also joined, moving from the Athenian League.

1920   There were no changes to the league's constitution.

1921   Wimbledon joined from the Athenian League and Wycombe Wanderers joined from the Spartan League.

1922   There were no changes to the league's constitution.

1923   West Norwood moved to the London League and St. Albans City joined from the Athenian League.

1924-28 There were no changes to the league's constitution.

1929 Civil Service moved to the Southern Amateur League and Kingstonian joined from the Athenian League.

1930-38 There were no changes to the league's constitution.

1939 London Caledonians resigned and disbanded after losing use of their ground. Romford and Walthamstow Avenue both joined from the Athenian League. Casuals merged with the Corinthians, who were not playing in a league, to form Corinthian Casuals. The merged club continued in the Isthmian League and also continued playing at Richmond Road, Kingston-upon-Thames which was Kingstonian's home ground and was where Casuals had been playing.

However, the league was immediately suspended when war broke out on 3rd September, 1939 after just 8 games of the 1939-40 season had been played.

1945 When the league restarted after the war, Nunhead were unable to continue because they had lost use of their ground. They finally disbanded completely in 1949 without ever resuming activity. The league thus began in 1945-46 with the remaining 14 pre-war members.

1946-49 There were no changes to the league's constitution.

1950 Tufnell Park had lost their ground at Tufnell Park, Holloway in 1939 and ground-shared with Golders Green (later Hendon) during the war. After the war they ground-shared with Cheshunt but in 1950, they merged with London League side Edmonton Borough. The newly merged club played at Edmonton Borough's Henry Barrass Stadium and continued in the Isthmian League as Tufnell Park, Edmonton.

1951 There were no changes to the league's constitution.

1952 Tufnell Park, Edmonton moved to the Spartan League. Barking and Bromley both joined from the Athenian League.

1953-55 There were no changes to the league's constitution.

1956 Tooting & Mitcham United joined from the Athenian League.

1957-58 There were no changes to the league's constitution.

1959 Romford moved to the Southern League and Maidstone joined from the Athenian League.

1960-62 There were no changes to the league's constitution.

1963 Enfield, Hendon, Hitchin Town and Sutton United all joined from the Athenian League.

1964 Wimbledon moved to the Southern League and Wealdstone joined from the Athenian League.

1965-70 There were no changes to the league's constitution.

1971 Maidstone United and Wealdstone both moved to the Southern League and Bishop's Stortford, Hayes and Walton & Hersham all joined from the Athenian League.

1972 Leatherhead joined from the Athenian League.

1973 A new Second Division was formed with 16 clubs, 15 of which came from the Athenian League. These were Aveley, Carshalton Athletic, Chesham United, Dagenham, Finchley, Hampton, Harlow Town, Harwich & Parkeston, Horsham, Maidenhead United, Slough Town, Southall, Staines Town, Tilbury and Wokingham Town. The 16th club was Hertford Town who joined from the Eastern Counties League, The existing 22 members all continued in the league and formed Division One. Promotion and relegation for two clubs was introduced.

1974 Promoted: Dagenham and Slough Town.

Relegated: Corinthian Casuals and St. Albans City.

Croydon and Boreham Wood both joined Division Two from the Athenian League.

1975 Promoted: Staines Town and Southall. After promotion, Southall changed their name to Southall & Ealing Borough

Relegated: Walton & Hersham and Bromley

Harrow Borough, Hornchurch, Ware and Wembley all joined Division Two from the Athenian League.

1976 Promoted: Tilbury and Croydon.   Relegated: Oxford City and Clapton

1977 Division One was renamed the Premier Division, Division Two was renamed Division One and a new Division Two was formed containing 17 clubs, 16 of which joined from the Athenian League.

These were: Camberley Town, Cheshunt, Eastbourne United, Egham Town, Epping Town, Epsom & Ewell, Farnborough Town, Feltham, Hemel Hempstead, Letchworth Garden City, Lewes, Molesey, Rainham Town, Tring Town, Willesden and Worthing. The 17th club were Metropolitan Police who joined from the Southern League. Milton Keynes City of the Southern League were also elected but withdrew their application before the start of the season and remained in the Southern League.

       Promoted to Premier Division from Division One: Boreham Wood and Carshalton Athletic.

       Relegated from Premier Division to Division One: Dulwich Hamlet and Ilford.

1978   Promoted to Premier Division from Division One: Oxford City and Dulwich Hamlet

       Relegated Premier Division to Division One: Southall & Ealing Borough, Bishops Stortford

       Promoted to Division One from Division Two: Epsom & Ewell and Metropolitan Police

       Relegated from Division One to Division Two: Hornchurch and Corinthian Casuals

Hungerford Town joined Division Two from the Hellenic League.

1979   Promoted to Premier Division from Division One: Harlow Town and Harrow Borough

       Relegated from Premier Division to Division One: Kingstonian

Leytonstone, who were due for relegation from the Premier Division to Division One, merged with Ilford of Division One. The two clubs had been ground-sharing at Leytonstone's Granleigh Road ground since 1977 and the merged club continued there, playing in Division One as Leytonstone and Ilford.

       Promoted to Division One from Division Two: Farnborough Town and Camberley Town

       Relegated from Division One to Division Two: Southall & Ealing Borough

Barton Rovers joined Division Two from the South Midlands League and Billericay Town joined Division Two from the Athenian League.

1980   Promoted to Premier Division from Division One: Leytonstone & Ilford and Bromley

       Relegated from Premier Division to Division One: Oxford City and Tilbury

       Promoted to Division One from Division Two: Billericay Town and Lewes

       Relegated from Division One to Division Two: Harwich & Parkeston and Horsham

Dorking Town joined Division Two from the Athenian League. Southall & Ealing Borough changed their name to Southall.

1981   Promoted to National League from Premier Division: Enfield and Dagenham

       Promoted to Premier Division from Division One: Bishops Stortford and Billericay Town

       Promoted to Division One from Division Two: Feltham and Hornchurch

       Relegated from Division One to Division Two: Camberley Town and Finchley

Bognor Regis Town joined Division One from the Southern League. Basildon United and Windsor & Eton both joined Division Two from the Athenian League. Willesden resigned from Division Two and disbanded after losing their ground.

1982   Promoted to Premier Division from Division One: Wokingham Town and Bognor Regis Town

       Relegated from Premier Division to Division One: Harlow Town and Boreham Wood

       Promoted to Division One from Division Two: Worthing and Cheshunt

       Relegated from Division One to Division Two: Clapton and Ware

Camberley Town moved to the Athenian League. Leyton Wingate and Uxbridge both joined Division Two from the Athenian League.

1983   Promoted to Premier Division from Division One: Worthing and Harlow Town

       Relegated from Premier Division to Division One: Woking and Leatherhead

Leytonstone & Ilford changed their name to Leytonstone/Ilford.

       Promoted to Division One from Division Two: Windsor & Eton and Clapton

       Relegated from Division One to Division Two: St. Albans City

Harwich & Parkeston moved to the Athenian League. Grays Athletic and Newbury Town both joined from the Athenian League. Dorking Town changed their name to Dorking.

1984   Promoted to Premier Division from Division One: Windsor & Eton and Epsom & Ewell

       Relegated from Premier Division to Division One: Bromley and Staines Town

       Promoted to Division One from Division Two: St. Albans City and Basildon United

Division Two expanded into two regional divisions, South (which would have 20 clubs) and North (which would have 21 clubs). 19 new clubs joined either one or the other of the new regional divisions, 13 of them from the Athenian League which closed down at the end of the 1983-84 season.

The 20 clubs selected to form Division Two (South) were made up of 12 from the former single Division Two: Corinthian Casuals, Dorking, Eastbourne United, Egham Town, Grays Athletic, Horsham, Hungerford Town, Molesey, Newbury Town, Rainham Town, Southall and Uxbridge; plus 5 from the Athenian League: Banstead Athletic, Camberley Town, Chertsey Town, Ruislip Manor and Whyteleafe; plus Feltham (relegated from Division One), Bracknell Town (from the London-Spartan League) and Petersfield United (from the Hampshire League). However Corinthian Casuals were unable to take part because they did not have a ground that met the criteria. They therefore moved to the London-Spartan League and Division Two (South) began with 19 clubs.

The 21 clubs selected to form Division Two (North) were made up of 8 from the former single Division Two: Barton Rovers, Epping Town, Finchley, Hemel Hempstead, Letchworth Garden City, Leyton Wingate, Tring Town and Ware; plus 8 from the Athenian League: Berkhamsted Town, Chalfont St. Peter, Flackwell Heath, Harefield United, Haringey Borough, Kingsbury Town, Marlow and Wolverton Town; plus Cheshunt (relegated from Division One), Heybridge Swifts (from the Essex Senior League), Royston Town (from the South Midlands League), Saffron Walden Town (from the Eastern Counties League) and Stevenage Borough (from the United Counties League).

1985   Promoted to National League from Premier Division: Wycombe Wanderers

Relegated from National League to Premier Division: Yeovil Town

Promoted to Premier Division from Division One: Farnborough Town and Kingstonian

Relegated from Premier Division to Division One: Leytonstone/Ilford and Harlow Town

Promoted to Division One from Division Two (North): Leyton Wingate and Finchley

Promoted to Division One from Division Two (South): Uxbridge and Grays Athletic

Relegated from Division One to Division Two (North): Hertford Town and Clapton

Relegated from Division One to Division Two (South): Metropolitan Police and Woking

Moved from Division Two (North) to Division Two (South): Flackwell Heath and Marlow

Moved from Division Two (South) to Division Two (North): Rainham Town

Epping Town did not play their final Division Two (North) game away to Heybridge Swifts and their record (P39 W13 D8 L17 F42 A59 P48) was deleted. They were expelled from the league and subsequently disbanded.

Vauxhall Motors joined Division Two (North) from the South Midlands League. Chertsey Town were relegated from Division Two (South) to the Combined Counties League, swapping places with Southwick.

1986   Promoted to National League from Premier Division: Sutton United

Relegated from National League to Premier Division: Wycombe Wanderers

Promoted to Premier Division from Division One: Bromley and St. Albans City

Relegated from Premier Division to Division One: Billericay Town and Epsom & Ewell

Promoted to Division One from Division Two (North):
                        Kingsbury Town and Stevenage Borough

Promoted to Division One from Division Two (South): Bracknell Town and Southwick

Relegated from Division One to Division Two (North):
                        Hornchurch, Chesham United, Harlow Town and Aveley

Moved from Division Two (North) to Division Two (South):
                        Chalfont St. Peter and Harefield United

Wivenhoe Town joined Division Two (North) from the Essex Senior League and Collier Row joined Division Two (North) from the London Spartan League. Chertsey Town joined Division Two (South) from the Combined Counties League.

1987   Promoted to National League from Premier Division: Wycombe Wanderers

Promoted to Premier Division from Division One: Leytonstone/Ilford and Leyton Wingate

Relegated from Premier Division to Division One: Worthing and Walthamstow Avenue

Basingstoke Town joined the Premier Division from the Southern League.

Promoted to Division One from Division Two (North): Wolverton Town and Chesham United
Promoted to Division One from Division Two (South): Marlow and Woking
Relegated from Division One to Division Two (North): Finchley and Tilbury
Relegated from Division One to Division Two (South): Epsom & Ewell, Maidenhead United

Cheshunt moved from Division Two (North) to the London-Spartan League and Witham Town joined Division Two (North) from the Essex Senior League. Yeading joined Division Two (South) from the London-Spartan League.

1988   Promoted to National League from Premier Division: Yeovil Town

Relegated from National League to Premier Division: Dagenham

Promoted to Premier Division from Division One: Grays Athletic and Marlow

Relegated from Premier Division to Division One: Hitchin Town and Basingstoke Town

Promoted to Division One from Division Two (North): Wivenhoe Town and Collier Row

Promoted to Division One from Division Two (South):
Metropolitan Police and Chalfont St. Peter

Relegated from Division One to Division Two (North):
Billericay Town, Stevenage Borough and Wolverton Town

Wolverton Town changed their name to Wolverton Town (Milton Keynes).

Walthamstow Avenue of Division One resigned and merged with Leytonstone/Ilford of the Premier Division who had been ground-sharing at Walthamstow's Green Pond Road ground since 1986. The merged club continued to play at Green Pond Road as Leytonstone/Ilford in the Premier Division.

Oxford City of Division One were evicted from their White House ground in May 1988 by their landlords, Brasenose College, for an alleged breech of lease. The club directors resigned and the ground was sold for housing. Oxford City resigned from all senior competitions but a new board was formed and a youth side played in the 1988-89 season. The senior side was re-formed in 1990 and joined the South Midlands League. Their new ground was at Cutteslowe Park.

Moved from Division Two (North) to Division Two (South): Finchley and Haringey Borough

Haringey Borough suffered a mass exodus of players and management shortly before the start of the 1988-89 season and were expelled as they could not field a team. After a season's inactivity, they joined the Spartan League in 1989-90. Purfleet joined Division Two (North) from the Essex Senior League.

1989   Promoted to National League from Premier Division: Farnborough Town

Relegated from National League to Premier Division: Aylesbury United

Promoted to Premier Division from Division One: Basingstoke Town and Staines Town

Relegated from Premier Division to Division One: Tooting & Mitcham United and Croydon

Leytonstone/Ilford of the Premier Division changed their name to Redbridge Forest.

Promoted to Division One from Division Two (North): Harlow Town and Purfleet

Promoted to Division One from Division Two (South): Dorking and Whyteleafe

Relegated from Division One to Division Two (North): Collier Row and Basildon United

Relegated from Division One to Division Two (South): Bracknell Town

Moved from Division Two (South) to Division Two (North): Finchley

Wolverton Town moved from Division One (North) to the South Midlands League. Malden Vale joined Division One (South) from the Combined Counties League and Abingdon Town joined Division One (South) from the Spartan League. Newport County were also elected to the league, subject to the consent of their liquidator, but were unable to take their place.

1990   Promoted to National League from Premier Division: Slough Town

Relegated from National League to Premier Division: Enfield

Promoted to Premier Division from Division One: Woking and Wivenhoe Town

Relegated from Premier Division to Division One: Bromley and Dulwich Hamlet

Promoted to Division One from Division Two (North): Aveley and Heybridge Swifts

Promoted to Division One from Division Two (South): Yeading and Molesey

Relegated from Division One to Division Two (North): Purfleet and Kingsbury Town

Relegated from Division One to Division Two (South): Hampton and Leatherhead

Letchworth Garden City moved from Division One (North) to the South Midlands League and Edgware Town joined Division One (North) from the Spartan League. Cove joined Division One (South) from the Combined Counties League.

1991   Promoted to National League from Premier Division: Redbridge Forest

        Relegated from National League to Premier Division: Sutton United

        Promoted to Premier Division from Division One: Chesham United and Bromley

        Relegated from Premier Division to Division One: Barking and Leyton Wingate

        Promoted to Division One from Division Two (North): Stevenage Borough

        Promoted to Division One from Division Two (South): Abingdon Town, Maidenhead United

Division Two (North) and Division Two (South) were re-organised as Division Two and Division Three.

Division Two was formed by the 18 clubs who finished between 3rd and 11th in the two regional divisions plus Southwick, Lewes, Metropolitan Police and Worthing who were all relegated from Division One.

Division Three was formed by the clubs who finished below 11th in the two regional leagues with the exception of 2 clubs from Division Two (North): Basildon United, who moved to the Essex Senior League because of the increased travelling that the re-organisation of the league would mean, and Finchley, who merged with Wingate of the South Midlands League as Wingate & Finchley and continued in that league but playing at Finchley's Summers Lane ground. It was renamed Harry Abrahams Stadium in honour of a long time Wingate supporter.

Hounslow of the Hellenic League had lost their Denbigh Road ground because the local council were building a school on the site and some elements of the club then merged with Feltham of Division Two (South). The merged club took Feltham's place in Division Three as Feltham & Hounslow Borough.

Thame United joined Division Three from the South Midlands League.

Vauxhall Motors had earned promotion from Division Two (North) to Division One but were expelled from the league because the club's parent company had decided to install an artificial pitch which was not allowed by league rules. The club withdrew from senior football and disbanded.

1992   Promoted to National League from Premier Division: Woking

        Promoted to Premier Division from Division One:

                Dulwich Hamlet, Stevenage Borough and Yeading

        Relegated from Premier Division to Division One: Bishops Stortford

Dagenham of the Premier Division merged with Redbridge Forest of the National League who had been sharing Dagenham's Victoria Road ground. The merged club continued at Victoria Road in the National League as Dagenham & Redbridge.

        Promoted to Division One from Division Two: Billericay Town, Lewes and Purfleet

Harlow Town of Division One were suspended from the league. They had had to vacate their Sportcentre Ground as it was not up to standard and plans for a new ground in Roydon Road had collapsed. The club did not compete in any league in 1992-93. Leyton Wingate of Division One changed their name to Leyton.

        Promoted to Division Two from Division Three:

                Chertsey Town, Hampton, Edgware Town and Tilbury

Southwick resigned from Division Two and Eastbourne United resigned from Division Three. Both moved to the Sussex County League.

East Thurrock United joined from the Essex Senior League, Leighton Town joined from the South Midlands League and Northwood joined from the Spartan League. Aldershot Town joined as a new club that was formed by supporters of Aldershot F.C. after the original club disbanded in March 1992.

1993   Promoted to Premier Division from Division One: Dorking, Hitchin Town and Molesey

        Relegated from Premier Division to Division One:

                Staines Town, Windsor & Eton and Bognor Regis Town

        Promoted to Division One from Division Two: Worthing, Berkhamsted Town, Ruislip Manor

        Relegated from Division One to Division Two: Lewes and Aveley

        Promoted to Division Two from Division Three: Aldershot Town, Thame United, Collier Row

Relegated from Division Two to Division Three: Harefield United and Southall

Petersfield United resigned from Division Three because of financial problems and travelling costs. They were refused permission to switch to the Wessex League and disbanded. A new club called Petersfield Town was formed as a replacement and joined the Wessex League.

Harlow Town had upgraded their Sportcentre Ground and rejoined the league in Division Three after a season's inactivity. Cheshunt joined Division Three from the Spartan League and Oxford City joined Division Three from the South Midlands League.

1994 Promoted to National League from the Premier Division: Stevenage Borough

Relegated from National League to the Premier Division: Slough Town

Promoted to Premier Division from Division One:
Bishops Stortford, Purfleet and Walton & Hersham

Relegated from Premier Division to Division One:
Basingstoke Town, Dorking and Wivenhoe Town

Promoted to Division One from Division Two:
Aldershot Town, Chertsey Town, Newbury Town

Relegated from Division One to Division Two: Chalfont St. Peter, Croydon, Windsor & Eton

Promoted to Division Two from Division Three: Oxford City, Bracknell Town and Cheshunt

Relegated from Division Two to Division Three: Lewes and Collier Row

Rainham Town disbanded having left their Deri Park ground in 1991 when they were planning to build a new ground using funds raised by selling Deri Park for housing. However, it was found to be too expensive to build houses at Deri Park so the club resigned from Division Two and disbanded at the end of the 1993-94 season with major financial problems.

Royston Town resigned from Division Three and joined the Spartan League. Bedford Town joined Division Three from the South Midlands League and Canvey Island joined Division Three from the Essex Senior League.

1995 Promoted to National League from the Premier Division: Slough Town

Relegated from National League to the Premier Division: Yeovil Town

Promoted to Premier Division from Division One: Boreham Wood, Chertsey Town, Worthing

Relegated Premier Division to Division One: Chesham United, Marlow, Wokingham Town

Promoted to Division One from Division Two: Barton Rovers, Oxford City and Thame United

Relegated from Division One to Division Two: Dorking and Wivenhoe Town

Leyton of Division One merged with Walthamstow Pennant of the Spartan League to form Leyton Pennant. The merged club continued in Division One playing at Walthamstow Pennant's Wadham Lodge ground.

Newbury Town resigned from Division One and disbanded shortly before the start of the 1995-96 season with severe financial problems.

Promoted to Division Two from Division Three: Canvey Island, Collier Row and Bedford Town

Relegated from Division Two to Division Three: Aveley and Windsor & Eton

Malden Vale of Division Two merged with Raynes Park of the Surrey County Premier League to form Raynes Park Vale. The merged club joined the Combined Counties League and played at Malden Vale's ground at Grand Drive, Raynes Park which became known as Prince George's playing field.

Feltham & Hounslow Borough of Division Three were expelled from the league as their ground had a plastic pitch which the league did not allow. They changed name to Feltham and joined the Combined Counties League.

Wealdstone joined Division Three from the Southern League – Southern Division and Wingate & Finchley joined Division Three from the South Midlands League.

1996 Promoted to National League from the Premier Division: Hayes

Relegated from National League to the Premier Division: Dagenham & Redbridge

Promoted to Premier Division from Division One: Heybridge Swifts, Oxford City, Staines Town

Relegated from Premier Division to Division One: Molesey, Walton & Hersham and Worthing

Promoted to Division One from Division Two: Hampton, Croydon and Canvey Island

Relegated from Division One to Division Two: Barking and Wembley

Ruislip Manor were to be relegated from Division One to Division Two but resigned and joined the Spartan League because of lack of finance to meet ground grading requirements.

Promoted to Division Two from Division Three: Horsham, Leighton Town, Windsor & Eton

Collier Row of Division Two merged with Romford of the Essex Senior League to form Collier Row & Romford. The merged club continued in Division Two playing at Collier Row's ground, Sungate in Collier Row Road.

Saffron Walden Town resigned from Division Two because of travelling costs and joined the Essex Senior League.

Harefield United resigned from Division Three and joined the Spartan League because of lack of finance to meet ground grading requirements.

Cove resigned from Division Three because of the costs and joined the Combined Counties League.

Braintree Town joined Division Three from the Southern League – Southern Division

1997   Promoted to National League from the Premier Division: Yeovil Town

Promoted to Premier Division from Division One:
Basingstoke Town, Chesham United and Walton & Hersham

Relegated Premier Division to Division One: Chertsey Town, Grays Athletic, Staines Town

Gravesend & Northfleet joined the Premier Division from the Southern League – Premier Division

Promoted to Division One from Division Two:
Collier Row & Romford, Leatherhead and Wembley

Collier Row & Romford changed their name to Romford

Relegated from Division One to Division Two:
Canvey Island, Marlow and Tooting & Mitcham United

Promoted to Division Two from Division Three: Braintree Town, Wealdstone and Northwood

Relegated from Division Two to Division Three: Ware, Dorking and Hemel Hempstead

Corinthian Casuals joined Division Three from the Combined Counties League, Croydon Athletic joined Division Three from the Spartan League and Ford United joined Division Three from the Essex Senior League.

1998   Promoted to National League from the Premier Division: Kingstonian

Relegated from National League to the Premier Division: Slough Town

Promoted to Premier Division from Division One: Aldershot town, Billericay Town, Hampton

Relegated from Premier Division to Division One: Yeading, Hitchin Town and Oxford City

Promoted to Division One from Division Two: Canvey Island, Braintree Town, Wealdstone

Relegated from Division One to Division Two:
Wokingham Town, Abingdon Town and Thame United

Promoted to Division Two from Division Three:
Hemel Hempstead, Hertford Town and Harlow Town

Relegated from Division Two to Division Three: Tilbury, Egham Town and Cheshunt

1999   Promoted to National League from the Premier Division: Sutton United

Relegated from National League to the Premier Division: Farnborough Town

Promoted to Premier Division from Division One: Canvey Island and Hitchin Town

Relegated from Premier Division to Division One: Bishops Stortford and Bromley

Hampton of the Premier Division changed their name to Hampton & Richmond Borough

Promoted to Division One from Division Two: Thame United, Bedford Town, Harlow Town

Relegated from Division One to Division Two: Molesey, Wembley and Berkhamsted Town

Promoted to Division Two from Division Three: Ford United, Wingate & Finchley, Cheshunt

Relegated from Division Two to Division Three:
Hertford Town, Bracknell Town and Abingdon Town

Hemel Hempstead of Division Two changed their name to Hemel Hempstead Town.

Great Wakering Rovers joined Division Three from the Essex Senior League.

2000   Promoted to National League from the Premier Division: Dagenham & Redbridge
Relegated from National League to the Premier Division: Sutton United
Promoted to Premier Division from Division One: Croydon, Grays Athletic, Maidenhead Utd.
Relegated from Premier Division to Division One:
Aylesbury United, Boreham Wood, Walton & Hersham
Promoted to Division One from Division Two: Ford United and Northwood
Relegated from Division One to Division Two: Chertsey Town and Leyton Pennant
Promoted to Division Two from Division Three:
East Thurrock United, Great Wakering Rovers and Tilbury
Relegated from Division Two to Division Three:
Wingate & Finchley, Witham Town and Chalfont St. Peter

Two Division Three games not played: Croydon Athletic v. Bracknell Town and Lewes v. Hertford Town.
Southall moved from Division Three to the Combined Counties League.

Ashford Town (Middlesex) joined Division Three from the Combined Counties League and Arlesey Town joined Division Three from the Spartan South Midlands League.

2001   Promoted to National League from the Premier Division: Farnborough Town
Relegated from National League to the Premier Division: Kingstonian
Promoted to Premier Division from Division One:
Braintree Town, Boreham Wood and Bedford Town
Relegated from Premier Division to Division One:
Slough Town, Carshalton Athletic and Dulwich Hamlet
Promoted to Division One from Division Two:
Tooting & Mitcham United, Windsor & Eton and Barking

Having achieved promotion from Division Two, Barking merged with East Ham United of the Essex Senior League to form Barking & East Ham United. The merged club played at Barking's ground at Mayesbrook Park, Lodge Avenue, Dagenham where East Ham United had been groundsharing.

Relegated from Division One to Division Two: Leatherhead, Romford and Barton Rovers
Promoted to Division Two from Division Three:
Arlesey Town, Lewes and Ashford Town (Middlesex)
Relegated from Division Two to Division Three:
Edgware Town, Leighton Town and Wokingham Town

2002   Promoted to National League from the Premier Division: Gravesend & Northfleet
Relegated from National League to the Premier Division: Hayes
Promoted to Premier Division from Division One:
Bishops Stortford, Ford United and Aylesbury United

Divisions One, Two and Three were re-organised so that there were two regional sections to Division One, North and South, and a new Division Two.

The new Division One (North) was created with 9 clubs from the former Division One: Barking & East Ham United, Harlow Town, Northwood, Oxford City, Slough Town, Thame United, Uxbridge, Wealdstone and Yeading; 11 clubs from the former Division Two: Arlesey Town, Barton Rovers, Berkhamsted Town, East Thurrock United, Great Wakering Rovers, Hemel Hempstead Town, Leyton Pennant, Marlow, Tilbury, Wembley and Wivenhoe Town; and 4 clubs from the former Division Three: Aveley, Hertford Town, Hornchurch and Wingate & Finchley.

The new Division One (South) was created with 10 clubs from the former Division One: Bognor Regis Town, Bromley, Carshalton Athletic, Dulwich Hamlet, Staines Town, Tooting & Mitcham United, Walton & Hersham, Whyteleafe, Windsor & Eton and Worthing; 8 clubs from the former Division Two: Ashford Town (Middlesex), Banstead Athletic, Chertsey Town, Horsham, Leatherhead, Lewes, Metropolitan Police and Molesey; 5 clubs from the former Division Three: Bracknell Town, Corinthian Casuals, Croydon Athletic, Egham Town and Epsom & Ewell. The final member was Croydon who were relegated from the Premier Division.

The new Division Two was created with 13 clubs from the former Division Three: Abingdon Town, Camberley Town, Chalfont St. Peter, Clapton, Dorking, Edgware Town, Flackwell Heath, Kingsbury

Town, Leighton Town, Tring Town, Ware, Witham Town and Wokingham Town; plus 2 clubs from the former Division Two: Cheshunt and Hungerford Town; Leyton joined from the Essex Senior League.

2003   Promoted to National League from the Premier Division: Aldershot Town

Relegated from National League to the Premier Division: Kettering Town

Promoted to Premier Division from Division One (North): Hornchurch and Northwood

Promoted to Premier Division from Division One (South):
                    Carshalton Athletic and Bognor Regis Town

Relegated from Premier Division to Division One (North):
                    Chesham United, Boreham Wood and Enfield

Relegated from Premier Division to Division One (South): Hampton & Richmond Borough

Purfleet of the Premier Division changed their name to Thurrock.

Promoted to Division One (North) from Division Two: Cheshunt and Leyton

Relegated from Division One (North) to Division Two: Wembley and Hertford Town

Moved from Division One (North) to Division One (South): Slough Town and Marlow

Leyton Pennant of Division One (North) changed their name to Waltham Forest.

Dunstable Town joined Division One (North) from the Spartan South Midlands League.

Relegated from Division One (South) to Division Two: Chertsey Town

Hungerford Town of Division Two moved to the Hellenic League.

Following a fire at their ground in March 2003, Tring Town of Division Two were in financial difficulties and resigned from the league shortly before the start of the 2003-04 season. An agreement was made with Tring Athletic of the Spartan South Midlands League whereby Tring Athletic left their Miswell Lane ground because they were unable to install floodlights. Tring Athletic then moved into Tring Town's Pendley ground and continued in the Spartan South Midlands League.

2004   The top levels of non-League football in England were restructured. The National League acquired two extra divisions, North and South which both fed into the National League itself and the two new regional divisions were in turn fed by the three leagues at the next level. These being the Isthmian League, Southern League and Northern Premier League. Additionally, clubs in those three leagues were re-allocated according to their geographical position.

As 2003-04 champions of the Isthmian League – Premier Division, Canvey Island were promoted to the National League while the remaining 23 clubs were re-allocated as follows: Basingstoke Town, Bishops Stortford, Bognor Regis Town, Carshalton Athletic, Ford United (who changed their name to Redbridge), Grays Athletic, Hayes, Hornchurch, Maidenhead United, St. Albans City, Sutton United and Thurrock (12 clubs) all moved to the National League (South). Kettering Town (1 club) moved to the National League (North). Aylesbury United, Bedford Town and Hitchin Town (3 clubs) moved to the Southern League – Premier Division while the remaining 7 clubs: Billericay Town, Braintree Town, Harrow Borough, Hendon, Heybridge Swifts, Kingstonian and Northwood remained in the Isthmian League – Premier Division.

The Premier Division was made up to 22 clubs by promoting 4 clubs from Division One (North): Cheshunt, Leyton, Wealdstone and Yeading and 5 clubs from Division One (South): Hampton & Richmond Borough, Slough Town, Staines Town, Windsor & Eton and Worthing. 2 clubs were transferred from the Southern League – Premier Division: Chelmsford City and Dover Athletic; and 4 clubs from the Southern League – Eastern Division: Eastleigh, Folkestone Invicta, Salisbury City and Tonbridge Angels.

Additionally, Divisions One (North) and (South) were scrapped and instead there was a single Division One of 22 clubs.

Apart from the 4 clubs promoted to the Premier Division (noted above), the remaining 20 Division One (North) clubs were re-allocated as follows: Chesham United, Dunstable Town and Hemel Hempstead Town (3 clubs) moved to the Southern League – Premier Division; Arlesey Town, Aveley, Barking & East Ham United, Barton Rovers, Berkhamsted Town, Boreham Wood, East Thurrock United, Great Wakering Rovers, Harlow Town, Tilbury, Uxbridge, Waltham Forest, Wingate & Finchley and Wivenhoe Town (14 clubs) all moved to the Southern League – Eastern Division; Oxford City and Thame United (2 clubs) both moved to the Southern League – Western Division; and Enfield were relegated to the Isthmian League – Division Two.

Apart from the 5 clubs promoted to the Premier Division (noted above), the remaining 19 Division One (South) clubs were re-allocated as follows: Lewes (1 club) were promoted to the National League (South); Ashford Town (Middlesex), Bracknell Town, Egham Town and Marlow (4 clubs) moved to the Southern League – Western Division; Banstead Athletic, Bromley, Corinthian Casuals, Croydon, Croydon Athletic, Dulwich Hamlet, Horsham, Leatherhead, Metropolitan Police, Molesey, Tooting & Mitcham United, Walton & Hersham and Whyteleafe (13 clubs) moved to the new Division One of the Isthmian League and Epsom & Ewell (1 club) were relegated to Division Two.

The new Division One thus consisted of 22 clubs, made up of 13 (noted above) from the previous Division One (South) plus Dorking who were promoted from Division Two, 6 clubs from the Southern League – Eastern Division: Ashford Town, Bashley, Burgess Hill Town, Fleet Town, Hastings United and Newport (IOW); AFC Wimbledon from the Combined Counties League and Cray Wanderers from the Kent League.

Division Two increased from 15 to 16 clubs. Dorking were promoted to the new Division One, Leighton Town moved to the Southern League – Eastern Division and Wokingham Town merged with Emmbrook Sports of the Reading League to form Wokingham & Emmbrook who then joined the Hellenic League. There were 4 new clubs in Division Two. Enfield were relegated from Division One (North) and Epsom & Ewell were relegated from Division One (South). Ilford joined from the Essex Senior League and Brook House joined from the Spartan South Midlands League.

2005   Promoted to National League (South) from Premier Division: Yeading and Eastleigh

Relegated from National League (South) to Premier Division: Margate and Redbridge

Promoted to Premier Division from Division One:
                    AFC Wimbledon, Walton & Hersham and Bromley

Relegated from Premier Division to Division One:
                    Tonbridge Angels, Dover Athletic and Kingstonian

Moved to Premier Division from Southern League (Eastern):
                    Fisher Athletic, East Thurrock United and Maldon Town

Moved from Premier Division to Southern League (Premier):
                    Salisbury City, Northwood and Cheshunt

Relegated from Division One to Division Two: Dorking and Croydon

Ramsgate joined Division One from the Kent League, Walton Casuals joined Division One from the Combined Counties League and Lymington & New Milton joined Division One from the Wessex League.

Ilford and Enfield both moved to the Southern League (Eastern) from Division Two and Abingdon Town moved to the Hellenic League from Division Two. Egham Town joined Division Two from the Southern League (Western).

2006   Promoted to National League (South) from Premier Division: Braintree Town, Fisher Athletic

Relegated from National League (South) to Premier Division: Carshalton Athletic

Promoted to Premier Division from Division One: Ramsgate, Horsham and Tonbridge Angels

Relegated from Premier Division to Division One (North): Maldon Town and Redbridge

Relegated from Premier to Southern League (South & West): Windsor & Eton

Moved to Premier Division from Southern League (Eastern): Boreham Wood

Moved to Premier Division from Southern League (Western): Ashford Town (Middlesex)

Moved from Premier Division to Southern League (Premier): Wealdstone

There was a re-organisation of divisions at the level immediately below the Premier Division. As a result, Division One was split into North and South sections as had existed prior to 2004 and Division Two was scrapped.

Of the 23 Division One clubs, 3 were promoted to the Premier Division (as noted above) while Bashley, Lymington & New Milton and Newport (IOW) moved to the Southern League (South & West). Banstead Athletic moved to the Combined Counties League and the remaining 16 clubs: Ashford Town, Burgess Hill Town, Corinthian Casuals, Cray Wanderers, Croydon Athletic, Dover Athletic, Dulwich Hamlet, Fleet Town, Hastings United, Kingstonian, Leatherhead, Metropolitan Police, Molesey, Tooting & Mitcham United, Walton Casuals and Whyteleafe all moved to the new Division One (South).

Apart from the 16 clubs noted above, the new Division One (South) was made up to 22 clubs by the addition of Chatham Town, Dartford and Sittingbourne (all from the Southern League – Eastern), Godalming Town from the Combined Counties League, Horsham YMCA from the Sussex County League and Maidstone United from the Kent League.

The new Division One (North) consisted of 22 clubs, 2 of which (Maldon Town and Redbridge) were relegated from the Premier Division as noted above while 3 clubs were promoted from Division Two – Flackwell Heath, Ware and Witham Town. Of the remaining 17 clubs, 11 came from the Southern League (Eastern) – Arlesey Town, Aveley, Enfield, Enfield Town, Great Wakering Rovers, Harlow Town, Ilford, Potters Bar Town, Waltham Forest, Wingate & Finchley and Wivenhoe Town – while 3 came from the Essex Senior League – AFC Hornchurch, Tilbury and Waltham Abbey – and 2 from the Eastern Counties League – AFC Sudbury and Bury Town. The final club was Canvey Island who were relegated from the National League.

Of the 16 Division Two clubs, 3 were promoted to Division One (North) as noted above while 6 – Camberley Town, Chertsey Town, Dorking, Egham Town, Epsom & Ewell and Wembley – moved to the Combined Counties League and 3 – Chalfont St. Peter, Edgware Town and Hertford Town – moved to the Spartan South Midlands League. Brook House moved to the Southern League (South & West), Clapton moved to the Essex Senior League and Croydon moved to the Kent League. Kingsbury Town merged with London Tigers of the Middlesex Premier League to form Kingsbury London Tigers who joined the Spartan South Midlands League, playing at Kingsbury Town's former ground – Silver Jubilee Park, Townsend Lane, Kingsbury.

2007 Promoted to National League (South) from Premier Division:
Bromley and Hampton & Richmond Borough

Promoted to Premier Division from Division One (North): AFC Hornchurch and Harlow Town

Promoted to Premier Division from Division One (South): Maidstone United, Hastings United

Relegated from Premier Division to Division One (South): Worthing and Walton & Hersham

Relegated from Premier Division to Southern League (S & W): Slough Town

Moved to Premier Division from Southern League (Premier): Wealdstone

Moved from Division One (South) to Division One (North): Dartford

Division One (North): Northwood joined after relegation from the Southern League – Premier Division, Brentwood Town joined from the Essex Senior League and Edgware Town joined from the Spartan South Midlands League. Flackwell Heath moved to the Hellenic League and Enfield disbanded because of financial problems. A replacement club called Enfield 1893 was formed almost immediately and joined the Essex Senior League in 2007-08.

Division One (South): Chipstead joined from the Combined Counties League, Eastbourne Town joined from the Sussex County League and Whitstable Town joined from the Kent League. Fleet Town and Godalming Town both moved to the Southern League (South & West).

2008 Promoted to National League (South) from Premier Division:
Chelmsford City and AFC Wimbledon

Relegated from National League (South) to Premier Division: Sutton United

Promoted to Premier Division from Division One (North): Dartford and Canvey Island

Promoted to Premier Division from Division One (South):
Dover Athletic and Tooting & Mitcham United

Relegated from Premier Division to Division One (North): East Thurrock United and Leyton

Relegated from Premier Division to Division One (South): Folkestone Invicta

Moved from Division One (South) to Division One (North): Chatham Town

Division One (North): Cheshunt joined after relegation from the Southern League – Premier Division, Hillingdon Borough joined from the Southern League (South & West), Concord Rangers joined from the Essex Senior League and Thamesmead Town joined from the Kent League. AFC Sudbury and Bury Town both moved to the Southern League (Midlands) and Wivenhoe Town moved to the Eastern Counties League. Edgware Town resigned and ceased playing at the end of the season because the council had sold their White Lion Ground for housing. Edgware though continued in membership of the Middlesex F.A. and in 2014, they resumed playing, in the Spartan South Midlands League at Silver Jubilee Park, Kingsbury.

Division One (South): Fleet Town and Godalming Town both joined from the Southern League – South & West Division, Merstham joined from the Combined Counties League and Crowborough Athletic joined from the Sussex County League. Horsham YMCA moved to the Sussex County League and Molesey moved to the Combined Counties League.

2009   Promoted to National League (South) from Premier Division: Dover Athletic, Staines Town

Relegated from National League (South) to Premier Division: Bognor Regis Town

Promoted to Premier Division from Division One (North): Aveley and Waltham Abbey

Promoted to Premier Division from Division One (South): Kingstonian and Cray Wanderers

Relegated from Premier Division to Division One (North): Harlow Town, Heybridge Swifts

Relegated from Premier Division to Division One (South): Ramsgate

Moved from Division One (North) to Division One (South): Chatham Town

Division One (North): Lowestoft Town joined from the Eastern Counties League, VCD Athletic joined from the Kent League and Romford joined from the Essex Senior League. Witham Town moved to the Essex Senior League and Hillingdon Borough moved to the Spartan South Midlands League.

Division One (South): Horsham YMCA joined from the Sussex County League and Crowborough Athletic moved to the Sussex County League.

2010   Promoted to National League (South) from Premier Division: Dartford and Boreham Wood

Promoted to Premier Division from Division One (North): Lowestoft Town, Concord Rangers

Promoted to Premier Division from Division One (South):
                                Croydon Athletic and Folkestone Invicta

Relegated from Premier Division to Division One (North): Waltham Abbey

Relegated from Premier Division to Division One (South): Bognor Regis Town

Bury Town joined the Premier Division from the Southern League – Midlands and Ashford Town (Middlesex) moved from the Premier Division to the Southern League – Central.

Division One (North): Maldon Town absorbed Tiptree United of the Essex Senior League who had been sharing Maldon's Wallace Binder Ground, to form Maldon & Tiptree. The new club continued at the Wallace Binder Ground in Division One (North).

Grays Athletic were placed in Division One (North) after finishing bottom of the National League and resigning from the competition. AFC Sudbury joined from the Southern League – Midlands and Needham Market joined from the Eastern Counties League. VCD Athletic were demoted to the Kent League because of ground-grading issues and Northwood moved to the Southern League – Central.

Division One (South): Ashford Town were banned from all competitions in 2010-11 because of an unpaid debt to another club. They later folded before being re-formed as Ashford United in 2011 when they joined the Kent Invicta League. Whitehawk joined from the Sussex County League and Faversham Town joined from the Kent League.

2011   Promoted to National League (South) from Premier Division:
                                Sutton United and Tonbridge Angels

Relegated from National League (South) to Premier Division: Lewes

Promoted to Premier Division from Division One (North):
                                East Thurrock United and Wingate & Finchley

Promoted to Premier Division from Division One (South):
                                Metropolitan Police and Leatherhead

Relegated from Premier Division to Division One (South):
                                Maidstone United, Croydon Athletic and Folkestone Invicta

Moved to Division One (North) from Division One (South): Chatham Town

Division One (North): Leyton resigned and disbanded due to financial problems on 14th January 2011 and their record (P19 W1 D6 L12 F13 A45 P9) was deleted. Soham Town Rangers joined from the Southern League – Central and Leiston joined from the Eastern Counties League.

Division One (South): Fleet Town moved to the Southern League – Central and Horsham YMCA moved to the Sussex County League. Hythe Town joined from the Kent league and Crawley Down joined from the Sussex County League.

2012   Promoted to National League (South) from Premier Division:
Billericay Town and AFC Hornchurch
Relegated from National League (South) to Premier Division:
Hampton & Richmond Borough and Thurrock
Promoted to Premier Division from Division One (North): Leiston and Enfield Town
Promoted to Premier Division from Division One (South): Whitehawk, Bognor Regis Town
Relegated from Premier Division to Division One (North): Aveley
Relegated from Premier Division to Division One (South):
Leatherhead, Tooting & Mitcham United and Horsham

Division One (North): Witham Town joined from the Essex Senior League and Wroxham joined from the Eastern Counties League. Great Wakering Rovers moved to the Essex Senior League.

Division One (South): Croydon Athletic resigned on 18th January 2012 and disbanded. They had had 10 points deducted for a series of financial irregularities and their record (P19 W3 D3 L13 F23 A44 P2) was deleted. Supporters of the club formed a new club called AFC Croydon Athletic who joined the Combined Counties League in 2012-13. Godalming Town moved to the Southern League – Central. Herne Bay joined from the Kent League and Three Bridges joined from the Sussex County League. Whyteleafe moved to the Kent League. Crawley Down changed name to Crawley Down Gatwick.

2013   Promoted to National League (South) from Premier Division: Whitehawk, Concord Rangers
Relegated from National League (South) to Premier Division:
AFC Hornchurch and Billericay Town
Promoted to Premier Division from Division One (North): Grays Athletic, Thamesmead Town
Promoted to Premier Division from Division One (South):
Dulwich Hamlet and Maidstone United
Relegated from Premier Division to Division One (North): Thurrock
Relegated from Premier Division to Division One (South): Hastings United

Division One (North): Potters Bar Town moved to the Southern League – Central and Ilford moved to the Essex Senior League. Burnham Ramblers and Barkingside both joined from the Essex Senior League, Erith & Belvedere and VCD Athletic both joined from the Kent League and Dereham Town joined from the Eastern Counties League.

Division One (South): Peacehaven & Telscombe and Redhill both joined from the Sussex County League and Guernsey joined from the Combined Counties League.

2014   Promoted to National League (South) from Premier Division: Wealdstone
Promoted to National League (North) from Premier Division: Lowestoft Town
Relegated from National League (South) to Premier Division: Tonbridge Angels
Promoted to Premier Division from Division One (North): VCD Athletic and Witham Town
Promoted to Premier Division from Division One (South):
Leatherhead and Peacehaven & Telscombe
Relegated from Premier Division to Division One (North):
Thamesmead Town and Cray Wanderers
Relegated from Premier Division to Division One (South): Carshalton Athletic

Division One (North): Great Wakering Rovers joined from the Essex Senior League and Brightlingsea Regent joined from the Eastern Counties League. Waltham Forest moved to the Essex Senior League and Erith & Belvedere moved to the Kent League.

Division One (South): Whyteleafe joined from the Southern Counties East League (formerly known as the Kent League), South Park joined from the Combined Counties League and East Grinstead Town joined from the Sussex County League. Crawley Down Gatwick and Eastbourne Town both moved to the Sussex County League.

2015   Promoted to National League (South) from Premier Division: Maidstone United and Margate
Relegated from National League (South) to Premier Division: Staines Town and Farnborough
Promoted to Premier Division from Division One (North):
Needham Market and Brentwood Town
Promoted to Premier Division from Division One (South): Merstham and Burgess Hill Town

Relegated from Premier Division to Division One (North):
Witham Town, AFC Hornchurch and Bury Town

Relegated from Premier Division to Division One (South): Peacehaven & Telscombe

Moved to Division One (South) from Division One (North): Chatham Town

Division One (North): Ware moved to the Southern League – Central and Burnham Ramblers moved to the Essex Senior League. Phoenix Sports joined from the Southern Counties East League and Haringey Borough joined from the Essex Senior League.

Division One (South): Dorking Wanderers joined from the Sussex County League and Molesey joined from the Combined Counties League. Redhill moved to the Combined Counties League and Horsham moved to the Southern Combination, which had changed name from Sussex County League.

2016   Promoted to National League (South) from Premier Division:
Hampton & Richmond Borough and East Thurrock United.

Relegated from National League (South) to Premier Division: Havant & Waterlooville

Relegated from National League (North) to Premier Division: Lowestoft Town

Promoted to Premier Division from Division One (North): Harlow Town and AFC Sudbury

Promoted to Premier Division from Division One (South): Worthing and Folkestone Invicta

Relegated from Premier Division to Division One (North): Brentwood Town and VCD Athletic

Relegated from Premier Division to Division One (South): Lewes

Farnborough moved from the Premier Division to the Southern League – Central.

Moved to Division One (South) from Division One (North): Cray Wanderers

Division One (North): Ware joined from the Southern League – Central, Bowers & Pitsea joined from the Essex Senior League and Norwich United joined from the Eastern Counties League. Barkingside and Redbridge both moved to the Essex Senior League. The division was renamed the North Division from the next season.

Division One (South): Godalming Town joined from the Southern League – Central, Greenwich Borough joined from the Southern Counties East League and Horsham joined from the Southern Combination. Walton & Hersham moved to the Combined Counties League, Whitstable Town moved to the Southern Counties East League and Peacehaven & Telscombe moved to the Southern Combination. The division was renamed the South Division from the next season.

2017   Promoted to National League (South) from Premier Division:
Havant & Waterlooville and Bognor Regis Town

Relegated from National League (South) to Premier Division: Margate

Promoted to Premier Division from Division One (North): Brightlingsea Regent and Thurrock

Promoted to Premier Division from Division One (South):
Dorking Wanderers and Tooting & Mitcham United

Relegated from Premier Division to Division One (North):
Canvey Island, Grays Athletic and AFC Sudbury

Moved to Division One (South) from Division One (North):
Phoenix Sports, VCD Athletic and Thamesmead Town

North Division: Potters Bar Town joined from the Southern League – Central, Barking joined from the Essex Senior League, Mildenhall Town joined from the Eastern Counties League and Hertford Town joined from the Spartan South Midlands League. Wroxham moved to the Eastern Counties League and Great Wakering Rovers moved to the Essex Senior League.

South Division: Chatham Town moved to the Southern Counties East League, Three Bridges moved to the Southern Combination and Godalming Town moved to the Combined Counties League. Ashford United joined from the Southern Counties East League and Shoreham joined from the Southern Combination. The division was renamed the South East Division from the next season.

2018   Promoted to National League (South) from Premier Division:
Billericay Town and Dulwich Hamlet

Relegated from National League (South) to Premier Division:
Whitehawk and Bognor Regis Town

Promoted to Premier Division from the North Division:
AFC Hornchurch, Potters Bar Town, Haringey Borough
Promoted to Premier Division from the South Division:
Carshalton Athletic, Lewes and Corinthian-Casuals
Moved from North Division to the new South Central Division:
Cheshunt, Hertford Town, Waltham Abbey and Ware
Moved from South Division to the new South Central Division:
Chipstead, Molesey and South Park

At the end of the season, there was a major reorganisation of Steps 3 and 4 of the Non-League pyramid with the creation of two new divisions. A new division at Step 3 was created after the Southern League Premier Division was split into two new divisions – the Central Division and South Division. In addition to this, the Isthmian League created the South Central Division at Step 4 to run alongside the North Division and the South Division. A large number of clubs were transferred between the various leagues operating at Step 3 and Step 4 to enable the reorganisation to take place.

Premier Division: Hendon, Staines Town, Metropolitan Police and Harrow Borough all moved to the Southern League – South Division. Leiston, Needham Market and Lowestoft Town transferred to the Southern League – Central. Tooting & Mitcham United were relegated into the new Isthmian League South Central Division and Thurrock resigned from the league at the end of the season before folding. Their Chairman had been forced to step down due to ill health and no buyer for the club was found.

Bishop's Stortford joined from the Southern League – Premier Division.

North Division: Coggeshall Town and Felixstowe & Walton United joined from the Eastern Counties League, which Norwich United joined and Basildon United and Great Wakering Rovers joined the Essex Senior League.

South East Division (formerly the South Division): Walton Casuals were promoted to the Southern League – South; Haywards Heath Town and Three Bridges joined from the Southern Combination and Sevenoaks Town and Whitstable Town joined from the Southern Counties East League.

South Central Division: This new Step 4 division comprised the following 20 teams: Cheshunt, Hertford Town, Waltham Abbey and Ware transferred from the North Division, Chipstead, Molesey and South Park transferred from the South Division and Tooting & Mitcham United joined from the Premier Division; Ashford Town, Chalfont St. Peter, Egham Town, Fleet Town, Hanwell Town, Hayes & Yeading United, Marlow, Northwood and Uxbridge all joined from the Southern League – East; Bedfont Sports and Westfield joined from the combined Counties League and Bracknell Town joined from the Hellenic League.

2019   Promoted to National League (South) from Premier Division:
Dorking Wanderers and Tonbridge Angels
Relegated from National League (South) to Premier Division: East Thurrock United
Promoted to Premier Division from the North Division: Bowers & Pitsea
Promoted to Premier Division from the South Central Division:
Hayes & Yeading United and Cheshunt
Promoted to Premier Division from the South East Division: Cray Wanderers and Horsham
Relegated from the Premier Division to the South East Division:
Burgess Hill Town and Whitehawk
Relegated from the Premier Division to the South Central Division: Harlow Town

North Division: Mildenhall Town were relegated to the Eastern Counties League from where Histon were promoted. Hullbridge Sports joined after winning promotion from the Essex Senior League. Barking transferred to the South Central Division and Cambridge City joined from the Southern Football League Division One (Central).

South Central Division: Egham Town and Molesey were relegated to the Combined Counties League from where Chertsey Town were promoted. Staines Town joined after relegation from the Southern Football League Premier Division South.

South East Division: Greenwich Borough were relegated to the Southern Counties East League from where Cray Valley Paper Mills were promoted. Chichester City won promotion from the Southern Combination League.

ISTHMIAN LEAGUE

1905-06

London Caledonians	10	7	1	2	25	8	15
Clapton	10	6	1	3	11	13	13
Casuals	10	3	4	3	14	14	10
Civil Service	10	4	1	5	16	20	9
Ealing Association	10	3	2	5	15	19	8
Ilford	10	1	3	6	5	12	5

1906-07

Ilford	10	8	2	0	26	9	18
London Caledonians	10	6	0	4	19	14	12
Clapton	10	4	3	3	18	11	11
Civil Service	10	3	1	6	11	19	7
Ealing Association	10	3	1	6	12	22	7
Casuals	10	2	1	7	15	26	5

1907-08

London Caledonians	10	5	2	3	20	15	12
Clapton	10	4	3	3	24	14	11
Ilford	10	5	1	4	28	22	11
Oxford City	10	5	1	4	20	20	11
Dulwich Hamlet	10	3	2	5	15	18	8
West Norwood	10	3	1	6	13	31	7

1908-09

Bromley	18	11	1	6	42	29	23
Leytonstone	18	9	4	5	43	31	22
Ilford	18	9	4	5	37	36	22
Dulwich Hamlet	18	9	2	7	39	30	20
Clapton	18	8	4	6	34	32	20
Oxford City	18	6	4	8	29	32	16
Nunhead	18	7	2	9	31	35	16
Shepherd's Bush	18	6	3	9	26	44	15
London Caledonians	18	4	6	8	25	34	14
West Norwood	18	5	2	11	40	43	12

1909-10

Bromley	18	11	4	3	32	10	26
Clapton	18	10	4	4	56	19	24
Nunhead	18	10	4	4	49	26	24
Ilford	18	10	3	5	31	17	23
Dulwich Hamlet	18	8	4	6	26	26	20
Leytonstone	18	7	3	8	44	46	17
Oxford City	18	5	4	9	28	45	14
London Caledonians	18	5	3	10	19	40	13
West Norwood	18	5	2	11	28	54	12
Shepherd's Bush	18	2	3	13	23	55	7

1910-11

Clapton	18	11	4	3	39	19	26
Leytonstone	18	12	1	5	47	30	25
Dulwich Hamlet	18	8	5	5	28	22	21
Oxford City	18	7	4	7	32	43	18
Ilford	18	8	1	9	41	32	17
Shepherd's Bush	18	7	3	8	31	27	17
Bromley	18	8	4	6	32	27	16
Nunhead	18	5	4	9	32	36	14
West Norwood	18	4	5	9	24	43	13
London Caledonians	18	3	3	12	18	45	9
Bromley had 4 points deducted							

1911-12

London Caledonians	20	11	7	2	39	25	29
Ilford	20	11	3	6	37	24	25
Nunhead	20	10	5	5	36	30	25
Dulwich Hamlet	20	8	5	7	33	23	21
West Norwood	20	9	3	8	38	38	21
Clapton	20	7	5	8	37	37	19
Woking	20	7	5	8	38	41	19
Shepherd's Bush	20	5	6	9	39	49	16
Leytonstone	20	5	6	9	28	38	16
Oxford City	20	5	5	10	33	36	15
Tunbridge Wells	20	5	4	11	23	40	14

1912-13

London Caledonians	20	14	5	1	38	12	33
Leytonstone	20	12	3	5	45	20	27
Nunhead	20	12	3	5	36	23	27
Clapton	20	7	7	6	23	20	21
Dulwich Hamlet	20	8	4	8	34	28	20
Woking	20	7	5	8	33	40	19
Oxford City	20	6	6	8	23	39	18
Ilford	20	6	5	9	27	37	17
Shepherd's Bush	20	5	5	10	26	38	15
Tunbridge Wells	20	5	4	11	22	36	14
West Norwood	20	3	3	14	23	37	9

1913-14

London Caledonians	20	12	6	2	55	23	30
Nunhead	20	11	6	3	49	27	28
Ilford	20	11	4	5	52	35	26
Dulwich Hamlet	20	10	4	6	34	22	24
New Crusaders	20	10	3	7	40	30	23
Oxford City	20	10	0	10	42	42	20
Leytonstone	20	8	4	8	29	32	20
Clapton	20	8	3	9	29	27	19
Shepherd's Bush	20	7	2	11	24	46	16
West Norwood	20	4	3	13	27	47	11
Woking	20	1	1	18	11	61	3

1919

Leytonstone	8	5	1	2	21	7	11
Ilford	8	4	2	2	22	16	10
Dulwich Hamlet	8	3	2	3	19	17	8
Nunhead	8	3	2	3	18	19	8
Clapton	8	0	3	5	14	35	3

1919-20

Dulwich Hamlet	22	15	3	4	58	16	33
Nunhead	22	14	5	3	48	26	33
Tufnell Park	22	12	4	6	45	32	28
Ilford	22	13	1	8	63	42	27
Oxford City	22	12	3	7	63	51	27
London Caledonians	22	10	3	9	32	30	23
Leytonstone	22	8	3	11	50	43	19
Clapton	22	8	3	11	38	44	19
Civil Service	22	7	4	11	35	40	18
Woking	22	6	3	13	36	42	15
West Norwood	22	5	4	13	19	53	14
Casuals	22	3	2	17	20	88	8

1920-21

Ilford	22	16	4	2	70	24	36
London Caledonians	22	13	5	4	45	17	31
Tufnell Park	22	14	3	5	43	24	31
Nunhead	22	12	5	5	53	33	29
Dulwich Hamlet	22	11	6	5	60	30	28
Oxford City	22	12	3	7	56	38	27
Leytonstone	22	8	6	8	36	29	22
Clapton	22	7	7	8	33	52	21
Civil Service	22	3	7	12	28	45	13
Woking	22	3	5	14	16	43	11
Casuals	22	3	3	16	31	87	9
West Norwood	22	2	2	18	18	67	6

1921-22

Ilford	26	17	4	5	66	34	38
Dulwich Hamlet	26	14	8	4	65	24	36
London Caledonians	26	16	4	6	41	21	36
Nunhead	26	12	5	9	65	41	29
Clapton	26	13	3	10	51	46	29
Tufnell Park	26	10	7	9	44	39	27
Oxford City	26	18	2	12	48	47	26
Wycombe Wanderers	26	18	2	12	61	64	26
Civil Service	26	9	8	9	60	48	26
Woking	26	10	6	10	39	49	26
Leytonstone	26	9	6	11	41	48	24
West Norwood	26	8	5	13	43	57	21
Wimbledon	26	7	4	15	52	56	18
Casuals	26	0	2	24	25	107	2

1922-23

Clapton	26	15	7	4	51	33	37
Nunhead	26	15	5	6	52	32	35
London Caledonians	26	13	7	6	43	26	33
Ilford	26	11	7	8	57	38	29
Casuals	26	12	5	9	68	51	29
Civil Service	26	9	10	7	39	36	28
Wycombe Wanderers	26	11	4	11	61	61	26
Dulwich Hamlet	26	9	7	10	60	44	25
Leytonstone	26	9	7	10	45	56	25
Tufnell Park	26	9	5	12	41	45	23
Wimbledon	26	10	2	14	49	50	22
Woking	26	7	6	13	42	67	20
Oxford City	26	6	5	15	45	68	17
West Norwood	26	5	5	16	25	71	15

1923-24

St Albans City	26	17	5	4	72	38	39
Dulwich Hamlet	26	15	6	5	49	28	36
Clapton	26	14	5	7	73	50	33
Wycombe Wanderers	26	14	5	7	88	65	33
London Caledonians	26	14	3	9	53	49	31
Civil Service	26	12	5	9	52	47	29
Casuals	26	13	1	12	65	54	27
Ilford	26	9	6	11	56	59	24
Nunhead	26	8	8	10	41	46	24
Wimbledon	26	8	4	14	43	62	20
Tufnell Park	26	8	2	16	38	53	18
Woking	26	5	8	13	31	62	18
Oxford City	26	7	2	17	53	74	16
Leytonstone	26	6	4	16	41	68	16

1924-25

London Caledonians	26	18	5	3	76	36	41
Clapton	26	19	1	6	64	34	39
St Albans City	26	16	2	8	69	39	34
Tufnell Park	26	11	4	11	47	41	26
Ilford	26	11	4	11	46	42	26
Leytonstone	26	12	2	12	55	63	26
The Casuals	26	12	1	13	55	58	25
Wycombe Wanderers	26	11	2	13	58	61	24
Civil Service	26	10	4	12	52	64	24
Nunhead	26	9	5	12	45	43	23
Wimbledon	26	10	2	14	50	54	22
Dulwich Hamlet	26	8	5	13	42	57	21
Oxford City	26	9	2	15	38	71	20
Woking	26	5	3	18	33	67	13

1925-26

Dulwich Hamlet	26	20	1	5	80	49	41
London Caledonians	26	18	1	7	81	44	37
Clapton	26	14	4	8	64	50	32
Wycombe Wanderers	26	14	3	9	97	83	31
St Albans City	26	12	6	8	76	54	30
Nunhead	26	13	4	9	49	43	30
Ilford	26	13	2	11	81	70	28
Leytonstone	26	12	1	13	75	63	25
Woking	26	8	6	12	56	73	22
Tufnell Park	26	8	5	13	36	53	21
The Casuals	26	8	4	14	48	61	20
Wimbledon	26	9	1	16	61	77	19
Oxford City	26	8	1	17	48	76	17
Civil Service	26	5	1	20	43	99	11

1926-27

St Albans City	26	20	1	5	96	34	41
Ilford	26	18	0	9	76	57	34
Wimbledon	26	15	3	8	72	45	33
Nunhead	26	11	8	7	51	33	30
Woking	26	12	6	8	68	60	30
London Caledonians	26	11	7	8	58	47	29
Clapton	26	11	4	11	58	60	26
Leytonstone	26	11	1	14	54	78	23
Dulwich Hamlet	26	9	4	13	60	58	22
Wycombe Wanderers	26	10	2	14	59	86	22
Tufnell Park	26	8	4	14	45	55	20
Oxford City	26	7	5	14	46	72	19
The Casuals	26	8	3	15	37	78	19
Civil Service	26	6	4	16	48	65	16

1927-28

St Albans City	26	15	5	6	86	50	35
London Caledonians	26	12	9	5	63	38	33
Ilford	26	14	4	8	72	54	32
Woking	26	13	5	8	72	56	31
Nunhead	26	13	2	11	57	54	28
Wimbledon	26	12	3	11	57	48	27
Leytonstone	26	13	1	12	53	56	27
Clapton	26	8	10	8	52	47	26
Dulwich Hamlet	26	8	9	9	56	49	25
The Casuals	26	8	8	10	54	58	24
Wycombe Wanderers	26	9	5	12	60	69	23
Oxford City	26	7	7	12	36	57	21
Civil Service	26	8	4	14	38	76	20
Tufnell Park	26	4	4	18	38	82	12

1928-29

Nunhead	26	15	6	5	47	35	36
London Caledonians	26	15	4	7	65	33	34
Dulwich Hamlet	26	14	6	6	65	34	34
Wimbledon	26	9	10	7	66	54	28
Ilford	26	12	3	11	67	52	27
Clapton	26	11	5	10	60	55	27
Tufnell Park	26	11	5	10	58	55	27
St Albans City	26	12	3	11	63	69	27
Leytonstone	26	11	3	12	56	79	25
Wycombe Wanderers	26	10	3	13	58	60	23
Oxford City	26	10	3	13	61	71	23
The Casuals	26	8	5	13	49	60	21
Woking	26	8	3	15	39	65	19
Civil Service	26	4	5	17	39	71	13

1929-30

Nunhead	26	19	3	4	69	36	41
Dulwich Hamlet	26	15	6	5	74	39	36
Kingstonian	26	15	4	7	57	37	34
Ilford	26	16	1	9	84	60	33
Woking	26	11	5	10	66	65	27
Wimbledon	26	11	2	13	64	66	24
Wycombe Wanderers	26	10	4	12	49	52	24
The Casuals	26	8	7	11	50	51	23
Oxford City	26	10	3	13	45	60	23
St Albans City	26	9	4	13	54	77	22
Clapton	26	8	4	14	47	57	20
London Caledonians	26	8	3	15	49	69	19
Leytonstone	26	8	3	15	48	68	19
Tufnell Park	26	6	7	13	35	54	19

1930-31

Wimbledon	26	18	6	2	69	37	42
Dulwich Hamlet	26	12	9	5	51	39	33
Wycombe Wanderers	26	12	6	8	67	45	30
The Casuals	26	12	6	8	71	56	30
St Albans City	26	11	7	8	67	66	29
Ilford	26	10	6	10	70	62	26
Oxford City	26	10	5	11	43	48	25
London Caledonians	26	8	8	10	43	53	24
Kingstonian	26	10	4	12	49	64	24
Tufnell Park	26	9	5	12	45	61	23
Nunhead	26	9	4	13	49	54	22
Woking	26	9	4	13	56	63	22
Clapton	26	7	4	15	62	75	18
Leytonstone	26	6	4	16	46	65	16

1931-32

Wimbledon	26	17	2	7	60	35	36
Ilford	26	13	9	4	71	45	35
Dulwich Hamlet	26	15	3	8	69	43	33
Wycombe Wanderers	26	14	5	7	72	50	33
Oxford City	26	15	2	9	63	49	32
Kingstonian	26	13	3	10	71	50	29
Tufnell Park	26	9	7	10	50	48	25
Nunhead	26	9	7	10	54	61	25
The Casuals	26	10	4	12	59	65	24
Clapton	26	9	5	12	50	57	23
Leytonstone	26	9	3	14	36	61	21
St Albans City	26	8	4	14	57	78	20
Woking	26	6	5	15	44	64	17
London Caledonians	26	2	7	17	24	74	11

1932-33

Dulwich Hamlet	26	15	6	5	71	45	36
Leytonstone	26	16	4	6	66	43	36
Kingstonian	26	15	2	9	77	49	32
Ilford	26	14	0	12	60	58	28
The Casuals	26	12	2	12	48	36	26
Tufnell Park	26	11	3	12	51	51	25
St Albans City	26	12	1	13	57	63	25
Clapton	26	10	5	11	51	65	25
Oxford City	26	9	6	11	49	54	24
Woking	26	10	4	12	53	61	24
Wycombe Wanderers	26	10	4	12	47	56	24
Nunhead	26	8	6	12	42	50	22
Wimbledon	26	8	5	13	55	67	21
London Caledonians	26	5	6	15	35	64	16

1933-34

Kingstonian	26	15	7	4	80	42	37
Dulwich Hamlet	26	15	5	6	68	36	35
Wimbledon	26	13	7	6	62	35	33
Tufnell Park	26	14	5	7	55	50	33
Ilford	26	15	2	9	60	56	32
The Casuals	26	13	5	8	47	32	31
Leytonstone	26	13	3	10	55	48	29
Nunhead	26	10	5	11	48	44	25
London Caledonians	26	7	8	11	29	51	22
Wycombe Wanderers	26	9	2	15	57	60	20
St Albans City	26	8	4	14	44	75	20
Oxford City	26	7	4	15	45	57	18
Clapton	26	5	6	15	35	62	16
Woking	26	6	1	19	43	81	13

1934-35

Wimbledon	26	14	7	5	63	30	35
Oxford City	26	14	4	8	69	50	32
Leytonstone	26	15	2	9	49	36	32
Dulwich Hamlet	26	11	7	8	66	45	29
Tufnell Park	26	11	7	8	53	44	29
Kingstonian	26	11	6	9	44	40	28
Nunhead	26	10	7	9	35	34	27
London Caledonians	26	9	7	10	40	41	25
St Albans City	26	9	6	11	61	80	24
Ilford	26	9	6	11	40	56	24
Clapton	26	7	7	12	46	48	21
Woking	26	9	3	14	44	68	21
Wycombe Wanderers	26	7	6	13	51	69	20
The Casuals	26	6	5	15	37	57	17

1935-36

Wimbledon	26	19	2	5	82	29	40
The Casuals	26	14	5	7	60	45	33
Ilford	26	13	3	10	67	47	29
Dulwich Hamlet	26	10	8	8	64	47	28
Nunhead	26	11	6	9	51	40	28
Wycombe Wanderers	26	13	2	11	60	68	28
Clapton	26	11	5	10	42	46	27
Oxford City	26	11	4	11	60	58	26
St Albans City	26	11	2	13	59	64	24
Woking	26	9	4	13	43	62	22
Tufnell Park	26	9	3	14	42	61	21
London Caledonians	26	9	3	14	35	52	21
Kingstonian	26	9	2	15	43	56	20
Leytonstone	26	7	3	16	34	67	17

1936-37

Kingstonian	26	18	3	5	63	43	39
Nunhead	26	17	3	6	77	32	37
Leytonstone	26	16	4	6	71	42	36
Ilford	26	14	5	7	86	39	33
Dulwich Hamlet	26	12	6	8	64	48	30
Wycombe Wanderers	26	10	5	11	55	52	25
Wimbledon	26	9	7	10	52	53	25
Clapton	26	10	5	11	42	51	25
The Casuals	26	10	3	13	46	58	23
Woking	26	9	4	13	53	69	22
Oxford City	26	8	5	13	56	89	21
St Albans City	26	7	5	14	44	62	19
Tufnell Park	26	4	7	15	43	74	15
London Caledonians	26	5	4	17	26	66	14

1937-38

Leytonstone	26	17	6	3	72	34	40
Ilford	26	17	3	6	70	39	37
Tufnell Park	26	15	2	9	62	47	32
Nunhead	26	14	3	9	52	44	31
Wycombe Wanderers	26	12	5	9	69	55	29
Dulwich Hamlet	26	13	3	10	57	46	29
Kingstonian	26	12	4	10	51	48	28
Clapton	26	9	6	11	49	53	24
Wimbledon	26	10	3	13	62	49	23
London Caledonians	26	9	4	13	44	55	22
Oxford City	26	7	7	12	35	71	21
The Casuals	26	8	3	15	51	74	19
Woking	26	7	2	17	41	72	16
St Albans City	26	4	5	17	31	60	13

1938-39

Leytonstone	26	18	4	4	68	32	40
Ilford	26	17	4	5	68	32	38
Kingstonian	26	17	3	6	62	39	37
Dulwich Hamlet	26	15	5	6	60	32	35
Wimbledon	26	14	3	9	88	56	31
Nunhead	26	11	6	9	54	44	28
The Casuals	26	11	6	9	54	51	28
Clapton	26	12	2	12	69	61	26
Wycombe Wanderers	26	10	6	10	62	62	26
St Albans City	26	8	5	13	44	50	21
Woking	26	9	2	15	35	56	20
Oxford City	26	4	4	18	44	84	12
Tufnell Park	26	4	4	18	33	87	12
London Caledonians	26	3	4	19	26	81	10

1945-46

Walthamstow Avenue	26	21	0	5	100	31	42
Oxford City	26	17	6	3	91	40	40
Romford	26	15	3	8	83	59	33
Dulwich Hamlet	26	14	2	10	63	59	30
Tufnell Park	26	12	4	10	70	55	28
Woking	26	10	7	9	56	54	27
Ilford	26	12	2	12	56	71	26
Leytonstone	26	11	3	12	61	75	25
Wycombe Wanderers	26	9	3	14	80	88	21
Wimbledon	26	7	6	13	52	72	20
Corinthian Casuals	26	8	4	14	58	83	20
Clapton	26	8	3	15	51	62	19
St Albans City	26	6	6	14	48	85	18
Kingstonian	26	6	3	17	48	86	15

1946-47

Leytonstone	26	19	2	5	92	36	40
Dulwich Hamlet	26	17	3	6	78	46	37
Romford	26	13	8	5	76	52	34
Walthamstow Avenue	26	13	4	9	64	37	30
Oxford City	26	12	6	8	70	51	30
Kingstonian	26	12	4	10	54	57	28
Wycombe Wanderers	26	9	8	9	62	62	26
Wimbledon	26	10	5	11	68	64	25
Ilford	26	7	7	12	66	78	21
Tufnell Park	26	8	5	13	45	69	21
Woking	26	7	7	12	34	62	21
Clapton	26	6	8	12	41	59	20
St Albans City	26	7	5	14	47	79	19
Corinthian Casuals	26	4	4	18	36	80	12

1947-48

Leytonstone	26	19	1	6	87	38	39
Kingstonian	26	16	6	4	74	39	38
Walthamstow Avenue	26	17	3	6	61	37	37
Dulwich Hamlet	26	17	2	7	71	39	36
Wimbledon	26	13	6	7	66	40	32
Romford	26	14	1	11	53	47	29
Oxford City	26	10	5	11	50	68	25
Woking	26	10	3	13	63	55	23
Ilford	26	7	8	11	51	59	22
St Albans City	26	9	2	15	43	56	20
Wycombe Wanderers	26	7	5	14	51	65	19
Tufnell Park	26	7	4	15	38	83	18
Clapton	26	5	4	17	35	69	14
Corinthian Casuals	26	5	2	19	33	81	12

1948-49

Dulwich Hamlet	26	15	6	5	60	31	36
Walthamstow Avenue	26	16	4	6	65	38	36
Wimbledon	26	15	4	7	64	41	34
Ilford	26	14	3	9	56	36	31
Oxford City	26	13	5	8	48	34	31
Leytonstone	26	12	6	8	49	41	30
Woking	26	14	1	11	64	59	29
Romford	26	11	3	12	47	54	25
Kingstonian	26	10	4	12	43	47	24
Corinthian Casuals	26	11	2	13	47	59	24
Wycombe Wanderers	26	11	2	13	49	61	24
St Albans City	26	6	6	14	40	60	16
Clapton	26	5	5	16	32	61	15
Tufnell Park	26	1	5	20	28	70	7

St Albans City had 2 points deducted

1949-50

Leytonstone	26	17	5	4	77	31	39
Wimbledon	26	18	2	6	72	51	38
Kingstonian	26	16	3	7	59	39	35
Walthamstow Avenue	26	14	6	6	73	42	34
Dulwich Hamlet	26	14	3	9	60	47	31
St Albans City	26	12	3	11	59	45	27
Woking	26	10	6	10	60	71	26
Wycombe Wanderers	26	9	7	10	51	52	25
Romford	26	10	4	12	45	49	24
Ilford	26	10	4	12	46	53	24
Clapton	26	8	6	12	51	59	22
Oxford City	26	6	6	14	35	54	18
Corinthian Casuals	26	4	5	17	41	69	13
Tufnell Park	26	3	2	21	24	91	8

1950-51

Leytonstone	26	20	3	3	72	26	43
Walthamstow Avenue	26	15	4	7	57	37	34
Romford	26	15	3	8	58	49	33
Wimbledon	26	13	5	8	58	39	31
Dulwich Hamlet	26	14	2	10	54	43	30
Woking	26	11	6	9	65	55	28
Ilford	26	12	4	10	44	45	28
Corinthian Casuals	26	13	0	13	62	60	26
St Albans City	26	11	4	11	32	36	26
Kingstonian	26	9	4	13	46	54	22
Wycombe Wanderers	26	8	3	15	46	64	19
Oxford City	26	7	4	15	47	65	18
Clapton	26	6	5	15	29	50	17
Tufnell Park Edmonton	26	4	1	21	24	73	9

1951-52

Leytonstone	26	13	9	4	63	36	35
Wimbledon	26	16	3	7	65	44	35
Walthamstow Avenue	26	15	4	7	71	43	34
Romford	26	14	4	8	64	42	32
Kingstonian	26	11	7	8	62	48	29
Wycombe Wanderers	26	12	5	9	64	59	29
Woking	26	11	5	10	60	71	27
Dulwich Hamlet	26	11	4	11	60	53	26
Corinthian Casuals	26	11	4	11	55	66	26
St Albans City	26	9	7	10	48	53	25
Ilford	26	8	5	13	32	47	21
Clapton	26	9	2	15	50	59	20
Oxford City	26	6	3	17	50	72	15
Tufnell Park Edmonton	26	2	6	18	25	73	10

1952-53

Walthamstow Avenue	28	19	6	3	53	25	44
Bromley	28	17	4	7	71	35	38
Leytonstone	28	14	6	8	60	38	34
Wimbledon	28	14	5	9	68	37	33
Kingstonian	28	13	6	9	62	50	32
Dulwich Hamlet	28	15	2	11	62	52	32
Romford	28	12	8	8	62	52	32
Wycombe Wanderers	28	14	2	12	54	62	30
St Albans City	28	11	6	11	43	57	28
Barking	28	9	7	12	42	51	25
Ilford	28	10	4	14	59	57	24
Woking	28	10	4	14	57	72	24
Corinthian Casuals	28	7	9	12	45	56	23
Oxford City	28	5	2	21	37	87	12
Clapton	28	2	5	21	27	71	9

1953-54

Bromley	28	18	3	7	76	45	39
Walthamstow Avenue	28	13	7	8	55	30	33
Wycombe Wanderers	28	15	3	10	65	44	33
Ilford	28	11	10	7	48	44	32
Corinthian Casuals	28	12	7	9	59	44	31
Woking	28	13	4	11	54	58	30
Leytonstone	28	12	5	11	58	48	29
St Albans City	28	11	6	11	54	55	28
Dulwich Hamlet	28	11	6	11	55	57	28
Romford	28	11	5	12	57	54	27
Clapton	28	11	5	12	42	56	27
Barking	28	11	2	15	59	84	24
Kingstonian	28	8	7	13	59	71	23
Wimbledon	28	7	8	13	43	59	22
Oxford City	28	4	6	18	49	84	14

1954-55

Walthamstow Avenue	28	21	1	6	80	38	43
St Albans City	28	18	3	7	61	41	39
Bromley	28	18	2	8	66	34	38
Wycombe Wanderers	28	16	3	9	68	43	35
Ilford	28	13	5	10	64	46	31
Barking	28	15	1	12	55	51	31
Woking	28	12	3	13	75	79	27
Kingstonian	28	10	7	11	47	57	27
Leytonstone	28	10	4	14	35	51	24
Oxford City	28	10	3	15	43	74	23
Clapton	28	9	4	15	41	50	22
Wimbledon	28	10	2	16	48	62	22
Corinthian Casuals	28	9	3	16	50	65	21
Dulwich Hamlet	28	7	5	16	48	60	19
Romford	28	4	10	14	43	73	18

1955-56

Wycombe Wanderers	28	19	5	4	82	36	43
Bromley	28	12	7	9	54	43	31
Leytonstone	28	12	7	9	50	44	31
Woking	28	14	3	11	62	60	31
Barking	28	12	7	9	41	45	31
Kingstonian	28	12	6	10	67	64	30
Walthamstow Avenue	28	13	3	12	61	45	29
Ilford	28	10	8	10	44	52	28
Oxford City	28	10	7	11	48	55	27
Clapton	28	9	8	11	45	48	26
Wimbledon	28	12	2	14	51	62	26
Corinthian Casuals	28	9	7	12	56	56	25
Dulwich Hamlet	28	9	6	13	55	67	24
Romford	28	9	6	13	42	55	24
St Albans City	28	2	10	16	36	62	14

1956-57

Wycombe Wanderers	30	18	6	6	86	53	42
Woking	30	20	1	9	104	47	41
Bromley	30	16	5	9	78	60	37
Oxford City	30	16	3	11	65	57	35
Ilford	30	12	8	10	59	65	32
Tooting & Mitcham United	30	10	11	9	53	48	31
Kingstonian	30	11	9	10	72	77	31
Walthamstow Avenue	30	11	8	11	48	46	30
Dulwich Hamlet	30	13	3	14	65	54	29
St Albans City	30	13	3	14	62	71	29
Leytonstone	30	11	6	13	50	50	28
Clapton	30	9	9	12	48	59	27
Wimbledon	30	10	5	15	47	66	25
Romford	30	10	5	15	53	81	25
Barking	30	7	6	17	48	72	20
Corinthian Casuals	30	7	4	19	46	78	18

1957-58

Tooting & Mitcham United	30	20	6	4	79	33	46
Wycombe Wanderers	30	19	4	7	78	42	42
Walthamstow Avenue	30	17	5	8	63	35	39
Bromley	30	13	9	8	66	51	35
Oxford City	30	13	6	11	59	48	32
Leytonstone	30	13	6	11	49	48	32
Wimbledon	30	15	2	13	64	66	32
Corinthian Casuals	30	12	8	10	62	68	32
Woking	30	12	7	11	70	58	31
Barking	30	10	6	14	49	61	26
St Albans City	30	11	3	16	56	76	25
Clapton	30	8	9	13	42	65	25
Kingstonian	30	7	8	15	45	66	22
Dulwich Hamlet	30	7	7	16	49	64	21
Ilford	30	8	4	18	46	70	20
Romford	30	6	8	16	45	71	20

1958-59

Wimbledon	30	22	3	5	91	38	47
Dulwich Hamlet	30	18	5	7	68	44	41
Wycombe Wanderers	30	18	4	8	93	50	40
Oxford City	30	17	4	9	87	58	38
Walthamstow Avenue	30	16	5	9	59	40	37
Tooting & Mitcham United	30	15	4	11	84	55	34
Barking	30	14	2	14	59	53	30
Woking	30	12	6	12	66	66	30
Bromley	30	11	7	12	56	55	29
Clapton	30	10	6	14	55	67	26
Ilford	30	10	6	14	46	67	26
Kingstonian	30	9	4	17	54	72	22
St Albans City	30	8	6	16	53	89	22
Leytonstone	30	7	6	17	40	87	20
Romford	30	7	5	18	54	76	19
Corinthian Casuals	30	7	5	18	44	92	19

1959-60

Tooting & Mitcham United	30	17	8	5	75	43	42
Wycombe Wanderers	30	19	3	8	84	46	41
Wimbledon	30	18	3	9	66	36	39
Kingstonian	30	18	3	9	76	51	39
Corinthian Casuals	30	18	1	11	69	61	37
Bromley	30	15	6	9	75	46	36
Dulwich Hamlet	30	14	6	10	65	47	34
Walthamstow Avenue	30	11	11	8	48	38	33
Oxford City	30	10	10	10	57	57	30
Leytonstone	30	10	8	12	43	46	28
Woking	30	10	6	14	54	61	26
St Albans City	30	10	6	14	50	65	26
Maidstone United	30	10	5	15	53	60	25
Barking	30	7	4	19	30	75	18
Ilford	30	5	6	19	34	86	16
Clapton	30	3	4	23	32	92	10

1960-61

Bromley	30	20	6	4	89	42	46
Walthamstow Avenue	30	20	5	5	87	38	45
Wimbledon	30	18	6	6	72	43	42
Dulwich Hamlet	30	17	4	9	71	59	35
Maidstone United	30	14	8	8	63	39	36
Leytonstone	30	15	6	9	46	34	36
Tooting & Mitcham United	30	14	3	13	69	51	31
Wycombe Wanderers	30	12	5	13	63	61	29
St Albans City	30	12	4	14	45	72	28
Oxford City	30	10	7	13	59	59	27
Corinthian Casuals	30	9	9	12	49	59	27
Kingstonian	30	10	6	14	55	61	26
Woking	30	10	6	14	58	71	26
Ilford	30	5	8	17	30	69	18
Barking	30	3	8	19	30	76	14
Clapton	30	3	5	22	25	77	11

1961-62

Wimbledon	30	19	6	5	68	24	44
Leytonstone	30	17	7	6	61	44	41
Walthamstow Avenue	30	14	8	8	51	31	36
Kingstonian	30	15	5	10	65	48	35
Tooting & Mitcham United	30	12	10	8	62	47	34
Oxford City	30	12	9	9	56	49	33
Wycombe Wanderers	30	12	7	11	57	51	31
Corinthian Casuals	30	12	7	11	45	51	31
St Albans City	30	10	9	11	55	55	29
Woking	30	9	9	12	51	60	27
Dulwich Hamlet	30	11	4	15	55	66	26
Barking	30	9	8	13	40	64	26
Ilford	30	7	10	13	59	59	24
Bromley	30	10	4	16	49	69	24
Clapton	30	6	8	16	45	67	20
Maidstone United	30	6	7	17	34	59	19

1962-63

Wimbledon	30	19	8	3	84	33	46
Kingstonian	30	18	8	4	79	37	44
Tooting & Mitcham United	30	17	8	5	65	37	42
Ilford	30	19	3	8	70	44	41
Walthamstow Avenue	30	14	7	9	51	44	35
Maidstone United	30	13	8	9	56	45	34
Bromley	30	12	10	8	57	51	34
Leytonstone	30	12	7	11	48	50	31
Wycombe Wanderers	30	10	10	10	56	61	30
St Albans City	30	11	5	14	54	49	27
Barking	30	8	10	12	39	50	26
Oxford City	30	8	9	13	55	64	25
Woking	30	8	6	16	42	66	22
Clapton	30	7	4	19	30	71	18
Dulwich Hamlet	30	4	5	21	30	71	13
Corinthian Casuals	30	4	4	22	28	71	12

1963-64

Wimbledon	38	27	6	5	87	44	60
Hendon	38	25	4	9	124	38	54
Kingstonian	38	24	4	10	100	62	52
Sutton United	38	23	5	10	99	64	51
Enfield	38	20	10	8	96	56	50
Oxford City	38	20	8	10	90	55	48
Tooting & Mitcham United	38	19	8	11	78	51	46
St Albans City	38	14	12	12	62	63	40
Ilford	38	16	8	14	75	79	40
Maidstone United	38	15	8	15	65	71	38
Walthamstow Avenue	38	15	6	17	70	66	36
Leytonstone	38	14	8	16	66	71	36
Wycombe Wanderers	38	13	6	19	74	80	32
Hitchin Town	38	14	4	20	67	100	32
Bromley	38	11	8	19	64	75	30
Barking	38	10	9	19	46	69	29
Woking	38	10	9	19	48	88	29
Corinthian Casuals	38	10	4	24	52	92	24
Dulwich Hamlet	38	6	12	20	47	97	24
Clapton	38	2	5	31	31	120	9

1964-65

Hendon	38	28	7	3	123	49	63
Enfield	38	29	5	4	98	35	63
Kingstonian	38	24	8	6	86	44	56
Leytonstone	38	24	5	9	115	62	53
Oxford City	38	20	7	11	76	51	47
St Albans City	38	18	9	11	63	43	45
Sutton United	38	17	11	10	74	57	45
Wealdstone	38	19	6	13	93	68	44
Bromley	38	14	11	13	71	80	39
Tooting & Mitcham United	38	15	7	16	71	66	37
Hitchin Town	38	13	9	16	61	66	35
Walthamstow Avenue	38	15	5	18	63	82	35
Wycombe Wanderers	38	13	7	18	70	85	33
Corinthian Casuals	38	13	7	18	56	77	33
Barking	38	10	8	20	58	80	28
Ilford	38	8	8	22	43	89	24
Maidstone United	38	8	6	24	49	86	22
Dulwich Hamlet	38	8	5	25	45	79	21
Clapton	38	8	3	27	43	91	19
Woking	38	7	4	27	45	113	18

Hendon beat Enfield in a play-off to decide the Championship

1965-66

Leytonstone	38	27	7	4	98	33	63
Hendon	38	27	5	6	111	55	59
Enfield	38	24	8	6	104	54	56
Wycombe Wanderers	38	25	6	7	100	65	56
Kingstonian	38	24	5	9	94	55	53
Wealdstone	38	20	6	12	90	64	46
Maidstone United	38	19	6	13	74	61	44
St Albans City	38	19	5	14	57	56	43
Sutton United	38	17	7	14	83	72	41
Tooting & Mitcham United	38	16	7	15	65	58	39
Corinthian Casuals	38	17	5	16	74	67	39
Woking	38	12	10	16	60	83	34
Walthamstow Avenue	38	12	9	17	81	75	33
Oxford City	38	10	9	19	49	72	29
Barking	38	10	7	21	51	72	27
Bromley	38	10	5	23	69	101	25
Ilford	38	7	10	21	50	84	24
Hitchin Town	38	6	8	24	57	118	20
Clapton	38	5	6	27	46	103	16
Dulwich Hamlet	38	5	5	28	30	95	15

1966-67

Sutton United	38	26	7	5	89	33	59
Walthamstow Avenue	38	22	12	4	89	47	56
Wycombe Wanderers	38	23	8	7	92	54	54
Enfield	38	25	2	11	87	33	52
Hendon	38	20	9	9	64	37	49
Tooting & Mitcham United	38	19	10	9	76	60	48
Leytonstone	38	19	9	10	67	38	47
St Albans City	38	16	12	10	59	45	44
Kingstonian	38	18	8	12	60	49	44
Oxford City	38	15	9	14	74	61	39
Woking	38	13	10	15	65	71	36
Wealdstone	38	13	8	17	72	73	34
Barking	38	11	12	15	56	61	34
Bromley	38	12	7	19	50	67	31
Clapton	38	10	8	20	49	92	28
Ilford	38	8	10	20	43	77	26
Corinthian Casuals	38	9	7	22	45	68	25
Maidstone United	38	6	10	22	43	90	22
Hitchin Town	38	8	6	24	39	89	22
Dulwich Hamlet	38	3	4	31	33	107	10

1967-68

Enfield	38	28	8	2	85	22	64
Sutton United	38	22	11	5	89	27	55
Hendon	38	23	6	9	90	36	52
Leytonstone	38	21	10	7	78	41	52
St Albans City	38	20	8	10	78	41	48
Walthamstow Avenue	38	19	9	10	81	64	47
Wealdstone	38	19	8	11	80	45	46
Tooting & Mitcham United	38	19	5	14	57	45	43
Barking	38	17	8	13	75	57	42
Oxford City	38	17	4	17	59	58	38
Kingstonian	38	14	10	14	56	61	38
Hitchin Town	38	14	9	15	61	73	37
Bromley	38	12	10	16	58	80	34
Wycombe Wanderers	38	13	5	20	73	85	31
Dulwich Hamlet	38	10	7	21	39	66	27
Clapton	38	10	7	21	51	88	27
Woking	38	8	8	22	50	90	24
Corinthian Casuals	38	7	10	21	40	80	24
Ilford	38	7	7	24	41	77	21
Maidstone United	38	3	4	31	26	131	10

1968-69

Enfield	38	27	7	4	103	28	61
Hitchin Town	38	23	10	5	67	41	56
Sutton United	38	22	9	7	83	29	53
Wycombe Wanderers	38	23	6	9	70	37	52
Wealdstone	38	20	11	7	73	48	51
Hendon	38	22	5	11	69	47	49
St Albans City	38	17	13	8	75	44	47
Barking	38	20	7	11	69	46	47
Oxford City	38	18	8	12	76	64	44
Tooting & Mitcham United	38	16	10	12	68	55	42
Leytonstone	38	18	4	16	71	53	40
Kingstonian	38	15	8	15	62	56	38
Walthamstow Avenue	38	10	10	18	47	71	30
Maidstone United	38	10	8	20	47	75	28
Clapton	38	10	7	21	52	76	27
Woking	38	8	7	23	45	77	23
Bromley	38	8	7	23	52	95	23
Dulwich Hamlet	38	6	9	23	31	77	21
Ilford	38	6	8	24	33	77	20
Corinthian Casuals	38	2	4	32	23	120	8

1969-70

Enfield	38	27	8	3	91	26	62
Wycombe Wanderers	38	25	11	2	85	24	61
Sutton United	38	24	9	5	75	35	57
Barking	38	21	9	8	93	47	51
Hendon	38	19	12	7	77	44	50
St Albans City	38	21	8	9	69	40	50
Hitchin Town	38	19	10	9	71	40	48
Tooting & Mitcham United	38	19	5	14	88	62	43
Leytonstone	38	17	7	14	57	41	41
Wealdstone	38	15	10	13	53	48	40
Oxford City	38	15	7	16	61	78	37
Kingstonian	38	13	9	16	55	57	35
Ilford	38	8	15	15	42	73	31
Dulwich Hamlet	38	8	12	18	46	66	28
Woking	38	10	7	21	46	69	27
Walthamstow Avenue	38	11	5	22	52	81	27
Clapton	38	9	7	22	45	87	25
Maidstone United	38	7	8	23	48	84	22
Corinthian Casuals	38	6	3	29	30	99	15
Bromley	38	3	4	31	28	111	10

1970-71

Wycombe Wanderers	38	28	6	4	93	32	62
Sutton United	38	29	3	6	76	35	61
St Albans City	38	23	10	5	87	26	56
Enfield	38	24	7	7	67	24	55
Ilford	38	21	7	10	74	51	49
Hendon	38	18	11	9	81	37	47
Barking	38	20	4	14	89	59	44
Leytonstone	38	17	10	11	68	50	44
Woking	38	18	6	14	57	50	42
Walthamstow Avenue	38	14	11	13	63	52	39
Oxford City	38	13	10	15	51	48	36
Hitchin Town	38	12	9	17	46	60	33
Wealdstone	38	12	8	18	45	64	32
Tooting & Mitcham United	38	11	9	18	44	66	31
Kingstonian	38	11	8	19	53	71	30
Bromley	38	10	6	22	34	77	26
Dulwich Hamlet	38	7	10	21	30	66	24
Maidstone United	38	7	6	25	42	84	20
Clapton	38	5	7	26	33	101	17
Corinthian Casuals	38	2	8	28	23	103	12

1971-72

Wycombe Wanderers	40	31	3	6	102	20	65
Enfield	40	26	8	6	90	41	60
Walton & Hersham	40	24	8	8	69	25	56
Hendon	40	23	10	7	79	35	56
Bishop's Stortford	40	24	5	11	61	37	53
Sutton United	40	21	10	9	77	43	52
St Albans City	40	23	4	13	74	47	50
Ilford	40	17	11	12	62	52	45
Barking	40	20	4	16	65	61	44
Hitchin Town	40	17	10	13	68	66	44
Bromley	40	16	10	14	67	64	42
Hayes	40	14	12	14	50	48	40
Oxford City	40	13	9	18	67	74	35
Woking	40	11	10	19	52	58	32
Kingstonian	40	10	12	18	49	59	32
Walthamstow Avenue	40	12	8	20	58	71	32
Leytonstone	40	11	8	21	48	68	30
Tooting & Mitcham United	40	6	9	25	38	93	21
Clapton	40	7	7	26	45	118	21
Dulwich Hamlet	40	4	12	24	35	81	20
Corinthian Casuals	40	3	4	33	21	116	10

1972-73

Hendon	42	34	6	2	88	18	74
Walton & Hersham	42	25	11	6	60	25	61
Leatherhead	42	23	10	9	76	32	56
Wycombe Wanderers	42	25	6	11	66	32	56
Walthamstow Avenue	42	20	12	10	66	48	52
Tooting & Mitcham United	42	20	11	11	73	39	51
Sutton United	42	21	9	12	69	48	51
Kingstonian	42	20	10	12	60	49	50
Enfield	42	20	8	14	90	54	48
Bishop's Stortford	42	18	12	12	58	51	48
Hayes	42	19	8	15	69	42	46
Dulwich Hamlet	42	18	9	15	59	52	45
Ilford	42	18	9	15	61	59	45
Leytonstone	42	17	11	14	55	54	45
Woking	42	18	8	16	61	56	44
Hitchin Town	42	15	9	18	52	64	39
Barking	42	8	7	27	45	88	23
St Albans City	42	5	12	25	34	76	22
Oxford City	42	6	7	29	30	101	19
Bromley	42	4	10	28	31	70	18
Clapton	42	3	11	28	31	100	17
Corinthian Casuals	42	3	8	31	30	106	14

1973-74   First Division

Wycombe Wanderers	42	27	9	6	96	34	90
Hendon	42	25	13	4	63	20	88
Bishop's Stortford	42	26	9	7	78	26	87
Dulwich Hamlet	42	22	11	9	71	38	77
Leatherhead	42	23	6	13	81	44	75
Walton & Hersham	42	20	12	10	68	50	72
Woking	42	22	6	14	63	55	72
Leytonstone	42	20	9	13	63	44	69
Ilford	42	20	8	14	60	44	68
Hayes	42	17	14	11	65	43	65
Oxford City	42	15	16	11	45	47	61
Sutton United	42	13	16	13	51	52	55
Hitchin Town	42	15	10	17	68	73	55
Barking	42	14	12	16	57	58	54
Kingstonian	42	12	15	15	47	46	51
Tooting & Mitcham United	42	14	9	19	57	62	51
Enfield	42	13	11	18	50	57	50
Walthamstow Avenue	42	11	13	18	46	62	46
Bromley	42	7	9	26	37	81	30
Clapton	42	8	3	31	36	128	27
St Albans City	42	4	7	31	30	92	19
Corinthian Casuals	42	3	4	35	31	107	13

Second Division

Dagenham	30	22	4	4	68	23	70
Slough Town	30	18	6	6	46	23	60
Hertford Town	30	17	5	8	46	29	56
Chesham Town	30	16	6	8	61	43	54
Aveley	30	16	5	9	50	28	53
Tilbury	30	14	5	11	47	36	47
Maidenhead United	30	12	11	7	36	30	47
Horsham	30	12	9	9	47	35	45
Harwich & Parkeston	30	11	9	10	46	41	42
Staines Town	30	10	8	12	34	41	38
Carshalton Athletic	30	8	8	14	34	51	32
Hampton	30	6	10	14	33	51	28
Harlow Town	30	6	9	15	33	48	27
Finchley	30	6	7	17	29	52	25
Southall	30	3	10	17	17	52	19
Wokingham Town	30	3	8	19	30	74	17

1974-75

First Division

Wycombe Wanderers	42	28	11	3	93	30	95
Enfield	42	29	8	5	78	26	95
Dagenham	42	28	5	9	95	44	89
Tooting & Mitcham United	42	25	9	8	78	46	84
Dulwich Hamlet	42	24	10	8	75	38	82
Leatherhead	42	23	10	9	83	42	79
Ilford	42	23	10	9	98	51	79
Oxford City	42	17	9	16	63	56	60
Slough Town	42	17	6	19	68	52	57
Sutton United	42	17	6	19	68	63	57
Bishop's Stortford	42	17	6	19	56	64	57
Hitchin Town	42	15	10	17	57	71	55
Hendon	42	15	7	20	59	74	52
Walthamstow Avenue	42	13	9	20	56	62	48
Woking	42	12	10	20	53	73	46
Hayes	42	10	14	18	52	66	44
Barking	42	12	8	22	57	81	44
Leytonstone	42	12	7	23	42	61	43
Kingstonian	42	13	4	25	48	73	43
Clapton	42	12	4	26	46	96	40
Walton & Hersham	42	9	4	29	37	108	31
Bromley	42	6	3	33	25	110	21

Second Division

Staines Town	34	23	2	9	65	23	71
Southall	34	20	3	11	55	41	63
Tilbury	34	19	5	10	64	36	60
Harwich & Parkeston	34	18	4	12	52	44	58
Chesham United	34	17	6	11	59	39	57
St Albans City	34	15	11	8	42	37	56
Harlow Town	34	16	6	12	53	47	54
Horsham	34	16	5	13	59	49	53
Maidenhead United	34	13	7	14	38	40	46
Hampton	34	12	7	15	44	42	43
Croydon	34	11	10	13	48	55	43
Hertford Town	34	10	7	17	35	52	37
Boreham Wood	34	7	15	12	41	49	36
Wokingham Town	34	10	6	18	32	43	36
Finchley	34	9	9	16	36	53	36
Carshalton Athletic	34	9	9	16	38	46	36
Aveley	34	9	7	18	34	63	34
Corinthian Casuals	34	8	9	17	35	59	33

Tilbury had 2 points deducted

1975-76 First Division

Team	P	W	D	L	F	A	Pts
Enfield	42	26	9	7	83	38	87
Wycombe Wanderers	42	24	10	8	71	41	82
Dagenham	42	25	6	11	89	55	81
Ilford	42	22	10	10	58	39	76
Dulwich Hamlet	42	22	5	15	67	41	71
Hendon	42	20	11	11	60	41	71
Tooting & Mitcham United	42	19	11	12	73	49	68
Leatherhead	42	19	10	13	63	53	67
Staines Town	42	19	9	14	46	37	66
Slough Town	42	17	12	13	58	45	63
Sutton United	42	17	11	14	71	60	62
Bishop's Stortford	42	15	12	15	51	47	57
Walthamstow Avenue	42	14	11	17	47	60	53
Woking	42	14	9	19	58	62	51
Barking	42	15	6	21	57	70	51
Hitchin Town	42	13	11	18	45	57	50
Hayes	42	10	19	13	44	48	49
Kingstonian	42	13	8	21	53	87	47
Southall & Ealing Borough	42	11	9	22	56	69	42
Leytonstone	42	10	10	22	41	63	40
Oxford City	42	9	8	25	29	65	35
Clapton	42	3	3	36	19	112	12

Second Division

Team	P	W	D	L	F	A	Pts
Tilbury	42	32	6	4	97	30	102
Croydon	42	28	14	0	81	27	98
Carshalton Athletic	42	28	6	8	75	37	90
Chesham United	42	21	12	9	91	51	75
Harwich & Parkeston	42	21	11	10	78	56	74
Hampton	42	21	9	12	72	52	72
St Albans City	42	18	12	12	59	48	66
Boreham Wood	42	17	12	13	68	50	63
Harrow Borough	42	15	12	15	71	74	57
Hornchurch	42	15	11	16	61	61	56
Horsham	42	14	13	15	60	55	55
Wembley	42	14	13	15	51	54	55
Wokingham Town	42	13	16	13	45	52	55
Walton & Hersham	42	14	12	16	61	56	54
Finchley	42	14	11	17	52	53	53
Bromley	42	11	11	20	64	86	44
Aveley	42	11	9	22	34	51	42
Harlow Town	42	11	9	22	50	73	42
Maidenhead United	42	6	17	19	32	65	35
Ware	42	7	12	23	50	95	33
Hertford Town	42	5	9	28	32	87	24
Corinthian Casuals	42	4	7	31	42	113	19

1976-77 First Division

Team	P	W	D	L	F	A	Pts
Enfield	42	24	12	6	63	34	84
Wycombe Wanderers	42	25	8	9	71	34	83
Dagenham	42	23	10	9	80	39	79
Hendon	42	19	10	13	60	48	67
Tilbury	42	18	13	11	57	49	67
Tooting & Mitcham	42	18	10	14	85	72	64
Walthamstow Avenue	42	19	7	16	61	55	64
Slough Town	42	18	9	15	51	46	63
Hitchin Town	42	19	6	17	60	66	63
Leatherhead	42	18	7	17	61	47	61
Staines Town	42	16	13	13	52	48	61
Leytonstone	42	16	11	15	59	57	59
Barking	42	16	9	17	63	61	57
Southall & Ealing Borough	42	15	8	19	52	64	53
Croydon	42	13	10	19	38	52	49
Sutton United	42	14	7	21	40	55	49
Kingstonian	42	13	7	22	45	60	46
Hayes	42	12	10	20	49	69	46
Woking	42	11	12	19	47	61	45
Bishop's Stortford	42	11	11	20	51	71	44
Dulwich Hamlet	42	11	8	23	52	68	41
Ilford	42	10	8	24	32	73	38

Second Division

Team	P	W	D	L	F	A	Pts
Boreham Wood	42	35	4	5	80	26	103
Carshalton Athletic	42	25	12	5	80	33	87
Harwich & Parkeston	42	23	8	11	93	61	77
Wembley	42	23	8	11	82	58	77
Harrow Borough	42	21	12	9	78	44	75
Horsham	42	23	5	14	67	56	74
Bromley	42	20	10	12	71	46	70
Oxford City	42	20	8	14	73	55	68
Hampton	42	20	8	14	62	45	68
Wokingham Town	42	16	14	12	60	44	62
Hornchurch	42	18	7	17	62	53	61
Chesham United	42	17	10	15	63	66	61
St Albans City	42	16	12	14	59	53	60
Walton & Hersham	42	17	9	16	57	56	60
Aveley	42	14	8	20	49	62	50
Corinthian Casuals	42	13	6	23	52	75	45
Harlow Town	42	11	8	23	39	77	41
Hertford Town	42	9	9	24	45	80	36
Maidenhead United	42	8	8	26	36	73	32
Clapton	42	7	9	28	43	87	30
Finchley	42	5	13	24	36	82	28
Ware	42	5	8	29	43	98	23

1977-78 Premier Division

Team	P	W	D	L	F	A	Pts
Enfield	42	35	5	2	96	27	110
Dagenham	42	24	7	11	78	55	79
Wycombe Wanderers	42	22	9	11	66	41	75
Tooting & Mitcham United	42	22	8	12	64	49	74
Hitchin Town	42	20	9	13	69	53	69
Sutton United	42	18	12	12	66	57	66
Leatherhead	42	18	11	13	62	48	65
Croydon	42	18	10	14	61	52	64
Walthamstow Avenue	42	17	12	13	64	61	63
Barking	42	17	7	18	76	66	58
Carshalton Athletic	42	15	11	16	60	62	56
Hayes	42	15	11	16	46	53	56
Hendon	42	16	7	19	57	55	55
Woking	42	14	11	17	62	62	53
Boreham Wood	42	15	8	19	48	65	53
Slough Town	42	14	8	20	52	69	0
Staines Town	42	12	13	17	46	60	49
Tilbury	42	11	12	19	57	68	45
Kingstonian	42	8	13	21	43	65	37
Leytonstone	42	7	15	20	44	71	36
Southall & Ealing Borough	42	6	15	21	43	74	33
Bishop's Stortford	42	7	8	27	36	83	29

First Division

Team	P	W	D	L	F	A	Pts
Dulwich Hamlet	42	28	9	5	91	25	93
Oxford City	42	26	5	11	85	44	83
Bromley	42	23	13	6	74	41	82
Walton & Hersham	42	22	11	9	69	41	77
Ilford	42	21	14	7	57	47	77
St Albans City	42	22	10	10	83	46	76
Wokingham Town	42	19	12	11	69	48	69
Harlow Town	42	19	8	15	63	49	65
Harrow Borough	42	17	10	15	59	54	61
Maidenhead United	42	16	13	13	55	54	61
Hertford Town	42	15	14	13	57	51	59
Chesham United	42	14	13	15	69	70	55
Hampton	42	13	13	16	49	53	52
Harwich & Parkeston	42	12	13	17	68	79	49
Wembley	42	15	3	24	56	82	48
Horsham	42	12	10	20	41	57	46
Finchley	42	11	13	18	41	68	46
Aveley	42	13	7	22	47	75	46
Ware	42	8	13	21	61	95	37
Clapton	42	10	6	26	46	78	36
Hornchurch	42	8	10	24	47	81	34
Corinthian Casuals	42	3	10	29	40	88	19

Second Division

Epsom & Ewell	32	21	5	6	65	34	68
Metropolitan Police	32	19	6	7	53	30	63
Farnborough Town	32	19	4	9	68	40	61
Molesey	32	17	8	7	47	27	59
Egham Town	32	15	9	8	52	34	54
Tring Town	32	14	11	7	62	32	53
Letchworth Garden City	32	14	11	7	67	48	53
Lewes	32	13	7	12	52	51	46
Rainham Town	32	13	6	13	42	50	45
Worthing	32	11	9	12	40	45	42
Eastbourne United	32	10	8	14	40	50	38
Cheshunt	32	9	6	17	43	60	33
Feltham	32	7	9	16	30	49	30
Camberley Town	32	6	11	15	32	49	29
Hemel Hempstead	32	6	9	17	33	50	27
Epping Town	32	7	6	19	37	64	27
Willesden	32	7	3	22	38	88	24

Second Division

Farnborough Town	34	26	3	5	77	34	81
Camberley Town	34	21	8	5	71	32	71
Molesey	34	19	11	4	55	33	68
Lewes	34	19	6	9	66	50	63
Feltham	34	16	7	11	47	36	55
Letchworth Garden City	34	14	10	10	56	48	52
Eastbourne United	34	16	4	14	47	45	52
Hemel Hempstead	34	13	11	10	46	37	50
Epping Town	34	14	7	13	49	44	49
Rainham Town	34	13	10	11	42	41	49
Cheshunt	34	11	8	15	43	49	41
Hungerford Town	34	11	8	15	48	58	41
Worthing	34	9	8	17	40	50	35
Hornchurch	34	9	8	17	39	62	35
Egham Town	34	7	12	15	48	54	33
Tring Town	34	6	8	20	33	56	26
Willesden	34	6	8	20	41	77	26
Corinthian Casuals	34	4	7	23	23	65	19

1978-79

Premier Division

Barking	42	28	9	5	92	50	93
Dagenham	42	25	6	11	83	63	81
Enfield	42	22	11	9	69	37	77
Dulwich Hamlet	42	21	13	8	69	39	76
Slough Town	42	20	12	10	61	44	72
Wycombe Wanderers	42	20	9	13	59	44	69
Woking	42	18	14	10	79	59	68
Croydon	42	19	9	14	61	51	66
Hendon	42	16	14	12	55	48	62
Leatherhead	42	17	9	16	57	45	60
Sutton United	42	17	9	16	62	51	60
Tooting & Mitcham United	42	15	14	13	52	52	59
Walthamstow Avenue	42	15	6	21	61	69	51
Tilbury	42	13	1	18	60	76	50
Boreham Wood	42	13	10	19	50	67	49
Hitchin Town	42	12	11	19	59	71	47
Carshalton Athletic	42	10	16	16	49	69	46
Hayes	42	9	18	15	45	58	45
Oxford City	42	12	7	23	50	80	43
Staines Town	42	6	16	20	40	64	34
Leytonstone	42	8	7	27	36	75	31
Kingstonian	42	3	15	24	35	72	24

1979-80

Premier Division

Enfield	42	25	9	8	74	32	84
Walthamstow Avenue	42	24	9	9	87	48	81
Dulwich Hamlet	42	21	16	5	66	37	79
Sutton United	42	20	13	9	67	40	73
Dagenham	42	20	13	9	82	56	73
Tooting & Mitcham United	42	21	6	15	62	59	69
Barking	42	19	10	13	72	51	67
Harrow Borough	42	17	15	10	64	51	66
Woking	42	17	13	12	78	59	64
Wycombe Wanderers	42	17	13	12	53	53	64
Harlow Town	42	14	12	16	55	61	54
Hitchin Town	42	13	15	14	55	69	54
Hendon	42	12	13	17	50	57	49
Slough Town	42	13	10	19	54	71	49
Boreham Wood	42	13	10	19	50	69	49
Staines Town	42	14	6	22	46	67	48
Hayes	42	12	9	21	48	68	45
Leatherhead	42	11	11	20	51	60	44
Carshalton Athletic	42	12	7	23	48	78	43
Croydon	42	10	10	22	51	59	40
Oxford City	42	10	9	23	49	87	39
Tilbury	42	7	11	24	41	90	30

Tilbury had 2 points deducted

First Division

Harlow Town	42	31	7	4	93	32	100
Harrow Borough	42	26	8	8	85	49	86
Maidenhead United	42	25	6	11	72	50	81
Bishop's Stortford	42	22	11	9	68	40	77
Horsham	42	23	7	12	63	47	76
Hertford Town	42	21	11	10	62	41	74
Harwich & Parkeston	42	22	5	15	90	57	71
Bromley	42	18	12	12	76	50	66
Hampton	42	17	11	14	59	47	62
Epsom & Ewell	42	18	7	17	69	57	61
Wembley	42	15	14	13	57	50	59
Aveley	42	17	6	19	57	67	57
Wokingham Town	42	17	8	17	64	68	56
Clapton	42	15	8	19	67	80	53
Metropolitan Police	42	12	13	17	58	55	49
Walton & Hersham	42	12	9	21	47	71	45
Ilford	42	13	5	24	48	80	44
Ware	42	11	10	21	46	69	43
Chesham United	42	11	9	22	46	66	42
Finchley	42	7	15	20	43	74	36
St Albans City	42	7	7	28	43	90	28
Southall & Ealing Borough	42	5	5	32	41	114	20

Wokingham Town had 3 points deducted

First Division

Leytonstone & Ilford	42	31	6	5	83	35	99
Bromley	42	24	10	8	93	44	82
Maidenhead United	42	24	8	10	81	46	80
Bishop's Stortford	42	24	8	10	74	47	80
Kingstonian	42	22	8	12	59	44	74
Chesham United	42	18	13	11	68	56	67
St Albans City	42	17	13	12	65	47	64
Farnborough Town	42	19	7	16	70	57	64
Epsom & Ewell	42	18	7	17	62	57	61
Camberley Town	42	16	10	16	43	38	58
Walton & Hersham	42	15	12	15	61	50	57
Wembley	42	16	8	18	46	52	56
Wokingham Town	42	14	11	17	45	49	53
Hertford Town	42	13	11	18	71	74	50
Aveley	42	12	13	17	45	55	49
Hampton	42	14	7	21	57	74	49
Finchley	42	13	9	20	44	59	48
Metropolitan Police	42	13	8	21	46	67	47
Ware	42	11	12	19	45	61	45
Clapton	42	14	3	25	48	77	45
Harwich & Parkeston	42	11	6	25	51	84	38
Horsham	42	6	4	32	29	113	22

Harwich & Parkeston had 1 point deducted

Second Division

Billericay Town	36	31	3	2	100	18	96
Lewes	36	24	7	5	82	33	79
Hungerford Town	36	21	8	7	78	36	71
Eastbourne United	36	21	6	9	77	45	69
Letchworth Garden City	36	21	6	9	63	32	69
Hornchurch	36	21	6	9	66	39	69
Molesey	36	15	9	12	67	60	54
Barton Rovers	36	15	7	14	49	49	52
Worthing	36	14	9	13	58	54	51
Cheshunt	36	13	7	16	47	52	46
Rainham Town	36	12	7	17	54	65	43
Egham Town	36	11	9	16	47	53	42
Southall & Ealing Borough	36	11	6	19	43	69	39
Feltham	36	8	11	17	23	49	35
Tring Town	36	7	13	16	38	55	34
Epping Town	36	10	4	22	44	69	34
Willesden	36	9	6	21	32	83	33
Hemel Hempstead	36	4	9	23	33	72	21
Corinthian Casuals	36	6	3	27	24	92	21

Second Division

Feltham	38	24	10	4	65	30	82
Hornchurch	38	25	6	7	74	35	81
Hungerford Town	38	23	10	5	84	29	79
Barton Rovers	38	19	11	8	61	25	68
Worthing	38	19	11	8	74	43	68
Cheshunt	38	19	11	8	57	33	68
Letchworth Garden City	38	18	7	13	49	40	61
Southall	38	14	11	13	48	52	53
Dorking Town	38	13	12	13	47	45	51
Horsham	38	16	3	19	47	47	51
Hemel Hempstead	38	14	7	17	47	54	49
Egham Town	38	13	9	16	45	62	48
Harwich & Parkeston	38	12	11	15	57	58	47
Rainham Town	38	11	13	14	44	45	46
Epping Town	38	12	7	19	37	50	43
Eastbourne United	38	11	10	17	59	75	43
Willesden	38	11	8	19	57	68	41
Tring Town	38	11	6	21	40	71	39
Molesey	38	4	9	25	31	83	21
Corinthian Casuals	38	1	8	29	17	95	11

1980-81 Premier Division

Slough Town	42	23	13	6	73	34	82
Enfield	42	23	11	8	81	43	80
Wycombe Wanderers	42	22	9	11	76	49	75
Leytonstone & Ilford	42	19	12	11	78	57	69
Sutton United	42	19	12	11	82	65	69
Hendon	42	18	10	14	66	58	64
Dagenham	42	17	11	14	79	66	62
Hayes	42	18	8	16	45	50	62
Harrow Borough	42	16	11	15	57	52	59
Bromley	42	16	9	17	63	69	57
Staines Town	42	15	9	18	60	61	54
Tooting & Mitcham United	42	15	8	19	49	53	53
Hitchin Town	42	14	10	18	64	62	52
Croydon	42	12	15	15	51	51	51
Dulwich Hamlet	42	13	12	17	62	67	51
Leatherhead	42	12	14	16	36	50	50
Carshalton Athletic	42	14	8	20	57	82	50
Barking	42	13	12	17	58	72	49
Harlow Town	42	11	15	16	53	66	48
Walthamstow Avenue	42	13	7	22	50	81	46
Boreham Wood	42	10	13	19	46	69	43
Woking	42	11	7	24	40	69	37

Barking had 1 point deducted
Woking had 3 points deducted

First Division

Bishop's Stortford	42	30	6	6	84	28	96
Billericay Town	42	29	6	7	67	34	93
Epsom & Ewell	42	24	12	6	80	36	84
Farnborough Town	42	23	11	8	75	39	80
St Albans City	42	24	5	13	85	61	77
Kingstonian	42	20	9	13	63	52	66
Oxford City	42	18	9	15	71	48	63
Wokingham Town	42	16	15	11	70	56	63
Metropolitan Police	42	18	7	17	61	58	61
Chesham United	42	17	7	18	64	64	58
Lewes	42	17	7	18	72	83	58
Maidenhead United	42	16	7	19	58	62	55
Walton & Hersham	42	12	15	15	46	53	51
Hertford Town	42	13	11	18	46	65	50
Hampton	42	12	13	17	46	53	49
Aveley	42	13	9	20	54	55	48
Wembley	42	13	8	21	47	61	47
Clapton	42	12	8	22	53	86	44
Ware	42	9	13	20	50	69	40
Tilbury	42	10	8	24	42	84	35
Camberley Town	42	8	7	27	42	88	31
Finchley	42	6	11	25	36	77	29

Kingstonian and Tilbury both had 3 points deducted

1981-82

Premier Division

Leytonstone & Ilford	42	26	5	11	91	52	83
Sutton United	42	22	9	11	72	49	75
Wycombe Wanderers	42	21	10	11	63	48	73
Staines Town	42	21	9	12	58	45	72
Walthamstow Avenue	42	21	7	14	81	62	70
Harrow Borough	42	18	13	11	77	55	67
Tooting & Mitcham United	42	19	10	13	58	47	67
Slough Town	42	17	13	12	64	54	64
Leatherhead	42	16	12	14	57	52	60
Hayes	42	16	10	16	58	52	58
Croydon	42	16	9	17	59	57	57
Barking	42	14	14	14	53	51	56
Hendon	42	13	13	16	56	65	52
Dulwich Hamlet	42	14	10	18	47	59	52
Bishop's Stortford	42	15	5	22	50	70	50
Carshalton Athletic	42	14	8	20	58	86	50
Billericay Town	42	11	16	15	41	50	49
Hitchin Town	42	12	11	19	56	77	47
Bromley	42	13	7	22	63	79	46
Woking	42	11	13	18	57	75	46
Harlow Town	42	10	11	21	50	73	41
Boreham Wood	42	8	13	21	47	58	37

First Division

Wokingham Town	40	29	5	6	86	30	92
Bognor Regis Town	40	23	10	7	65	34	79
Metropolitan Police	40	22	11	7	75	48	77
Oxford City	40	21	11	8	82	47	74
Feltham	40	20	8	12	65	49	68
Lewes	40	19	7	14	73	66	64
Hertford Town	40	16	10	14	62	54	58
Wembley	40	14	15	11	69	55	57
Farnborough Town	40	15	11	14	71	57	56
Epsom & Ewell	40	16	8	16	52	44	56
Kingstonian	40	16	7	17	57	56	55
Hampton	40	15	9	16	52	52	54
Hornchurch	40	13	15	12	42	50	54
Aveley	40	14	10	16	46	58	52
St Albans City	40	14	9	17	55	55	51
Maidenhead United	40	11	10	19	49	70	43
Tilbury	40	9	15	16	49	66	42
Walton & Hersham	40	10	11	19	43	65	41
Chesham United	40	9	9	22	41	71	36
Clapton	40	9	7	24	44	75	34
Ware	40	5	2	33	29	105	17

Second Division

Worthing	40	29	6	5	95	25	93
Cheshunt	40	25	7	8	79	33	82
Hungerford Town	40	22	10	8	89	42	74
Barton Rovers	40	22	8	10	65	32	74
Windsor & Eton	40	22	6	12	69	49	72
Corinthian Casuals	40	19	12	9	67	50	69
Harwich & Parkeston	40	19	12	9	64	47	69
Letchworth Garden City	40	15	11	14	67	55	56
Dorking Town	40	13	17	10	52	44	56
Hemel Hempstead	40	15	9	16	54	49	54
Basildon United	40	16	5	19	64	51	53
Finchley	40	14	9	17	57	68	51
Southall	40	12	14	14	36	42	50
Epping Town	40	12	11	17	48	62	47
Molesey	40	13	7	20	61	73	46
Egham Town	40	11	9	20	56	64	42
Rainham Town	40	11	9	20	53	83	42
Tring Town	40	9	13	18	49	78	40
Eastbourne United	40	9	12	19	51	73	39
Horsham	40	10	9	21	42	79	39
Camberley Town	40	3	2	35	21	140	11

Hungerford Town had 2 points deducted

Second Division

Clapton	42	30	4	8	96	46	94
Windsor & Eton	42	27	7	8	98	43	88
Barton Rovers	42	26	6	10	86	48	84
Leyton Wingate	42	25	8	9	111	41	83
Basildon United	42	23	13	6	92	42	82
Uxbridge	42	22	12	8	80	42	78
Hungerford Town	42	22	10	10	82	39	76
Corinthian Casuals	42	23	6	13	95	48	75
Egham Town	42	21	8	13	77	67	71
Tring Town	42	20	10	12	86	59	70
Letchworth Garden City	42	18	13	11	68	53	66
Southall	42	18	7	17	81	80	61
Molesey	42	17	9	16	73	56	60
Dorking Town	42	15	9	18	56	75	54
Hemel Hempstead	42	12	14	16	53	59	50
Rainham Town	42	14	4	24	57	94	46
Eastbourne United	42	10	6	26	54	104	36
Epping Town	42	6	8	28	29	89	26
Ware	42	6	6	30	34	97	24
Finchley	42	4	12	26	28	92	24
Horsham	42	5	7	30	32	106	22
Harwich & Parkeston	42	5	7	30	42	130	22

Letchworth Garden City had 1 point deducted

1982-83 Premier Division

Wycombe Wanderers	42	26	7	9	79	47	85
Leytonstone & Ilford	42	24	9	9	71	39	81
Harrow Borough	42	24	7	11	91	58	79
Hayes	42	23	9	10	63	41	78
Sutton United	42	20	8	14	96	71	68
Dulwich Hamlet	42	18	14	10	59	52	68
Slough Town	42	18	13	11	73	36	67
Bognor Regis Town	42	19	8	15	53	48	65
Tooting & Mitcham United	42	18	9	15	65	62	63
Billericay Town	42	17	10	15	54	51	61
Croydon	42	17	9	16	68	58	60
Hendon	42	18	6	18	68	61	60
Bishop's Stortford	42	17	9	16	61	58	60
Barking	42	14	14	14	47	55	56
Bromley	42	14	12	16	51	50	54
Carshalton Athletic	42	15	9	18	58	60	54
Wokingham Town	42	13	9	20	37	51	48
Walthamstow Avenue	42	12	11	19	48	64	47
Staines Town	42	12	11	19	62	79	47
Hitchin Town	42	11	9	22	49	77	42
Woking	42	6	6	30	30	79	24
Leatherhead	42	4	5	33	35	121	17

First Division

Worthing	40	25	6	9	76	39	81
Harlow Town	40	21	11	8	84	55	74
Farnborough Town	40	20	13	7	69	39	73
Hertford Town	40	20	11	9	70	61	71
Oxford City	40	19	13	8	70	49	70
Boreham Wood	40	21	6	13	62	42	69
Metropolitan Police	40	19	9	12	77	57	66
Walton & Hersham	40	17	6	17	65	59	57
Hampton	40	15	10	15	62	60	55
Wembley	40	14	10	16	62	61	52
Aveley	40	15	7	18	52	62	52
Kingstonian	40	13	12	15	53	53	51
Tilbury	40	12	10	18	41	47	46
Feltham	40	11	12	17	45	54	45
Chesham United	40	13	6	21	43	70	45
Epsom & Ewell	40	10	14	16	44	49	44
Lewes	40	12	8	20	47	71	44
Cheshunt	40	10	13	17	41	49	43
Hornchurch	40	11	8	21	45	74	41
Maidenhead United	40	10	10	20	57	87	40
St Albans City	40	10	9	21	52	79	37

St Albans City had 2 points deducted

1983-84 Premier Division

Harrow Borough	42	25	13	4	73	42	88
Worthing	42	20	11	11	89	72	71
Slough Town	42	20	9	13	73	56	69
Sutton United	42	18	12	12	67	45	66
Hayes	42	17	13	12	56	41	64
Hitchin Town	42	16	15	11	58	57	63
Wycombe Wanderers	42	16	14	12	63	52	62
Wokingham Town	42	18	10	14	78	55	61
Hendon	42	17	10	15	62	51	61
Dulwich Hamlet	42	16	11	15	61	64	59
Bishop's Stortford	42	15	13	14	56	52	58
Harlow Town	42	15	11	16	64	70	56
Bognor Regis Town	42	14	13	15	62	69	55
Staines Town	42	15	9	18	63	72	54
Billericay Town	42	15	8	19	53	73	53
Barking	42	13	13	16	60	64	52
Croydon	42	14	10	18	52	58	52
Walthamstow Avenue	42	13	10	19	53	67	49
Leytonstone & Ilford	42	13	9	20	54	67	48
Carshalton Athletic	42	11	10	21	59	72	43
Tooting & Mitcham United	42	10	13	19	50	63	43
Bromley	42	7	11	24	33	72	32

Wokingham Town had 3 points deducted

First Division

Windsor & Eton	42	26	7	9	89	44	85
Epsom & Ewell	42	23	9	10	73	51	78
Wembley	42	21	11	10	65	32	74
Maidenhead United	42	22	8	12	67	42	74
Boreham Wood	42	22	7	13	74	43	73
Farnborough Town	42	18	12	12	78	60	66
Hampton	42	18	12	12	65	49	66
Metropolitan Police	42	20	5	17	79	64	65
Chesham United	42	18	8	16	64	57	62
Tilbury	42	17	10	15	54	64	61
Leatherhead	42	15	10	17	67	56	55
Aveley	42	15	10	17	49	53	55
Woking	42	16	7	19	66	73	55
Hertford Town	42	15	9	18	56	73	54
Oxford City	42	14	9	19	57	56	51
Lewes	42	13	12	17	49	65	51
Walton & Hersham	42	13	10	19	52	70	49
Hornchurch	42	13	10	19	43	63	49
Kingstonian	42	13	9	20	47	67	48
Clapton	42	12	11	19	49	67	47
Cheshunt	42	12	8	22	45	64	44
Feltham	42	7	4	31	31	106	25

Second Division

Basildon United	42	30	7	5	88	27	97
St Albans City	42	29	9	5	100	46	96
Leyton Wingate	42	29	4	9	97	41	91
Tring Town	42	23	11	8	89	44	80
Corinthian Casuals	42	23	11	8	75	47	80
Hungerford Town	42	21	12	9	94	47	75
Uxbridge	42	18	15	9	61	36	69
Grays Athletic	42	20	9	13	72	57	69
Dorking	42	21	5	16	66	54	68
Southall	42	20	8	14	79	60	65
Egham Town	42	16	15	11	59	49	63
Epping Town	42	15	16	11	61	50	61
Molesey	42	13	14	15	59	68	53
Barton Rovers	42	15	8	19	54	64	53
Letchworth Garden City	42	15	7	20	48	66	52
Newbury Town	42	14	5	23	60	82	47
Hemel Hempstead	42	12	9	21	63	69	45
Rainham Town	42	7	5	30	38	114	26
Finchley	42	5	9	28	28	78	24
Eastbourne United	42	7	3	32	36	98	24
Ware	42	6	6	30	48	114	24
Horsham	42	7	4	31	40	104	23

Southall had 2 points deducted
Horsham had 3 points deducted

1984-85

Premier Division

Sutton United	42	23	15	4	115	55	84
Worthing	42	24	8	10	89	59	80
Wycombe Wanderers	42	24	6	12	68	46	78
Wokingham Town	42	20	13	9	74	54	73
Windsor & Eton	42	19	10	13	65	55	67
Bognor Regis Town	42	20	6	16	67	58	66
Dulwich Hamlet	42	16	17	9	82	57	65
Harrow Borough	42	18	8	16	70	56	62
Hayes	42	17	8	17	60	56	59
Tooting & Mitcham United	42	16	11	15	64	66	59
Walthamstow Avenue	42	15	11	16	64	65	56
Croydon	42	15	12	15	62	63	54
Epsom & Ewell	42	13	14	15	65	62	53
Slough Town	42	13	12	17	69	74	51
Carshalton Athletic	42	14	8	20	55	68	50
Bishop's Stortford	42	12	12	18	48	67	48
Hendon	42	9	19	14	62	65	46
Billericay Town	42	11	14	17	53	74	46
Barking	42	13	7	22	43	75	46
Hitchin Town	42	10	15	17	55	70	45
Leytonstone & Ilford	42	11	10	21	37	72	43
Harlow Town	42	5	12	25	45	95	27

Billericay Town had 1 point deducted
Croydon had 3 points deducted

First Division

Farnborough Town	42	26	8	8	101	45	86
Kingstonian	42	23	10	9	67	39	79
Leatherhead	42	23	10	9	109	61	76
Chesham United	42	22	8	12	78	46	74
Wembley	42	20	10	12	59	40	70
St Albans City	42	19	10	13	79	60	67
Tilbury	42	18	13	11	86	68	67
Bromley	42	18	9	15	71	64	63
Hampton	42	17	11	14	75	62	62
Staines Town	42	16	11	15	59	53	59
Maidenhead United	42	17	8	17	65	64	59
Walton & Hersham	42	16	8	18	60	69	55
Aveley	42	16	7	19	62	78	55
Oxford City	42	14	12	16	62	53	54
Lewes	42	15	9	18	70	72	54
Basildon United	42	15	8	19	55	61	53
Boreham Wood	42	15	7	20	72	83	52
Hornchurch	42	15	6	21	55	74	51
Woking	42	15	6	21	60	91	51
Metropolitan Police	42	10	12	20	65	92	42
Clapton	42	5	11	26	50	124	26
Hertford Town	42	5	10	27	36	97	25

Walton & Hersham had 1 point deducted
Leatherhead had 3 points deducted

Second Division North

Leyton Wingate	38	24	9	5	98	50	81
Finchley	38	24	8	6	66	31	79
Heybridge Swifts	38	22	9	7	71	33	75
Stevenage Borough	38	23	6	9	79	49	75
Saffron Walden Town	38	22	8	8	73	31	74
Tring Town	38	19	11	8	76	41	68
Chalfont St Peter	38	17	10	11	72	41	61
Flackwell Heath	38	16	11	11	54	40	59
Berkhamsted Town	38	15	12	11	50	42	57
Letchworth Garden City	38	17	6	15	66	69	57
Royston Town	38	13	9	16	47	77	48
Cheshunt	38	14	5	19	52	57	47
Marlow	38	13	6	19	64	81	45
Hemel Hempstead	38	11	7	20	49	65	40
Barton Rovers	38	9	8	21	40	62	35
Wolverton Town	38	9	8	21	38	77	35
Kingsbury Town	38	9	7	22	53	72	34
Harefield United	38	7	9	22	51	81	30
Haringey Borough	38	6	12	20	38	79	30
Ware	38	7	5	26	40	100	26

Finchley had 1 point deducted
The record of Epping Town was expunged

Second Division South

Grays Athletic	36	24	9	3	84	25	81
Uxbridge	36	22	10	4	81	20	76
Molesey	36	20	5	11	62	42	65
Hungerford Town	36	18	9	9	71	49	63
Whyteleafe	36	17	10	9	66	34	61
Egham Town	36	17	7	12	54	42	58
Southall	36	18	3	15	54	57	57
Bracknell Town	36	15	7	14	54	48	52
Banstead Athletic	36	14	8	14	63	70	50
Horsham	36	13	10	13	44	39	49
Ruislip Manor	36	13	10	13	48	49	49
Dorking	36	12	11	13	45	50	47
Rainham Town	36	12	8	16	58	61	44
Feltham	36	10	13	13	44	58	43
Camberley Town	36	10	12	14	44	54	42
Eastbourne United	36	10	9	17	66	72	39
Petersfield Town	36	9	5	22	41	80	32
Newbury Town	36	8	7	21	35	69	16
Chertsey Town	36	2	3	31	23	118	6

Chertsey Town had 3 points deducted
Newbury Town had 15 points deducted

1985-86

Premier Division

Sutton United	42	29	8	5	109	39	95
Yeovil Town	42	28	7	7	92	48	91
Farnborough Town	42	23	8	11	90	50	77
Croydon	42	23	7	12	70	50	76
Harrow Borough	42	21	8	13	76	66	71
Slough Town	42	18	8	16	66	68	62
Bishop's Stortford	42	17	10	15	55	61	61
Kingstonian	42	15	15	12	57	56	60
Dulwich Hamlet	42	17	9	16	64	79	60
Wokingham Town	42	16	10	16	67	64	58
Windsor & Eton	42	17	7	18	58	75	58
Tooting & Mitcham United	42	14	11	17	65	76	53
Walthamstow Avenue	42	12	14	16	69	70	50
Worthing	42	13	10	19	72	82	49
Bognor Regis Town	42	15	6	21	63	70	48
Hayes	42	10	17	15	36	42	47
Hitchin Town	42	11	14	17	53	69	47
Barking	42	11	13	18	45	55	46
Hendon	42	10	13	19	59	77	43
Carshalton Athletic	42	9	13	20	56	79	40
Billericay Town	42	9	12	21	59	78	39
Epsom & Ewell	42	8	12	22	63	90	36

Bognor Regis Town had 3 points deducted

First Division

St Albans City	42	23	11	8	92	61	80
Bromley	42	24	8	10	68	41	80
Wembley	42	22	12	8	59	30	78
Oxford City	42	22	11	9	75	51	77
Hampton	42	21	11	10	63	45	74
Leyton Wingate	42	21	10	11	77	56	73
Uxbridge	42	20	8	14	64	49	68
Staines Town	42	18	10	14	69	66	64
Boreham Wood	42	15	16	11	62	54	61
Walton & Hersham	42	16	10	16	68	71	58
Lewes	42	16	8	18	61	75	56
Leytonstone & Ilford	42	13	15	14	57	67	54
Finchley	42	12	17	13	61	59	53
Grays Athletic	42	13	11	18	69	75	50
Leatherhead	42	14	8	20	62	68	50
Tilbury	42	13	11	18	60	66	50
Maidenhead United	42	13	7	22	61	67	46
Basildon United	42	12	9	21	52	72	45
Hornchurch	42	11	11	20	44	59	44
Chesham United	42	12	6	24	51	87	42
Harlow Town	42	8	14	20	53	70	38
Aveley	42	8	6	28	59	98	30

Second Division North

Stevenage Borough	38	26	6	6	71	24	84
Kingsbury Town	38	25	8	5	84	35	83
Heybridge Swifts	38	20	8	10	65	46	68
Cheshunt	38	18	10	10	60	40	64
Hertford Town	38	17	7	14	60	50	58
Chalfont St Peter	38	15	11	12	53	50	56
Tring Town	38	14	13	11	58	46	55
Royston Town	38	13	13	12	59	57	52
Saffron Walden Town	38	13	12	13	61	65	51
Berkhamsted Town	38	14	8	16	45	52	50
Haringey Borough	38	14	7	17	49	51	49
Letchworth Garden City	38	13	8	17	46	52	47
Rainham Town	38	14	4	20	54	91	46
Hemel Hempstead	38	12	9	17	50	66	45
Ware	38	11	11	16	56	61	44
Vauxhall Motors	38	11	10	17	58	62	43
Barton Rovers	38	12	7	19	50	60	43
Harefield United	38	9	12	17	56	72	39
Clapton	38	10	7	21	51	90	37
Wolverton Town	38	8	11	19	42	58	35

Second Division South

Southwick	38	25	8	5	86	34	83
Bracknell Town	38	24	9	5	80	23	81
Woking	38	23	9	6	94	45	78
Newbury Town	38	22	7	9	86	53	73
Whyteleafe	38	21	10	7	61	41	73
Molesey	38	21	8	9	59	39	71
Metropolitan Police	38	20	6	12	72	48	66
Southall	38	19	7	12	76	58	64
Dorking	38	18	10	10	70	57	64
Feltham	38	16	7	15	65	60	55
Banstead Athletic	38	15	8	15	60	66	53
Petersfield United	38	12	9	17	61	71	45
Hungerford Town	38	11	6	21	57	78	39
Flackwell Heath	38	11	6	21	46	72	39
Eastbourne United	38	9	8	21	51	81	35
Camberley Town	38	9	7	22	53	64	34
Egham Town	38	7	8	23	41	83	29
Horsham	38	6	10	22	33	74	28
Ruislip Manor	38	5	12	21	44	87	27
Marlow	38	6	5	27	47	108	23

1986-87

Premier Division

Wycombe Wanderers	42	32	5	5	103	32	101
Yeovil Town	42	28	8	6	71	27	92
Slough Town	42	23	8	11	70	44	77
Hendon	42	22	7	13	67	53	73
Bognor Regis Town	42	20	10	12	85	61	70
Harrow Borough	42	20	10	12	68	44	70
Croydon	42	18	10	14	51	48	64
Barking	42	16	14	12	76	56	62
Farnborough Town	42	17	11	14	66	72	62
Bishop's Stortford	42	15	15	12	62	57	60
Bromley	42	16	11	15	63	72	59
Kingstonian	42	16	9	17	58	50	57
Windsor & Eton	42	13	15	14	47	52	54
St Albans City	42	14	9	19	61	70	51
Carshalton Athletic	42	13	9	20	55	68	48
Wokingham Town	42	14	6	22	47	61	48
Hayes	42	12	12	18	45	68	48
Dulwich Hamlet	42	12	10	20	62	71	46
Tooting & Mitcham United	42	12	9	21	41	53	45
Hitchin Town	42	13	5	24	56	69	44
Worthing	42	8	9	25	58	107	33
Walthamstow Avenue	42	4	6	32	36	113	18

First Division

Leytonstone & Ilford	42	30	5	7	78	29	95
Leyton Wingate	42	23	13	6	68	31	82
Bracknell Town	42	24	9	9	92	48	81
Southwick	42	23	7	12	80	66	76
Wembley	42	21	9	12	61	47	72
Grays Athletic	42	19	10	13	76	64	67
Kingsbury Town	42	20	7	15	69	67	67
Boreham Wood	42	20	6	16	59	52	66
Uxbridge	42	18	9	15	60	59	63
Leatherhead	42	17	11	14	45	48	62
Hampton	42	18	5	19	57	55	59
Basildon United	42	16	10	16	58	60	58
Billericay Town	42	14	12	16	57	52	54
Staines Town	42	13	13	16	40	51	52
Lewes	42	15	6	21	55	65	51
Stevenage Borough	42	12	11	19	61	67	47
Oxford City	42	11	10	21	64	72	43
Walton & Hersham	42	11	10	21	53	74	43
Tilbury	42	12	7	23	46	70	43
Epsom & Ewell	42	12	7	23	44	64	43
Maidenhead United	42	11	4	27	44	76	37
Finchley	42	6	11	25	44	90	29

Second Division North

Chesham United	42	28	6	8	81	48	90
Wolverton Town	42	23	14	5	74	32	83
Haringey Borough	42	22	13	7	86	40	79
Heybridge Swifts	42	21	11	10	81	54	74
Aveley	42	19	13	10	68	50	70
Letchworth Garden City	42	19	11	12	77	62	68
Barton Rovers	42	18	11	13	49	39	65
Tring Town	42	19	7	16	69	49	64
Collier Row	42	19	5	18	67	65	62
Ware	42	17	8	17	51	50	59
Saffron Walden Town	42	14	14	14	56	54	56
Wivenhoe Town	42	15	11	16	61	61	56
Vauxhall Motors	42	15	10	17	61	57	55
Hornchurch	42	13	16	13	60	60	55
Hertford Town	42	14	13	15	52	53	55
Berkhamsted Town	42	12	16	14	62	64	52
Harlow Town	42	13	11	18	45	55	50
Rainham Town	42	12	11	19	53	70	47
Clapton	42	10	11	21	45	63	41
Hemel Hempstead	42	9	12	21	48	77	39
Royston Town	42	4	12	26	37	109	24
Cheshunt	42	5	6	31	43	114	21

Second Division South

Woking	40	27	7	6	110	32	88
Marlow	40	28	4	8	78	36	88
Dorking	40	24	12	4	78	30	84
Feltham	40	25	3	12	79	34	78
Ruislip Manor	40	22	10	8	85	47	76
Chertsey Town	40	18	11	11	56	44	65
Metropolitan Police	40	16	13	11	70	61	61
Chalfont St Peter	40	17	10	13	60	55	61
Hungerford Town	40	14	14	12	55	48	56
Harefield United	40	14	14	12	53	47	56
Eastbourne United	40	15	10	15	72	59	55
Whyteleafe	40	12	15	13	52	63	51
Horsham	40	14	8	18	54	61	50
Egham Town	40	14	6	20	45	77	48
Camberley Town	40	13	3	24	62	89	42
Flackwell Heath	40	9	11	20	34	63	38
Banstead Athletic	40	7	15	18	44	61	36
Petersfield United	40	9	8	23	45	84	34
Molesey	40	7	12	21	37	89	33
Newbury Town	40	6	14	20	51	83	32
Southall	40	6	6	28	28	85	24

1987-88　Premier Division

Yeovil Town	42	24	9	9	66	34	81
Bromley	42	23	7	12	68	40	76
Slough Town	42	21	9	12	67	41	72
Leytonstone & Ilford	42	20	11	11	59	43	71
Wokingham Town	42	21	7	14	62	52	70
Hayes	42	20	9	13	62	48	69
Windsor & Eton	42	16	17	9	59	43	65
Farnborough Town	42	17	11	14	63	60	62
Carshalton Athletic	42	16	13	13	49	41	61
Hendon	42	16	12	14	62	58	60
Tooting & Mitcham United	42	15	14	13	57	59	59
Harrow Borough	42	15	11	16	53	58	56
Bishop's Stortford	42	15	10	17	55	58	55
Kingstonian	42	14	12	16	47	53	54
St Albans City	42	15	6	21	60	69	51
Bognor Regis Town	42	14	9	19	41	57	51
Leyton Wingate	42	14	8	20	58	64	50
Croydon	42	11	13	18	40	52	46
Barking	42	11	12	19	44	57	45
Dulwich Hamlet	42	10	11	21	46	64	41
Hitchin Town	42	10	8	24	46	79	38
Basingstoke Town	42	6	17	19	37	71	35

First Division

Marlow	42	32	5	5	100	44	101
Grays Athletic	42	30	10	2	74	25	100
Woking	42	25	7	10	91	52	82
Boreham Wood	42	21	9	12	65	45	72
Staines Town	42	19	11	12	71	48	68
Wembley	42	18	11	13	54	46	65
Basildon United	42	18	9	15	65	58	63
Walton & Hersham	42	15	16	11	53	44	61
Hampton	42	17	10	15	59	54	61
Leatherhead	42	16	11	15	64	53	59
Southwick	42	13	12	17	59	63	51
Oxford City	42	13	12	17	70	77	51
Worthing	42	14	8	20	67	73	50
Kingsbury Town	42	11	17	14	62	69	50
Walthamstow Avenue	42	13	11	18	53	63	50
Lewes	42	12	13	17	83	77	49
Uxbridge	42	11	16	15	41	47	49
Chesham United	42	12	10	20	69	77	46
Bracknell Town	42	12	9	21	54	80	45
Billericay Town	42	11	11	20	58	88	44
Stevenage Borough	42	11	9	22	36	64	42
Wolverton Town	42	3	3	36	23	124	12

Second Division North

Wivenhoe Town	42	26	10	6	105	42	88
Collier Row	42	22	13	7	71	39	79
Tilbury	42	18	15	9	61	40	69
Berkhamsted Town	42	19	12	11	71	53	69
Harlow Town	42	17	16	9	67	36	67
Ware	42	17	15	10	63	58	66
Witham Town	42	17	14	11	69	47	65
Vauxhall Motors	42	16	17	9	56	42	65
Heybridge Swifts	42	17	13	12	56	50	64
Tring Town	42	18	6	18	69	67	60
Letchworth Garden City	42	18	5	19	59	64	59
Finchley	42	16	10	16	67	54	58
Clapton	42	14	15	13	50	62	57
Hornchurch	42	13	15	14	56	65	54
Barton Rovers	42	13	10	19	43	60	49
Rainham Town	42	12	12	18	63	66	48
Royston Town	42	13	8	21	49	70	47
Saffron Walden Town	42	13	7	22	34	67	46
Hemel Hempstead	42	11	12	19	38	71	45
Haringey Borough	42	11	8	23	54	78	41
Aveley	42	8	13	21	42	65	37
Hertford Town	42	8	4	30	45	92	28

Second Division South

Chalfont St Peter	42	26	9	7	81	35	87
Metropolitan Police	42	23	17	2	80	32	86
Dorking	42	25	11	6	86	39	86
Feltham	42	21	12	9	74	41	75
Epsom & Ewell	42	21	11	10	71	49	74
Chertsey Town	42	22	7	13	63	47	73
Whyteleafe	42	20	11	11	84	55	71
Hungerford Town	42	21	7	14	66	54	70
Ruislip Manor	42	21	5	16	74	57	68
Yeading	42	19	10	13	83	56	67
Maidenhead United	42	18	12	12	69	54	66
Eastbourne United	42	18	10	14	67	57	64
Harefield Town	42	18	6	18	59	60	60
Egham Town	42	12	12	18	45	55	48
Horsham	42	12	10	20	45	66	46
Southall	42	13	7	22	45	72	46
Molesey	42	11	11	20	42	63	44
Newbury Town	42	8	13	21	40	81	37
Camberley Town	42	9	9	24	51	94	36
Flackwell Heath	42	6	8	28	42	96	26
Banstead Athletic	42	6	7	29	34	81	25
Petersfield United	42	6	7	29	45	102	25

1988-89 Premier Division

Team	P	W	D	L	F	A	Pts
Leytonstone & Ilford	42	26	11	5	76	36	89
Farnborough Town	42	24	9	9	85	61	81
Slough Town	42	24	6	12	72	42	78
Carshalton Athletic	42	19	15	8	59	36	72
Grays Athletic	42	19	13	10	62	47	70
Kingstonian	42	19	11	12	54	37	68
Bishop's Stortford	42	20	6	16	70	56	66
Hayes	42	18	12	12	61	47	66
Bognor Regis Town	42	17	11	14	38	49	62
Barking	42	16	13	13	49	45	61
Wokingham Town	42	15	11	16	60	54	56
Hendon	42	13	17	12	51	68	56
Windsor & Eton	42	14	13	15	52	50	55
Bromley	42	13	15	14	61	48	54
Leyton Wingate	42	13	15	14	55	56	54
Dulwich Hamlet	42	12	12	18	58	57	48
St Albans City	42	12	9	21	51	59	45
Dagenham	42	11	12	19	53	68	45
Harrow Borough	42	9	13	20	53	75	40
Marlow	42	9	11	22	48	83	38
Tooting & Mitcham United	42	10	6	26	41	81	36
Croydon	42	4	9	29	27	81	21

First Division

Team	P	W	D	L	F	A	Pts
Staines Town	40	26	9	5	79	29	87
Basingstoke Town	40	25	8	7	85	36	83
Woking	40	24	10	6	72	30	82
Hitchin Town	40	21	11	8	60	32	74
Wivenhoe Town	40	22	6	12	62	44	72
Lewes	40	21	8	11	72	54	71
Walton & Hersham	40	21	7	12	56	36	70
Kingsbury Town	40	20	7	13	65	41	67
Uxbridge	40	19	7	14	60	54	64
Wembley	40	18	6	16	45	58	60
Boreham Wood	40	16	9	15	57	52	57
Leatherhead	40	14	8	18	56	58	50
Metropolitan Police	40	13	9	18	52	68	48
Chesham United	40	12	9	19	54	67	45
Southwick	40	9	15	16	44	58	42
Chalfont St Peter	40	11	9	20	56	82	42
Hampton	40	7	14	19	37	62	35
Worthing	40	8	10	22	49	80	32
Collier Row	40	8	7	25	37	82	31
Bracknell Town	40	8	6	26	38	70	30
Basildon United	40	6	7	27	34	77	25

Worthing had 2 points deducted.

Second Division North

Team	P	W	D	L	F	A	Pts
Harlow Town	42	27	9	6	83	38	90
Purfleet	42	22	12	8	60	42	78
Tring Town	42	22	10	10	65	44	76
Stevenage Borough	42	20	13	9	84	55	73
Heybridge Swifts	42	21	9	12	64	43	72
Billericay Town	42	19	11	12	65	52	68
Clapton	42	18	11	13	65	56	65
Barton Rovers	42	18	11	13	58	50	65
Aveley	42	18	10	14	54	52	64
Hertford Town	42	16	13	13	62	49	59
Ware	42	17	8	17	60	65	59
Hemel Hempstead	42	16	10	16	55	58	58
Witham Town	42	16	7	19	69	67	55
Vauxhall Motors	42	15	9	18	53	57	54
Berkhamsted Town	42	14	10	18	57	70	52
Hornchurch	42	11	16	15	59	61	49
Tilbury	42	13	10	19	53	60	49
Royston Town	42	12	7	23	46	72	43
Rainham Town	42	9	15	18	49	62	42
Saffron Walden Town	42	8	16	18	54	72	40
Letchworth Garden City	42	4	18	20	34	71	30
Wolverton Town	42	5	7	30	42	95	13

Hertford Town 2 points deducted, Wolverton Town 9 points deducted.

Second Division South

Team	P	W	D	L	F	A	Pts
Dorking	40	32	4	4	109	35	100
Whyteleafe	40	25	9	6	86	41	84
Finchley	40	21	9	10	70	45	72
Molesey	40	19	13	8	58	42	70
Harefield United	40	19	7	14	56	45	64
Hungerford Town	40	17	13	10	55	45	64
Ruislip Manor	40	16	9	15	56	43	57
Feltham	40	16	9	15	58	53	57
Epsom & Ewell	40	16	8	16	55	55	56
Egham Town	40	16	7	17	54	58	55
Eastbourne United	40	15	9	16	68	61	54
Chertsey Town	40	13	14	13	55	58	53
Flackwell Heath	40	13	11	16	51	49	50
Camberley Town	40	15	5	20	51	71	50
Yeading	40	13	9	18	47	63	46
Banstead Athletic	40	12	8	20	50	65	44
Maidenhead United	40	10	13	17	44	61	43
Southall	40	11	10	19	41	73	43
Newbury Town	40	11	8	21	47	65	41
Horsham	40	7	14	19	36	68	35
Petersfield United	40	5	7	28	36	87	22

Yeading had 2 points deducted.

1989-90 Premier Division

Team	P	W	D	L	F	A	Pts
Slough Town	42	27	11	4	85	38	92
Wokingham Town	42	26	11	5	67	34	89
Aylesbury United	42	25	9	8	86	30	84
Kingstonian	42	24	9	9	87	51	81
Grays Athletic	42	19	13	10	59	44	70
Dagenham	42	17	15	10	54	43	66
Leyton Wingate	42	20	6	16	54	48	66
Basingstoke Town	42	18	9	15	65	55	63
Bishop's Stortford	42	19	6	17	60	59	63
Carshalton Athletic	42	19	5	18	63	59	59
Redbridge Forest	42	16	11	15	65	62	59
Hendon	42	15	10	17	54	63	55
Windsor & Eton	42	13	15	14	51	47	54
Hayes	42	14	11	17	61	59	53
St Albans City	42	13	10	19	49	59	49
Staines Town	42	14	6	22	53	69	48
Marlow	42	11	13	18	42	59	46
Harrow Borough	42	11	10	21	51	79	43
Bognor Regis Town	42	9	14	19	37	67	41
Barking	42	7	11	24	53	86	32
Bromley	42	7	11	24	32	69	32
Dulwich Hamlet	42	6	8	28	32	80	26

Carshalton Athletic had 3 points deducted.

First Division

Team	P	W	D	L	F	A	Pts
Wivenhoe Town	42	31	7	4	94	36	100
Woking	42	30	8	4	102	29	98
Southwick	42	23	15	4	68	30	84
Hitchin Town	42	22	13	7	60	30	79
Walton & Hersham	42	20	10	12	68	50	70
Dorking	42	19	12	11	66	41	69
Boreham Wood	42	17	13	12	60	59	64
Harlow Town	42	16	13	13	60	53	61
Metropolitan Police	42	16	11	15	54	59	59
Chesham United	42	15	12	15	46	49	57
Chalfont St Peter	42	14	13	15	50	59	55
Tooting & Mitcham United	42	14	13	15	42	51	55
Worthing	42	15	8	19	56	63	53
Whyteleafe	42	11	16	15	50	65	49
Lewes	42	12	11	19	55	65	47
Wembley	42	11	10	21	57	68	43
Croydon	42	9	16	17	43	57	43
Uxbridge	42	11	10	21	52	75	43
Hampton	42	8	13	21	28	51	37
Leatherhead	42	7	10	25	34	77	31
Purfleet	42	7	8	27	33	78	29
Kingsbury Town	42	8	10	24	45	78	25

Kingsbury Town had 9 points deducted

Second Division North

Heybridge Swifts	42	26	9	7	79	29	87
Aveley	42	23	16	3	68	24	85
Hertford Town	42	24	11	7	92	51	83
Stevenage Borough	42	21	16	5	70	31	79
Barton Rovers	42	22	6	14	60	45	72
Tilbury	42	20	9	13	68	54	69
Basildon United	42	13	20	9	50	44	59
Collier Row	42	15	13	14	43	45	58
Royston Town	42	15	11	16	63	72	56
Saffron Walden Town	42	15	11	16	60	73	56
Vauxhall Motors	42	14	13	15	55	54	55
Clapton	42	13	16	13	50	46	54
Ware	42	14	11	17	53	59	53
Hemel Hempstead	42	12	15	15	58	70	51
Billericay Town	42	13	11	18	49	58	50
Hornchurch	42	12	12	18	49	64	48
Berkhamsted Town	42	9	16	17	44	68	43
Finchley	42	11	10	21	50	75	43
Tring Town	42	10	9	23	48	70	39
Witham Town	42	8	14	20	44	56	38
Rainham Town	42	9	11	22	48	75	38
Letchworth Garden City	42	7	12	23	30	68	33

Clapton had 1 point deducted

Second Division South

Yeading	40	29	4	7	86	37	91
Molesey	40	24	11	5	76	30	83
Abingdon Town	40	22	9	9	64	39	75
Ruislip Manor	40	20	12	8	60	32	72
Maidenhead United	40	20	12	8	66	39	72
Southall	40	22	5	13	56	33	71
Newbury Town	40	21	7	12	50	36	70
Flackwell Heath	40	16	11	13	69	65	59
Hungerford Town	40	14	16	10	54	51	58
Egham Town	40	12	14	14	39	38	50
Banstead Athletic	40	14	8	18	46	47	50
Harefield United	40	13	9	18	44	46	48
Chertsey Town	40	13	9	18	53	58	48
Epsom & Ewell	40	13	9	18	49	54	48
Malden Vale	40	13	7	20	36	67	46
Eastbourne United	40	11	10	19	47	65	43
Camberley Town	40	11	9	20	44	66	42
Feltham	40	11	7	22	47	80	40
Bracknell Town	40	10	9	21	40	57	39
Petersfield United	40	10	8	22	48	93	38
Horsham	40	4	8	28	29	70	20

1990-91   Premier Division

Redbridge Forest	42	29	6	7	74	43	93
Enfield	42	26	11	5	83	30	89
Aylesbury United	42	24	11	7	90	47	83
Woking	42	24	10	8	84	39	82
Kingstonian	42	21	12	9	86	57	75
Grays Athletic	42	20	8	14	66	53	68
Marlow	42	18	13	11	72	49	67
Hayes	42	20	5	17	60	57	65
Carshalton Athletic	42	19	7	16	80	67	64
Wivenhoe Town	42	16	11	15	69	66	59
Wokingham Town	42	15	13	14	58	54	58
Windsor & Eton	42	15	10	17	48	63	55
Bishop's Stortford	42	14	12	16	54	49	54
Dagenham	42	13	11	18	62	68	50
Hendon	42	12	10	20	48	62	46
St Albans City	42	11	12	19	60	74	45
Bognor Regis Town	42	12	8	22	44	71	44
Basingstoke Town	42	12	7	23	57	95	43
Staines Town	42	10	10	22	46	79	39
Harrow Borough	42	10	8	24	57	84	38
Barking	42	8	10	24	41	85	34
Leyton Wingate	42	7	7	28	44	91	28

Staines Town had 1 point deducted

First Division

Chesham United	42	27	8	7	102	37	89
Bromley	42	22	14	6	62	37	80
Yeading	42	23	8	11	75	45	77
Aveley	42	21	9	12	76	43	72
Hitchin Town	42	21	9	12	78	50	72
Tooting & Mitcham United	42	20	12	10	71	48	72
Walton & Hersham	42	21	8	13	73	48	71
Molesey	42	22	5	15	65	46	71
Whyteleafe	42	21	6	15	62	53	69
Dorking	42	20	5	17	78	67	65
Chalfont St Peter	42	19	5	18	56	63	62
Dulwich Hamlet	42	16	11	15	67	54	59
Harlow Town	42	17	8	17	73	64	59
Boreham Wood	42	15	8	19	46	53	53
Wembley	42	13	12	17	62	59	51
Uxbridge	42	15	5	22	45	61	50
Croydon	42	15	5	22	44	85	50
Heybridge Swifts	42	13	10	19	46	59	49
Southwick	42	13	8	21	49	75	47
Lewes	42	10	8	24	49	82	38
Metropolitan Police	42	9	6	27	55	76	33
Worthing	42	2	4	36	28	157	10

Second Division North

Stevenage Borough	42	34	5	3	122	29	107
Vauxhall Motors	42	24	10	8	82	50	82
Billericay Town	42	22	8	12	70	41	74
Ware	42	22	8	12	78	51	74
Berkhamsted Town	42	19	11	12	60	51	68
Witham Town	42	19	10	13	70	59	67
Purfleet	42	17	14	11	68	57	65
Rainham Town	42	19	7	16	57	46	64
Hemel Hempstead	42	16	14	12	62	56	62
Barton Rovers	42	17	10	15	61	58	61
Saffron Walden Town	42	16	13	13	72	77	61
Collier Row	42	16	11	15	63	63	59
Kingsbury Town	42	17	8	17	64	72	59
Edgware Town	42	17	7	18	73	65	58
Hertford Town	42	16	10	16	69	70	58
Royston Town	42	14	15	13	78	62	57
Tilbury	42	14	6	22	70	79	48
Basildon United	42	11	10	21	61	90	43
Hornchurch	42	10	9	23	53	87	39
Clapton	42	9	10	23	54	93	34
Finchley	42	6	7	29	50	112	24
Tring Town	42	1	9	32	30	99	12

Finchley had 1 point deducted. Clapton had 3 points deducted

Second Division South

Abingdon Town	42	29	7	6	95	28	94
Maidenhead United	42	28	8	6	85	33	92
Egham Town	42	27	6	9	100	46	87
Malden Vale	42	26	5	11	72	44	83
Ruislip Manor	42	25	5	12	93	44	80
Southall	42	23	10	9	84	43	79
Harefield United	42	23	10	9	81	56	79
Newbury Town	42	23	8	11	71	45	77
Hungerford Town	42	16	13	13	84	69	61
Leatherhead	42	17	9	16	82	55	60
Banstead Athletic	42	15	13	14	58	62	58
Hampton	42	14	15	13	62	43	57
Epsom & Ewell	42	15	12	15	49	50	57
Chertsey Town	42	15	9	18	76	72	54
Horsham	42	14	7	21	58	67	49
Flackwell Heath	42	11	11	20	56	78	44
Bracknell Town	42	11	7	24	60	97	40
Feltham	42	10	8	24	45	80	38
Cove	42	10	7	25	51	94	37
Eastbourne United	42	10	7	25	53	109	37
Petersfield United	42	6	3	33	35	119	21
Camberley Town	42	1	6	35	27	143	9

1991-92

Premier Division

Woking	42	30	7	5	96	25	97
Enfield	42	24	7	11	59	45	79
Sutton United	42	19	13	10	88	51	70
Chesham United	42	20	10	12	67	48	70
Wokingham Town	42	19	10	13	73	58	67
Marlow	42	20	7	15	56	50	67
Aylesbury United	42	16	17	9	69	46	65
Carshalton Athletic	42	18	8	16	64	67	62
Dagenham	42	15	16	11	70	59	61
Kingstonian	42	17	8	17	71	65	59
Windsor & Eton	42	15	11	16	56	56	56
Bromley	42	14	12	16	51	57	54
St Albans City	42	14	11	17	66	70	53
Basingstoke Town	42	14	11	17	56	65	53
Grays Athletic	42	14	11	17	53	68	53
Wivenhoe Town	42	16	4	22	56	81	52
Hendon	42	13	9	20	59	73	48
Harrow Borough	42	11	13	18	58	78	46
Hayes	42	10	14	18	52	63	44
Staines Town	42	11	10	21	43	73	43
Bognor Regis Town	42	9	11	22	51	89	38
Bishop's Stortford	42	7	12	23	41	68	33

First Division

Stevenage Borough	40	30	6	4	95	37	96
Yeading	40	24	10	6	83	34	82
Dulwich Hamlet	40	22	9	9	71	40	75
Boreham Wood	40	22	7	11	65	40	73
Wembley	40	21	6	13	54	43	69
Abingdon Town	40	19	8	13	60	47	65
Tooting & Mitcham United	40	16	13	11	57	45	61
Hitchin Town	40	17	10	13	55	45	61
Walton & Hersham	40	15	13	12	62	50	58
Molesey	40	16	9	15	55	61	57
Dorking	40	16	7	17	68	65	55
Barking	40	14	11	15	51	54	53
Chalfont St Peter	40	15	6	19	62	70	51
Leyton Wingate	40	13	11	16	53	56	50
Uxbridge	40	13	8	19	47	62	47
Maidenhead United	40	13	7	20	52	61	46
Harlow Town	40	11	9	20	50	70	42
Croydon	40	11	6	23	44	68	39
Heybridge Swifts	40	8	9	23	33	71	33
Whyteleafe	40	7	10	23	42	78	31
Aveley	40	8	3	29	33	95	27

Second Division

Purfleet	42	27	8	7	97	48	89
Lewes	42	23	14	5	74	36	83
Billericay Town	42	24	8	10	75	44	80
Leatherhead	42	23	6	13	68	40	75
Ruislip Manor	42	20	9	13	74	51	69
Egham Town	42	19	12	11	81	62	69
Metropolitan Police	42	20	9	13	76	58	69
Saffron Walden Town	42	19	11	12	86	67	68
Hemel Hempstead	42	18	10	14	63	50	64
Hungerford Town	42	18	7	17	53	58	61
Barton Rovers	42	17	8	17	61	64	59
Worthing	42	17	8	17	67	72	59
Witham Town	42	16	11	15	56	61	59
Banstead Athletic	42	16	10	16	69	58	58
Malden Vale	42	15	12	15	63	48	57
Rainham Town	42	14	13	15	53	48	55
Ware	42	14	9	19	58	62	51
Berkhamsted Town	42	13	11	18	56	57	50
Harefield United	42	11	7	24	47	66	40
Southall	42	8	7	27	39	93	31
Southwick	42	6	2	34	29	115	20
Newbury Town	42	4	8	30	30	117	20

Third Division

Edgware Town	40	30	3	7	106	44	93
Chertsey Town	40	29	4	7	115	44	91
Tilbury	40	26	9	5	84	40	87
Hampton	40	26	5	9	93	35	83
Horsham	40	23	8	9	92	51	77
Cove	40	21	9	10	74	49	72
Flackwell Heath	40	19	12	9	78	50	69
Thame United	40	19	7	14	73	46	64
Epsom & Ewell	40	17	11	12	55	50	62
Collier Row	40	17	9	14	67	59	60
Royston Town	40	17	7	16	59	58	58
Kingsbury Town	40	12	10	18	54	61	46
Hertford Town	40	12	10	18	55	73	46
Petersfield United	40	12	9	19	45	67	45
Camberley Town	40	11	8	21	52	69	41
Feltham & Hounslow	40	11	2	22	53	78	40
Bracknell Town	40	10	7	23	48	90	37
Hornchurch	40	8	7	25	40	87	31
Tring Town	40	9	4	27	35	94	31
Clapton	40	9	3	28	47	92	30
Eastbourne United	40	5	5	30	34	121	20

1992-93

Premier Division

Chesham United	42	30	8	4	104	34	98
St Albans City	42	28	9	5	103	50	93
Enfield	42	25	6	11	94	48	81
Carshalton Athletic	42	22	10	10	96	56	76
Sutton United	42	18	14	10	74	57	68
Grays Athletic	42	18	11	13	61	64	65
Stevenage Borough	42	18	8	16	62	60	62
Harrow Borough	42	16	14	12	59	60	62
Hayes	42	16	13	13	64	59	61
Aylesbury United	42	18	6	18	70	77	60
Hendon	42	12	18	12	52	54	54
Basingstoke Town	42	12	17	13	49	45	53
Kingstonian	42	14	10	18	59	58	52
Dulwich Hamlet	42	12	14	16	52	66	50
Marlow	42	12	11	19	72	73	47
Wokingham Town	42	11	13	18	62	81	46
Bromley	42	11	13	18	51	72	46
Wivenhoe Town	42	13	7	22	41	75	46
Yeading	42	11	12	19	58	66	45
Staines Town	42	10	13	19	59	77	43
Windsor & Eton	42	8	7	27	40	90	31
Bognor Regis Town	42	5	10	27	46	106	25

First Division

Hitchin Town	40	25	7	8	67	29	82
Molesey	40	23	11	6	81	38	80
Dorking	40	23	9	8	73	40	78
Purfleet	40	19	12	9	67	42	69
Bishop's Stortford	40	19	10	11	63	42	67
Abingdon Town	40	17	13	10	65	47	64
Tooting & Mitcham United	40	17	12	11	68	46	63
Billericay Town	40	18	6	16	67	61	60
Wembley	40	14	15	11	44	34	57
Walton & Hersham	40	14	12	14	58	54	54
Boreham Wood	40	12	14	14	44	43	50
Maidenhead United	40	10	18	12	45	50	48
Leyton	40	11	14	15	56	61	47
Whyteleafe	40	12	10	18	63	71	46
Uxbridge	40	11	13	16	50	59	46
Heybridge Swifts	40	11	9	20	47	62	42
Croydon	40	11	9	20	54	82	42
Chalfont St Peter	40	7	17	16	48	70	38
Barking	40	10	8	22	42	80	38
Lewes	40	9	10	21	34	80	37
Aveley	40	9	7	24	45	87	34

Second Division

Worthing	42	28	7	7	105	50	91
Ruislip Manor	42	25	12	5	78	33	87
Berkhamsted Town	42	24	8	10	77	55	80
Hemel Hempstead	42	22	12	8	84	52	78
Metropolitan Police	42	22	6	14	84	51	72
Malden Vale	42	20	9	13	78	54	69
Chertsey Town	42	20	7	15	84	60	67
Saffron Walden Town	42	19	10	13	63	49	67
Newbury Town	42	14	18	10	53	51	60
Hampton	42	16	11	15	59	59	59
Edgware Town	42	16	10	16	84	75	58
Egham Town	42	16	9	17	60	71	57
Banstead Athletic	42	14	13	15	67	52	55
Leatherhead	42	14	11	17	66	61	53
Ware	42	12	11	19	68	76	47
Witham Town	42	10	16	16	54	65	46
Tilbury	42	12	8	22	55	101	44
Barton Rovers	42	9	14	19	40	66	41
Hungerford Town	42	11	8	23	37	93	41
Rainham Town	42	9	10	23	56	80	37
Harefield United	42	10	7	25	37	72	37
Southall	42	7	7	28	43	106	28

Third Division

Aldershot Town	38	28	8	2	90	35	92
Thame United	38	21	11	6	84	38	74
Collier Row	38	21	11	6	68	30	74
Leighton Town	38	21	10	7	89	47	73
Cove	38	21	8	9	69	42	71
Northwood	38	19	11	8	84	68	68
Royston Town	38	17	8	13	59	42	59
East Thurrock United	38	17	7	14	69	58	58
Kingsbury Town	38	15	9	14	62	59	54
Hertford Town	38	14	10	14	61	64	52
Flackwell Heath	38	15	6	17	82	76	51
Tring Town	38	12	11	15	59	63	47
Hornchurch	38	11	13	14	53	52	46
Horsham	38	12	7	19	63	72	43
Epsom & Ewell	38	10	11	17	52	67	41
Bracknell Town	38	7	13	18	52	94	34
Clapton	38	8	7	23	46	74	31
Camberley Town	38	8	7	23	37	72	31
Petersfield United	38	6	12	20	36	90	30
Feltham & Hounslow	38	5	4	29	47	119	19

1993-94

Premier Division

Stevenage Borough	42	31	4	7	88	39	97
Enfield	42	28	8	6	80	28	92
Marlow	42	25	7	10	90	67	82
Chesham United	42	24	8	10	73	45	80
Sutton United	42	23	10	9	77	31	79
Carshalton Athletic	42	22	7	13	81	53	73
St Albans City	42	21	10	11	81	54	73
Hitchin Town	42	21	7	14	81	56	70
Harrow Borough	42	18	11	13	54	56	65
Kingstonian	42	18	9	15	101	64	63
Hendon	42	18	9	15	61	51	63
Aylesbury United	42	17	7	18	64	67	58
Hayes	42	15	8	19	63	72	53
Grays Athletic	42	15	5	22	56	69	50
Bromley	42	14	7	21	56	69	49
Dulwich Hamlet	42	13	8	21	52	74	47
Yeading	42	11	13	18	58	66	46
Molesey	42	11	11	20	44	62	44
Wokingham Town	42	11	6	25	38	67	39
Dorking	42	9	4	29	58	104	31
Basingstoke Town	42	5	12	25	38	86	27
Wivenhoe Town	42	5	3	34	38	152	18

First Division

Bishop's Stortford	42	24	13	5	83	31	85
Purfleet	42	22	12	8	70	44	78
Walton & Hersham	42	22	11	9	81	53	77
Tooting & Mitcham United	42	21	12	9	66	37	75
Heybridge Swifts	42	20	11	11	72	45	71
Billericay Town	42	20	11	11	70	51	71
Abingdon Town	42	20	10	12	61	50	70
Worthing	42	19	11	12	79	46	68
Leyton	42	20	8	14	88	66	68
Boreham Wood	42	17	15	10	69	50	66
Staines Town	42	18	9	15	85	56	63
Bognor Regis Town	42	15	14	13	57	48	59
Wembley	42	16	10	16	66	52	58
Barking	42	15	11	16	63	69	56
Uxbridge	42	15	8	19	57	58	53
Whyteleafe	42	15	6	21	71	90	51
Maidenhead United	42	12	13	17	52	48	49
Berkhamsted Town	42	12	9	21	65	77	45
Ruislip Manor	42	10	8	24	42	79	38
Chalfont St Peter	42	7	10	25	40	79	31
Windsor & Eton	42	8	7	27	47	94	31
Croydon	42	3	3	36	37	198	12

Second Division

Newbury Town	42	32	7	3	115	36	103
Chertsey Town	42	33	3	6	121	48	102
Aldershot Town	42	30	7	5	78	27	97
Barton Rovers	42	25	8	9	68	37	83
Witham Town	42	21	10	11	68	51	73
Malden Vale	42	20	10	12	70	49	70
Thame United	42	19	12	11	87	51	69
Metropolitan Police	42	20	9	13	75	54	69
Banstead Athletic	42	19	9	14	56	53	66
Aveley	42	19	5	18	60	66	62
Edgware Town	42	16	10	16	88	75	58
Saffron Walden Town	42	17	7	18	61	62	58
Hemel Hempstead	42	14	11	17	47	43	53
Egham Town	42	14	8	20	48	65	50
Ware	42	14	7	21	48	76	49
Hungerford Town	42	13	7	22	56	66	46
Tilbury	42	13	3	26	59	81	42
Hampton	42	12	5	25	42	70	41
Leatherhead	42	10	6	26	46	92	36
Lewes	42	8	11	24	38	85	34
Collier Row	42	7	8	27	37	88	29
Rainham Town	42	4	2	36	24	116	14

Third Division

Bracknell Town	40	25	8	7	78	29	83
Cheshunt	40	23	12	5	62	34	81
Oxford City	40	24	6	10	94	55	78
Harlow Town	40	22	11	7	61	36	77
Southall	40	17	12	11	66	53	63
Camberley Town	40	18	7	15	56	50	61
Hertford Town	40	18	6	16	67	65	60
Royston Town	40	15	11	14	44	41	56
Northwood	40	15	11	14	78	77	56
Epsom & Ewell	40	15	9	16	63	62	54
Harefield United	40	12	15	13	45	55	51
Cove	40	15	6	19	59	74	51
Kingsbury Town	40	12	14	14	57	54	50
Feltham & Hounslow	40	14	7	19	60	63	49
Leighton Town	40	12	11	17	51	64	47
East Thurrock Town	40	10	15	15	66	64	45
Clapton	40	12	9	19	51	65	45
Hornchurch	40	12	8	20	42	60	44
Tring Town	40	10	11	19	48	64	41
Flackwell Heath	40	9	11	20	44	83	38
Horsham	40	6	8	26	43	86	26

1994-95 Premier Division

Enfield	42	28	9	5	106	43	93
Slough Town	42	22	13	7	82	56	79
Hayes	42	20	14	8	66	47	74
Aylesbury United	42	21	6	15	86	59	69
Hitchin Town	42	18	12	12	68	59	66
Bromley	42	18	11	13	76	67	65
St Albans City	42	17	13	12	96	81	64
Molesey	42	18	8	16	65	61	62
Yeading	42	14	15	13	60	59	57
Harrow Borough	42	17	6	19	64	67	57
Dulwich Hamlet	42	16	9	17	70	82	57
Carshalton Athletic	42	16	9	17	69	84	57
Kingstonian	42	16	8	18	62	57	56
Walton & Hersham	42	14	11	17	75	73	53
Sutton United	42	13	12	17	74	69	51
Purfleet	42	13	12	17	76	90	51
Hendon	42	12	14	16	57	65	50
Grays Athletic	42	11	16	15	57	61	49
Bishop's Stortford	42	12	11	19	53	76	47
Chesham United	42	12	9	21	60	87	45
Marlow	47	10	9	23	57	84	39
Wokingham Town	42	6	9	27	39	86	27

First Division

Boreham Wood	42	31	5	6	90	38	98
Worthing	42	21	13	8	93	49	76
Chertsey Town	42	21	11	10	109	57	74
Aldershot Town	42	23	5	14	80	53	74
Billericay Town	42	20	9	13	68	52	69
Staines Town	42	17	12	13	83	65	63
Basingstoke Town	42	17	10	15	81	71	61
Tooting & Mitcham United	42	15	14	13	58	48	59
Wembley	42	16	11	15	70	61	59
Abingdon Town	42	16	11	15	67	69	59
Whyteleafe	42	17	7	18	70	78	58
Maidenhead United	42	15	12	15	73	76	57
Uxbridge	42	15	11	16	54	62	56
Leyton	42	15	10	17	67	66	55
Barking	42	16	7	19	74	77	55
Heybridge Swifts	42	16	6	20	73	78	54
Ruislip Manor	42	14	11	17	70	75	53
Bognor Regis Town	42	13	14	15	57	63	53
Berkhamsted Town	42	14	10	18	54	70	52
Newbury Town	42	12	15	15	58	71	51
Wivenhoe Town	42	8	7	27	47	94	31
Dorking	42	3	3	36	40	163	12

Second Division

Thame United	42	30	3	9	97	49	93
Barton Rovers	42	25	7	10	93	51	82
Oxford City	42	24	8	10	86	47	80
Bracknell Town	42	23	9	10	86	47	78
Metropolitan Police	42	19	12	11	81	65	69
Hampton	42	20	9	13	79	74	69
Croydon	42	20	5	17	85	65	65
Banstead Athletic	42	18	10	14	73	59	64
Saffron Walden Town	42	17	13	12	64	59	64
Chalfont St Peter	42	17	12	13	54	53	63
Witham Town	42	18	9	15	75	64	63
Leatherhead	42	16	12	14	71	75	60
Edgware Town	42	16	10	16	70	66	58
Tilbury	42	15	9	18	62	82	54
Cheshunt	42	13	13	16	66	81	52
Ware	42	14	7	21	61	81	49
Egham Town	42	11	14	17	60	65	47
Hemel Hempstead	42	10	11	21	45	76	41
Hungerford Town	42	11	7	24	55	81	40
Windsor & Eton	42	10	8	24	58	84	38
Aveley	42	9	5	28	48	95	32
Malden Vale	42	5	9	28	46	108	24

Third Division

Collier Row	40	30	5	5	86	23	95
Canvey Island	40	28	4	8	88	42	88
Bedford Town	40	22	11	7	90	50	77
Northwood	40	22	8	10	80	47	74
Horsham	40	22	6	12	84	61	72
Southall	40	21	8	11	87	59	71
Leighton Town	40	20	8	12	66	43	68
Camberley Town	40	19	8	13	59	39	65
Kingsbury Town	40	18	11	1	72	54	65
Hornchurch	40	17	8	15	64	63	59
Clapton	40	14	11	15	69	61	53
Tring Town	40	13	12	15	68	69	51
East Thurrock United	40	14	8	18	60	79	50
Epsom & Ewell	40	13	10	17	58	62	49
Harlow Town	40	13	8	19	53	83	47
Harefield United	40	12	8	20	51	79	44
Hertford Town	40	11	10	19	56	78	43
Feltham & Hounslow	40	13	4	23	64	87	43
Flackwell Heath	40	8	4	28	50	99	28
Lewes	40	6	5	29	34	104	23
Cove	40	3	5	32	37	94	14

1995-96 Premier Division

Hayes	42	24	14	4	76	32	86
Enfield	42	26	8	8	78	35	86
Boreham Wood	42	24	11	7	69	29	83
Yeovil Town	42	23	11	8	83	51	80
Dulwich Hamlet	42	23	11	8	85	59	80
Carshalton Athletic	42	22	8	12	68	49	74
St Albans City	42	20	12	10	70	41	72
Kingstonian	42	20	11	11	62	38	71
Harrow Borough	42	19	10	13	70	56	67
Sutton United	42	17	14	11	71	56	65
Aylesbury United	42	17	12	13	71	58	63
Bishop's Stortford	42	16	9	17	61	62	57
Yeading	42	11	14	17	48	60	47
Hendon	42	12	10	20	52	65	46
Chertsey Town	42	13	6	23	45	71	45
Purfleet	42	12	8	22	48	67	44
Grays Athletic	42	11	11	20	43	63	44
Hitchin Town	42	10	10	22	41	74	40
Bromley	42	10	7	25	52	91	37
Molesey	42	9	9	24	46	81	36
Walton & Hersham	42	9	7	26	42	79	34
Worthing	42	4	7	31	42	106	19

First Division

Oxford City	42	28	7	7	98	60	91
Heybridge Swifts	42	27	7	8	97	43	88
Staines Town	42	23	11	8	82	59	80
Leyton Pennant	42	22	7	13	77	57	73
Aldershot Town	42	21	9	12	81	46	72
Billericay Town	42	19	9	14	58	58	66
Bognor Regis Town	42	18	11	13	71	53	65
Marlow	42	19	5	18	72	75	62
Basingstoke Town	42	16	13	13	70	60	61
Uxbridge	42	16	12	14	46	49	60
Wokingham Town	42	16	10	16	62	65	58
Chesham United	42	15	12	15	51	44	57
Thame United	42	14	13	15	64	73	55
Maidenhead United	42	12	14	16	50	63	50
Whyteleafe	42	12	13	17	71	81	49
Abingdon Town	42	13	9	20	63	80	48
Barton Rovers	42	12	10	20	69	87	46
Berkhamsted Town	42	11	11	20	52	68	44
Tooting & Mitcham United	42	11	10	21	45	64	43
Ruislip Manor	42	11	9	22	55	77	42
Wembley	42	11	8	23	49	66	41
Barking	42	4	12	26	35	90	24

Second Division

Canvey Island	40	25	12	3	91	36	87
Croydon	40	25	6	9	78	42	81
Hampton	40	23	10	7	74	44	79
Banstead Athletic	40	21	11	8	72	36	74
Collier Row	40	21	11	8	73	41	74
Wivenhoe Town	40	21	8	11	82	57	71
Metropolitan Police	40	18	10	12	57	45	64
Bedford Town	40	18	10	12	69	59	64
Bracknell Town	40	18	8	14	69	50	62
Edgware Town	40	16	9	15	72	67	57
Tilbury	40	12	11	17	52	62	47
Ware	40	13	8	19	55	80	47
Chalfont St Peter	40	11	13	16	58	63	46
Leatherhead	40	12	10	18	71	77	46
Saffron Walden Town	40	11	12	17	56	58	45
Cheshunt	40	10	12	18	56	90	42
Hemel Hempstead	40	10	10	20	46	62	40
Egham Town	40	12	3	25	42	74	39
Witham Town	40	8	10	22	35	68	34
Hungerford Town	40	9	7	24	44	79	34
Dorking	40	8	5	27	44	104	29

Third Division

Horsham	40	29	5	6	95	40	92
Leighton Town	40	28	5	7	95	34	89
Windsor & Eton	40	27	6	7	117	46	87
Wealdstone	40	23	8	9	104	39	77
Harlow Town	40	22	10	8	85	62	76
Northwood	40	20	9	11	76	56	69
Epsom & Ewell	40	18	14	8	95	57	68
Kingsbury Town	40	15	16	9	61	48	61
East Thurrock United	40	17	8	15	61	50	59
Aveley	40	16	10	14	62	53	58
Wingate & Finchley	40	16	7	17	74	70	55
Lewes	40	14	7	19	56	72	49
Flackwell Heath	40	14	5	21	60	84	47
Hornchurch	40	11	8	21	55	77	41
Harefield United	40	11	7	22	49	89	40
Tring Town	40	10	8	22	40	78	38
Camberley Town	40	9	9	22	45	81	36
Hertford Town	40	10	5	25	72	103	35
Cove	40	8	10	22	37	89	34
Clapton	40	9	6	25	48	89	33
Southall	40	9	5	26	34	104	32

1996-97

Premier Division

Yeovil Town	42	31	8	3	83	34	101
Enfield	42	28	11	3	91	29	98
Sutton United	42	18	13	11	87	70	67
Dagenham & Redbridge	42	18	11	13	57	43	65
Yeading	42	17	14	11	58	47	65
St Albans City	42	18	11	13	65	55	65
Aylesbury United	42	18	11	13	64	54	65
Purfleet	42	17	11	14	67	63	62
Heybridge Swifts	42	16	14	12	62	62	62
Boreham Wood	42	15	13	14	56	52	58
Kingstonian	42	16	8	18	79	79	56
Dulwich Hamlet	42	14	13	15	57	57	55
Carshalton Athletic	42	14	11	17	51	56	53
Hitchin Town	42	15	7	20	67	73	52
Oxford City	42	14	10	18	67	83	52
Hendon	42	13	12	17	53	59	51
Harrow Borough	42	12	14	16	58	62	50
Bromley	42	13	9	20	67	72	48
Bishop's Stortford	42	10	13	19	43	64	43
Staines Town	42	10	8	24	46	71	38
Grays Athletic	42	8	9	25	43	78	33
Chertsey Town	42	8	7	27	40	98	31

First Division

Chesham United	42	27	6	9	80	46	87
Basingstoke Town	42	22	13	7	81	38	79
Walton & Hersham	42	21	13	8	67	41	76
Hampton	42	21	12	9	62	39	75
Billericay Town	42	21	12	9	69	49	75
Bognor Regis Town	42	21	9	12	63	44	72
Aldershot Town	42	19	14	9	67	45	71
Uxbridge	42	15	17	10	65	48	62
Whyteleafe	42	18	7	17	71	68	61
Molesey	42	17	9	16	50	53	60
Abingdon Town	42	15	11	16	44	42	56
Leyton Pennant	42	14	12	16	71	72	54
Maidenhead United	42	15	10	17	57	57	52
Wokingham Town	42	14	10	18	41	45	52
Thame United	42	13	10	19	57	69	49
Worthing	42	11	11	20	58	77	44
Barton Rovers	42	11	11	20	31	58	44
Croydon	42	11	10	21	40	57	43
Berkhamsted Town	42	11	9	22	47	66	42
Canvey Island	42	9	14	19	52	71	41
Marlow	42	11	6	25	41	84	39
Tooting & Mitcham United	42	8	8	26	40	85	32

Maidenhead United had 3 points deducted

Second Division

Collier Row & Romford	42	28	12	2	93	33	96
Leatherhead	42	30	5	7	116	45	95
Wembley	42	23	11	8	92	45	80
Barking	42	22	13	7	69	40	79
Horsham	42	22	11	9	78	48	77
Edgware Town	42	20	14	8	74	50	74
Bedford Town	42	21	8	13	77	43	71
Banstead Athletic	42	21	5	16	75	52	68
Windsor & Eton	42	17	13	12	65	62	64
Leighton Town	42	17	12	13	64	52	63
Bracknell Town	42	17	9	16	78	71	60
Wivenhoe Town	42	17	9	16	69	62	60
Chalfont St Peter	42	14	13	15	53	61	55
Hungerford Town	42	14	13	15	68	77	55
Metropolitan Police	42	14	7	21	72	75	49
Tilbury	42	14	7	21	68	77	49
Witham Town	42	11	10	21	39	67	43
Egham Town	42	10	9	23	47	86	39
Cheshunt	42	9	3	30	37	101	30
Ware	42	7	8	27	44	80	29
Dorking	42	7	6	29	40	100	27
Hemel Hempstead	42	5	6	31	34	125	21

Third Division

Wealdstone	32	24	3	5	72	24	75
Braintree Town	32	23	5	4	99	29	74
Northwood	32	18	10	4	60	31	64
Harlow Town	32	19	4	9	60	41	61
Aveley	32	17	6	9	64	39	57
East Thurrock United	32	16	6	10	58	51	54
Camberley Town	32	15	6	11	55	44	51
Wingate & Finchley	32	11	7	14	52	63	40
Hornchurch	32	11	6	15	35	51	39
Clapton	32	11	6	15	31	49	39
Lewes	32	10	8	14	45	53	38
Kingsbury Town	32	11	4	17	41	54	37
Hertford Town	32	10	6	16	55	65	36
Epsom & Ewell	32	8	5	19	62	78	29
Flackwell Heath	32	8	5	19	36	71	29
Tring Town	32	7	3	22	33	74	24
Southall	32	6	4	22	28	69	22

1997-98 Premier Division

Kingstonian	42	25	12	5	84	35	87
Boreham Wood	42	23	11	8	81	42	80
Sutton United	42	22	12	8	83	56	78
Dagenham & Redbridge	42	21	10	11	73	50	73
Hendon	42	21	10	11	69	50	73
Heybridge Swifts	42	18	11	13	74	62	65
Enfield	42	18	8	16	66	58	62
Basingstoke Town	42	17	11	14	56	60	62
Walton & Hersham	42	18	6	18	50	70	60
Purfleet	42	15	13	14	57	58	58
St Albans City	42	17	7	18	54	59	58
Harrow Borough	42	15	10	17	60	67	55
Gravesend & Northfleet	42	15	8	19	65	67	53
Chesham United	42	14	10	18	71	70	52
Bromley	42	13	13	16	53	53	52
Dulwich Hamlet	42	13	11	18	56	67	50
Carshalton Athletic	42	13	9	20	54	77	48
Aylesbury United	42	13	8	21	55	70	47
Bishop's Stortford	42	14	5	23	53	69	47
Yeading	42	12	11	19	49	65	47
Hitchin Town	42	8	15	19	45	62	39
Oxford City	42	7	9	26	35	76	30

First Division

Aldershot Town	42	28	8	6	89	36	92
Billericay Town	42	25	6	11	78	44	81
Hampton	42	22	15	5	75	47	81
Maidenhead United	42	25	5	12	76	37	80
Uxbridge	42	23	6	13	66	59	75
Grays Athletic	42	21	10	11	79	49	73
Romford	42	21	8	13	92	59	71
Bognor Regis Town	42	20	9	13	77	45	69
Leatherhead	42	18	11	13	70	51	65
Leyton Pennant	42	17	11	14	66	58	62
Chertsey Town	42	16	13	13	83	70	61
Worthing	42	17	6	19	64	71	57
Berkhamsted Town	42	15	8	19	59	69	53
Staines Town	42	13	10	19	54	71	49
Croydon	42	13	10	19	47	64	49
Barton Rovers	42	11	13	18	53	72	46
Wembley	42	10	15	17	38	61	45
Molesey	42	10	11	21	47	65	41
Whyteleafe	42	10	10	22	48	83	40
Wokingham Town	42	7	10	25	41	74	31
Abingdon Town	42	9	4	29	47	101	31
Thame United	42	7	9	26	33	96	30

Second Division

Canvey Island	42	30	8	4	116	41	98
Braintree Town	42	29	11	2	117	45	98
Wealdstone	42	24	11	7	81	46	83
Bedford Town	42	22	12	8	55	25	78
Metropolitan Police	42	21	8	13	80	65	71
Wivenhoe Town	42	18	12	12	84	66	66
Edgware Town	42	18	10	14	81	65	64
Chalfont St Peter	42	17	13	12	63	60	64
Northwood	42	17	11	14	65	69	62
Windsor & Eton	42	17	7	18	75	72	58
Tooting & Mitcham United	42	16	9	17	58	56	57
Barking	42	15	12	15	62	75	57
Banstead Athletic	42	15	9	18	60	63	54
Marlow	42	16	5	21	64	78	53
Horsham	42	13	9	20	67	75	48
Bracknell Town	42	13	8	21	68	93	47
Leighton Town	42	13	6	23	45	78	45
Hungerford Town	42	11	11	20	66	77	44
Witham Town	42	9	13	20	55	68	40
Tilbury	42	9	12	21	57	88	39
Egham Town	42	9	5	28	47	101	32
Cheshunt	42	4	10	28	31	90	32

Third Division

Hemel Hempstead	38	27	6	5	86	28	87
Hertford Town	38	26	5	7	77	31	83
Harlow Town	38	24	11	3	81	43	83
Camberley Town	38	24	7	7	93	43	79
Ford United	38	23	9	6	90	34	78
East Thurrock United	38	23	7	8	70	40	76
Epsom & Ewell	38	17	6	15	69	57	57
Ware	38	17	6	15	69	57	57
Aveley	38	16	7	15	65	57	55
Corinthian Casuals	38	16	6	16	59	57	54
Hornchurch	38	12	9	17	55	68	45
Clapton	38	13	6	19	46	61	45
Flackwell Heath	38	12	9	17	50	76	45
Croydon Athletic	38	12	7	19	58	63	43
Tring Town	38	12	7	19	51	69	43
Southall	38	10	6	22	41	85	36
Dorking	38	9	6	23	49	94	33
Wingate & Finchley	38	7	8	23	46	80	29
Lewes	38	7	5	26	34	88	26
Kingsbury Town	38	5	3	30	35	93	18

1998-99 Premier Division

Sutton United	42	27	7	8	89	39	88
Aylesbury United	42	23	8	11	67	38	77
Dagenham & Redbridge	42	20	13	9	71	44	73
Purfleet	42	22	7	13	71	52	73
Enfield	42	21	9	12	73	49	72
St Albans City	42	17	17	8	71	52	68
Aldershot Town	42	16	14	12	83	48	62
Basingstoke Town	42	17	10	15	63	53	61
Harrow Borough	42	17	9	16	72	66	60
Gravesend & Northfleet	42	18	6	18	54	53	60
Slough Town	42	16	11	15	60	53	59
Billericay Town	42	15	13	14	54	56	58
Hendon	42	16	9	17	70	71	57
Boreham Wood	42	14	15	13	59	63	57
Chesham United	42	15	9	18	58	79	54
Dulwich Hamlet	42	14	8	20	53	63	50
Heybridge Swifts	42	13	9	20	51	85	48
Walton & Hersham	42	12	7	23	50	77	43
Hampton	42	10	12	20	41	71	42
Carshalton Athletic	42	10	10	22	47	82	40
Bishop's Stortford	42	9	10	23	49	90	37
Bromley	42	8	11	23	50	72	35

First Division

Canvey Island	42	28	6	8	76	41	90
Hitchin Town	42	25	10	7	75	38	85
Wealdstone	42	26	6	10	75	48	84
Braintree Town	42	20	10	12	75	48	70
Bognor Regis Town	42	20	8	14	63	44	68
Grays Athletic	42	19	11	12	56	42	68
Oxford City	42	16	14	12	58	51	62
Croydon	42	16	13	13	53	53	61
Chertsey Town	42	14	16	12	57	57	58
Romford	42	14	15	13	58	63	57
Maidenhead United	42	13	15	14	50	46	54
Worthing	42	13	13	16	47	61	52
Leyton Pennant	42	13	12	17	62	70	51
Uxbridge	42	13	11	18	54	51	50
Barton Rovers	42	11	15	16	43	49	48
Yeading	42	12	10	20	51	55	46
Leatherhead	42	12	9	21	48	59	45
Whyteleafe	42	13	6	23	51	72	45
Staines Town	42	10	15	17	33	57	45
Molesey	42	8	20	14	35	52	44
Wembley	42	10	10	22	36	71	40
Berkhamsted Town	42	10	7	25	53	81	37

Second Division

Bedford Town	42	29	7	6	89	31	94
Harlow Town	42	27	8	7	100	47	89
Thame United	42	26	8	8	89	50	86
Hemel Hempstead	42	21	12	9	90	50	75
Windsor & Eton	42	22	6	14	87	55	72
Banstead Athletic	42	21	8	13	83	62	71
Northwood	42	20	7	15	67	68	67
Tooting & Mitcham United	42	19	9	14	63	62	66
Chalfont St Peter	42	16	12	14	70	71	60
Metropolitan Police	42	17	8	17	61	58	59
Leighton Town	42	16	10	16	60	64	58
Horsham	42	17	6	19	74	67	57
Marlow	42	16	9	17	72	68	57
Edgware Town	42	14	10	18	65	68	52
Witham Town	42	12	15	15	64	64	51
Hungerford Town	42	13	12	17	59	61	51
Wivenhoe Town	42	14	8	20	71	83	50
Wokingham Town	42	14	4	24	44	79	46
Barking	42	10	11	21	50	75	41
Hertford Town	42	11	2	29	44	96	35
Bracknell Town	42	7	10	25	48	92	31
Abingdon Town	42	6	6	30	48	124	24

Third Division

Ford United	38	27	5	6	110	42	86
Wingate & Finchley	38	25	5	8	79	38	80
Cheshunt	38	23	10	5	70	41	79
Lewes	38	25	3	10	86	45	78
Epsom & Ewell	38	19	5	14	61	51	62
Ware	38	19	4	15	79	60	61
Tilbury	38	17	8	13	74	52	59
Croydon Athletic	38	16	10	12	82	59	58
East Thurrock United	38	15	13	10	74	56	58
Egham Town	38	16	8	14	65	58	56
Corinthian Casuals	38	16	7	15	70	71	55
Southall	38	14	9	15	68	66	51
Camberley Town	38	14	8	16	66	77	50
Aveley	38	12	7	19	50	67	43
Flackwell Heath	38	11	9	18	59	70	42
Hornchurch	38	10	9	19	48	73	39
Clapton	38	11	6	21	48	89	39
Dorking	38	8	7	23	52	98	31
Kingsbury Town	38	6	3	29	40	98	21
Tring Town	38	5	6	27	38	108	21

1999-2000

Premier Division

Dagenham & Redbridge	42	32	5	5	97	35	101
Aldershot Town	42	24	5	13	71	51	77
Chesham United	42	20	10	12	64	50	70
Purfleet	42	18	15	9	70	48	69
Canvey Island	42	21	6	15	70	53	69
St Albans City	42	19	10	13	75	55	67
Billericay Town	42	18	12	12	62	62	66
Hendon	42	18	8	16	61	64	62
Slough Town	42	17	9	16	61	59	60
Dulwich Hamlet	42	17	5	20	62	68	56
Gravesend & Northfleet	42	15	10	17	66	67	55
Farnborough Town	42	14	11	17	52	55	53
Hampton & Richmond Borough	42	13	13	16	49	57	52
Enfield	42	13	11	18	64	68	50
Heybridge Swifts	42	13	11	18	57	65	50
Hitchin Town	42	13	11	18	59	72	50
Carshalton Athletic	42	12	12	18	55	65	48
Basingstoke Town	42	13	9	20	56	71	48
Harrow Borough	42	14	6	22	54	70	48
Aylesbury United	42	13	9	20	64	81	48
Boreham Wood	42	11	10	21	44	71	43
Walton & Hersham	42	11	8	23	44	70	41

First Division

Croydon	42	25	9	8	85	47	84
Grays Athletic	42	21	12	9	80	44	75
Maidenhead United	42	20	15	7	72	45	75
Thame United	42	20	13	9	61	38	73
Worthing	42	19	12	11	80	60	69
Staines Town	42	19	12	11	63	52	69
Whyteleafe	42	20	9	13	60	49	69
Bedford Town	42	17	12	13	59	52	63
Bromley	42	17	9	16	62	65	60
Uxbridge	42	15	13	14	60	44	58
Bishop's Stortford	42	16	10	16	57	62	58
Barton Rovers	42	16	8	18	64	83	56
Oxford City	42	17	4	21	57	55	55
Braintree Town	42	15	10	17	65	74	55
Yeading	42	12	18	12	53	54	54
Wealdstone	42	13	12	17	51	58	51
Bognor Regis Town	42	12	13	17	47	53	49
Harlow Town	42	11	13	18	62	76	46
Romford	42	12	9	21	51	70	45
Leatherhead	42	9	13	20	47	70	40
Chertsey Town	42	9	5	28	50	84	32
Leyton Pennant	42	7	9	26	34	85	30

Second Division

Hemel Hempstead	42	31	8	3	98	27	101
Northwood	42	29	9	4	109	40	96
Ford United	42	28	8	6	108	41	92
Berkhamsted Town	42	22	8	12	75	52	74
Windsor & Eton	42	20	13	9	73	53	73
Wivenhoe Town	42	20	9	13	61	47	69
Barking	42	18	13	11	70	51	67
Marlow	42	20	4	18	86	66	64
Metropolitan Police	42	18	7	17	75	71	61
Banstead Athletic	42	16	11	15	56	56	59
Tooting & Mitcham United	42	16	7	19	72	74	55
Wokingham Town	42	15	9	18	58	80	54
Wembley	42	14	11	17	47	53	53
Edgware Town	42	13	11	18	72	71	50
Hungerford Town	42	13	10	19	61	78	49
Cheshunt	42	12	12	18	53	65	48
Horsham	42	13	8	21	66	81	47
Leighton Town	42	13	8	21	65	84	47
Molesey	42	10	12	20	54	69	42
Wingate & Finchley	42	11	7	24	54	97	40
Witham Town	42	7	9	26	39	110	30
Chalfont St Peter	42	2	8	32	39	124	14

Third Division

East Thurrock United	40	26	7	7	89	42	85
Great Wakering Rovers	40	25	7	8	81	41	82
Tilbury	40	21	12	7	67	39	75
Hornchurch	40	19	12	9	72	57	69
Croydon Athletic	40	19	11	10	85	52	68
Epsom & Ewell	40	18	12	10	67	46	66
Lewes	40	18	10	12	73	51	64
Bracknell Town	40	15	16	9	81	64	61
Aveley	40	17	10	13	73	64	61
Corinthian Casuals	40	16	10	14	59	51	58
Flackwell Heath	40	17	6	17	74	76	57
Ware	40	16	8	16	74	62	56
Egham Town	40	14	13	13	48	43	55
Hertford Town	40	15	10	15	63	60	55
Abingdon Town	40	10	12	18	48	64	42
Kingsbury Town	40	11	8	21	55	86	41
Camberley Town	40	11	7	22	44	79	40
Tring Town	40	10	9	21	37	64	39
Dorking	40	9	10	21	53	69	37
Clapton	40	9	7	24	50	93	34
Southall	40	3	5	32	33	123	14

2000-2001 Premier Division

	P	W	D	L	F	A	Pts
Farnborough Town	42	31	6	5	86	27	99
Canvey Island	42	27	8	7	79	41	89
Basingstoke Town	42	22	13	7	73	40	79
Aldershot Town	41	21	11	9	73	39	74
Chesham United	42	22	6	14	78	52	72
Gravesend & Northfleet	42	22	5	15	63	46	71
Heybridge Swifts	42	18	13	11	74	60	67
Billericay Town	41	18	13	10	62	54	67
Hampton & Richmond Borough	42	18	12	12	73	60	66
Hitchin Town	42	18	5	19	72	69	59
Purfleet	42	14	13	15	55	55	55
Hendon	40	16	6	18	62	62	54
Sutton United	41	14	11	16	74	70	53
St Albans City	42	15	5	22	50	69	50
Grays Athletic	42	14	8	20	49	68	50
Maidenhead United	42	15	2	25	47	63	47
Croydon	42	12	10	20	55	77	46
Enfield	42	12	9	21	48	74	45
Harrow Borough	41	10	11	20	62	91	41
Slough Town	42	10	9	23	40	62	39
Carshalton Athletic	42	10	6	26	40	85	36
Dulwich Hamlet	42	4	10	28	33	84	22

First Division

	P	W	D	L	F	A	Pts
Boreham Wood	42	26	7	9	82	49	85
Bedford Town	42	22	16	4	81	40	82
Braintree Town	42	25	6	11	112	60	81
Bishop's Stortford	42	24	6	12	103	76	78
Thame United	42	22	8	12	86	54	74
Ford United	42	19	12	11	70	58	69
Uxbridge	42	21	5	16	73	55	68
Northwood	42	20	8	14	89	81	68
Whyteleafe	42	20	6	16	62	69	66
Oxford City	42	16	13	13	64	49	61
Harlow Town	42	15	16	11	70	66	61
Worthing	42	16	9	17	69	69	57
Staines Town	42	16	8	18	60	66	56
Aylesbury United	42	17	4	21	65	55	55
Yeading	42	15	9	18	72	74	54
Bognor Regis Town	42	13	11	18	71	71	50
Walton & Hersham	42	14	8	20	59	80	50
Bromley	42	14	6	22	63	86	48
Wealdstone	42	12	9	21	54	73	45
Leatherhead	42	12	4	26	37	87	40
Romford	42	9	4	29	53	113	31
Barton Rovers	42	2	9	31	30	94	15

Second Division

	P	W	D	L	F	A	Pts
Tooting & Mitcham United	42	26	11	5	92	35	89
Windsor	42	24	10	8	70	40	82
Barking	42	23	13	6	82	54	82
Berkhamsted Town	42	24	8	10	99	49	80
Wivenhoe Town	42	23	11	8	78	52	80
Hemel Hempstead	42	22	10	10	74	44	76
Horsham	42	19	9	14	84	61	66
Chertsey Town	42	18	9	15	59	59	63
Great Wakering Rovers	42	16	13	13	69	59	61
Tilbury	42	18	6	18	61	67	60
Banstead Athletic	42	17	8	17	69	58	59
East Thurrock United	42	16	11	15	72	64	59
Metropolitan Police	42	18	4	20	64	77	58
Marlow	42	15	11	16	62	61	56
Molesey	42	14	9	19	53	61	51
Wembley	42	12	10	20	39	63	46
Hungerford Town	42	11	9	22	40	73	42
Leyton Pennant	42	10	11	21	47	74	41
Cheshunt	42	11	6	25	48	77	39
Edgware Town	42	9	9	24	41	77	36
Leighton Town	42	8	10	24	44	87	34
Wokingham Town	42	3	12	27	39	94	20

Wokingham Town had 1 point deducted

Third Division

	P	W	D	L	F	A	Pts
Arlesey Town	42	34	6	2	138	37	108
Lewes	41	25	11	5	104	34	86
Ashford Town	42	26	7	9	102	49	85
Flackwell Heath	42	24	10	8	93	51	82
Corinthian Casuals	42	24	10	8	83	50	82
Aveley	42	24	3	15	85	61	75
Epsom & Ewell	42	23	4	15	76	52	73
Witham Town	42	21	9	12	76	57	72
Bracknell Town	41	19	10	12	90	70	67
Croydon Athletic	41	15	12	14	78	63	57
Ware	42	17	6	19	75	76	57
Tring Town	42	16	9	17	60	71	57
Egham Town	42	15	11	16	60	60	56
Hornchurch	42	14	13	15	73	60	55
Wingate & Finchley	42	15	7	20	75	75	52
Kingsbury Town	42	11	8	23	74	100	41
Abingdon Town	42	12	7	23	53	102	40
Dorking	42	10	9	23	59	99	39
Hertford Town	41	9	8	24	57	97	35
Camberley Town	42	8	8	26	53	107	32
Clapton	42	5	9	28	48	121	24
Chalfont St Peter	42	4	1	37	30	150	13

Abingdon Town had 3 points deducted

2001-2002 Premier Division

	P	W	D	L	F	A	Pts
Gravesend & Northfleet	42	31	6	5	90	33	99
Canvey Island	42	30	5	7	107	41	95
Aldershot Town	42	22	7	13	76	51	73
Braintree Town	42	23	4	15	66	61	73
Purfleet	42	19	15	8	67	44	72
Grays Athletic	42	20	10	12	65	55	70
Chesham United	42	19	10	13	69	53	67
Hendon	42	19	5	18	66	54	62
Billericay Town	42	16	13	13	59	60	61
St Albans City	42	16	9	17	71	60	57
Hitchin Town	42	15	10	17	73	81	55
Sutton United	42	13	15	14	62	62	54
Heybridge Swifts	42	15	9	18	68	85	54
Kingstonian	42	13	13	16	50	56	52
Boreham Wood	42	15	6	21	49	62	51
Maidenhead United	42	15	5	22	51	63	50
Bedford Town	42	12	12	18	64	69	48
Basingstoke Town	42	11	15	16	50	68	48
Enfield	42	11	9	22	48	77	42
Hampton & Richmond Borough	42	9	13	20	51	71	40
Harrow Borough	42	8	10	24	50	89	34
Croydon	42	7	5	30	36	93	26

First Division

	P	W	D	L	F	A	Pts
Ford United	42	27	7	8	92	56	88
Bishop's Stortford	42	26	9	7	104	51	87
Aylesbury United	42	23	10	9	96	64	79
Bognor Regis Town	42	20	13	9	74	55	73
Northwood	42	19	11	12	92	64	68
Carshalton Athletic	42	17	16	9	64	53	67
Harlow Town	42	19	9	14	77	65	66
Slough Town	42	17	11	14	68	51	62
Uxbridge	42	18	6	18	68	65	60
Oxford City	42	17	9	16	59	66	60
Thame United	42	15	14	13	75	61	59
Tooting & Mitcham United	42	16	11	15	70	70	59
Walton & Hersham	42	16	10	16	75	70	58
Yeading	42	16	10	16	84	90	58
Worthing	42	15	8	19	69	65	53
Staines Town	42	12	11	19	45	60	47
Dulwich Hamlet	42	11	13	18	64	76	46
Wealdstone	42	11	12	19	60	82	45
Bromley	42	10	11	21	44	74	41
Whyteleafe	42	10	11	21	46	86	41
Barking & East Ham United	42	8	7	27	61	123	31
Windsor & Eton	42	7	5	30	53	93	26

2002-2003

Second Division

Lewes	42	29	9	4	108	31	96
Horsham	42	27	9	6	104	44	90
Berkhamstead Town	42	23	10	9	82	51	79
Arlesey Town	42	23	6	13	89	55	75
Banstead Athletic	42	22	8	12	83	54	74
Leyton Pennant	42	22	8	12	84	60	74
Great Wakering Rovers	42	21	8	13	64	37	71
East Thurrock United	42	21	8	13	67	59	71
Marlow	42	18	13	11	73	63	67
Hemel Hempstead Town	42	18	10	14	82	66	64
Leatherhead	42	17	6	19	72	62	57
Ashford Town	42	15	11	16	58	71	56
Metropolitan Police	42	16	7	19	84	84	55
Barton Rovers	42	15	9	18	54	60	54
Hungerford Town	42	14	9	19	56	75	51
Tilbury	42	15	6	21	55	74	51
Chertsey Town	42	10	14	18	79	112	44
Wembley	42	9	10	23	51	82	37
Molesey	42	10	6	26	40	93	36
Cheshunt	42	7	13	22	51	84	34
Wivenhoe Town	42	8	9	25	55	111	33
Romford	42	4	7	31	42	105	19

Third Division

Croydon Athletic	42	30	5	7	138	41	95
Hornchurch	42	25	11	6	96	46	86
Aveley	42	26	6	10	109	55	84
Bracknell Town	42	25	8	9	96	54	83
Epsom & Ewell	42	20	15	7	79	51	75
Egham Town	42	21	11	10	72	59	74
Wingate & Finchley	42	20	9	13	80	60	69
Dorking	42	18	14	10	77	66	68
Tring Town	42	19	11	12	64	62	68
Corinthian-Casuals	42	18	13	11	69	44	67
Hertford Town	42	20	7	15	88	74	67
Witham Town	42	15	10	17	66	72	55
Ware	42	14	10	18	74	76	52
Chalfont St Peter	42	15	4	23	69	92	49
Wokingham Town	42	14	6	22	79	105	48
Abingdon Town	42	13	7	22	61	75	46
Leighton Town	42	8	12	22	56	95	36
Kingsbury Town	42	8	11	23	58	91	35
Edgware Town	42	9	7	26	65	101	34
Flackwell Heath	42	9	8	25	53	99	32
Clapton	42	9	4	29	45	118	31
Camberley Town	42	7	9	26	37	95	30

Premier Division

Aldershot Town	46	33	6	7	81	36	105
Canvey Island	46	28	8	10	112	56	92
Hendon	46	22	13	11	70	56	79
St. Albans City	46	23	8	15	73	65	77
Basingstoke Town	46	23	7	16	80	60	76
Sutton United	46	22	9	15	77	62	75
Hayes	46	20	13	13	67	54	73
Purfleet	46	19	15	12	68	48	72
Bedford Town	46	21	9	16	66	58	72
Maidenhead United	46	16	17	13	75	63	65
Kingstonian	46	16	17	13	71	64	65
Billericay Town	46	17	11	18	46	44	62
Bishop's Stortford	46	16	11	19	74	72	59
Hitchin Town	46	15	13	18	69	67	58
Ford United	46	15	12	19	78	84	57
Braintree Town	46	14	12	20	59	71	54
Aylesbury United	46	13	15	18	62	75	54
Harrow Borough	46	15	9	22	54	75	54
Grays Athletic	46	14	11	21	53	59	53
Heybridge Swifts	46	13	14	19	52	80	53
Chesham United	46	14	10	22	56	81	52
Boreham Wood	46	11	15	20	50	58	48
Enfield	46	9	11	26	47	101	38
Hampton & Richmond Borough	46	3	14	29	35	86	23

Division One North

Northwood	46	28	7	11	109	56	91
Hornchurch	46	25	15	6	85	48	90
Hemel Hempstead Town	46	26	7	13	70	55	85
Slough Town	46	22	14	10	86	59	80
Uxbridge	46	23	10	13	62	41	79
Aveley	46	21	14	11	66	48	77
Berkhamsted Town	46	21	13	12	92	68	76
Thame United	46	20	12	14	84	51	72
Wealdstone	46	21	9	16	85	69	72
Harlow Town	46	20	12	14	66	53	72
Marlow	46	19	10	17	74	63	67
Barking & East Ham United	46	19	9	18	73	76	66
Yeading	46	18	11	17	77	69	65
Great Wakering Rovers	46	17	14	15	64	70	65
Oxford City	46	17	13	16	55	51	64
Arlesey Town	46	17	12	17	69	71	63
East Thurrock United	46	17	10	19	75	79	61
Wingate & Finchley	46	15	11	20	70	74	56
Barton Rovers	46	15	7	24	53	65	52
Tilbury	46	14	7	25	55	96	49
Wivenhoe Town	46	9	11	26	56	94	38
Leyton Pennant	46	9	7	30	38	81	34
Wembley	46	7	11	28	57	111	32
Hertford Town	46	6	6	34	46	119	24

Division One South

Carshalton Athletic	46	28	8	10	73	44	92
Bognor Regis Town	46	26	10	10	92	34	88
Lewes	46	24	16	6	106	50	88
Dulwich Hamlet	46	23	12	11	73	49	81
Whyteleafe	46	21	13	12	74	51	76
Bromley	46	21	13	12	70	53	76
Walton & Hersham	46	20	13	13	87	63	73
Horsham	46	21	9	16	80	58	72
Epsom & Ewell	46	19	12	15	67	66	69
Egham Town	46	19	10	17	62	71	67
Tooting & Mitcham United	46	18	9	19	83	78	63
Worthing	46	17	12	17	78	75	63
Windsor & Eton	46	18	9	19	66	65	63
Leatherhead	46	16	13	17	71	66	61
Staines Town	46	14	16	16	57	63	58
Banstead Athletic	46	14	15	17	58	59	57
Ashford Town (Middlesex)	46	14	11	21	47	70	53
Croydon	46	15	8	23	56	87	53
Croydon Athletic	46	13	13	20	52	66	52
Bracknell Town	46	12	16	18	57	74	52
Corinthian Casuals	46	12	14	20	50	68	50
Molesey	46	13	9	24	52	79	48
Metropolitan Police	46	12	10	24	50	76	46
Chertsey Town	46	3	7	36	43	139	16

Division Two

Cheshunt	30	25	3	2	91	29	78
Leyton	30	21	5	4	77	22	68
Flackwell Heath	30	17	3	10	52	44	54
Abingdon Town	30	14	11	5	65	42	53
Hungerford Town	30	12	12	6	49	36	48
Leighton Town	30	14	3	13	61	43	45
Witham Town	30	12	8	10	40	43	44
Ware	30	12	5	13	47	53	41
Clapton	30	12	5	13	40	47	41
Tring Town	30	11	5	14	49	58	38
Kingsbury Town	30	9	11	10	38	48	38
Edgware Town	30	10	3	17	49	65	33
Wokingham Town	30	7	7	16	34	59	28
Dorking	30	6	6	18	49	63	24
Chalfont St. Peter	30	6	5	19	34	63	23
Camberley Town	30	4	4	22	23	61	16

2003-2004

Premier Division

Canvey Island	46	32	8	6	106	42	104
Sutton United	46	25	10	11	94	56	85
Thurrock	46	24	11	11	87	45	83
Hendon	46	25	8	13	68	47	83
Hornchurch	46	24	11	11	63	35	82
Grays Athletic	46	22	15	9	82	39	81
Carshalton Athletic	46	24	9	13	66	55	81
Hayes	46	21	11	14	56	46	74
Kettering Town	46	20	11	15	63	63	71
Bognor Regis Town	46	20	10	16	69	67	70
Bishop's Stortford	46	20	9	17	78	61	69
Maidenhead United	46	18	9	19	60	68	63
Ford United	46	16	14	16	69	63	62
Basingstoke Town	46	17	9	20	58	64	60
Bedford Town	46	14	13	19	62	63	55
Heybridge Swifts	46	14	11	21	57	78	53
Harrow Borough	46	12	14	20	47	63	50
Kingstonian	46	12	13	21	40	56	49
St. Albans City	46	12	12	22	55	83	48
Hitchin Town	46	13	8	25	55	89	47
Northwood	46	12	9	25	65	95	45
Billericay Town	46	11	11	24	51	66	44
Braintree Town	46	11	6	29	41	88	39
Aylesbury United	46	5	14	27	41	101	29

Hornchurch had 1 point deducted.

Division One North

Yeading	46	32	7	7	112	54	103
Leyton	46	29	9	8	90	53	96
Cheshunt	46	27	10	9	119	54	91
Chesham United	46	24	9	13	104	60	81
Dunstable Town	46	23	9	14	86	61	78
Hemel Hempstead Town	46	22	12	12	75	72	78
Wealdstone	46	23	7	16	81	51	76
Arlesey Town	46	23	7	16	95	70	76
Boreham Wood	46	20	13	13	82	59	73
Harlow Town	46	20	10	16	75	51	70
Wingate & Finchley	46	19	13	14	68	63	70
East Thurrock United	46	19	11	16	62	54	68
Uxbridge	46	15	14	17	59	57	59
Aveley	46	15	14	17	67	71	59
Thame United	46	16	9	21	72	83	57
Waltham Forest	46	15	13	18	62	60	55
Wivenhoe Town	46	15	10	21	79	104	55
Barton Rovers	46	16	6	24	52	80	54
Oxford City	46	14	11	21	55	65	53
Berkhamstead Town	46	12	10	24	66	88	46
Great Wakering Rovers	46	10	13	23	47	97	43
Tilbury	46	10	9	27	56	100	39
Barking & East Ham United	46	8	7	31	37	100	31
Enfield	46	5	7	34	44	138	22

Waltham Forest had 3 points deducted.

Division One South

Lewes	46	29	7	10	113	61	94
Worthing	46	26	14	6	87	46	92
Windsor & Eton	46	26	13	7	75	39	91
Slough Town	46	28	6	12	103	63	90
Hampton & Richmond Borough	46	26	11	9	82	45	89
Staines Town	46	26	9	11	85	52	87
Dulwich Hamlet	46	23	15	8	77	57	84
Bromley	46	22	10	14	80	58	76
Walton & Hersham	46	20	14	12	76	55	74
Croydon Athletic	46	20	10	16	70	54	70
Tooting & Mitcham United	46	20	9	17	82	68	69
Ashford Town (Middlesex)	46	18	13	15	69	62	67
Leatherhead	46	19	9	18	83	88	66
Bracknell Town	46	19	6	21	81	87	63
Horsham	46	16	11	19	71	69	59
Marlow	46	16	11	19	50	64	59
Whyteleafe	46	17	4	25	66	93	55
Banstead Athletic	46	15	8	23	56	73	53
Molesey	46	12	6	28	45	84	42
Metropolitan Police	46	9	14	23	58	84	41
Croydon	46	10	10	26	57	88	40
Egham Town	46	8	8	30	55	92	32
Corinthian Casuals	46	6	6	34	48	110	24
Epsom & Ewell	46	5	8	33	40	117	23

Division Two

Leighton Town	42	28	7	7	111	36	91
Dorking	42	27	8	7	87	47	89
Hertford Town	42	24	9	9	74	35	81
Chertsey Town	42	22	9	11	75	53	75
Flackwell Heath	42	22	5	15	71	53	71
Witham Town	42	20	10	12	75	54	70
Kingsbury Town	42	14	11	17	60	64	53
Ware	42	14	10	18	67	60	52
Abingdon Town	42	15	6	21	83	81	51
Camberley Town	42	15	6	21	51	71	51
Wembley	42	13	9	20	46	67	48
Wokingham Town	42	12	7	23	55	94	43
Edgware Town	42	12	6	24	62	88	42
Chalfont St. Peter	42	12	6	24	57	89	42
Clapton	42	8	5	29	47	129	29

2004-2005

Premier Division

Yeading	42	25	11	6	74	48	86
Billericay Town	42	23	11	8	78	40	80
Eastleigh	42	22	13	7	84	49	79
Braintree Town	42	19	17	6	67	33	74
Leyton	42	21	8	13	71	57	71
Hampton & Richmond	42	21	8	13	64	53	71
Heybridge Swifts	42	18	9	15	76	65	63
Chelmsford City	42	17	11	14	63	58	62
Staines Town	42	17	9	16	59	53	60
Worthing	42	16	11	15	50	45	59
Hendon	42	17	7	18	48	60	58
Salisbury City	42	16	9	17	60	64	57
Slough Town	42	15	10	17	61	66	55
Folkestone Invicta	42	14	10	18	51	53	52
Windsor & Eton	42	12	14	16	48	62	50
Harrow Borough	42	13	10	19	41	54	49
Northwood	42	14	7	21	49	66	49
Wealdstone	42	13	8	21	60	73	47
Cheshunt	42	12	11	19	58	71	47
Tonbridge Angels	42	11	10	21	47	73	43
Dover Athletic	42	10	9	23	50	66	39
Kingstonian	42	7	5	30	43	93	26

Division One

AFC Wimbledon	42	29	10	3	91	33	97
Walton & Hersham	42	28	4	10	69	34	88
Horsham	42	24	6	12	90	61	78
Bromley	42	22	9	11	69	44	75
Metropolitan Police	42	22	8	12	72	51	74
Cray Wanderers	42	19	16	7	95	54	73
Leatherhead	42	20	13	9	73	55	73
Tooting & Mitcham United	42	18	15	9	92	60	69
Whyteleafe	42	20	6	16	60	59	66
Burgess Hill Town	42	19	6	17	73	62	63
Hastings United	42	15	11	16	55	57	56
Croydon Athletic	42	13	16	13	66	65	55
Corinthian-Casuals	42	15	9	18	56	64	54
Bashley	42	13	13	16	68	74	52
Dulwich Hamlet	42	10	14	18	61	64	44
Molesey	42	12	8	22	46	70	44
Banstead Athletic	42	10	10	22	50	64	40
Newport IOW	42	10	10	22	50	88	40
Fleet Town	42	11	5	26	47	86	38
Ashford Town	42	8	12	22	47	85	36
Dorking	42	8	11	23	43	89	35
Croydon	42	5	10	27	37	91	25

Division Two

Ilford	30	22	3	5	62	23	69
Enfield	30	21	3	6	64	33	66
Brook House	30	20	4	6	65	25	64
Hertford Town	30	17	7	6	65	40	58
Witham Town	30	16	3	11	67	53	51
Chertsey Town	30	15	6	9	55	48	51
Abingdon Town	30	13	9	8	65	42	48
Edgware Town	30	12	3	15	40	41	39
Flackwell Heath	30	11	5	14	50	55	38
Ware	30	9	10	11	41	55	37
Chalfont St Peter	30	9	7	14	41	52	34
Camberley Town	30	9	5	16	36	44	32
Wembley	30	8	5	17	41	55	29
Epsom & Ewell	30	8	4	18	41	64	28
Kingsbury Town	30	5	4	21	35	76	19
Clapton	30	3	6	21	20	82	15

2005-2006

Premier Division

Braintree Town	42	28	10	4	74	32	94
Heybridge Swifts	42	28	3	11	70	46	87
Fisher Athletic	42	26	7	9	84	46	85
AFC Wimbledon	42	22	11	9	67	36	77
Hampton & Richmond	42	24	3	15	73	54	75
Staines Town	42	20	10	12	74	56	70
Billericay Town	42	19	12	11	69	45	69
Worthing	42	19	10	13	71	60	67
Walton & Hersham	42	19	7	16	55	50	64
Chelmsford City	42	18	10	14	57	62	64
Bromley	42	16	14	12	57	49	62
East Thurrock United	42	18	5	19	60	60	59
Folkestone Invicta	42	16	10	16	47	51	58
Margate	42	11	17	14	49	55	50
Leyton	42	13	9	20	58	61	48
Harrow Borough	42	13	9	20	56	73	48
Slough Town	42	13	8	21	63	75	47
Wealdstone	42	13	5	24	68	82	44
Hendon	42	9	12	21	44	64	39
Maldon Town	42	8	11	23	41	73	35
Windsor & Eton	42	8	8	26	37	75	32
Redbridge	42	3	5	34	28	97	14

Division One

Ramsgate	44	24	14	6	84	38	86
Horsham	44	25	11	8	94	55	86
Tonbridge Angels	44	24	8	12	71	48	80
Metropolitan Police	44	24	7	13	72	46	79
Dover Athletic	44	21	14	9	69	46	77
Tooting & Mitcham United	44	22	9	13	93	62	75
Kingstonian	44	20	14	10	82	56	74
Croydon Athletic	44	20	13	11	56	41	73
Bashley	44	20	10	14	63	61	70
Leatherhead	44	18	14	12	64	50	68
Cray Wanderers	44	20	8	16	80	74	68
Hastings United	44	19	10	15	65	58	67
Dulwich Hamlet	44	19	8	17	55	43	65
Fleet Town	44	13	19	12	50	56	58
Walton Casuals	44	16	10	18	68	75	58
Lymington & New Milton	44	12	11	21	61	80	47
Molesey	44	12	10	22	56	79	46
Whyteleafe	44	10	14	20	50	66	44
Burgess Hill Town	44	10	10	24	57	83	40
Banstead Athletic	44	8	13	23	43	71	37
Ashford Town	44	8	11	25	41	81	35
Newport IOW	44	6	11	27	38	97	29
Corinthian Casuals	44	6	9	29	39	85	27

Division Two

Ware	30	19	4	7	77	36	61
Witham Town	30	17	7	6	61	30	58
Brook House	30	17	7	6	63	33	58
Flackwell Heath	30	15	7	8	54	49	52
Egham Town	30	15	5	10	39	36	50
Chertsey Town	30	14	7	9	47	37	49
Edgware Town	30	13	5	12	46	41	44
Chalfont St Peter	30	13	2	15	50	53	41
Dorking	30	11	8	11	48	51	41
Croydon	30	11	7	12	43	43	40
Wembley	30	11	6	13	44	43	39
Kingsbury Town	30	9	10	11	32	37	37
Hertford Town	30	7	10	13	35	54	31
Camberley Town	30	5	8	17	31	57	23
Epsom & Ewell	30	5	6	19	32	64	21
Clapton	30	4	9	17	33	71	16

Clapton had 5 points deducted.

2006-2007 Premier Division

Hampton & Richmond	42	24	10	8	77	53	82
Bromley	42	23	11	8	83	43	80
Chelmsford City	42	23	8	11	96	51	77
Billericay Town	42	22	11	9	71	42	77
AFC Wimbledon	42	21	15	6	76	37	75
Margate	42	20	11	11	79	48	71
Boreham Wood	42	19	12	11	71	49	69
Horsham	42	18	14	10	70	57	68
Ramsgate	42	20	5	17	63	63	65
Heybridge Swifts	42	17	13	12	57	40	64
Tonbridge Angels	42	20	4	18	74	72	64
Staines Town	42	15	12	15	64	64	57
Carshalton Athletic	42	14	12	16	54	59	54
Hendon	42	16	6	20	53	64	54
Leyton	42	13	10	19	55	77	49
East Thurrock United	42	14	6	22	56	70	48
Ashford Town (Middlesex)	42	11	13	18	59	71	46
Folkestone Invicta	42	12	10	20	45	66	46
Harrow Borough	42	13	6	23	61	71	45
Worthing	42	8	11	23	57	82	35
Walton & Hersham	42	9	6	27	38	83	33
Slough Town	42	4	6	32	26	123	18

AFC Wimbledon had 3 points deducted.

Division One North

AFC Hornchurch	42	32	7	3	96	27	103
Harlow Town	42	24	10	8	71	31	82
Enfield Town	42	24	7	11	74	39	79
Maldon Town	42	20	11	11	50	42	71
AFC Sudbury	42	19	13	10	67	41	70
Canvey Island	42	19	10	13	65	47	67
Ware	42	19	10	13	70	56	67
Waltham Forest	42	17	14	11	60	56	65
Wingate & Finchley	42	16	11	15	58	49	59
Waltham Abbey	42	15	13	14	65	51	58
Wivenhoe Town	42	16	9	17	50	52	57
Great Wakering Rovers	42	16	9	17	57	64	57
Enfield	42	16	6	20	65	63	54
Potters Bar Town	42	14	9	19	60	62	51
Aveley	42	14	9	19	47	57	51
Redbridge	42	15	5	22	42	48	50
Bury Town	42	13	11	18	57	69	50
Arlesey Town	42	13	11	18	44	63	50
Tilbury	42	11	10	21	43	72	43
Witham Town	42	10	7	25	52	90	37
Ilford	42	9	5	28	36	97	32
Flackwell Heath	42	7	9	26	37	90	30

Division One South

Maidstone United	42	23	11	8	79	47	80
Tooting & Mitcham	42	22	13	7	70	41	79
Dover Athletic	42	22	11	9	77	41	77
Hastings United	42	22	10	10	79	56	76
Fleet Town	42	21	12	9	65	52	75
Metropolitan Police	42	18	15	9	65	48	69
Dartford	42	19	11	12	86	65	68
Dulwich Hamlet	42	18	13	11	83	56	67
Horsham YMCA	42	17	7	18	59	69	58
Sittingbourne	42	14	15	13	68	63	57
Leatherhead	42	15	10	17	58	63	55
Cray Wanderers	42	14	12	16	67	69	54
Kingstonian	42	13	13	16	60	63	52
Burgess Hill Town	42	13	12	17	58	81	51
Molesey	42	12	13	17	52	63	49
Chatham Town	42	12	11	19	52	62	47
Walton Casuals	42	11	13	18	57	71	46
Ashford Town	42	10	14	18	52	65	44
Croydon Athletic	42	12	8	22	44	77	44
Whyteleafe	42	9	15	18	52	65	42
Corinthian-Casuals	42	8	10	24	53	88	34
Godalming Town	42	8	9	25	45	76	33

2007-2008

Premier Division

Chelmsford City	42	26	9	7	84	39	87
Staines Town	42	22	12	8	85	54	78
AFC Wimbledon	42	22	9	11	81	47	75
AFC Hornchurch	42	20	10	12	68	44	70
Ramsgate	42	19	11	12	67	53	68
Ashford Town (Middlesex)	42	20	6	16	79	65	66
Hendon	42	18	11	13	79	67	65
Tonbridge Angels	42	17	12	13	77	57	63
Margate	42	17	11	14	71	68	62
Billericay Town	42	16	12	14	66	57	60
Horsham	42	18	5	19	63	63	59
Heybridge Swifts	42	14	13	15	64	64	55
Wealdstone	42	15	9	18	68	75	54
Hastings United	42	15	8	19	58	67	53
Harlow Town	42	13	13	16	56	52	52
Harrow Borough	42	15	7	20	61	74	52
Maidstone United	42	16	4	22	56	79	52
Carshalton Athletic	42	14	8	20	52	65	50
Doreham Wood	42	15	5	22	56	73	50
East Thurrock United	42	14	9	19	48	67	50
Folkestone Invicta	42	13	10	19	49	70	49
Leyton	42	4	4	34	35	123	16

East Thurrock United had one point deducted.

Division One North

Dartford	42	27	8	7	107	42	89
AFC Sudbury	42	24	8	10	86	40	80
Redbridge	42	24	9	9	70	43	80
Ware	42	23	10	9	110	58	79
Canvey Island	42	23	10	9	82	39	79
Brentwood Town	42	22	11	9	70	49	77
Bury Town	42	22	9	11	76	53	75
Edgware Town	42	20	14	8	53	39	74
Maldon Town	42	19	10	13	78	63	67
Northwood	42	18	12	12	71	61	66
Aveley	42	18	12	12	68	65	66
Enfield Town	42	18	9	15	60	63	63
Great Wakering Rovers	42	13	9	20	64	66	48
Waltham Abbey	42	12	10	20	42	78	46
Arlesey Town	42	12	9	21	64	84	45
Witham Town	42	12	5	25	75	109	41
Potters Bar Town	42	10	9	23	45	77	39
Wingate & Finchley	42	8	11	23	45	72	35
Waltham Forest	42	7	12	23	44	74	33
Tilbury	42	7	12	23	49	96	32
Ilford	42	8	8	26	47	95	32
Wivenhoe Town	42	8	7	27	46	86	31

Redbridge and Tilbury both had one point deducted.

Division One South

Dover Athletic	42	30	8	4	84	29	98
Tooting & Mitcham	42	26	8	8	88	41	86
Cray Wanderers	42	25	11	6	87	42	86
Metropolitan Police	42	24	3	15	69	47	75
Worthing	42	22	7	13	77	49	73
Dulwich Hamlet	42	20	10	12	68	47	70
Kingstonian	42	20	10	12	66	52	70
Ashford Town	42	19	10	13	64	51	67
Sittingbourne	42	20	7	15	56	58	67
Walton & Hersham	42	15	12	15	65	62	57
Whyteleafe	42	17	5	20	57	62	56
Burgess Hill Town	42	18	8	16	61	57	54
Croydon Athletic	42	14	9	19	65	76	51
Whitstable Town	42	14	8	20	69	84	50
Chipstead	42	15	5	22	58	76	50
Walton Casuals	42	11	15	16	55	68	48
Leatherhead	42	13	7	22	52	63	46
Chatham Town	42	12	10	20	58	70	46
Eastbourne Town	42	11	11	20	58	84	44
Corinthian-Casuals	42	11	11	20	51	77	44
Horsham YMCA	42	7	6	29	36	85	27
Molesey	42	3	9	30	36	100	18

Burgess Hill Town had 8 points deducted.

Division One North

Aveley	42	29	9	4	81	40	96
East Thurrock United	42	30	5	7	112	50	95
Brentwood Town	42	26	10	6	77	32	88
Waltham Abbey	42	25	7	10	85	45	82
Concord Rangers	42	23	10	9	83	34	79
Northwood	42	22	12	8	65	39	78
Wingate & Finchley	42	19	10	13	67	51	67
Redbridge	42	18	10	14	61	50	64
Ware	42	19	4	19	69	75	61
Chatham Town	42	18	6	18	58	60	60
Tilbury	42	16	10	16	62	53	58
Enfield Town	42	17	7	18	71	68	58
Great Wakering Rovers	42	16	10	16	56	62	58
Cheshunt	42	17	5	20	60	71	56
Leyton	42	12	15	15	63	56	51
Maldon Town	42	13	9	20	48	63	45
Ilford	42	12	5	25	27	68	41
Thamesmead Town	42	10	10	22	46	73	40
Potters Bar Town	42	9	10	23	52	73	36
Waltham Forest	42	9	7	26	39	81	34
Witham Town	42	6	9	27	37	103	27
Hillingdon Borough	42	4	4	34	35	107	16

Maldon Town had 3 points deducted.
Potters Bar Town had 1 point deducted.

2008-2009

Premier Division

Dover Athletic	42	33	5	4	91	34	104
Staines Town	42	23	13	6	75	41	82
Tonbridge Angels	42	20	13	9	82	54	73
Carshalton Athletic	42	19	11	12	64	63	68
Sutton United	42	18	13	11	57	53	67
AFC Hornchurch	42	19	8	15	60	51	65
Wealdstone	42	18	8	16	70	56	62
Dartford	42	17	11	14	62	49	62
Tooting & Mitcham United	42	16	10	16	57	57	58
Ashford Town (Middlesex)	42	18	2	22	64	66	56
Billericay Town	42	15	11	16	54	66	56
Canvey Island	42	16	7	19	65	70	55
Horsham	42	16	7	19	49	60	55
Harrow Borough	42	14	12	16	56	73	54
Maidstone United	42	14	11	17	46	51	53
Hendon	42	15	6	21	69	65	51
Hastings United	42	14	7	21	52	68	49
Boreham Wood	42	12	12	18	48	61	48
Margate	42	13	7	22	51	64	46
Harlow Town	42	13	6	23	61	77	42
Heybridge Swifts	42	10	11	21	41	63	41
Ramsgate	42	8	11	23	47	79	31

Harlow town had 3 points deducted.
Ramsgate had 4 points deducted.

Division One South

Kingstonian	42	26	8	8	91	48	86
Cray Wanderers	42	24	7	11	87	54	79
Fleet Town	42	21	15	6	82	43	78
Metropolitan Police	42	21	14	7	72	45	77
Worthing	42	21	13	8	77	48	76
Sittingbourne	42	19	13	10	63	54	70
Ashford Town	42	16	15	11	68	54	63
Merstham	42	18	10	14	57	54	63
Godalming Town	42	17	11	14	71	50	62
Croydon Athletic	42	16	14	12	67	54	62
Folkestone Invicta	42	16	11	15	54	46	59
Dulwich Hamlet	42	15	15	12	64	50	57
Eastbourne Town	42	17	6	19	66	72	57
Walton & Hersham	42	13	11	18	46	55	50
Leatherhead	42	14	8	20	57	74	50
Whitstable Town	42	14	8	20	58	77	50
Walton Casuals	42	12	8	22	43	60	44
Whyteleafe	42	11	10	21	48	64	43
Burgess Hill Town	42	10	13	19	49	66	43
Corinthian-Casuals	42	11	10	21	61	91	43
Chipstead	42	8	12	22	57	96	36
Crowborough Athletic	42	4	4	34	42	125	13

Merstham had one point deducted.
Dulwich Hamlet and Crowborough Athletic had 3 points deducted.

2009-2010

Premier Division

Dartford	42	29	6	7	101	45	93
Sutton United	42	22	9	11	65	45	75
Aveley	42	21	7	14	83	62	70
Boreham Wood	42	20	8	14	54	44	68
Kingstonian	42	20	8	14	73	69	68
Wealdstone	42	17	14	11	65	65	65
Hastings United	42	18	9	15	68	56	63
Tonbridge Angels	42	18	8	16	69	67	62
AFC Hornchurch	42	16	13	13	51	47	61
Hendon	42	18	6	18	61	59	60
Horsham	42	16	8	18	65	67	56
Tooting & Mitcham United	42	15	10	17	60	64	55
Billericay Town	42	14	12	16	44	42	54
Harrow Borough	42	13	14	15	66	63	53
Cray Wanderers	42	14	9	19	54	70	51
Canvey Island	42	13	11	18	57	62	50
Carshalton Athletic	42	12	13	17	58	64	49
Maidstone United	42	13	10	19	39	57	49
Margate	42	11	12	19	50	72	45
Ashford Town (Middlesex)	42	11	11	20	62	80	44
Waltham Abbey	42	12	8	22	49	74	44
Bognor Regis Town	42	9	14	19	45	65	41

Division One South

Croydon Athletic	42	27	8	7	92	39	89
Folkestone Invicta	42	28	8	6	54	23	82
Worthing	42	25	5	12	83	53	80
Godalming Town	42	26	5	11	71	44	80
Leatherhead	42	22	8	12	78	45	74
Fleet Town	42	22	6	14	74	49	72
Burgess Hill Town	42	19	10	13	64	50	67
Walton & Hersham	42	18	8	16	55	54	62
Sittingbourne	42	18	7	17	63	48	61
Metropolitan Police	42	17	9	16	59	50	60
Horsham YMCA	42	15	14	13	67	61	59
Dulwich Hamlet	42	14	12	16	57	64	54
Corinthian-Casuals	42	17	3	22	66	79	54
Ramsgate	42	13	14	15	55	61	53
Whyteleafe	42	15	6	21	60	64	51
Merstham	42	12	12	18	62	80	48
Chatham Town	42	14	4	24	55	75	46
Whitstable Town	42	14	3	25	41	85	45
Chipstead	42	11	10	21	47	65	43
Ashford Town (Kent)	42	9	11	22	49	90	38
Walton Casuals	42	8	10	24	41	66	34
Eastbourne Town	42	6	11	25	29	77	29

Folkestone Invicta had 10 points deducted.
Godalming Town had 3 points deducted.

Division One North

Lowestoft Town	42	32	5	5	115	37	101
Concord Rangers	42	26	8	8	94	42	86
Wingate & Finchley	42	24	9	9	88	55	81
Enfield Town	42	23	11	8	81	47	80
East Thurrock United	42	23	8	11	102	59	77
Heybridge Swifts	42	21	8	13	67	56	71
Thamesmead Town	42	20	7	15	67	56	67
VCD Athletic (R)	42	19	10	13	61	53	67
Great Wakering Rovers	42	18	10	14	67	70	64
Northwood	42	17	10	15	65	61	61
Tilbury	42	15	11	16	61	60	56
Brentwood Town	42	15	7	20	53	53	52
Romford	42	15	7	20	71	88	52
Potters Bar Town	42	14	8	20	51	67	50
Cheshunt	42	16	2	24	57	83	50
Waltham Forest	42	13	9	20	51	75	48
Maldon Town	42	13	6	23	54	74	45
Ilford	42	11	10	21	47	72	43
Redbridge	42	9	15	18	42	62	42
Ware	42	11	9	22	57	84	42
Leyton	42	5	15	22	40	84	30
Harlow Town	42	6	7	29	46	98	15

VCD Athletic were relegated at the end of the season due to their failure to meet ground grading requirements.
Harlow Town had 10 points deducted for entering administration but were reprieved from relegation.

2010-2011

Premier Division

Sutton United	42	26	9	7	76	33	87
Tonbridge Angels	42	22	10	10	71	45	76
Bury Town	42	22	10	10	67	49	76
Lowestoft Town	42	20	15	7	68	30	75
Harrow Borough	42	22	7	13	77	51	73
Canvey Island	42	21	10	11	69	51	73
Kingstonian	42	21	9	12	66	50	72
Concord Rangers	42	21	8	13	72	55	71
Cray Wanderers	42	20	9	13	72	46	69
AFC Hornchurch	42	19	12	11	60	46	69
Billericay Town	42	20	9	13	56	45	69
Wealdstone	42	16	10	16	58	54	58
Carshalton Athletic	42	14	10	18	49	57	52
Tooting & Mitcham United	42	13	10	19	63	85	49
Hendon	42	12	10	20	61	81	46
Margate	42	11	12	19	52	64	45
Horsham	42	11	11	20	43	77	44
Hastings United	42	9	11	22	50	65	38
Aveley	42	10	8	24	35	62	38
Maidstone United	42	9	10	23	43	75	37
Croydon Athletic	42	10	4	28	44	95	31
Folkestone Invicta	42	5	12	25	34	68	27

Croydon Athletic had 3 points deducted.

2011-2012

Division One North

East Thurrock United	40	30	5	5	92	38	95
Needham Market	40	26	9	5	95	49	87
Wingate & Finchley	40	21	9	10	72	54	72
Harlow Town	40	21	8	11	61	51	71
Brentwood Town	40	20	9	11	75	55	69
Enfield Town	40	21	5	14	76	44	68
AFC Sudbury	40	18	12	10	82	64	66
Maldon & Tiptree	40	18	9	13	70	67	63
Heybridge Swifts	40	17	10	13	81	59	61
Grays Athletic	40	17	10	13	69	51	61
Waltham Abbey	40	16	10	14	75	63	58
Romford	40	16	7	17	63	66	55
Potters Bar Town	40	14	9	17	60	68	51
Ware	40	13	6	21	57	77	45
Great Wakering Rovers	40	13	5	22	60	82	44
Redbridge	40	10	9	21	51	79	39
Thamesmead Town	40	11	6	23	42	71	39
Cheshunt	40	10	8	22	49	81	38
Tilbury	40	11	4	25	41	66	37
Ilford	40	8	8	24	42	81	32
Waltham Forest	40	6	8	26	43	90	26

Leyton withdrew from Division One North on 14th January 2011 and were subsequently expelled from the League. The club's record was expunged when it stood at: 19 1 6 12 13 45 9
Waltham Forest were reprieved from relegation due to this withdrawal.

Premier Division

Billericay Town	42	24	13	5	82	38	85
AFC Hornchurch	42	26	4	12	68	35	82
Lowestoft Town	42	25	7	10	80	53	82
Wealdstone	42	20	15	7	76	39	75
Bury Town	42	22	9	11	85	55	75
Lewes	42	21	10	11	55	47	73
Hendon	42	21	9	12	69	44	72
Canvey Island	42	22	5	15	66	55	71
Cray Wanderers	42	20	8	14	74	55	68
East Thurrock United	42	18	8	16	70	65	62
Kingstonian	42	18	7	17	58	64	61
Metropolitan Police	42	18	6	18	63	46	60
Wingate & Finchley	42	16	11	15	63	79	59
Concord Rangers	42	16	9	17	72	66	57
Margate	42	15	9	18	66	65	54
Carshalton Athletic	42	14	10	18	48	55	52
Harrow Borough	42	13	8	21	53	70	47
Hastings United	42	13	8	21	43	61	47
Leatherhead	42	11	8	23	46	62	41
Aveley	42	5	12	25	41	88	27
Tooting & Mitcham United	42	7	6	29	47	116	27
Horsham	42	3	6	33	38	105	14

Horsham had 1 point deducted for fielding an ineligible player.

Division One South

Metropolitan Police	42	30	6	6	102	41	96
Bognor Regis Town	42	29	9	4	103	43	96
Whitehawk	42	26	10	6	109	44	88
Leatherhead	42	27	7	8	100	41	88
Dulwich Hamlet	42	19	8	15	79	59	65
Walton & Hersham	42	18	8	16	69	58	62
Burgess Hill Town	42	16	14	12	69	60	62
Ramsgate	42	16	12	14	65	63	60
Faversham Town	42	14	17	11	55	48	59
Chipstead	42	15	12	15	63	67	57
Sittingbourne	42	16	8	18	52	66	56
Walton Casuals	42	15	8	19	65	71	53
Fleet Town	42	14	10	18	68	90	52
Worthing	42	12	14	16	76	72	50
Whitstable Town	42	12	13	17	58	75	49
Whyteleafe	42	14	3	25	65	94	45
Godalming Town	42	13	6	23	52	82	45
Eastbourne Town	42	11	11	20	60	78	44
Merstham	42	10	15	17	60	85	44
Corinthian-Casuals	42	11	9	22	53	80	42
Chatham Town	42	10	10	22	52	80	40
Horsham YMCA	42	5	8	29	41	119	23

Merstham had one point deducted.
Chatham Town were reprieved from relegation after transferring to the Isthmian League Division One North for the next season.

Division One North

Leiston	42	28	7	7	99	41	91
Enfield Town	42	27	9	6	96	46	90
Tilbury	42	23	11	8	82	62	80
Needham Market	42	23	8	11	104	56	77
Grays Athletic	42	24	8	10	80	47	77
Redbridge	42	21	10	11	79	59	73
Harlow Town	42	21	8	13	70	49	71
AFC Sudbury	42	20	9	13	65	57	69
Brentwood Town	42	18	8	16	58	42	62
Thamesmead Town	42	17	7	18	68	70	58
Maldon & Tiptree	42	16	10	16	62	66	58
Potters Bar Town	42	16	9	17	67	76	57
Romford	42	15	12	15	64	73	57
Waltham Abbey	42	15	10	17	79	76	55
Chatham Town	42	16	6	20	54	63	54
Heybridge Swifts	42	15	7	20	59	64	52
Waltham Forest	42	12	7	23	59	95	43
Cheshunt	42	9	12	21	42	83	39
Soham Town Rangers	42	7	13	22	55	93	34
Ilford	42	8	6	28	47	85	30
Ware	42	8	6	28	40	78	30
Great Wakering Rovers	42	6	11	25	43	91	29

Grays Athletic had 3 points deducted for fielding an ineligible player.

Division One South

Whitehawk	40	29	6	5	82	26	90
Bognor Regis Town	40	26	10	4	105	37	88
Dulwich Hamlet	40	26	8	6	73	26	86
Folkestone Invicta	40	23	7	10	82	53	76
Godalming Town	40	22	7	11	77	53	73
Maidstone United	40	20	7	13	68	50	67
Worthing	40	18	10	12	69	45	64
Hythe Town	40	17	8	15	62	62	59
Merstham	40	17	8	15	63	69	59
Chipstead	40	16	8	16	59	57	56
Ramsgate	40	16	7	17	61	72	55
Walton & Hersham	40	14	8	18	54	52	50
Corinthian-Casuals	40	12	12	16	49	63	48
Eastbourne Town	40	11	13	16	49	63	46
Walton Casuals	40	12	6	22	51	74	42
Crawley Down	40	12	5	23	65	81	41
Faversham Town	40	10	10	20	43	67	40
Whitstable Town	40	12	4	24	46	87	40
Sittingbourne	40	6	12	22	36	75	30
Burgess Hill Town	40	9	6	25	39	90	30
Whyteleafe	40	6	10	24	38	67	28

Whitehawk had 3 points deducted for fielding an ineligible player.
Burgess Hill Town had 3 points deducted for fielding an ineligible player.
Croydon Athletic had 10 points deducted for financial irregularities and then resigned from the League on 18th January 2012. The club's record was expunged when it stood as follows: 19 3 3 13 23 44 2
Godalming Town transferred to the Southern Football League Division One Central at the end of the season.

Division One North

Grays Athletic	42	32	6	4	96	38	102
Maldon & Tiptree	42	27	8	7	101	47	89
Thamesmead Town	42	28	4	10	85	49	88
Witham Town	42	24	7	11	71	47	79
Aveley	42	24	6	12	92	58	78
Heybridge Swifts	42	21	10	11	102	55	73
Soham Town Rangers	42	22	7	13	95	75	73
Romford	42	19	7	16	72	72	64
Tilbury	42	18	9	15	69	62	63
Brentwood Town	42	17	8	17	63	62	59
Potters Bar Town	42	15	13	14	64	68	58
Cheshunt	42	16	10	16	75	73	55
Waltham Abbey	42	15	8	19	60	70	53
Chatham Town	42	13	13	16	59	65	52
Wroxham	42	12	14	16	68	64	50
Needham Market	42	12	13	17	61	62	49
A.F.C. Sudbury	42	12	9	21	57	84	45
Waltham Forest	42	10	10	22	54	72	40
Ware	42	10	6	26	59	105	36
Redbridge	42	7	6	29	42	105	26
Harlow Town	42	9	8	25	45	82	25
Ilford	42	4	8	30	32	105	20

Redbridge had one point deducted for fielding an ineligible player.
Cheshunt had 3 points deducted for fielding an ineligible player.
Harlow Town had 10 points deducted for failing to notify the league that they had failed to make repayments under their company voluntary arrangement and had extended the term of their CVA.

2012-2013

Premier Division

Whitehawk	42	25	13	4	88	42	88
Lowestoft Town	42	23	11	8	71	38	80
Wealdstone	42	22	13	7	70	38	79
Concord Rangers	42	22	10	10	80	54	76
East Thurrock United	42	18	16	8	65	45	70
Metropolitan Police	42	20	10	12	65	56	70
Bury Town	42	19	9	14	66	64	66
Canvey Island	42	18	10	14	60	55	64
Margate	42	17	11	14	61	49	62
Hendon	42	16	12	14	48	50	60
Kingstonian	42	18	5	19	63	62	59
Leiston	42	13	17	12	55	57	56
Hampton & Richmond	42	13	14	15	58	56	53
Bognor Regis Town	42	15	8	19	48	58	53
Harrow Borough	42	12	9	21	53	71	45
Enfield Town	42	13	5	24	60	83	44
Cray Wanderers	42	10	13	19	60	85	43
Wingate & Finchley	42	12	6	24	56	82	42
Lewes	42	9	13	20	59	75	40
Carshalton Athletic	42	12	4	26	55	76	40
Hastings United	42	8	15	19	39	62	39
Thurrock	42	11	8	23	40	62	38

Thurrock had three points deducted after the end of the season for fielding an ineligible player. A subsequent appeal was rejected.

Division One South

Dulwich Hamlet	42	28	5	9	91	42	89
Maidstone United	42	26	10	6	96	39	88
Faversham Town	42	22	11	9	74	57	77
Hythe Town	42	22	10	10	78	55	76
Folkestone Invicta	42	19	14	9	73	49	71
Leatherhead	42	22	4	16	66	44	70
Ramsgate	42	20	10	12	60	44	70
Burgess Hill Town	42	16	15	11	54	46	63
Sittingbourne	42	16	13	13	67	56	61
Worthing	42	16	9	17	77	74	57
Eastbourne Town	42	16	9	17	62	61	57
Merstham	42	16	8	18	67	76	56
Crawley Down Gatwick	42	15	10	17	72	70	55
Corinthian-Casuals	42	10	16	16	39	54	46
Horsham	42	12	9	21	54	77	45
Tooting & Mitcham United	42	12	9	21	52	75	45
Whitstable Town	42	12	8	22	53	71	44
Walton & Hersham	42	11	11	20	48	77	44
Herne Bay	42	10	13	19	44	69	43
Chipstead	42	11	9	22	54	80	42
Three Bridges	42	11	7	24	58	83	40
Walton Casuals	42	9	10	23	50	90	37

2013-2014

Premier Division

Wealdstone	46	28	12	6	99	43	96
Kingstonian	46	25	10	11	80	44	85
Bognor Regis Town	46	26	7	13	95	65	85
Lowestoft Town	46	24	12	10	76	40	84
AFC Hornchurch	46	24	11	11	83	53	83
Dulwich Hamlet	46	25	7	14	96	65	82
Maidstone United	46	23	12	11	92	57	81
Hendon	46	21	7	18	84	69	70
Leiston	46	19	10	17	73	71	67
Billericay Town	46	19	9	18	66	64	66
Margate	46	18	10	18	70	67	64
Hampton & Richmond Borough	46	18	10	18	72	70	64
Canvey Island	46	17	11	18	65	65	62
Grays Athletic	46	17	10	19	74	82	61
Bury Town	46	17	9	20	60	65	60
Lewes	46	14	17	15	67	67	59
Metropolitan Police	46	15	13	18	58	59	58
Harrow Borough	46	15	13	18	66	72	58
Enfield Town	46	13	12	21	64	90	51
East Thurrock United	46	13	10	23	66	84	49
Wingate & Finchley	46	14	7	25	57	84	49
Thamesmead Town	46	12	10	24	61	90	46
Carshalton Athletic	46	8	6	32	40	101	30
Cray Wanderers	46	7	5	34	40	138	26

Division One South

Peacehaven & Telscombe	46	33	8	5	128	55	107
Folkestone Invicta	46	27	8	11	102	59	89
Leatherhead	46	28	8	10	93	46	86
Guernsey	46	23	12	11	93	65	81
Hastings United	46	24	7	15	73	62	79
Burgess Hill Town	46	22	11	13	88	67	77
Merstham	46	23	7	16	81	63	76
Hythe Town	46	22	7	17	87	71	73
Walton Casuals	46	22	4	20	89	93	70
Faversham Town	46	18	14	14	78	69	68
Tooting & Mitcham United	46	17	12	17	79	75	63
Ramsgate	46	18	8	20	84	79	62
Chipstead	46	18	8	20	79	83	62
Sittingbourne	46	16	13	17	69	75	61
Worthing	46	17	8	21	80	98	59
Horsham	46	15	11	20	66	78	56
Corinthian-Casuals	46	15	10	21	69	73	55
Herne Bay	46	15	9	22	69	72	54
Three Bridges	46	15	8	23	71	88	53
Whitstable Town	46	14	11	21	61	78	53
Walton & Hersham	46	14	9	23	75	92	51
Redhill	46	13	6	27	72	96	45
Crawley Down Gatwick	46	9	6	31	51	139	33
Eastbourne Town	46	6	11	29	60	121	29

Leatherhead had 6 points deducted for a registration irregularity.

Division One North

VCD Athletic	46	32	3	11	116	54	99
Witham Town	46	30	8	8	109	54	98
Heybridge Swifts	46	28	9	9	108	59	93
Harlow Town	46	27	10	9	105	59	91
Needham Market	46	25	12	9	85	44	87
Thurrock	46	26	9	11	99	60	87
Dereham Town	46	22	11	13	98	65	77
Soham Town Rangers	46	24	4	18	92	75	76
Maldon & Tiptree	46	21	13	12	82	68	76
AFC Sudbury	46	21	13	12	76	63	76
Romford	46	21	5	20	76	69	68
Chatham Town	46	20	8	18	74	76	68
Aveley	46	20	5	21	81	81	65
Redbridge	46	16	11	19	78	84	59
Cheshunt	46	12	17	17	74	75	53
Tilbury	46	14	11	21	56	74	53
Burnham Ramblers	46	14	10	22	69	100	52
Waltham Abbey	46	14	8	24	71	90	50
Brentwood Town	46	11	13	22	71	92	46
Barkingside	46	12	10	24	76	120	46
Ware	46	12	9	25	73	93	45
Wroxham	46	10	6	30	77	123	36
Waltham Forest	46	6	7	33	43	118	25
Erith & Belvedere	46	6	4	36	44	137	22

2014-2015

Premier Division

Maidstone United	46	29	11	6	85	41	98
Hendon	46	27	14	5	82	55	95
Margate	46	25	10	11	94	58	85
Dulwich Hamlet	46	21	13	12	66	51	76
Metropolitan Police	46	21	12	13	72	51	75
Grays Athletic	46	22	8	16	70	57	74
Enfield Town	46	24	4	18	70	56	73
Billericay Town	46	20	8	18	73	65	68
Leiston	46	18	13	15	73	58	67
Leatherhead	46	19	10	17	72	62	67
Kingstonian	46	18	13	15	63	56	67
Wingate & Finchley	46	20	7	19	72	70	67
East Thurrock United	46	17	15	14	66	71	66
Bognor Regis Town	46	17	12	17	71	64	63
Hampton & Richmond	46	16	9	21	62	79	57
Harrow Borough	46	15	8	23	64	77	53
Canvey Island	46	14	11	21	61	77	53
VCD Athletic	46	14	11	21	53	70	53
Lewes	46	14	11	21	45	67	53
Tonbridge Angels	46	13	13	20	63	67	52
Peacehaven & Telscombe	46	13	9	24	58	85	48
Witham Town	46	9	15	22	61	84	42
AFC Hornchurch	46	10	10	26	46	70	40
Bury Town	46	7	11	28	35	86	32

Enfield Town had 3 points deducted for fielding an ineligible player.

2015-2016

Premier Division

Hampton & Richmond Borough	46	28	11	7	105	52	95
Bognor Regis Town	46	29	7	10	95	42	94
East Thurrock United	46	26	13	7	107	53	91
Tonbridge Angels	46	24	13	9	90	49	85
Dulwich Hamlet	46	23	12	11	93	58	81
Enfield Town	46	24	8	14	74	47	80
Kingstonian	46	21	10	15	78	64	73
Leiston	46	20	12	14	72	57	72
Billericay Town	46	18	17	11	76	53	71
Merstham	46	18	8	20	74	80	62
Leatherhead	46	18	8	20	67	81	62
Metropolitan Police	46	17	10	19	60	79	61
Wingate & Finchley	46	17	9	20	66	70	60
Canvey Island	46	17	9	20	69	89	60
Grays Athletic	46	15	12	19	63	74	57
Staines Town	46	15	10	21	53	74	55
Harrow Borough	46	15	9	22	66	80	54
Farnborough	46	16	5	25	65	88	53
Hendon	46	13	13	20	68	85	52
Needham Market	46	13	12	21	51	76	51
Burgess Hill Town	46	12	14	20	57	73	50
Brentwood Town	46	10	10	26	51	80	40
Lewes	46	6	16	24	48	87	34
VCD Athletic	46	8	10	28	46	103	34

Farnborough were demoted at the end of the season after financial irregularities were discovered.

Division One North

Needham Market	46	33	5	8	101	41	104
Harlow Town	46	31	10	5	108	58	103
AFC Sudbury	46	28	6	12	89	51	90
Brentwood Town	46	25	10	11	83	63	85
Thurrock	46	25	9	12	104	57	84
Brightlingsea Regent	46	25	7	14	88	57	82
Dereham Town	46	25	6	15	82	63	81
Wroxham	46	23	10	13	97	58	79
Aveley	46	21	7	18	86	75	70
Ware	46	16	16	14	76	60	64
Soham Town Rangers	46	19	6	21	74	86	63
Heybridge Swifts	46	17	11	18	70	75	62
Thamesmead Town	46	16	10	20	61	69	58
Tilbury	46	16	10	20	64	76	58
Great Wakering Rovers	46	14	10	22	80	87	52
Cray Wanderers	46	14	10	22	77	86	52
Waltham Abbey	46	14	10	22	76	90	52
Cheshunt	46	13	13	20	63	78	52
Maldon & Tiptree	46	13	10	23	57	78	49
Romford	46	13	9	24	69	99	48
Chatham Town	46	12	11	23	52	75	47
Barkingside	46	12	9	25	59	98	45
Redbridge	46	13	6	27	64	111	45
Burnham Ramblers	46	5	7	34	50	138	22

Division One South

Burgess Hill Town	46	33	10	3	105	39	109
Folkestone Invicta	46	29	11	6	106	47	98
Faversham Town	46	30	7	9	111	52	97
Merstham	46	27	12	7	107	51	93
Whyteleafe	46	23	12	11	91	61	81
Worthing	46	22	10	14	92	65	76
Three Bridges	46	21	9	16	94	95	72
Whitstable Town	46	20	11	15	82	77	71
Herne Bay	46	20	9	17	62	65	69
Guernsey	46	19	7	20	92	94	64
Tooting & Mitcham United	46	15	14	17	77	66	59
Sittingbourne	46	16	11	19	55	69	59
Corinthian-Casuals	46	16	10	20	64	82	58
South Park	46	16	8	22	76	105	56
Chipstead	46	15	9	22	67	84	54
Hythe Town	46	14	11	21	82	79	53
Walton & Hersham	46	14	11	21	59	75	53
Walton Casuals	46	16	5	25	62	94	53
Hastings United	46	12	12	22	57	70	48
Carshalton Athletic	46	13	9	24	61	79	48
Ramsgate	46	13	9	24	61	86	48
East Grinstead Town	46	13	6	27	55	94	45
Redhill	46	10	11	25	69	101	41
Horsham	46	10	6	30	50	107	36

Division One North

AFC Sudbury	46	33	6	7	90	49	105
Thurrock	46	30	6	10	99	52	96
Harlow Town	46	29	9	8	92	47	96
Cray Wanderers	46	27	9	10	98	52	90
AFC Hornchurch	46	25	11	10	87	35	86
Cheshunt	46	22	14	10	88	50	80
Maldon & Tiptree	46	22	12	12	89	66	78
Brightlingsea Regent	46	22	11	13	76	55	77
Dereham Town	46	21	11	14	82	61	74
Thamesmead Town	46	21	11	14	74	63	74
Tilbury	46	20	9	17	85	66	69
Aveley	46	20	8	18	84	71	68
Bury Town	46	16	14	16	74	68	62
Phoenix Sports	46	16	8	22	60	74	56
Haringey Borough	46	12	14	20	61	76	50
Romford	46	12	12	22	59	83	48
Soham Town Rangers	46	13	9	24	61	90	48
Great Wakering Rovers	46	12	11	23	69	103	47
Witham Town	46	12	9	25	59	96	45
Heybridge Swifts	46	12	8	26	59	87	44
Waltham Abbey	46	11	8	27	54	80	41
Wroxham	46	10	10	26	50	89	40
Barkingside	46	9	10	27	55	97	37
Redbridge	46	8	4	34	46	141	28

Division One South

Team	P	W	D	L	F	A	Pts
Folkestone Invicta	46	36	6	4	102	34	114
Dorking Wanderers	46	27	9	10	99	56	90
Worthing	46	27	7	12	96	56	88
Hythe Town	46	27	6	13	74	49	87
Faversham Town	46	25	8	13	76	45	83
Corinthian-Casuals	46	26	7	13	75	52	82
Hastings United	46	25	6	15	99	64	81
Herne Bay	46	22	10	14	79	54	76
Molesey	46	23	6	17	87	83	75
Carshalton Athletic	46	21	9	16	83	74	72
South Park	46	21	9	16	78	71	72
Ramsgate	46	21	8	17	92	76	71
Guernsey	46	21	5	20	94	88	68
Three Bridges	46	20	6	20	59	67	66
Whyteleafe	46	19	5	22	69	77	62
Walton Casuals	46	18	6	22	74	85	60
Tooting & Mitcham United	46	16	10	20	66	71	58
Sittingbourne	46	16	6	24	63	77	54
Chatham Town	46	13	7	26	61	70	46
East Grinstead Town	46	12	7	27	55	84	43
Chipstead	46	11	6	29	54	92	39
Walton & Hersham	46	9	6	31	50	113	30
Whitstable Town	46	8	2	36	52	118	26
Peacehaven & Telscombe	46	6	7	33	48	129	25

Walton & Hersham and Corinthian-Casuals both had 3 points deducted for fielding an ineligible player.

Division One North

Team	P	W	D	L	F	A	Pts
Brightlingsea Regent	46	32	7	7	114	57	103
Maldon & Tiptree	46	29	4	13	107	51	91
Thurrock	46	27	8	11	84	39	89
AFC Hornchurch	46	24	13	9	78	42	85
Haringey Borough	46	24	7	15	107	74	79
Bowers & Pitsea	46	23	9	14	102	66	78
Aveley	46	21	13	12	75	64	76
Norwich United	46	24	6	16	70	60	75
Phoenix Sports	46	22	9	15	71	72	75
Cheshunt	46	20	11	15	85	72	71
Bury Town	46	20	9	17	74	66	69
Tilbury	46	17	13	16	67	73	64
Witham Town	46	16	11	19	77	80	59
Brentwood Town	46	17	5	24	63	77	56
VCD Athletic	46	15	11	20	53	76	56
Romford	46	15	11	20	59	90	56
Thamesmead Town	46	16	6	24	70	78	54
Dereham Town	46	15	9	22	70	89	54
Soham Town Rangers	46	14	11	21	62	78	53
Waltham Abbey	46	14	9	23	57	73	51
Heybridge Swifts	46	13	12	21	64	81	51
Ware	46	15	6	25	66	84	51
Wroxham	46	6	7	33	42	103	25
Great Wakering Rovers	46	6	7	33	49	121	25

Norwich United had 3 points deducted for fielding an ineligible player.
Ware were reprieved from relegation after Worcester City requested relegation to Level 5.

2016-2017

Premier Division

Team	P	W	D	L	F	A	Pts
Havant & Waterlooville	46	28	10	8	88	43	94
Bognor Regis Town	46	27	11	8	87	41	92
Dulwich Hamlet	46	22	14	10	89	55	80
Enfield Town	46	21	13	12	86	57	76
Wingate & Finchley	46	23	6	17	63	61	75
Tonbridge Angels	46	21	11	14	66	55	74
Leiston	46	21	10	15	98	66	73
Billericay Town	46	21	9	16	77	56	72
Needham Market	46	20	12	14	76	80	72
Harlow Town	46	20	7	19	76	72	67
Lowestoft Town	46	18	10	18	63	73	64
Staines Town	46	16	13	17	78	68	61
Leatherhead	46	16	12	18	72	72	57
Worthing	46	16	8	22	73	85	56
Folkestone Invicta	46	15	10	21	75	82	55
Kingstonian	46	16	7	23	65	73	55
Metropolitan Police	46	15	9	22	54	72	54
Hendon	46	14	12	20	68	88	54
Burgess Hill Town	46	14	12	20	59	80	54
Merstham	46	15	11	20	70	72	53
Harrow Borough	46	14	11	21	60	80	53
Canvey Island	46	13	13	20	63	92	52
AFC Sudbury	46	12	10	24	57	85	46
Grays Athletic	46	11	5	30	46	101	38

Leatherhead were deducted three points for fielding an ineligible player in their win over Hendon on 10 December.
Merstham were deducted three points for fielding an ineligible player in their win over Leiston on 28 February.
Harrow Borough were reprieved from relegation after Worcester City requested relegation to Level 5.

Division One South

Team	P	W	D	L	F	A	Pts
Tooting & Mitcham United	46	33	6	7	120	54	105
Dorking Wanderers	46	33	6	7	103	44	105
Greenwich Borough	46	30	5	11	102	52	95
Corinthian-Casuals	46	29	6	11	99	59	93
Hastings United	46	23	13	10	128	64	82
Carshalton Athletic	46	24	9	13	106	69	81
Hythe Town	46	23	9	14	87	65	78
South Park	46	24	4	18	95	80	76
Lewes	46	23	7	16	88	75	76
Faversham Town	46	22	8	16	89	58	74
Cray Wanderers	46	19	11	16	88	86	68
Ramsgate	46	18	11	17	79	75	65
Walton Casuals	46	19	8	19	98	99	65
Whyteleafe	46	19	7	20	81	75	64
Sittingbourne	46	17	11	18	71	86	62
Horsham	46	17	10	19	79	80	61
Herne Bay	46	13	12	21	74	98	51
East Grinstead Town	46	14	5	27	82	121	47
Molesey	46	11	10	25	61	116	43
Chipstead	46	11	8	27	68	99	41
Guernsey	46	9	11	26	66	112	38
Chatham Town	46	7	10	29	57	120	31
Three Bridges	46	7	8	31	59	114	29
Godalming Town	46	8	3	35	49	128	24

Godalming Town had 3 points deducted after fielding an ineligible player.

2017-2018

Premier Division

Billericay Town	46	30	9	7	110	50	99
Dulwich Hamlet	46	28	11	7	91	41	95
Hendon	46	25	10	11	96	59	85
Folkestone Invicta	46	25	10	11	104	71	85
Leiston	46	23	10	13	82	53	79
Leatherhead	46	24	7	15	68	49	79
Margate	46	20	17	9	77	53	77
Staines Town	46	21	12	13	106	83	75
Wingate & Finchley	46	20	9	17	63	71	69
Metropolitan Police	46	19	12	15	76	71	66
Tonbridge Angels	46	19	7	20	58	63	64
Harrow Borough	46	19	6	21	69	76	63
Kingstonian	46	18	5	23	57	70	59
Dorking Wanderers	46	16	10	20	77	80	58
Thurrock	46	17	6	23	68	79	57
Worthing	46	15	12	19	71	84	57
Enfield Town	46	14	14	18	72	80	56
Merstham	46	15	11	20	69	80	56
Needham Market	46	13	10	23	65	84	49
Brightlingsea Regent	46	13	9	24	67	89	48
Harlow Town	46	13	8	25	55	88	47
Lowestoft Town	46	12	7	27	52	92	43
Burgess Hill Town	46	9	9	28	64	102	36
Tooting & Mitcham United	46	9	9	28	52	101	36

Metropolitan Police had 3 points deducted for fielding an ineligible player.
Thurrock resigned from the league at the end of the season.

South Division

Carshalton Athletic	46	31	9	6	99	55	102
Lewes	46	30	9	7	93	38	99
Cray Wanderers	46	25	14	7	112	46	89
Greenwich Borough	46	25	12	9	99	46	87
Corinthian-Casuals	46	26	9	11	86	47	87
Walton Casuals	46	25	11	10	98	52	86
Hythe Town	46	25	11	10	92	63	86
Whyteleafe	46	20	13	13	87	69	73
Hastings United	46	20	13	13	84	67	73
Thamesmead Town	46	20	12	14	103	81	72
Phoenix Sports	46	20	9	17	79	68	69
Herne Bay	46	21	5	20	81	89	68
South Park	46	19	6	21	79	91	63
Sittingbourne	46	18	8	20	68	72	62
Horsham	46	16	8	22	71	90	56
Ramsgate	46	15	9	22	79	85	54
VCD Athletic	46	15	7	24	69	91	52
Guernsey	46	13	10	23	65	98	49
Faversham Town	46	13	9	24	61	73	48
Chipstead	46	12	10	24	64	78	46
Ashford United	46	10	8	28	60	111	38
East Grinstead Town	46	9	9	28	63	128	36
Molesey	46	7	12	27	55	103	30
Shoreham	46	3	5	38	33	138	8

Molesey had 3 points deducted for fielding an ineligible player.
Shoreham had 6 points deducted for fielding an ineligible player.

At the end of the season, the South Division was renamed the South East Division and a new South Central Division was also formed.

North Division

AFC Hornchurch	46	32	7	7	97	35	103
Potters Bar Town	46	28	9	9	87	42	90
Bowers & Pitsea	46	28	5	13	94	48	89
Haringey Borough	46	27	8	11	84	49	89
Heybridge Swifts	46	26	9	11	105	53	87
Canvey Island	46	24	8	14	100	65	80
Maldon & Tiptree	46	20	9	17	94	83	69
Dereham Town	46	20	11	15	75	63	68
Bury Town	46	17	14	15	67	65	65
Barking	46	18	10	18	63	63	64
Witham Town	46	18	8	20	59	66	62
AFC Sudbury	46	15	14	17	57	66	59
Soham Town Rangers	46	16	10	20	67	73	58
Aveley	46	15	12	19	61	67	57
Hertford Town	46	16	9	21	55	85	57
Grays Athletic	46	14	14	18	72	80	56
Tilbury	46	16	8	22	73	95	56
Cheshunt	46	14	8	24	72	103	50
Waltham Abbey	46	13	10	23	73	87	49
Ware	46	13	9	24	49	81	48
Brentwood Town	46	12	10	24	71	96	46
Mildenhall Town	46	11	13	22	54	86	46
Romford	46	10	11	25	51	97	41
Norwich United	46	8	16	22	63	95	40

Potters Bar Town had 3 points deducted for fielding an ineligible player.
Dereham Town had 3 points deducted for fielding an ineligible player.

2018-2019

Premier Division

Dorking Wanderers	42	28	9	5	87	31	93
Carshalton Athletic	42	21	8	13	70	49	71
Haringey Borough	42	21	8	13	73	54	71
Tonbridge Angels	42	21	7	14	59	46	70
Merstham	42	20	10	12	60	46	70
Folkestone Invicta	42	21	6	15	77	58	69
Bishop's Stortford	42	20	7	15	70	57	67
Leatherhead	42	19	8	15	56	42	65
Worthing	42	18	11	13	72	63	65
Enfield Town	42	17	10	15	76	56	61
Lewes	42	16	12	14	61	53	60
Margate	42	16	11	15	45	48	59
Brightlingsea Regent	42	16	11	15	49	54	59
Bognor Regis Town	42	14	15	13	71	62	56
AFC Hornchurch	42	12	14	16	57	59	50
Potters Bar Town	42	13	10	19	51	56	49
Corinthian-Casuals	42	13	8	21	48	74	47
Kingstonian	42	13	6	23	60	78	45
Wingate & Finchley	42	12	7	23	57	86	43
Whitehawk	42	10	11	21	50	72	41
Burgess Hill Town	42	9	10	23	44	91	37
Harlow Town	42	9	7	26	53	107	34

Bognor Regis Town had 1 point deducted.

North Division

Bowers & Pitsea	38	29	5	4	96	25	92
Aveley	38	24	8	6	84	49	80
Maldon & Tiptree	38	24	7	7	86	46	79
Coggeshall Town	38	22	8	8	79	43	74
Heybridge Swifts	38	23	5	10	70	51	74
Bury Town	38	17	8	13	72	63	59
Grays Athletic	38	14	11	13	65	64	53
AFC Sudbury	38	16	4	18	71	72	52
Canvey Island	38	15	6	17	51	50	51
Tilbury	38	13	11	14	64	64	50
Felixstowe & Walton United	38	14	8	16	56	66	50
Barking	38	13	8	17	49	63	47
Brentwood Town	38	12	9	17	71	77	45
Dereham Town	38	14	5	19	71	82	44
Great Wakering Rovers	38	11	8	19	55	72	41
Soham Town Rangers	38	12	4	22	44	64	40
Basildon United	38	11	6	21	37	71	39
Witham Town	38	9	7	22	38	68	34
Romford	38	10	4	24	48	82	34
Mildenhall Town	38	5	12	21	47	82	27

Dereham Town had 3 points deducted for fielding an ineligible player in two games.

South Central Division

Hayes & Yeading United	38	29	6	3	129	36	93
Bracknell Town	38	23	8	7	102	49	77
Cheshunt	38	22	10	6	79	43	76
Marlow	38	21	10	7	66	37	73
Westfield	38	21	7	10	77	54	70
Tooting & Mitcham United	38	18	11	9	66	52	65
Ware	38	18	9	11	90	59	63
Hanwell Town	38	16	12	10	71	65	60
Waltham Abbey	38	18	2	18	63	68	56
Northwood	38	16	6	16	65	71	54
Ashford Town	38	15	5	18	55	70	50
Bedfont Sports	38	13	9	16	75	76	48
Chipstead	38	13	6	19	54	63	45
Chalfont St Peter	38	10	13	15	52	60	43
Uxbridge	38	11	9	18	50	71	42
FC Romania	38	11	3	24	46	86	36
South Park	38	9	6	23	47	92	33
Hertford Town	38	6	13	19	55	85	31
Molesey	38	7	7	24	36	76	28
Egham Town	38	4	6	28	29	94	18

South East Division

Cray Wanderers	36	25	7	4	79	35	82
Horsham	36	23	5	8	73	38	74
Hastings United	36	21	7	8	78	45	70
Ashford United	36	21	5	10	74	36	68
Haywards Heath Town	36	18	9	9	65	52	63
VCD Athletic	36	20	2	14	74	66	62
Hythe Town	36	14	10	12	66	59	52
Whyteleafe	36	14	7	15	59	51	49
Phoenix Sports	36	13	10	13	65	65	49
Sevenoaks Town	36	13	8	15	49	54	47
Ramsgate	36	11	12	13	54	53	45
Whitstable Town	36	11	10	15	36	55	43
East Grinstead Town	36	11	8	17	65	72	41
Three Bridges	36	12	5	19	51	69	41
Herne Bay	36	11	5	20	65	85	38
Sittingbourne	36	11	4	21	49	72	37
Faversham Town	36	10	7	19	55	85	37
Guernsey	36	7	9	20	50	77	30
Greenwich Borough	36	6	6	22	40	78	27

Greenwich Borough had 3 points deducted for fielding an ineligible player. Thamesmead Town folded during October 2018 and their record was expunged.

2019-2020

Premier Division

Worthing	34	21	8	5	72	41	71
Cray Wanderers	33	18	10	5	63	45	64
Carshalton Athletic	35	18	9	8	59	38	63
Hornchurch	33	17	11	5	62	28	62
Folkestone Invicta	32	18	8	6	60	34	62
Horsham	33	17	6	10	51	35	57
Enfield Town	32	16	8	8	61	51	56
Bognor Regis Town	32	16	5	11	58	46	53
Leatherhead	31	15	7	9	48	42	52
Kingstonian	31	11	14	6	42	36	47
East Thurrock United	30	14	4	12	47	40	46
Margate	33	11	10	12	47	54	43
Potters Bar Town	32	11	8	13	47	56	41
Bowers & Pitsea	33	11	7	15	49	42	40
Haringey Borough	30	6	13	44	47	39
Lewes	34	8	7	19	35	55	31
Bishop's Stortford	32	8	4	20	37	63	28
Cheshunt	31	8	3	20	39	59	27
Corinthian-Casuals	31	6	8	17	33	44	26
Wingate & Finchley	33	5	10	18	34	58	25
Merstham	33	6	7	20	34	70	25
Brightlingsea Regent	34	5	10	19	24	62	25

North Division

Maldon & Tiptree	26	22	2	2	65	20	65
Bury Town	31	15	7	9	49	41	52
Aveley	26	14	9	3	66	31	51
Heybridge Swifts	30	15	6	9	54	43	51
Tilbury	27	15	5	7	49	30	50
Coggeshall Town	26	12	10	4	40	24	46
Great Wakering Rovers	28	13	4	11	45	36	43
Dereham Town	29	11	8	10	52	43	41
Cambridge City	28	12	3	13	42	39	39
Canvey Island	27	11	5	11	49	54	38
AFC Sudbury	26	11	4	11	42	42	37
Histon	28	10	6	12	40	53	36
Soham Town Rangers	28	10	4	14	41	47	34
Grays Athletic	29	9	4	16	41	47	31
Witham Town	28	8	5	15	36	63	29
Hullbridge Sports	27	7	7	13	33	53	28
Brentwood Town	29	7	6	16	41	54	27
Felixstowe & Walton United	29	6	7	16	40	62	25
Romford	25	7	3	15	41	66	24
Basildon United	25	6	5	14	29	47	23

Maldon & Tiptree had 3 points deducted for fielding an ineligible player.

South Central Division

Ware	30	19	7	4	81	44	64
Hanwell Town	28	17	7	4	72	32	58
Uxbridge	29	16	7	6	59	35	55
Chertsey Town	28	15	7	6	74	40	52
Westfield	28	15	7	6	65	32	52
Bracknell Town	26	15	5	6	63	33	50
Waltham Abbey	29	15	5	9	68	52	50
Tooting & Mitcham United	27	14	5	8	53	29	47
Barking	29	14	4	11	51	45	46
Chipstead	28	13	6	9	53	40	45
Marlow	28	11	10	7	39	30	43
Bedfont Sports	29	10	9	10	42	44	39
Chalfont St. Peter	30	10	7	13	45	59	37
Harlow Town	29	10	4	15	42	57	34
South Park	26	6	9	11	37	52	27
Hertford Town	29	6	4	19	39	81	22
Ashford Town	29	5	5	19	30	70	20
Northwood	29	6	2	21	34	81	20
FC Romania	28	4	4	20	35	84	16
Staines Town	29	2	8	19	39	81	14

South East Division

Hastings United	28	18	8	2	53	21	62
Ashford United	30	19	2	9	75	41	59
Cray Valley Paper Mills	28	17	6	5	53	29	57
Whitehawk	28	16	8	4	61	33	56
Herne Bay	28	15	6	7	53	40	51
Chichester City	25	13	6	6	46	34	45
Whyteleafe	28	13	6	9	47	40	45
VCD Athletic	30	12	6	12	48	53	42
Phoenix Sports	27	13	2	12	46	40	41
Sevenoaks Town	29	11	8	10	43	37	41
Hythe Town	29	11	7	11	34	37	40
Haywards Heath Town	27	10	9	8	37	33	39
Guernsey	28	9	9	10	39	47	36
Whitstable Town	28	9	8	11	38	41	35
Burgess Hill Town	27	9	4	14	47	60	31
Sittingbourne	29	8	4	17	31	42	28
Faversham Town	30	7	7	16	30	51	28
Ramsgate	30	4	8	18	35	68	20
Three Bridges	29	5	3	21	35	68	18
East Grinstead Town	26	1	7	18	25	61	10

Play was suspended during mid-March 2020 due to the effects of the Covid-19 pandemic and the season was subsequently abandoned.

The tables shown are correct to the final match played in each division.

NORTHERN PREMIER LEAGUE

Since the early years of the 20th century, the Southern League had been recognised as the top competition for non-League clubs in the southern half of the country. However there was no equivalent in the North where the Cheshire County League and the Lancashire Combination were the strongest leagues in the North-West while the Midland League covered the East Midlands and Yorkshire. In the North-East, the top amateur teams played in the Northern League while after the closure of the North-Eastern League in 1958, a handful of semi-professional clubs played in the North Regional League. There had been calls in the past for a single league to cater for the strongest clubs in these other leagues but it was not until 1966 that positive steps were taken to form such a competition.

After a meeting held in Altrincham that was attended by more than 200 clubs, a steering committee was set up to form the Northern Premier League. It was decided that invitations to join the new competition would be sent to those clubs with the best record in the three previous seasons. As the initial membership would be restricted to 20, there would inevitably be many who would miss out and so a system was set up of promotion and relegation between the Northern Premier League and three "feeders", the Lancashire Combination, the Cheshire County League and the Midland League. This, in effect, was the start of the present non-League pyramid and it was hoped that the top clubs in the new league would have improved their chances of election to the Football League.

The finishing positions in their previous leagues for 19 of the 20 clubs who formed the league are shown below.

Cheshire League

	1965-66	1966-67	1967-68
Altrincham	1	1	2
Bangor City	4	7	3
Hyde United	8	4	10
Macclesfield Town	3	5	1
Northwich Victoria	7	3	7
Runcorn	5	9	13
Wigan Athletic	2	2	8

Lancashire Combination

	1965-66	1966-67	1967-68
Chorley	2	4	11
Fleetwood	13	5	4
Morecambe	7	1	1
Netherfield	6	3	8
South Liverpool	1	6	7

Midland League

	1965-66	1966-67	1967-68
Gainsborough Trinity	6	1	4
Goole Town	9	9	5
Scarborough	11	6	7
Worksop Town	1	2	9

North Regional League

	1965-66	1966-67	1967-68
Ashington	6	4	5
Gateshead	10	9	6
South Shields	4	1	4

The 20th founder member were Boston United who were champions of the United Counties League in 1965-66 and champions of the West Midlands (Regional) League in 1966-67 and 1967-68.

Northern Premier League changes 1969-2020

Note: The Northern Premier League had been known by a variety of titles since its formation in 1959. For clarity, it is referred to throughout this book as "The Northern Premier League".

1969   Chorley were relegated to the Lancashire Combination from where Great Harwood were promoted, Worksop Town were relegated to the Midland League from where Matlock Town were promoted and Ashington were relegated to the Northern Alliance. Stafford Rangers joined after promotion from the Cheshire League.

1970   Hyde United resigned because of the high travel costs and joined the Cheshire League instead while Gateshead were relegated to the Wearside League. Bradford Park Avenue joined after failing to win re-election to the Football League while Chorley, Lancaster City and Kirkby Town all joined after promotion from the Lancashire Combination.

1971   Skelmersdale United and Ellesmere Port Town both joined after promotion from the Cheshire League.

1972   Kirkby Town were relegated to the Lancashire Combination and Chorley moved to the Cheshire League. Mossley joined after promotion from the Cheshire League and Barrow joined after failing to win re-election to the Football League.

1973   Ellesmere Port Town resigned for financial reasons and joined the Lancashire Combination. Buxton were promoted from the Cheshire League and replaced them.

1974   Bradford Park Avenue were liquidated on 3rd May 1974 but a Sunday football team was quickly formed that carried on the club name. Worksop Town joined after promotion from the Midland League. South Shields sold their ground at Simonside Hall with the intention of moving back to their previous ground at Horsley Hill. However, they were unable to finalise that move and so moved instead to the Gateshead Youth Stadium and changed their name to Gateshead United

1975   There were no changes to the constitution of the league.

1976   Fleetwood were wound up by the High Court on 8th June 1976 following a cash crisis and a petition from the Inland Revenue. A replacement club called Fleetwood Town was formed in April 1977 and played in junior football in 1977-78. Skelmersdale United moved to the Lancashire Combination and Frickley Athletic joined after promotion from the Midland League. From the 1976-77 season, goal difference was used instead of goal average to decide final placings where necessary.

1977   Workington joined after failing to win re-election to the Football League. Gateshead United disbanded but a replacement club called Gateshead was formed and took Gateshead United's place in the league for 1977-78, continuing to play at the Gateshead Youth Stadium.

1978   Great Harwood disbanded after a financial crisis. A junior club in the town called Harwood Wellington took over residency of their Showground home, changed their name to Great Harwood Town and joined the West Lancashire League in 1978-79. Wigan Athletic left after being elected to the Football League, replacing Southport who took their place in the Northern Premier League.

1979   Altrincham, Bangor City, Barrow, Boston United, Northwich Victoria, Scarborough and Stafford Rangers all left to become founder members of the National League. Marine and Witton Albion joined after promotion from the Cheshire League and Burton Albion, Grantham, Oswestry Town and Tamworth all joined from the Southern League.

1980   Frickley Athletic were promoted to the National League. King's Lynn joined from the Southern League.

1981   Runcorn were promoted to the National League from where Bangor City were relegated.

1982   Bangor City were promoted to the National League and Lancaster City moved to the North-West Counties League because of financial problems. Hyde United and Chorley joined after promotion from the Cheshire League. From the 1982-83 season onwards, a win was worth 3 points instead of 2.

1983   Gateshead were promoted to the National League from where Barrow and Stafford Rangers were relegated. Netherfield were relegated to the North-West Counties League from where Rhyl and Horwich RMI were promoted. Kings Lynn moved to the Southern League – Premier Division and Tamworth were relegated to the Southern League – Division One (Midland).

1984   Barrow were promoted to the National League from where Bangor City were relegated.

1985   Stafford Rangers were promoted to the National League from where Gateshead were relegated. Grantham were relegated to the Southern League – Division One (Midland) and Caernarfon Town joined after promotion from the North-West Counties League.

1986   Gateshead were promoted to the National League from where Barrow were relegated.

1987   Macclesfield Town were promoted to the National League from where Gateshead and Frickley Athletic were relegated. Burton Albion moved to the Southern League.

Expansion to two divisions

A second division was formed. The existing division became the Premier Division and the new division was named Division One.

The 19 clubs who formed the new Division One were selected on the basis of ground facilities and recent league positions in the Northern Counties East League and North-West Counties League. Those clubs are listed below together with their league positions in the three previous seasons.

Northern Counties East League Premier Division

	1984-85	1985-86	1986-87
Alfreton Town	4	6	1
Eastwood Town	2	5	13
Farsley Celtic	1*	8	2
Harrogate Town	2*	3*	9
Sutton Town	12	7	5

* In 1984-85, Farsley Celtic were champions of Division One (North) and promoted to the Premier Division. Harrogate Town were 2nd in Division One (North) in 1984-85 and 3rd in Division One in 1985-86 after which they were promoted to the Premier Division.

North-West Counties League Division One

	1984-85	1985-86	1986-87
Accrington Stanley	15	11	2
Congleton Town	10	2	11
Curzon Ashton	6	8	19
Eastwood Hanley	5	3	14
Fleetwood Town	8	5	8
Irlam Town	2*	6	18
Leek Town	9	7	16
Netherfield	18	17	17
Penrith	20	16	9
Radcliffe Borough	1	14	15
Stalybridge Celtic	4	4	1
Winsford United	7	13	7

* In 1984-85, Irlam Town were 2nd in Division Two and promoted to Division One.

North-West Counties League Division Two

	1984-85	1985-86	1986-87
Droylsden	5	10	1
Lancaster City	19*	12	13

* In 1984-85, Lancaster City were 19th in Division One and relegated to Division Two.

1988   Premier Division: In an attempt to ease their financial position, Oswestry Town sold their Victoria Road ground to a house building company called Sunley. However they were unable to find a new ground and had to disband. Shepshed Charterhouse joined from the Southern League.

Promoted from the Premier Division to the National League	Chorley
Promoted to the Premier Division from Division One	Fleetwood Town, Stalybridge Celtic
Relegated from the Premier Division to Division One	Workington
Promoted to Division One from the North-West Counties League	Colne Dynamoes
Promoted to Division One from the Northern League	Bishop Auckland, Whitley Bay
Promoted to Division One from the Central Wales League	Newtown

1989

Promoted from the Premier Division to the National League	Barrow
Promoted to the Premier Division from Division One	Colne Dynamoes, Bishop Auckland
Relegated from the Premier Division to Division One	Worksop Town
Promoted to Div. One from the North-West Counties League	Rossendale United
Promoted to Div. One from the Northern Counties East League	Emley
Relegated from Div. One to the Northern Counties East League	Sutton Town

1990   Premier Division: Despite becoming Northern Premier League champions, Colne Dynamoes were refused entry to the National League because their Holt House ground did not meet the required standards. They were unable to find a new ground or an appropriate ground-share and so owner, financial backer and founder of the club, Graham White, decided to close it down.

Promoted from the Premier Division to the National League	Gateshead
Relegated to the Premier Division from the National League	Chorley
Promoted to the Premier Division from Division One	Droylsden, Leek Town
Relegated from the Premier Division to Division One	Caernarfon Town, Rhyl
Promoted to Division One from the North-West Counties League	Warrington Town
Promoted to Div. One from the Northern Counties East League	Bridlington Town
Relegated from Div. One to the North-West Counties League	Eastwood Hanley, Penrith

1991   Premier Division: South Liverpool disbanded. Their Holly Park ground suffered an arson attack in 1990 and vandals also damaged the pitch. They played the 1990-91 season at Bootle's ground at Buck's Park but lost support because of the distance and disbanded at the end of the season because the club was no longer financially viable. Shepshed Charterhouse changed name to Shepshed Albion.

Promoted from the Premier Division to the National League	Witton Albion
Promoted to the Premier Division from Division One	Accrington Stanley, Emley, Whitley Bay
Promoted to Division One from the North-West Counties League	Colwyn Bay, Knowsley United
Promoted to Div. One from the Northern Counties East League	Guiseley

1992   Premier Division: Bangor City moved to the Welsh football pyramid and joined it at its highest level, the newly formed League of Wales.

Promoted from the Premier Division to the National League	Stalybridge Celtic
Relegated to the Premier Division from the National League	Barrow
Promoted to the Premier Division from Division One	Colwyn Bay, Winsford United
Relegated from the Premier Division to Division One	Shepshed Albion

Division One: Newtown and Rhyl both moved to the Welsh football pyramid. Newtown joined it at its highest level, the newly formed League of Wales but Rhyl were late in putting in their application and so were placed in the Cymru Alliance.

Promoted to Div One from the North-West Counties League	Ashton United, Great Harwood Town
Promoted to Division One from the Northern League	Gretna
Relegated from Division One to the North-West Counties League	Irlam Town

Note: North Shields were promoted to Division One from the Northern Counties East League but had considerable debts and planned to sell their Appleby Park ground and ground-share at Whitley Bay, an arrangement that the Northern Premier League had approved. However, during the summer of 1992, the value of Appleby Park dropped so that the club could neither clear its debts nor pay Whitley Bay for the ground-share. The club played pre-season friendlies but disbanded a week before the start of the 1992-93 season. A replacement club was quickly formed, also called North Shields, and were admitted into the Wearside League – Division Two, initially playing at Appleby Park.

1993

Promoted from the Premier Division to the National League	Southport
Relegated to the Premier Division from the National League	Boston United
Promoted to the Premier Division from Division One	Bridlington Town, Knowsley United
Relegated from the Premier Division to Division One	Mossley, Goole Town
Promoted to Div. One from the North-West Counties League	Bamber Bridge
Promoted to Div One from the Northern Counties East League	Spennymoor United
Relegated from Division One to the North-West Counties League	Rossendale United
Relegated from Division One to the Midland Combination	Shepshed Albion

1994   Premier Division: Due to legal wrangles, Bridlington Town had been playing their home games more than 60 miles away at Doncaster Rovers. Support dropped and the club disbanded in the summer of 1994. A local pub team called Greyhound FC negotiated a lease for Town's Queensgate ground, changed their name to Bridlington Town and joined the Driffield & District League, playing their first game on 10th September. Leek Town moved to the Southern League.

Relegated to the Premier Division from the National League	Witton Albion
Promoted to the Premier Division from Division One	Spennymoor United, Guiseley
Relegated from the Premier Division to Division One changed their name to Fleetwood.	Fleetwood Town who subsequently
Promoted to Division One from the North-West Counties League	Atherton Laburnum Rovers
Promoted to Division One from the Northern League	Blyth Spartans

1995   Premier Division: Leek Town joined from the Southern League.

Promoted from the Premier Division to the National League	Morecambe
Promoted to the Premier Division from Division One	Blyth Spartans, Bamber Bridge
Relegated from the Premier Division to Division One subsequently changed their name to Leigh RMI)	Whitley Bay, Horwich RMI (who

Division One: Caernarfon Town moved to the Welsh football pyramid at the highest level, the League of Wales.

Promoted to Div. One from the North-West Counties League	Bradford Park Avenue
Promoted to Div. One from the Northern Counties East League	Lincoln United
Relegated from Div. One to the North-West Counties League	Mossley
Relegated from Div. One to the Northern Counties East League	Goole Town

1996

Relegated to the Premier Division from the National League	Runcorn
Promoted to the Premier Division from Division One	Alfreton Town, Lancaster City
Relegated from the Premier Division to Division One	Droylsden, Matlock Town

Division One: Fleetwood were expelled after their parent company went into liquidation. They subsequently disbanded and in 1997, a new club was formed called Fleetwood Wanderers. They changed their name to Fleetwood Freeport after obtaining a 5-year sponsorship and joined the North-West Counties League.

Promoted to Div One from the North-West Counties League	Flixton
Promoted to Div One from the Northern Counties East League	Stocksbridge Park Steels

1997   Premier Division: Knowsley United disbanded because the lease on their council-owned Alt Park had run out and the very poorly supported club could not afford to renew it.

Promoted from the Premier Division to the National League	Leek Town
Relegated to the Premier Division from the National League	Altrincham
Promoted to the Premier Division from Division One	Radcliffe Borough, Leigh RMI
Relegated from the Premier Division to Division One	Witton Albion, Buxton
Promoted to Div. One from the North-West Counties League	Trafford
Promoted to Div. One from the Northern Counties East League	Belper Town
Promoted to Division One from the Northern League	Whitby Town
Relegated from Div. One to the North-West Counties League Laburnum Rovers	Warrington Town, Atherton
Relegated from Div. One to the Northern Counties East League	Curzon Ashton

1998   Premier Division: Boston United moved to the Southern League.

Promoted from the Premier Division to the National League	Barrow
Relegated to the Premier Division from the National League	Gateshead, Stalybridge Celtic
Promoted to the Premier Division from Division One	Whitby Town, Worksop Town
Relegated from the Premier Division to Division One	Radcliffe Borough, Alfreton Town

Division One: Netherfield changed their name to Netherfield Kendal.

Promoted to Div. One from the North-West Counties League	Burscough

Promoted to Div. One from the Northern Counties East League	Hucknall Town
Relegated from Div. One to the North-West Counties League	Workington
Relegated from Div. One to the Northern Counties East League	Buxton

1999

Promoted from the Premier Division to the National League	Altrincham
Relegated to the Premier Division from the National League	Barrow, Leek Town
Promoted to the Premier Division from Division One	Hucknall Town, Droylsden
Relegated from the Premier Division to Division One	Chorley, Accrington Stanley
Promoted to Div. One from the North-West Counties League	Workington
Promoted to Div. One from the Northern Counties East League	Ossett Town
Relegated from Div. One to the North-West Counties League	Great Harwood Town
Relegated from Div. One to the Northern Counties East League	Alfreton Town

2000

Promoted from the Premier Division to the National League	Leigh RMI
Relegated to the Premier Division from the National League	Altrincham
Promoted to the Premier Division from Division One	Burscough, Accrington Stanley
Relegated from the Premier Division to Division One	Guiseley, Winsford United
Division One: Netherfield Kendal changed their name to Kendal Town	
Promoted to Div. One from the North-West Counties League	Vauxhall Motors
Promoted to Div. One from the Northern Counties East League	North Ferriby United
Relegated from Division One to the North-West Counties League	Flixton
Relegated from Division One to the Northern League	Whitley Bay

2001 Premier Division: Burton Albion joined from the Southern League. Runcorn changed their name to Runcorn FC Halton.

Promoted from the Premier Division to the National League	Stalybridge Celtic
Promoted to the Premier Division from Division One	Bradford Park Avenue, Vauxhall Motors
Relegated from the Premier Division to Division One	Leek Town, Spennymoor United
Promoted to Div. One from the North-West Counties League	Rossendale United
Promoted to Div. One from the Northern Counties East League	Ossett Albion
Relegated from Div. One to the North-West Counties League	Winsford United, Congleton Town

2002 Premier Division: Bishop Auckland were relegated to Division One because they proposed to ground-share at Shildon whose Dean Street ground did not meet Premier Division standards. Emley changed their name to Wakefield & Emley.

Promoted from the Premier Division to the National League	Burton Albion
Relegated to the Premier Division from the National League	Stalybridge Celtic
Promoted to the Premier Division from Division One	Harrogate Town, Ashton United
Relegated from the Premier Division to Division One	Bamber Bridge
Division One: Gretna moved to the Scottish League – Division Three	
Promoted to Div. One from the North-West Counties League	Kidsgrove Athletic
Promoted to Div. One from the Northern Counties East League	Alfreton Town
Relegated from Div. One to the Northern Counties East League	Ossett Albion

2003

Promoted from the Premier Division to the National League	Accrington Stanley
Relegated to the Premier Division from the National League	Southport
Promoted to the Premier Division from Division One	Alfreton Town, Spennymoor United, Radcliffe Borough
Relegated from the Premier Division to Division One	Gateshead, Colwyn Bay, Hyde United

Promoted to Div. One from the North-West Counties League	Prescot Cables
Promoted to Div. One from the Northern Counties East League	Bridlington Town
Relegated from Div. One to the Northern Counties East League	Eastwood Town
Relegated from Div. One to the North-West Counties League	Trafford

2004   Premier Division: The following 15 clubs all left to become founder members of the new North Division of the National League: Alfreton Town, Altrincham, Ashton United, Barrow, Bradford Park Avenue, Droylsden, Gainsborough Trinity, Harrogate Town, Hucknall Town, Lancaster City, Runcorn FC Halton, Southport, Stalybridge Celtic, Vauxhall Motors and Worksop Town.

Wakefield & Emley changed their name to Wakefield-Emley.

Promoted to the Premier Division from Division One   As a result, the following 14 clubs were promoted: Bamber Bridge, Bishop Auckland, Bridlington Town, Farsley Celtic, Gateshead, Guiseley, Hyde United, Leek Town, Lincoln United, Matlock Town, Ossett Town, Prescot Cables, Witton Albion and Workington.

Promoted to Div. One from the North-West Counties League	Clitheroe, Mossley, Warrington Town, Woodley Sports
Promoted to Div. One from the Northern Counties East League	Brigg Town, Eastwood Town, Ossett Albion
Promoted to Division One from the Midland Alliance	Rocester, Willenhall Town
Promoted to Division One from the United Counties League	Spalding United

Gresley Rovers, Ilkeston Town, Shepshed Dynamo all joined from the Southern League. AFC Telford United also joined, being newly formed as a replacement for Telford United of the National League who had been liquidated during the summer with large debts. The new club continued to play at the previous club's Buck's Head ground.

2005   Premier Division: Spennymoor United resigned and disbanded at the beginning of April. The club had been in financial trouble for some time and had failed to fulfil three games during the season because they were unable to raise a team, incurring a number of fines. They were also in dispute with the local council over the lease for the ground, so with poor levels of support and increasing debts, the owner decided to close the club down. Evenwood Town moved into Spennymoor's Brewery Field ground and continued playing in the Northern League, changing name to Spennymoor Town.

Promoted from the Premier Division to the National League – North	Hyde United, Workington
Relegated to the Premier Division from the National League – North	Ashton United, Bradford Park Avenue, Runcorn FC Halton
Promoted to the Premier Division from Division One	AFC Telford United, Ilkeston Town, North Ferriby United
Relegated from the Premier Division to Division One	Bishop Auckland, Bamber Bridge, Bridlington Town

Division One: Willenhall Town moved to the Southern League

Promoted to Div. One from the North-West Counties League	Fleetwood Town
Promoted to Div. One from the Northern Counties East League	Goole
Relegated from Division One to the Midland Alliance	Rocester

2006   Premier Division: Runcorn FC Halton had been in financial difficulty for some time and had been ground-sharing since 2000. With support dwindling, they could no longer afford to pay their players during 2005-06 and they resigned and disbanded at the end of the season. Wakefield-Emley changed their name to Wakefield. Grantham joined from the Southern League.

Promoted from the Premier Division to the National League – North	Blyth Spartans, Farsley Celtic
Relegated to the Premier Division from the National League – North	Hednesford Town
Promoted to the Premier Division from Division One	Kendal Town, Mossley, Fleetwood Town
Relegated from the Premier Division to Division One	Bradford Park Avenue, Wakefield

Division One: Spalding United Town moved to the Southern League.

Promoted to Div. One from the North-West Counties League	Alsager Town, Cammell Laird, Skelmersdale United

Promoted to Div. One from the Northern Counties East League   Buxton, Harrogate Railway Athletic
Relegated from Division One to the Northern League   Bishop Auckland

2007   Premier Division: Stamford joined from the Southern League.
Promoted from the Premier Division to the National League – North   Burscough, AFC Telford United
Relegated to the Premier Division from the National League – North   Worksop Town
Promoted to the Premier Division from Division One   Buxton, Eastwood Town
Relegated from the Premier Division to Division One   Grantham Town, Radcliffe Borough, Mossley
Division One split into two sections, North and South
The following 11 Division One clubs joined Division One (North): Bamber Bridge, Bradford Park
Avenue, Bridlington Town, Chorley, Clitheroe, Harrogate Railway Athletic, Ossett Albion, Rossendale
United, Skelmersdale United, Wakefield, Woodley Sports
The following 11 Division One clubs joined Division One (South): Alsager Town, Belper Town, Brigg
Town, Cammell Laird, Colwyn Bay, Goole, Gresley Rovers, Kidsgrove Athletic, Shepshed Dynamo,
Stocksbridge Park Steels, Warrington Town
          Division One (North): Lancaster City joined following relegation from the National League –
North, Mossley and Radcliffe Borough joined after relegation from the Premier Division, FC United of
Manchester and Curzon Ashton joined after promotion from the North-West Counties League, Garforth
Town joined after promotion from the Northern Counties East League and Newcastle Blue Star joined
after promotion from the Northern League.
          Division One (South): Grantham Town joined after relegation from the Premier Division,
Nantwich Town joined after promotion from the North-West Counties League, Carlton Town, Retford
United and Sheffield all joined after promotion from the Northern Counties East League, Quorn joined
after promotion from the Midland Alliance. Spalding United joined from the Southern League.

2008
Promoted from the Premier Division to the National League – North   Fleetwood Town, Gateshead
Relegated to the Premier Division from the National League – North   Boston United, Leigh Genesis
Promoted to the Premier Division from Div. One (North)   FC United of Manchester, Bradford
Park Avenue
Promoted to the Premier Division from Div. One (South)   Nantwich Town, Cammell Laird
Relegated from the Premier Division to Div. One (South)   Leek Town, Stamford, Lincoln United
Moved to Division One (North) from Division One (South)   Colwyn Bay, Warrington Town
Relegated to Div. One (North) from the National League – North   Boston United, Leigh Genesis
Promoted to Div. One (North) from the North-West Counties League   Trafford, Salford City
Promoted to Div. One (North) from the Northern League   Durham City
Relegated from Div. One (North) to the Northern Counties East League   Bridlington Town
          Division One (South): Rushall Olympic and Willenhall Town both joined from the Southern
League.
Promoted to Div. One (South) from the Northern Counties East League   Glapwell
Promoted to Div. One (South) from the Midland Alliance   Loughborough Dynamo
Relegated from Div. One (South) to the North-West Counties League   Alsager Town

2009
          Premier Division: Hednesford Town moved to the Southern League.
Promoted from the Premier Division to the National League – North   Eastwood Town, Ilkeston Town
Relegated to the Premier Division from the National League – North   Hucknall Town, Kings Lynn,
Burscough
Promoted to the Premier Division from Division One (North)   Durham City
Relegated from the Premier Division to Division One (North)   Leigh Genesis, Prescot Cables
Promoted to the Premier Division from Div. One (South)   Retford United, Stocksbridge Park Steels
Relegated from the Premier Division to Div. One (South)   Witton Albion. Cammell Laird were
also relegated as their Kirklands stadium did not meet ground criteria.

Division One (North): Newcastle Blue Star won promotion to the Premier Division but disbanded before taking their place. The club had been awarded £61,000 by the Football Stadia Improvement Fund to renovate their Wheatsheaf ground. However, the club decided to ground-share with Newcastle Falcons RUFC instead and the FSIF demanded their money back, a decision backed by the Football Association. Unable to pay, Blue Star closed down on 26th June 2009.

Promoted to Div. One (North) from the North-West Counties League   AFC Fylde

Division One (South): Gresley Rovers were liquidated with financial difficulties at the end of the season. A replacement club called Gresley FC was formed immediately, continuing to play at the Moat Ground and joined the East Midlands Counties League in 2009-10. Chasetown joined from the Southern League.

Promoted to Div. One (South) from the Northern Counties East League   Mickleover Sports
Promoted to Div. One (South) from the Midland Alliance   Market Drayton Town

2010   Premier Division: King's Lynn were wound up by the High Court on 25th November with unpaid taxes of £65,000. A replacement club called King's Lynn Town was formed, continuing to play at The Walks ground and joining the United Counties League in 2009-10.

Promoted from the Premier Division to the National League – North   Guiseley, Boston United
Relegated to the Premier Division from the National League – North   Northwich Victoria
Promoted to the Premier Division from Div. One (North)   FC Halifax Town, Colwyn Bay
Relegated from the Premier Division to Div. One (North)   Durham City
Promoted to the Premier Division from Div. One (South)   Chasetown, Mickleover Sports
Moved to Div. One (North) from Div. One (South)   Cammell Laird, Witton Albion

Division One (North): Chester joined as a new club, having been formed as a successor to Chester City who had been disbanded in March 2010. The new club took over at the Deva Stadium.

Relegated from Div. One (North) to the North-West Counties League   Rossendale United

Division One (South): Romulus and Sutton Coldfield Town joined from the Southern League.

Promoted to Div. One (South) from the North-West Counties League   Newcastle Town
Promoted to Div. One (South) from the Northern Counties East League   Rainworth Miners Welfare
Promoted to Div. One (South) from the Midland Alliance   Barwell
Relegated from Div. One (South) to the Midland Alliance   Willenhall Town

2011   Premier Division: Retford United decided to move to the Northern Counties East League to reduce costs and Hednesford Town joined from the Southern League.

Promoted from the Premier Division to the National League – North   FC Halifax Town, Colwyn Bay
Relegated to the Premier Division from the National League – North   Stafford Rangers
Promoted to the Premier Division from Division One (North)   Chester, Chorley
Relegated from the Premier Division to Division One (North)   Ossett Town
Promoted to the Premier Division from Division One (South)   Rushall Olympic
Relegated from the Premier Division to Division One (South)   Hucknall Town

Division One (North): Leigh Genesis were to be relegated to the North-West Counties League but decided to withdraw from senior football instead. They continued to run youth and women's teams and in 2012, they returned to senior football by joining the South Lancashire Counties League, a Sunday League not part of the non-League pyramid.

Promoted to Div. One (North) from the Northern Counties East League   Farsley

Division One (South): Glapwell resigned because they were unable to find a ground that met league requirements and so moved to the Central Midlands League. Ilkeston joined as a new club, having been formed as a successor to Ilkeston Town who had been liquidated in September 2010. Barwell were promoted to the Southern League – Premier Division.

Promoted to Div. One (South) from the North-West Counties League   New Mills
Promoted to Div. One (South) from the Midland Alliance   Barwell
Relegated from Div. One (South) to the United Counties League   Spalding United

2012
Promoted from the Premier Division to the National League – North   Chester, Bradford Park Avenue
Relegated to the Premier Division from the National League – North   Blyth Spartans, Eastwood Town
Promoted to the Premier Division from Division One (North)   Witton Albion, AFC Fylde
Relegated from the Premier Division to Division One (North)   Burscough
Promoted to the Premier Division from Division One (South)   Ilkeston, Grantham Town
Relegated from the Premier Division to Division One (South)   Chasetown, Mickleover Sports. Also Northwich Victoria for breaking league rules regarding their finances.
Moved to Division One (North) from Division One (South)   Goole, New Mills
          Division One (North): Woodley Sports were relegated because of ground grading issues. They changed their name to Stockport Sports and joined the North-West Counties League. Durham City resigned and moved to the Northern League in order to reduce costs.
Promoted to Div. One (North) from the North-West Counties League   Ramsbottom United
          Division One (South): Halesowen Town joined from the Southern League.
Promoted to Div. One (South) from the Midland Alliance   Gresley
Promoted to Div. One (South) from the United Counties League   Kings Lynn Town
Relegated from Div. One (South) to the United Counties League   Quorn, Shepshed Dynamo

2013   Premier Division: Barwell joined from the Southern League.
Promoted from the Premier Division to the National League – North   North Ferriby United, Hednesford Town
Relegated to the Premier Division from the National League – North   Droylsden
Promoted to the Premier Division from Division One (North)   Skelmersdale United, Trafford
Relegated from the Premier Division to Division One (North)   Kendal Town
Promoted to the Premier Division from Division One (South)   King's Lynn Town, Stamford
Relegated from the Premier Division to Division One (South)   Eastwood Town
Moved from Division One (North) to Division One (South)   Goole
Moved from Division One (South) to Division One (North)   Northwich Victoria
Promoted to Div. One (North) from the North-West Counties League   Padiham
Promoted to Div. One (North) from the Northern League   Darlington 1883
Relegated from Div. One (North) to the Northern Counties East League   Garforth Town
          Division One (South): Bedworth United joined after relegation from the Southern League – Premier Division. Hucknall Town decided to drop down to the Central Midlands League to reduce costs.
Promoted to Div. One (South) from the Northern Counties East League   Scarborough Athletic

2014   Premier Division: Worksop Town decided to drop down to the Northern Counties East League to reduce costs after their owner and main financial backer withdrew his support. Stourbridge joined from the Southern League.
Promoted from the Premier Division to the National League – North   Chorley, AFC Fylde
Relegated to the Premier Division from the National League – North   Workington
Promoted to the Premier Division from Division One (North)   Curzon Ashton, Ramsbottom United
Relegated from the Premier Division to Division One (North)   Droylsden
Promoted to the Premier Division from Division One (South)   Halesowen Town, Belper Town
Relegated from the Premier Division to Div. One (South)   Stafford Rangers, Stocksbridge Park Steels
Moved from Division One (South) to Division One (North)   Scarborough Athletic
          Division One (North): Cammell Laird resigned because of ownership issues. A replacement club called Cammell Laird 1907 was formed and joined the North-West Counties League – Division One in 2014-15. Wakefield resigned because they were unable to find a ground to meet the required standards and difficulties finding a different ground resulted in the club disbanding in June 2014.
Promoted to Div. One (North) from the Northern Counties East League   Brighouse Town
Promoted to Division One (North) from the Northern League   Spennymoor Town

Division One (South): Eastwood Town resigned on 9th March 2014 and disbanded shortly afterwards. The local council had locked up Eastwood's Coronation Park ground as there were considerable rent arrears. A replacement club called Eastwood Community was formed soon afterwards and joined the Central Midlands League in 2014-15. Bedworth United moved to the Southern League.

Promoted to Div. One (South) from the North-West Counties League   Norton United

Promoted to Div. One (South) from the Midland Alliance   Tividale

Promoted to Div. One (South) from the United Counties League   Spalding United

2015   Premier Division: King's Lynn Town moved to the Southern League.

Promoted from the Premier Division to the National League – North   Curzon Ashton, FC United of Manchester

Relegated to the Premier Division from the National League – North   Colwyn Bay, Hyde United who changed their name to Hyde.

Promoted to the Premier Division from Division One (North)   Darlington 1883, Salford City

Relegated from the Premier Division to Division One (North)   Witton Albion, Trafford

Promoted to the Premier Division from Division One (South)   Mickleover Sports, Sutton Coldfield Town

Relegated from the Premier Division to Division One (South)   Belper Town

Division One (North): Farsley changed their name to Farsley Celtic.

Promoted to Div. One (North) from the North-West Counties League   Glossop North End

Relegated from Div. One (North) to the North-West Counties League   Padiham

Division One (South): Norton United disbanded at the end of the season as they could not afford the rent of their Community Drive ground. Rugby Town and Daventry Town joined from the Southern League.

Promoted to Div. One (South) from the Northern Counties East League   Shaw Lane Aquaforce

Relegated from Div. One (South) to the Northern Counties East League   Rainworth Miners Welfare, Brigg Town

Promoted to Div. One (South) from the Midland Football League   Basford United

2016

Promoted from the Premier Division to the National League – North   Darlington 1883, Salford City

Relegated to the Premier Division from the National League – North   Corby Town, Hednesford Town

Promoted to the Premier Division from Division One (North)   Spennymoor Town, Warrington Town

Relegated from the Premier Division to Division One (North)   Ramsbottom United, Hyde United, Colwyn Bay

Promoted to the Premier Division from Division One (South)   Stafford Rangers, Coalville Town

Relegated from the Premier Division to Division One (South)   Stamford

Moved from Division One (North) to Division One (South)   Northwich Victoria, Witton Albion

Moved from Division One (South) to Division One (North)   Goole

Promoted to Division One (North) from the North-West Counties League   Colne

Relegated from Div. One (North) to the North-West Counties League   New Mills

Promoted to Div. One (North) from the Northern Counties East League   Tadcaster Albion

Relegated from Div. One (North) to the Northern Counties East League   Harrogate Railway Athletic

Division One (South): Bedworth United joined from the Southern League – Premier Division and AFC Rushden & Diamonds joined from the Southern League – Division One (Central).

Relegated from Div. One (South) to the Midland Football League   Tividale

Relegated from Div. One (South) to the United Counties League   Daventry Town

2017

Promoted from the Premier Division to the National League – North   Blyth Spartans and Spennymoor Town

Relegated to the Premier Division from the National League – North   Altrincham, Stalybridge Celtic
Promoted to the Premier Division from Division One (North)   Lancaster City, Farsley Celtic
Relegated from the Premier Division to Division One (North)   Corby Town, Frickley Athletic, Skelmersdale United
Promoted to the Premier Division from Division One (South)   Shaw Lane, Witton Albion
Relegated from the Premier Division to Division One (South)   Ilkeston
Promoted to Division One (North) from the North-West Counties League   Atherton Collieries
Promoted to Division One (North) from the Northern League – Division One   South Shields
Relegated from Div. One (North) to the North-West Counties League   Burscough
Relegated from Div. One (North) to the Northern Counties East League   Harrogate Railway Athletic
          Division One (South): Ilkeston were wound up before the start of the 2017/18 season due to unpaid debts. AFC Rushden & Diamonds transferred to the Southern League – League One Central.
Promoted to Div. One (South) from the Midland Football League   Alvechurch
Promoted to Div. One (South) from the Northern Counties East League   Cleethorpes Town
Promoted to Div. One (South) from the United Counties League   Peterborough Sports
Relegated from Div. One (South) to the Midland Football League   Rugby Town
Relegated from Div. One (South) to the North-West Counties League   Northwich Victoria

2018
Promoted from the Premier Division to the National League – North   Altrincham, Ashton United
Relegated to the Premier Division from the National League – North   Gainsborough Trinity and North Ferriby United
Promoted to the Premier Division from Division One (North)   Bamber Bridge, Hyde United, Scarborough Athletic and South Shields
Promoted to the Premier Division from Division One (South)   Basford United
Relegated from the Premier Division to Southern League East Division   Sutton Coldfield Town
Promoted to the Southern League – Central from Division One (South)   Alvechurch, Bedworth United
Promoted to Division One (West) from the North-West Counties League   Runcorn Linnets and Widnes
Promoted to Division One (East) from Northern League – Division One   Marske United, Morpeth Town
Relegated from Div. One (North) to the Northern Counties East League   Goole
Promoted to Div. One (East) from the Northern Counties East League   AFC Mansfield, Pickering Town and Pontefract Collieries
Promoted to Div. One (East) from the United Counties League   Wisbech Town
Relegated from Div. One (South) to the Midland Football League   Romulus
At the end of the 2017-18 season, there was a major reorganisation of Steps 3 and 4 of the Non-League pyramid as two new divisions were created. The Southern League Premier Division split to become the Southern League Central Division and the Southern League South Division, both at Step 3. At the same time, the Isthmian League created a new South Central division at Step 4.

As part of this reorganisation the Northern Premier League voted to realign their two divisions at Step 4 and Division One (North) became Division One (West) whilst Division One (South) became Division One (East). This led to a number of clubs moving between the two divisions and several clubs from the Premier Division also transferred to the Southern League.

Northern Premier League changes were as follows: Barwell, Coalville Town, Halesowen Town, Hednesford Town, Rushall Olympic, Stourbridge all transferred from the NPL Premier Division to the Southern League Central Division whilst Shaw Lane folded in the close season; Brighouse Town and Tadcaster Albion transferred from Division One (North) to Division One (East). In addition, Ossett Albion and Ossett Town merged to become Ossett United and this new club also moved across to Division One (East); Chasetown, Kidsgrove Athletic, Leek Town, Market Drayton Town and Newcastle Town all moved from Division One (South) to join Division One (West); Corby Town and Peterborough Sports transferred from Division One (South) to the Southern League East Division.

2019

Promoted from the Premier Division to the National League – North   Farsley Celtic

Relegated to the Premier Division from the National League – North   Ashton United and FC United of Manchester

Promoted to the Premier Division from Division One (West)   Atherton Collieries and Radcliffe

Promoted to the Premier Division from Division One (East)   Morpeth Town

Hednesford Town transferred from the NPL Premier League to the Southern Football League Premier Division (Central).

At the end of the 2018-19 season, Division One (West) and Division One (East) were realigned to become Division One (North West) and Division One (South East). This led to a number of clubs transferring between the two divisions. Please see below for further details of these transfers.

Relegated from the Premier Division to Division One (North West)   Marine and Workington

Promoted to Division One (North West) from the North-West Counties League   City of Liverpool

Relegated from Division One (North West) to the North-West Counties League   Skelmersdale United

Promoted to Division One (North West) from Northern League – Division One   Dunston UTS

Promoted to Division One (South East) from the Midland League   Ilkeston Town

Promoted to Division One (South East) from the Northern Counties East League   Worksop Town

Relegated from Division One (South East) to the Midland Football League   Gresley

As part of the realignment of Division One, the following clubs transferred from Division One (West) to Division One (South East): Chasetown, Glossop North End, Kidsgrove Athletic, Leek Town, Market Drayton Town and Newcastle Town. Colwyn Bay also left Division One (West) to rejoin Welsh football.

The following clubs transferred from Division One (East) to Division One (North West): Brighouse Town, Marske United, Ossett United, Pontefract Collieries, Pickering Town and Tadcaster Albion.

AFC Mansfield were demoted from Division One (East) to the Northern Counties East League after their ground failed grading regulations. Sutton Coldfield Town transferred to Division One (South East) from the Southern Football League Division One (Central).

2020

Due to the effects of the Covid-19 pandemic, the season was abanoned on 26th March 2020 so no promotion or relegation into or out of the Northern Premier League took place.

1968-69

Macclesfield Town	38	27	6	5	82	38	60
Wigan Athletic	38	18	12	8	59	41	48
Morecambe	38	16	14	8	64	37	46
Gainsborough Trinity	38	19	8	11	64	43	46
South Shields	38	19	8	11	78	56	46
Bangor City	38	18	9	11	102	64	45
Hyde United	38	16	10	12	71	65	42
Goole Town	38	15	10	13	80	78	40
Altrincham	38	14	10	14	69	52	38
Fleetwood	38	16	6	16	58	58	38
Gateshead	38	14	9	15	42	48	37
South Liverpool	38	12	13	13	56	66	37
Northwich Victoria	38	16	5	17	59	82	37
Boston United	38	14	8	16	59	65	36
Runcorn	38	12	11	15	59	63	35
Netherfield	38	12	4	22	51	69	28
Scarborough	38	9	10	19	49	68	28
Ashington	38	10	8	20	48	74	28
Chorley	38	8	9	21	46	75	25
Worksop Town	38	6	8	24	34	88	20

1969-70

Macclesfield Town	38	22	8	8	72	41	52
Wigan Athletic	38	20	12	6	56	32	52
Boston United	38	21	8	9	65	33	50
Scarborough	38	20	10	8	74	39	50
South Shields	38	19	7	12	66	43	45
Gainsborough Trinity	38	16	11	11	64	49	43
Stafford Rangers	38	16	7	15	59	52	39
Bangor City	38	15	9	14	68	63	39
Northwich Victoria	38	15	8	15	60	66	38
Netherfield	38	14	9	15	56	54	37
Hyde United	38	15	7	16	59	59	37
Altrincham	38	14	8	16	62	65	36
Fleetwood	38	13	10	15	53	60	36
Runcorn	38	11	13	14	57	72	35
Morecambe	38	10	13	15	41	51	33
South Liverpool	38	11	11	16	44	55	33
Great Harwood	38	10	9	19	63	92	29
Matlock Town	38	8	12	18	52	67	28
Goole Town	38	10	6	22	50	71	26
Gateshead	38	5	12	21	37	94	22

1970-71

Wigan Athletic	42	27	13	2	91	32	67
Stafford Rangers	42	27	7	8	87	51	61
Scarborough	42	23	12	7	83	40	58
Boston United	42	22	12	8	69	31	56
Macclesfield Town	42	23	10	9	84	45	56
Northwich Victoria	42	22	5	15	71	55	49
Bangor City	42	19	10	13	72	61	48
Altrincham	42	19	10	13	80	76	48
South Liverpool	42	15	15	12	67	57	45
Chorley	42	14	14	14	58	61	42
Gainsborough Trinity	42	15	11	16	65	63	41
Morecambe	42	14	11	17	67	79	39
South Shields	42	12	14	16	67	66	38
Bradford Park Avenue	42	15	8	19	54	73	38
Lancaster City	42	12	12	18	53	76	36
Netherfield	42	13	9	20	59	57	35
Matlock Town	42	10	13	19	58	80	33
Fleetwood	42	10	11	21	56	90	31
Great Harwood	42	8	13	21	66	98	29
Runcorn	42	10	5	27	58	84	25
Kirkby Town	42	6	13	23	57	93	25
Goole Town	42	10	4	28	44	98	24

1971-72

Stafford Rangers	46	30	11	5	91	32	71
Boston United	46	28	13	5	87	37	69
Wigan Athletic	46	27	10	9	70	43	64
Scarborough	46	21	15	10	75	46	57
Northwich Victoria	46	20	14	12	65	59	54
Macclesfield Town	46	18	15	13	61	50	51
Gainsborough Trinity	46	21	9	16	93	79	51
South Shields	46	18	14	14	75	57	50
Bangor City	46	20	8	18	93	74	48
Altrincham	46	18	11	17	72	58	47
Skelmersdale United	46	19	9	18	61	58	47
Matlock Town	46	20	7	19	67	75	47
Chorley	46	17	12	17	66	59	46
Lancaster City	46	15	14	17	85	84	44
Great Harwood	46	15	14	17	60	74	44
Ellesmere Port Town	46	17	9	20	67	71	43
Morecambe	46	15	10	21	51	64	40
Bradford Park Avenue	46	13	13	20	54	71	39
Netherfield	46	16	5	25	51	73	37
Fleetwood	46	11	15	20	43	67	37
South Liverpool	46	12	12	22	61	73	36
Runcorn	46	8	14	24	48	80	30
Goole Town	46	9	10	27	51	97	28
Kirkby Town	46	6	12	28	38	104	24

1972-73

Boston United	46	27	16	3	88	34	70
Scarborough	46	26	9	11	72	39	61
Wigan Athletic	46	23	14	9	69	38	60
Altrincham	46	22	16	8	75	55	60
Bradford Park Avenue	46	19	17	10	63	50	55
Stafford Rangers	46	20	11	15	63	46	51
Gainsborough Trinity	46	18	13	15	70	50	49
Northwich Victoria	46	17	15	14	74	62	49
Netherfield	46	20	9	17	68	65	49
Macclesfield Town	46	16	16	14	58	47	48
Ellesmere Port Town	46	18	11	17	52	56	47
Skelmersdale United	46	15	16	15	58	59	46
Bangor City	46	16	13	17	70	60	45
Mossley	46	17	11	18	70	73	45
Morecambe	46	17	11	18	62	70	45
Great Harwood	46	14	15	17	63	74	43
South Liverpool	46	12	19	15	47	57	43
Runcorn	46	15	12	19	75	78	42
Goole Town	46	13	13	20	64	73	39
South Shields	46	17	4	25	64	81	38
Matlock Town	46	11	11	24	42	80	33
Lancaster City	46	10	11	25	53	78	31
Barrow	46	12	6	28	52	101	30
Fleetwood	46	5	15	26	31	77	25

1973-74

Boston United	46	27	11	8	69	32	65
Wigan Athletic	46	28	8	10	96	39	64
Altrincham	46	26	11	9	77	34	63
Stafford Rangers	46	27	9	10	101	45	63
Scarborough	46	22	14	10	62	43	58
South Shields	46	25	6	15	87	48	56
Runcorn	46	21	14	11	72	47	56
Macclesfield Town	46	18	15	13	48	47	51
Bangor City	46	19	11	16	65	56	49
Gainsborough Trinity	46	18	11	17	77	64	47
South Liverpool	46	16	15	15	55	47	47
Skelmersdale United	46	16	13	17	50	59	45
Goole Town	46	14	15	17	60	69	43
Fleetwood	46	14	15	17	48	68	43
Mossley	46	15	11	20	53	65	41
Northwich Victoria	46	14	13	19	68	75	41
Morecambe	46	13	13	20	62	84	39
Buxton	46	14	10	22	45	71	38
Matlock Town	46	11	14	21	50	79	36
Great Harwood	46	10	14	22	52	74	34
Bradford Park Avenue	46	9	15	22	42	84	33
Barrow	46	13	7	26	46	94	33
Lancaster City	46	10	12	24	52	67	32
Netherfield	46	11	5	30	42	88	27

1975-76

Runcorn	46	29	10	7	95	42	68
Stafford Rangers	46	26	15	5	81	41	67
Scarborough	46	26	10	10	84	43	62
Matlock Town	46	26	9	11	96	63	61
Boston United	46	27	6	13	95	58	60
Wigan Athletic	46	21	15	10	81	42	57
Altrincham	46	20	14	12	77	57	54
Bangor City	46	21	12	13	80	70	54
Mossley	46	21	11	14	70	58	53
Goole Town	46	20	13	13	58	49	53
Northwich Victoria	46	17	17	12	79	59	51
Lancaster City	46	18	9	19	61	70	45
Worksop Town	46	17	10	19	63	56	44
Gainsborough Trinity	46	13	17	16	58	69	43
Macclesfield Town	46	15	12	19	50	64	42
Gateshead United	46	17	7	22	64	63	41
Buxton	46	11	13	22	37	62	35
Skelmersdale United	46	12	10	24	45	74	34
Netherfield	46	11	11	24	55	76	33
Morecambe	46	11	11	24	47	67	33
Great Harwood	46	13	7	26	58	86	33
South Liverpool	46	12	9	25	45	78	33
Barrow	46	12	9	25	47	84	33
Fleetwood	46	3	9	34	36	131	15

1974-75

Wigan Athletic	46	33	6	7	94	38	72
Runcorn	46	30	8	8	102	42	68
Altrincham	46	26	12	8	87	43	64
Stafford Rangers	46	25	13	8	81	39	63
Scarborough	46	24	12	10	75	45	60
Mossley	46	23	11	12	78	52	57
Gateshead United	46	22	12	12	74	48	56
Goole Town	46	19	12	15	75	71	50
Northwich Victoria	46	18	12	16	83	71	48
Great Harwood	46	17	14	15	69	66	48
Matlock Town	46	19	8	19	87	79	46
Boston United	46	16	14	16	64	63	46
Morecambe	46	14	15	17	71	87	43
Worksop Town	46	14	14	18	69	66	42
South Liverpool	46	14	14	18	59	71	42
Buxton	46	11	17	18	50	77	39
Macclesfield Town	46	11	14	21	46	62	36
Lancaster City	46	13	10	23	53	76	36
Bangor City	46	13	9	24	56	67	35
Gainsborough Trinity	46	10	15	21	46	79	35
Skelmersdale United	46	13	7	26	63	93	33
Barrow	46	9	15	22	45	72	33
Netherfield	46	12	8	26	42	91	32
Fleetwood	46	5	10	31	26	97	20

1976-77

Boston United	44	27	11	6	82	35	65
Northwich Victoria	44	27	11	6	85	43	65
Matlock Town	44	26	11	7	108	57	63
Bangor City	44	22	11	11	87	52	55
Scarborough	44	21	12	11	77	66	54
Goole Town	44	23	6	15	64	50	52
Lancaster City	44	21	9	14	71	58	51
Gateshead United	44	18	12	14	80	64	48
Mossley	44	17	14	13	74	59	48
Altrincham	44	19	9	16	60	53	47
Stafford Rangers	44	16	14	14	60	55	46
Runcorn	44	15	14	15	57	49	44
Worksop Town	44	16	12	16	50	58	44
Wigan Athletic	44	14	15	15	62	54	43
Morecambe	44	13	11	20	59	75	37
Gainsborough Trinity	44	13	10	21	58	74	36
Great Harwood	44	11	14	19	63	84	36
Buxton	44	11	13	20	48	63	35
Macclesfield Town	44	8	15	21	41	68	31
Frickley Athletic	44	11	8	25	53	93	30
Barrow	44	11	6	27	56	87	28
South Liverpool	44	10	8	26	51	104	28
Netherfield	44	9	8	27	47	92	26

1977-78

Boston United	46	31	9	6	85	35	71
Wigan Athletic	46	25	15	6	83	45	65
Bangor City	46	26	10	10	92	50	62
Scarborough	46	26	10	10	80	39	62
Altrincham	46	22	15	9	84	49	59
Northwich Victoria	46	22	14	10	83	55	58
Stafford Rangers	46	22	13	11	71	41	57
Runcorn	46	19	18	9	70	44	56
Mossley	46	22	11	13	85	73	55
Matlock Town	46	21	12	13	79	60	54
Lancaster City	46	15	14	17	66	82	44
Frickley Athletic	46	15	12	19	77	81	42
Barrow	46	14	12	20	58	61	40
Goole Town	46	15	9	22	60	68	39
Great Harwood	46	13	13	20	66	83	39
Gainsborough Trinity	46	14	10	22	61	74	38
Gateshead	46	16	5	25	65	74	37
Netherfield	46	11	13	22	50	80	35
Workington	46	13	8	25	48	80	34
Worksop Town	46	12	10	24	45	84	34
Morecambe	46	11	11	24	67	92	33
Macclesfield Town	46	12	9	25	60	92	33
Buxton	46	13	6	27	60	95	32
South Liverpool	46	9	7	30	53	111	25

1978-79

Mossley	44	32	5	7	117	48	69
Altrincham	44	25	11	8	93	39	61
Matlock Town	44	24	8	12	100	59	56
Scarborough	44	19	14	11	61	44	52
Southport	44	19	14	11	62	49	52
Boston United	44	17	18	9	40	33	52
Runcorn	44	21	9	14	79	54	51
Stafford Rangers	44	18	14	12	67	41	50
Goole Town	44	17	15	12	56	61	49
Northwich Victoria	44	18	11	15	64	52	47
Lancaster City	44	17	12	15	62	54	46
Bangor City	44	15	14	15	65	66	44
Worksop Town	44	13	14	17	55	67	40
Workington	44	16	7	21	62	74	39
Netherfield	44	13	11	20	39	69	37
Barrow	44	14	9	21	47	78	37
Gainsborough Trinity	44	12	12	20	52	67	36
Morecambe	44	11	13	20	55	65	35
Frickley Athletic	44	13	9	22	58	70	35
South Liverpool	44	12	10	22	48	85	34
Gateshead	44	11	11	22	42	63	33
Buxton	44	11	9	24	50	84	31
Macclesfield Town	44	8	10	26	40	92	26

1979-80

Mossley	42	28	9	5	96	41	65
Witton Albion	42	28	8	6	89	30	64
Frickley Athletic	42	24	13	5	93	48	61
Burton Albion	42	25	6	11	83	42	56
Matlock Town	42	18	17	7	87	53	53
Buxton	42	21	9	12	61	48	51
Worksop Town	42	20	10	12	65	52	50
Macclesfield Town	42	18	11	13	67	53	47
Grantham	42	18	8	16	71	65	44
Marine	42	16	10	16	65	57	42
Goole Town	42	14	13	15	61	63	41
Lancaster City	42	13	13	16	74	77	39
Oswestry Town	42	12	14	16	44	60	38
Gainsborough Trinity	42	14	8	20	64	75	36
Runcorn	42	11	11	20	46	63	33
Gateshead	42	11	11	20	50	77	33
Morecambe	42	10	12	20	40	59	32
Netherfield	42	7	15	20	37	66	29
Southport	42	8	13	21	30	75	29
South Liverpool	42	7	14	21	51	84	28
Workington	42	8	12	22	50	85	28
Tamworth	42	8	9	25	26	77	25

1980-81

Runcorn	42	32	7	3	99	22	71
Mossley	42	24	7	11	95	55	55
Marine	42	22	10	10	66	41	54
Buxton	42	21	7	14	64	50	49
Gainsborough Trinity	42	17	13	12	80	57	47
Burton Albion	42	19	8	15	63	54	46
Witton Albion	42	19	8	15	70	62	46
Goole Town	42	14	16	12	56	50	44
South Liverpool	42	19	6	17	59	64	44
Workington	42	15	13	14	57	48	43
Gateshead	42	12	18	12	65	61	42
Worksop Town	42	15	11	16	66	61	41
Macclesfield Town	42	13	13	16	52	69	39
Grantham	42	14	9	19	57	74	37
Matlock Town	42	12	12	18	57	80	36
Lancaster City	42	13	9	20	48	70	35
Netherfield	42	11	12	19	73	81	34
Oswestry Town	42	13	8	21	54	67	34
King's Lynn	42	8	18	16	46	65	34
Southport	42	11	11	20	42	68	33
Morecambe	42	11	8	23	42	74	30
Tamworth	42	9	12	21	38	76	30

1981-82

Bangor City	42	27	8	7	108	60	62
Mossley	42	24	11	7	76	43	59
Witton Albion	42	22	10	10	75	44	54
Gateshead	42	19	14	9	65	49	52
King's Lynn	42	19	12	11	61	36	50
Grantham	42	18	13	11	65	53	49
Burton Albion	42	19	9	14	71	62	47
Southport	42	16	14	12	63	55	46
Marine	42	17	12	13	64	57	46
Macclesfield Town	42	17	9	16	67	58	43
Workington	42	18	7	17	62	60	43
Worksop Town	42	15	13	14	52	60	43
South Liverpool	42	13	16	13	55	57	39
Goole Town	42	13	13	16	56	60	39
Oswestry Town	42	14	11	17	55	59	39
Buxton	42	14	11	17	48	56	39
Lancaster City	42	13	12	17	47	50	38
Gainsborough Trinity	42	10	13	19	60	69	33
Tamworth	42	10	9	23	31	56	29
Morecambe	42	9	11	22	43	86	29
Matlock Town	42	7	12	23	38	72	26
Netherfield	42	5	9	28	31	91	19

1982-83

Gateshead	42	32	4	6	114	43	100
Mossley	42	25	9	8	77	42	84
Burton Albion	42	24	9	9	81	53	81
Chorley	42	23	11	8	77	49	80
Macclesfield Town	42	24	8	10	71	49	80
Marine	42	17	17	8	81	57	68
Workington	42	19	10	13	71	55	67
Hyde United	42	18	12	12	91	63	66
King's Lynn	42	17	13	12	62	44	64
Matlock Town	42	18	10	14	70	65	64
Witton Albion	42	17	12	13	82	52	63
Buxton	42	17	9	16	60	62	60
Morecambe	42	16	11	15	75	66	59
Grantham	42	15	13	14	49	50	58
Southport	42	11	14	17	58	65	47
Goole Town	42	13	7	22	52	66	46
Gainsborough Trinity	42	11	9	22	60	71	42
Oswestry Town	42	10	8	24	56	99	38
South Liverpool	42	7	15	20	57	91	36
Tamworth	42	7	8	27	44	97	29
Worksop Town	42	5	10	27	50	98	25
Netherfield	42	2	9	31	28	129	15

1983-84

Barrow	42	29	10	3	92	38	97
Matlock Town	42	23	8	11	72	48	77
South Liverpool	42	22	11	9	55	44	77
Grantham	42	20	8	14	64	51	68
Burton Albion	42	17	13	12	61	47	64
Macclesfield Town	42	18	10	14	65	55	64
Rhyl	42	19	6	17	64	55	63
Horwich RMI	42	18	9	15	64	59	63
Gainsborough Trinity	42	17	11	14	82	66	62
Stafford Rangers	42	15	17	10	65	52	62
Hyde United	42	17	8	17	61	63	59
Marine	42	16	10	16	63	68	58
Witton Albion	42	14	14	14	64	57	56
Chorley	42	14	11	17	68	65	53
Workington	42	14	9	19	53	57	51
Southport	42	14	8	20	57	74	50
Worksop Town	42	13	8	21	57	74	47
Goole Town	42	12	10	20	59	80	46
Morecambe	42	11	12	19	59	75	45
Oswestry Town	42	11	8	23	66	97	41
Buxton	42	11	6	25	52	91	39
Mossley	42	9	9	24	47	74	33

Mossley had 3 points deducted

1984-85

Stafford Rangers	42	26	8	8	81	40	86
Macclesfield Town	42	23	13	6	67	39	82
Witton Albion	42	22	8	12	57	39	74
Hyde United	42	21	8	13	68	52	71
Marine	42	18	15	9	59	34	69
Burton Albion	42	18	15	9	70	49	69
Worksop Town	42	19	10	13	68	56	67
Workington	42	18	9	15	59	53	63
Horwich RMI	42	16	14	12	67	50	62
Bangor City	42	17	9	16	70	61	60
Gainsborough Trinity	42	14	14	14	72	73	56
Southport	42	15	9	18	65	66	54
Matlock Town	42	14	9	19	56	66	51
Oswestry Town	42	14	9	19	59	75	51
Mossley	42	14	9	19	45	65	51
Goole Town	42	13	11	18	60	65	50
Rhyl	42	11	14	17	52	63	47
Morecambe	42	11	14	17	51	67	47
Chorley	42	12	10	20	47	63	46
South Liverpool	42	9	15	18	43	71	42
Grantham	42	8	13	21	41	69	36
Buxton	42	8	6	28	38	79	30

Grantham had 1 point deducted

1985-86

Gateshead	42	24	10	8	85	51	82
Marine	42	23	11	8	63	35	80
Morecambe	42	17	17	8	59	39	68
Gainsborough Trinity	42	18	14	10	66	52	68
Burton Albion	42	18	12	12	64	47	66
Southport	42	17	11	14	70	66	62
Worksop Town	42	17	10	15	51	48	61
Workington	42	14	18	10	54	46	59
Macclesfield Town	42	17	8	17	67	65	59
Hyde United	42	14	15	13	63	62	57
Witton Albion	42	15	13	14	56	59	57
Mossley	42	13	16	13	56	60	55
Bangor City	42	13	15	14	51	51	54
Rhyl	42	14	10	18	65	71	52
South Liverpool	42	11	17	14	43	44	50
Horwich RMI	42	15	6	21	53	63	50
Caernarfon Town	42	11	17	14	51	63	50
Oswestry Town	42	12	13	17	51	60	49
Buxton	42	11	12	19	55	76	45
Chorley	42	9	15	18	56	64	42
Matlock Town	42	9	15	18	59	75	42
Goole Town	42	7	11	24	37	78	31

Workington, Witton Albion, Horwich and Goole Town all had 1 point deducted.

1986-87

Macclesfield Town	42	26	10	6	80	47	88
Bangor City	42	25	12	5	74	35	87
Caernarfon Town	42	20	16	6	67	40	76
Marine	42	21	10	11	70	43	73
South Liverpool	42	21	10	11	58	40	73
Morecambe	42	20	12	10	66	49	72
Matlock Town	42	20	10	12	81	67	70
Southport	42	19	11	12	67	49	68
Chorley	42	16	12	14	58	59	60
Mossley	42	15	12	15	57	52	57
Hyde United	42	15	10	17	81	70	55
Burton Albion	42	16	6	20	56	68	54
Buxton	42	13	14	15	71	68	53
Witton Albion	42	15	8	19	68	79	53
Barrow	42	15	7	20	42	57	52
Goole Town	42	13	12	17	58	62	51
Oswestry Town	42	14	8	20	55	83	50
Rhyl	42	10	15	17	56	74	45
Worksop Town	42	9	13	20	56	74	40
Gainsborough Trinity	42	9	10	23	53	77	37
Workington	42	5	14	23	38	70	28
Horwich RMI	42	3	12	27	36	85	20

Workington and Horwich RMI both had 1 point deducted.

1987-88

Premier Division

Chorley	42	26	10	6	78	35	88
Hyde United	42	25	10	7	91	52	85
Caernarfon Town	42	22	10	10	56	34	76
Morecambe	42	19	15	8	61	41	72
Barrow	42	21	8	13	70	41	71
Worksop Town	42	20	11	11	74	55	71
Bangor City	42	20	10	12	72	55	70
Rhyl	42	18	13	11	70	42	67
Marine	42	19	10	13	67	45	67
Frickley Athletic	42	18	11	13	61	55	65
Witton Albion	42	16	12	14	61	47	60
Goole Town	42	17	9	16	71	61	60
Horwich RMI	42	17	9	16	46	42	60
Southport	42	15	12	15	43	48	57
South Liverpool	42	10	19	13	56	64	49
Buxton	42	11	14	17	72	76	47
Mossley	42	11	11	20	54	75	44
Gateshead	42	11	7	24	52	71	40
Matlock Town	42	10	8	24	58	89	38
Gainsborough Trinity	42	8	10	24	38	81	34
Oswestry Town	42	6	10	26	44	101	28
Workington	42	6	3	33	28	113	21

First Division

Fleetwood Town	36	22	7	7	85	45	73
Stalybridge Celtic	36	22	6	8	72	42	72
Leek Town	36	20	10	6	63	38	70
Accrington Stanley	36	21	6	9	71	39	69
Farsley Celtic	36	18	9	9	64	48	60
Droylsden	36	16	10	10	63	48	58
Eastwood Hanley	36	14	12	10	50	37	54
Winsford United	36	15	6	15	59	47	51
Congleton Town	36	12	16	8	43	39	51
Harrogate Town	36	13	9	14	51	50	48
Alfreton Town	36	13	8	15	53	54	47
Radcliffe Borough	36	11	13	12	66	62	46
Irlam Town	36	12	10	14	39	45	46
Penrith	36	11	11	14	46	51	44
Sutton Town	36	11	5	20	51	96	38
Lancaster City	36	10	6	20	45	72	36
Eastwood Town	36	8	10	18	45	65	34
Curzon Ashton	36	8	4	24	43	73	28
Netherfield	36	4	4	28	35	93	16

Congleton Town had 1 point deducted
Farsley Celtic had 3 points deducted

1988-89

Premier Division

Barrow	42	26	9	7	69	35	87
Hyde United	42	24	8	10	77	44	80
Witton Albion	42	22	13	7	67	39	79
Bangor City	42	22	10	10	77	48	76
Marine	42	23	7	12	69	48	76
Goole Town	42	22	7	13	75	60	73
Fleetwood Town	42	19	16	7	58	44	73
Rhyl	42	18	10	14	75	65	64
Frickley Athletic	42	17	10	15	64	53	61
Mossley	42	17	9	16	56	58	60
South Liverpool	42	15	13	14	65	57	58
Caernarfon Town	42	15	10	17	49	63	55
Matlock Town	42	16	5	21	65	73	53
Southport	42	13	12	17	66	52	51
Buxton	42	12	14	16	61	63	50
Morecambe	42	13	9	20	55	60	47
Gainsborough Trinity	42	12	11	19	56	73	47
Shepshed Charterhouse	42	14	8	20	49	60	44
Stalybridge Celtic	42	9	13	20	46	81	40
Horwich RMI	42	7	14	21	42	70	35
Gateshead	42	7	13	22	36	70	34
Worksop Town	42	6	5	31	42	103	23

Morecambe had 1 point deducted
Shepshed Charterhouse had 6 points deducted

First Division

Colne Dynamoes	42	30	11	1	102	21	98
Bishop Auckland	42	28	5	9	78	28	89
Leek Town	42	25	11	6	74	41	85
Droylsden	42	25	9	8	84	48	84
Whitley Bay	42	23	6	13	77	49	75
Accrington Stanley	42	21	10	11	81	60	73
Lancaster City	42	21	8	13	76	54	71
Harrogate Town	42	19	7	16	68	61	64
Newtown	42	15	12	15	65	59	57
Congleton Town	42	15	11	16	62	66	56
Workington	42	17	3	22	59	74	54
Eastwood Town	42	14	10	18	55	61	52
Curzon Ashton	42	13	11	18	74	72	50
Farsley Celtic	42	12	13	17	52	73	49
Irlam Town	42	11	14	17	53	63	47
Penrith	42	14	5	23	58	93	45
Radcliffe Borough	42	12	10	20	62	86	46
Eastwood Hanley	42	11	12	19	46	67	45
Winsford United	42	13	6	23	58	93	45
Alfreton Town	42	8	11	23	44	92	35
Netherfield	42	8	9	25	57	90	32
Sutton Town	42	7	6	29	70	109	23

Leek Town and Netherfield both had 1 point deducted
Colne Dynamo had 3 points deducted
Sutton Town had 4 points deducted

1989-90

Premier Division

Colne Dynamoes	42	32	6	4	86	40	102
Gateshead	42	22	10	10	78	58	76
Witton Albion	42	22	7	13	67	39	73
Hyde United	42	21	8	13	73	50	71
South Liverpool	42	20	9	13	89	79	69
Matlock Town	42	18	12	12	61	42	66
Southport	42	17	14	11	54	48	65
Fleetwood Town	42	17	12	13	73	66	63
Marine	42	16	14	12	59	55	62
Bangor City	42	15	15	12	64	58	60
Bishop Auckland	42	17	8	17	72	64	59
Frickley Athletic	42	16	8	18	56	61	56
Horwich RMI	42	15	13	14	66	69	55
Morecambe	42	15	9	18	58	70	54
Gainsborough Trinity	42	16	8	18	59	55	53
Buxton	42	15	8	19	59	72	53
Stalybridge Celtic	42	12	9	21	48	61	45
Mossley	42	11	10	21	61	82	43
Goole Town	42	12	5	25	54	77	41
Shepshed Charterhouse	42	11	7	24	55	82	40
Caernarfon Town	42	10	8	24	56	86	38
Rhyl	42	7	10	25	43	77	30

Rhyl had 1 point deducted
Horwich and Gainsborough Trinity both had 3 points deducted

First Division

Leek Town	42	26	8	8	70	31	86
Droylsden	42	27	6	9	81	46	80
Accrington Stanley	42	22	10	10	80	53	76
Whitley Bay	42	21	11	10	93	59	74
Emley	42	20	9	13	70	42	69
Congleton Town	42	20	12	10	65	53	69
Winsford United	42	18	10	14	65	53	64
Curzon Ashton	42	17	11	14	66	60	62
Harrogate Town	42	17	9	16	68	62	60
Lancaster City	42	15	14	13	73	54	59
Eastwood Town	42	16	11	15	61	64	59
Farsley Celtic	42	17	6	19	71	75	57
Rossendale United	42	15	9	18	73	69	54
Newtown	42	14	12	16	49	62	54
Irlam Town	42	14	11	17	61	66	53
Workington	42	14	8	20	56	64	50
Radcliffe Borough	42	14	7	21	47	63	49
Alfreton Town	42	13	8	21	59	85	47
Worksop Town	42	13	5	24	56	95	44
Netherfield	42	11	6	25	56	89	39
Eastwood Hanley	42	10	6	26	45	76	36
Penrith	42	9	9	24	44	88	36

Congleton Town 3 points deducted. Droylsden 7 points deducted.

1990-91

Premier Division

Witton Albion	40	28	9	3	81	31	93
Stalybridge Celtic	40	22	11	7	44	26	77
Morecambe	40	19	16	5	72	44	73
Fleetwood Town	40	20	9	11	69	44	69
Southport	40	18	14	8	66	48	68
Marine	40	18	11	11	56	39	65
Bishop Auckland	40	17	10	13	62	56	61
Buxton	40	17	11	12	61	63	59
Leek Town	40	15	11	14	48	44	56
Frickley Athletic	40	16	6	18	64	62	54
Hyde United	40	14	11	15	73	63	53
Goole Town	40	14	10	16	68	74	52
Droylsden	40	12	11	17	67	70	47
Chorley	40	12	10	18	55	55	46
Mossley	40	13	10	17	55	68	45
Horwich RMI	40	13	6	21	62	81	45
Matlock Town	40	12	7	21	52	70	43
Bangor City	40	9	12	19	52	70	39
South Liverpool	40	10	9	21	58	92	39
Gainsborough Trinity	40	9	11	20	57	84	38
Shepshed Charterhouse	40	6	7	27	38	83	25

Buxton had 3 points deducted. Mossley had 4 points deducted.

First Division

Whitley Bay	42	25	10	7	95	38	85
Emley	42	24	12	6	78	37	84
Worksop Town	42	25	7	10	85	56	82
Accrington Stanley	42	21	13	8	83	57	76
Rhyl	42	21	7	14	62	63	70
Eastwood Town	42	17	11	14	70	60	62
Warrington Town	42	17	10	15	68	52	61
Lancaster City	42	19	8	15	58	56	61
Bridlington Town	42	15	15	12	72	52	60
Curzon Ashton	42	14	14	14	49	57	56
Congleton Town	42	14	12	16	57	71	54
Netherfield	42	14	11	17	67	66	53
Newtown	42	13	12	17	68	75	51
Caernarfon Town	42	13	10	19	51	64	49
Rossendale United	42	12	13	17	66	67	48
Radcliffe Borough	42	12	12	18	50	69	48
Irlam Town	42	12	11	19	55	76	47
Winsford United	42	11	13	18	51	66	46
Harrogate Town	42	11	13	18	55	73	46
Workington	42	11	11	20	54	67	41
Farsley Celtic	42	11	9	22	49	78	39
Alfreton Town	42	7	12	23	41	84	33

Lancaster City had 4 points deducted. Farsley Celtic and Workington both had 3 points deducted. Rossendale United had 1 point deducted.

1991-92

Premier Division

Stalybridge Celtic	42	26	14	2	84	33	92
Marine	42	23	9	10	64	32	78
Morecambe	42	21	13	8	70	44	76
Leek Town	42	21	10	11	62	49	73
Buxton	42	21	9	12	65	47	72
Emley	42	18	11	13	69	47	65
Southport	42	16	17	9	57	48	65
Accrington Stanley	42	17	12	13	78	62	63
Hyde United	42	17	9	16	69	67	60
Fleetwood Town	42	17	8	17	67	64	59
Bishop Auckland	42	16	9	17	48	58	57
Goole Town	42	15	9	18	60	72	54
Horwich RMI	42	13	14	15	44	52	53
Frickley Athletic	42	12	16	14	61	57	52
Droylsden	42	12	14	16	62	72	50
Mossley	42	15	4	23	51	73	49
Whitley Bay	42	13	9	20	53	79	48
Gainsborough Trinity	42	11	13	18	48	63	46
Matlock Town	42	12	9	21	59	87	45
Bangor City	42	11	10	21	46	57	43
Chorley	42	11	9	22	61	82	42
Shepshed Albion	42	6	8	28	46	79	26

First Division

Colwyn Bay	42	30	4	8	99	49	94
Winsford United	42	29	6	7	96	41	93
Worksop Town	42	25	5	12	101	51	80
Guiseley	42	22	12	8	93	56	78
Caernarfon Town	42	23	9	10	78	47	78
Bridlington Town	42	22	9	11	86	46	75
Warrington Town	42	20	8	14	79	64	68
Knowsley United	42	18	10	14	69	52	64
Netherfield	42	18	7	17	54	61	61
Harrogate Town	42	14	16	12	73	69	58
Curzon Ashton	42	15	9	18	71	83	54
Farsley Celtic	42	15	9	18	79	101	53
Radcliffe Borough	42	15	9	18	67	72	51
Newtown	42	15	6	21	60	95	51
Eastwood Town	42	13	11	18	59	70	50
Lancaster City	42	10	19	13	55	62	49
Congleton Town	42	14	5	23	59	81	47
Rhyl	42	11	10	21	59	69	43
Rossendale United	42	9	11	22	61	90	38
Alfreton Town	42	12	2	28	63	98	38
Irlam Town	42	9	7	26	45	95	33
Workington	42	7	8	27	45	99	28

Farsley Celtic, Irlam Town and Workington all had 1 point deducted.
Radcliffe Borough had 3 points deducted.

1992-93

Premier Division

Southport	42	29	9	4	103	31	96
Winsford United	42	27	9	6	91	43	90
Morecambe	42	25	11	6	93	51	86
Marine	42	26	8	8	83	47	86
Leek Town	42	21	11	10	86	51	74
Accrington Stanley	42	20	13	9	79	45	73
Frickley Athletic	42	21	6	15	62	52	69
Barrow	42	18	11	13	71	55	65
Hyde United	42	17	13	12	87	71	64
Bishop Auckland	42	17	11	14	63	52	62
Gainsborough Trinity	42	17	8	17	63	66	59
Colwyn Bay	42	16	6	20	80	79	54
Horwich RMI	42	14	10	18	72	79	52
Buxton	42	13	10	19	60	75	49
Matlock Town	42	13	11	18	56	79	47
Emley	42	13	6	23	62	91	45
Whitley Bay	42	11	8	23	57	96	41
Chorley	42	10	10	22	52	93	40
Fleetwood Town	42	10	7	25	50	77	37
Droylsden	42	10	7	25	47	84	37
Mossley	42	7	8	27	53	95	29
Goole Town	42	6	9	27	47	105	27

Matlock Town had 3 points deducted

First Division

Bridlington Town	40	25	11	4	84	35	86
Knowsley United	40	23	7	10	86	48	76
Ashton United	40	22	8	10	81	54	74
Guiseley	40	20	10	10	90	64	70
Warrington Town	40	19	10	11	85	57	67
Gretna	40	17	12	11	64	47	63
Curzon Ashton	40	16	15	9	69	63	63
Great Harwood Town	40	17	9	14	66	57	60
Alfreton Town	40	15	9	16	80	80	54
Harrogate Town	40	14	12	14	77	81	54
Worksop Town	40	15	9	16	66	70	54
Radcliffe Borough	40	13	14	13	66	69	53
Workington	40	13	13	14	51	61	52
Eastwood Town	40	13	11	16	49	52	50
Netherfield	40	11	14	15	68	63	47
Caernarfon Town	40	13	8	19	66	74	47
Farsley Celtic	40	12	8	20	64	77	44
Lancaster City	40	10	12	18	49	76	42
Shepshed Albion	40	9	12	19	46	66	39
Congleton Town	40	10	7	23	58	95	37
Rossendale United	40	5	5	30	50	126	20

1993-94

Premier Division

Marine	42	27	9	6	106	62	90
Leek Town	42	27	8	7	79	50	89
Boston United	42	23	9	10	90	43	78
Bishop Auckland	42	23	9	10	73	58	78
Frickley Athletic	42	21	12	9	90	51	75
Colwyn Bay	42	18	14	10	74	51	68
Morecambe	42	20	7	15	90	56	67
Barrow	42	18	10	14	59	51	64
Hyde United	42	17	10	15	80	71	61
Chorley	42	17	10	15	70	67	61
Whitley Bay	42	17	9	16	61	72	60
Gainsborough Trinity	42	15	11	16	64	66	56
Emley	42	12	16	14	63	71	52
Matlock Town	42	13	12	17	71	76	51
Buxton	42	13	10	19	67	73	49
Accrington Stanley	42	14	7	21	63	85	49
Droylsden	42	11	14	17	57	82	47
Knowsley United	42	11	11	20	52	66	44
Winsford United	42	9	11	22	50	74	38
Horwich RMI	42	8	12	22	50	75	35
Bridlington Town	42	7	10	25	41	91	28
Fleetwood Town	42	7	7	28	55	114	28

Horwich RMI 1 point deducted. Bridlington Town 3 points deducted

First Division

Guiseley	40	29	6	5	87	37	93
Spennymoor United	40	25	6	9	95	50	81
Ashton United	40	24	7	9	85	41	79
Lancaster City	40	20	10	10	74	46	70
Netherfield	40	20	6	14	68	60	66
Alfreton Town	40	18	10	12	83	70	64
Warrington Town	40	17	11	12	52	48	62
Goole Town	40	16	11	13	72	58	59
Great Harwood Town	40	15	14	11	56	60	59
Gretna	40	16	7	17	64	65	55
Workington	40	14	10	16	70	74	52
Worksop Town	40	14	9	17	79	87	51
Bamber Bridge	40	13	11	16	62	59	50
Curzon Ashton	40	13	8	19	62	71	47
Congleton Town	40	12	9	19	53	68	45
Radcliffe Borough	40	10	14	16	62	75	44
Mossley	40	10	12	18	44	68	39
Caernarfon Town	40	9	11	20	54	88	38
Farsley Celtic	40	6	16	18	42	77	34
Harrogate Town	40	8	9	23	40	86	33
Eastwood Town	40	7	11	22	47	63	32

Mossley had 3 points deducted

1994-95

Premier Division

Marine	42	29	11	2	83	27	98
Morecambe	42	28	10	4	99	34	94
Guiseley	42	28	9	5	96	50	93
Hyde United	42	22	10	10	89	59	76
Boston United	42	20	11	11	80	43	71
Spennymoor United	42	20	11	11	66	52	71
Buxton	42	18	9	15	65	62	63
Gainsborough Trinity	42	16	13	13	69	61	61
Bishop Auckland	42	16	12	14	68	55	57
Witton Albion	42	14	14	14	54	56	56
Barrow	42	17	5	20	68	71	56
Colwyn Bay	42	16	8	18	71	80	56
Emley	42	14	13	15	62	68	55
Matlock Town	42	15	5	22	62	72	50
Accrington Stanley	42	12	13	17	55	77	49
Knowsley United	42	11	14	17	64	83	47
Winsford United	42	10	11	21	56	75	41
Chorley	42	11	7	24	64	87	40
Frickley Athletic	42	10	10	22	53	79	40
Droylsden	42	10	8	24	56	93	38
Whitley Bay	42	8	8	26	46	97	32
Horwich RMI	42	9	4	29	49	94	31

Bishop Auckland had 3 points deducted

First Division

Blyth Spartans	42	26	9	7	95	55	87
Bamber Bridge	42	25	10	7	101	51	85
Warrington Town	42	25	9	8	74	40	84
Alfreton Town	42	25	7	10	94	49	82
Lancaster City	42	23	10	9	81	44	79
Worksop Town	42	19	14	9	95	68	71
Radcliffe Borough	42	18	10	14	76	70	64
Ashton United	42	18	8	16	80	70	62
Netherfield	42	17	7	18	54	56	58
Eastwood Town	42	14	13	15	67	61	55
Gretna	42	14	13	15	64	66	55
Atherton Laburnum Rovers	42	14	8	20	60	67	50
Harrogate Town	42	14	8	20	57	78	50
Caernarfon Town	42	13	10	19	59	62	49
Curzon Ashton	42	10	16	16	64	80	46
Great Harwood Town	42	11	13	18	64	87	46
Congleton Town	42	11	13	18	52	75	46
Fleetwood	42	12	11	19	51	74	44
Farsley Celtic	42	12	7	23	66	100	43
Workington	42	12	6	24	61	91	42
Goole Town	42	11	7	24	46	81	40
Mossley	42	11	5	26	52	90	37

Mossley had 1 point deducted. Fleetwood had 3 points deducted

1995-96

Premier Division

Bamber Bridge	42	20	16	6	81	49	76
Boston United	42	23	6	13	86	59	75
Hyde United	42	21	11	10	86	51	74
Barrow	42	20	13	9	69	42	73
Gainsborough Trinity	42	20	13	9	60	41	73
Blyth Spartans	42	17	13	12	75	61	64
Accrington Stanley	42	17	14	11	62	54	62
Emley	42	17	10	15	57	53	61
Spennymoor United	42	14	18	10	67	61	60
Guiseley	42	15	14	13	62	57	59
Bishop Auckland	42	16	11	15	60	55	59
Marine	42	15	14	13	59	54	59
Witton Albion	42	17	8	17	60	62	59
Chorley	42	14	9	19	67	74	48
Knowsley United	42	14	6	22	61	89	48
Winsford United	42	10	16	16	56	79	46
Leek Town	42	10	15	17	52	55	45
Colwyn Bay	42	8	21	13	43	57	45
Frickley Athletic	42	11	14	17	63	87	44
Buxton	42	9	11	22	43	72	38
Droylsden	42	10	8	24	58	100	38
Matlock Town	42	8	11	23	71	86	35

Accrington Stanley, Chorley & Frickley Town all had 3 points deducted

First Division

Lancaster City	40	24	11	5	79	38	83
Alfreton Town	40	23	9	8	79	47	78
Lincoln United	40	22	7	11	80	56	73
Curzon Ashton	40	20	7	13	73	53	67
Farsley Celtic	40	19	9	12	66	61	66
Radcliffe Borough	40	17	13	10	70	48	64
Eastwood Town	40	18	9	13	60	47	63
Whitley Bay	40	18	8	14	72	62	62
Ashton United	40	19	7	14	73	65	60
Atherton Laburnum Rovers	40	15	12	13	60	61	57
Worksop Town	40	16	8	16	84	90	56
Gretna	40	13	13	14	75	65	52
Warrington Town	40	13	10	17	75	72	49
Leigh RMI	40	14	7	19	53	59	49
Netherfield	40	13	10	17	64	73	49
Workington	40	11	12	17	50	62	45
Bradford Park Avenue	40	9	14	17	57	72	41
Congleton Town	40	11	11	18	36	59	41
Great Harwood Town	40	9	7	24	44	78	33
Fleetwood	40	7	10	23	41	81	31
Harrogate Town	40	7	10	23	54	96	31

Great Harwood Town had 1 point deducted, Congleton Town had 3 points deducted and Ashton United had 4 points deducted

1996-97

Premier Division

Leek Town	44	28	9	7	71	35	93
Bishop Auckland	44	23	14	7	88	43	83
Hyde United	44	22	16	6	93	46	82
Emley	44	23	12	9	89	54	81
Barrow	44	23	11	10	71	45	80
Boston United	44	22	13	9	74	47	79
Blyth Spartans	44	22	11	11	74	49	77
Marine	44	20	15	9	53	37	75
Guiseley	44	20	11	13	63	54	71
Gainsborough Trinity	44	18	12	14	65	46	66
Accrington Stanley	44	18	12	14	77	70	66
Runcorn	44	15	15	14	63	62	60
Chorley	44	16	9	19	69	66	57
Winsford United	44	13	14	17	50	56	53
Knowsley United	44	12	14	18	58	79	49
Colwyn Bay	44	11	13	20	60	76	46
Lancaster City	44	12	9	23	48	75	45
Frickley Athletic	44	12	8	24	62	91	44
Spennymoor United	44	10	10	24	52	68	40
Bamber Bridge	44	11	7	26	59	99	40
Alfreton Town	44	8	13	23	48	83	37
Witton Albion	44	5	14	25	41	91	29
Buxton	44	5	12	27	33	86	27

Knowsley United had 1 point deducted

First Division

Radcliffe Borough	42	26	7	9	77	33	85
Leigh RMI	42	24	11	7	65	33	83
Lincoln United	42	25	8	9	78	47	83
Farsley Celtic	42	23	8	11	75	48	77
Worksop Town	42	20	12	10	68	38	69
Stocksbridge Park Steels	42	19	11	12	66	54	68
Bradford Park Avenue	42	20	8	14	58	50	68
Ashton United	42	17	14	11	73	52	65
Great Harwood Town	42	16	12	14	56	46	60
Droylsden	42	15	14	13	69	67	59
Matlock Town	42	16	10	16	61	69	58
Whitley Bay	42	14	12	16	47	54	54
Flixton	42	15	7	20	57	72	52
Netherfield	42	12	14	16	54	56	50
Eastwood Town	42	12	14	16	42	50	50
Gretna	42	10	18	14	55	68	48
Harrogate Town	42	13	8	21	55	76	47
Congleton Town	42	12	9	21	47	64	45
Workington	42	10	12	20	45	63	42
Curzon Ashton	42	8	10	24	48	79	34
Warrington Town	42	5	18	19	42	79	33
Atherton Laburnum Rovers	42	7	9	26	45	85	30

Worksop Town had 3 points deducted

1997-98

Premier Division

Barrow	42	25	8	9	61	29	83
Boston United	42	22	12	8	55	40	78
Leigh RMI	42	21	13	8	63	41	76
Runcorn	42	22	9	11	80	50	75
Gainsborough Trinity	42	22	9	11	60	39	75
Emley	42	22	8	12	81	61	74
Winsford United	42	19	12	11	54	43	69
Altrincham	42	18	11	13	76	44	65
Guiseley	42	16	16	10	61	53	64
Bishop Auckland	42	17	12	13	78	60	63
Marine	42	15	11	16	56	59	56
Hyde United	42	13	16	13	60	55	55
Colwyn Bay	42	15	9	18	53	57	54
Spennymoor United	42	14	11	17	58	72	52
Chorley	42	14	7	21	51	70	49
Frickley Athletic	42	12	12	18	45	62	48
Lancaster City	42	13	8	21	55	74	47
Blyth Spartans	42	12	13	17	52	63	39
Bamber Bridge	42	9	12	21	51	74	39
Accrington Stanley	42	8	14	20	49	68	38
Radcliffe Borough	42	6	12	24	39	70	30
Alfreton Town	42	3	13	26	32	86	22

Spennymoor United had 1 point deducted
Blyth Spartans had 10 points deducted

1998-99

Premier Division

Altrincham	42	23	11	8	67	33	80
Worksop Town	42	22	10	10	66	48	76
Guiseley	42	21	9	12	64	47	72
Bamber Bridge	42	18	15	9	63	48	69
Gateshead	42	18	11	13	69	58	65
Gainsborough Trinity	42	19	8	15	65	59	65
Whitby Town	42	17	13	12	77	62	64
Leigh RMI	42	16	15	11	63	54	63
Hyde United	42	16	11	15	61	48	59
Stalybridge Celtic	42	16	11	15	71	63	59
Winsford United	42	14	15	13	56	52	57
Runcorn	42	12	19	11	46	49	55
Emley	42	12	17	13	47	49	53
Blyth Spartans	42	14	9	19	56	64	51
Colwyn Bay	42	12	13	17	60	71	49
Frickley Athletic	42	11	15	16	55	71	48
Marine	42	10	17	15	61	69	47
Spennymoor United	42	12	11	19	52	71	47
Lancaster City	42	11	13	18	50	62	46
Bishop Auckland	42	10	15	17	49	67	45
Chorley	42	8	15	19	45	68	39
Accrington Stanley	42	9	9	24	47	77	36

First Division

Whitby Town	42	30	8	4	99	48	98
Worksop Town	42	28	7	7	93	44	91
Ashton United	42	26	9	7	93	43	87
Droylsden	42	24	8	10	70	49	80
Lincoln United	42	20	11	11	76	62	71
Farsley Celtic	42	20	10	12	72	66	70
Witton Albion	42	19	9	14	77	55	66
Eastwood Town	42	18	12	12	68	51	66
Bradford Park Avenue	42	18	11	13	62	46	65
Belper Town	42	18	7	17	68	66	61
Stocksbridge Park Steels	42	17	9	16	68	63	60
Trafford	42	16	6	20	59	61	54
Whitley Bay	42	14	12	16	60	63	54
Matlock Town	42	14	11	17	68	65	53
Gretna	42	13	9	20	58	64	48
Netherfield	42	12	11	19	55	75	47
Flixton	42	10	12	20	45	73	42
Congleton Town	42	11	8	23	65	101	41
Harrogate Town	42	8	14	20	57	80	38
Great Harwood Town	42	8	12	22	42	88	36
Workington	42	8	7	27	38	84	31
Buxton	42	7	3	32	41	87	24

First Division

Droylsden	42	26	8	8	97	55	86
Hucknall Town	42	26	11	5	80	38	86
Ashton United	42	22	12	8	79	46	78
Lincoln United	42	20	12	10	94	65	72
Eastwood Town	42	20	8	14	65	69	68
Radcliffe Borough	42	19	8	15	78	62	65
Burscough	42	19	8	15	67	61	65
Witton Albion	42	18	9	15	70	63	63
Bradford Park Avenue	42	17	11	14	64	55	62
Stocksbridge Park Steels	42	16	13	13	64	60	61
Harrogate Town	42	17	7	18	75	77	58
Gretna	42	16	10	16	73	80	58
Belper Town	42	15	11	16	58	57	56
Trafford	42	14	11	17	50	58	53
Netherfield Kendal	42	13	10	19	51	64	49
Flixton	42	12	12	18	50	64	48
Matlock Town	42	14	6	22	53	72	48
Farsley Celtic	42	11	13	18	56	73	46
Whitley Bay	42	10	9	23	53	77	39
Congleton Town	42	8	15	19	65	91	39
Great Harwood Town	42	10	8	24	51	73	38
Alfreton Town	42	9	8	25	53	86	35

Hucknall Town had 3 points deducted

1999-2000

Premier Division

Leigh RMI	44	28	8	8	91	45	92
Hyde United	44	24	13	7	77	44	85
Gateshead	44	23	13	8	79	41	82
Marine	44	21	16	7	78	46	79
Emley	44	20	12	12	54	41	72
Lancaster City	44	20	11	13	65	55	71
Stalybridge Celtic	44	18	12	14	64	54	66
Bishop Auckland	44	18	11	15	63	61	65
Runcorn	44	18	10	16	64	55	64
Worksop Town	44	19	6	19	78	65	63
Gainsborough Trinity	44	16	15	13	59	49	63
Whitby Town	44	15	13	16	66	66	58
Barrow	44	14	15	15	65	59	57
Blyth Spartans	44	15	9	20	62	67	54
Droylsden	44	14	12	18	53	60	54
Frickley Athletic	44	15	9	20	64	85	54
Bamber Bridge	44	14	11	19	70	67	53
Hucknall Town	44	14	11	19	55	61	53
Leek Town	44	14	10	20	58	79	52
Colwyn Bay	44	12	12	20	46	85	48
Spennymoor United	44	10	13	21	41	71	42
Guiseley	44	8	17	19	52	72	41
Winsford United	44	3	7	34	40	116	16

Spennymoor United had 1 point deducted

First Division

Accrington Stanley	42	25	9	8	96	43	84
Burscough	42	22	18	2	81	35	84
Witton Albion	42	23	15	4	88	46	84
Bradford Park Avenue	42	23	9	10	77	48	78
Radcliffe Borough	42	22	12	8	71	48	78
Farsley Celtic	42	19	11	12	66	52	68
Matlock Town	42	17	16	9	72	55	67
Ossett Town	42	17	8	17	77	55	59
Stocksbridge Park Steels	42	16	8	18	55	70	56
Eastwood Town	42	15	11	16	64	65	55
Harrogate Town	42	14	12	16	65	67	54
Congleton Town	42	14	12	16	63	73	54
Chorley	42	13	15	14	53	64	54
Ashton United	42	12	16	14	65	67	52
Workington	42	13	13	16	49	55	52
Lincoln United	42	13	12	17	52	80	51
Belper Town	42	13	11	18	59	72	50
Trafford	42	11	12	19	55	63	45
Gretna	42	11	7	24	48	78	40
Netherfield Kendal	42	8	9	25	46	82	33
Flixton	42	7	9	26	47	85	30
Whitley Bay	42	7	9	26	41	87	30

Eastwood Town had 1 point deducted

2000-2001

Premier Division

Stalybridge Celtic	44	31	9	4	96	32	102
Emley	44	31	8	5	87	42	101
Bishop Auckland	44	26	7	11	88	53	85
Lancaster City	44	24	9	11	84	60	81
Worksop Town	44	20	13	11	102	60	73
Barrow	44	21	9	14	83	63	72
Altrincham	44	20	10	14	80	58	70
Gainsborough Trinity	44	17	14	13	59	56	65
Accrington Stanley	44	18	10	16	72	67	64
Hucknall Town	44	17	12	15	57	63	63
Gateshead	44	16	12	16	68	61	60
Bamber Bridge	44	17	8	19	63	65	59
Runcorn	44	15	10	19	56	70	55
Blyth Spartans	44	15	9	20	61	64	54
Burscough	44	14	10	20	59	68	52
Hyde United	44	13	12	19	72	79	51
Whitby Town	44	13	11	20	60	76	50
Marine	44	12	13	19	62	78	49
Colwyn Bay	44	12	10	22	68	102	46
Frickley Athletic	44	10	15	19	50	79	45
Droylsden	44	13	6	25	50	80	45
Leek Town	44	12	8	24	45	70	44
Spennymoor United	44	4	5	35	32	108	17

First Division

Bradford Park Avenue	42	28	5	9	83	40	89
Vauxhall Motors	42	23	10	9	95	50	79
Ashton United	42	23	9	10	91	49	78
Stocksbridge Park Steels	42	19	13	10	80	60	70
Trafford	42	20	9	13	70	62	68
Belper Town	42	18	11	13	71	62	65
Witton Albion	42	15	16	11	51	50	61
Ossett Town	42	16	12	14	66	58	60
Radcliffe Borough	42	17	8	17	72	71	59
Chorley	42	15	14	13	71	70	59
Harrogate Town	42	15	10	17	60	70	55
Matlock Town	42	14	10	18	70	74	52
North Ferriby United	42	14	10	18	64	73	52
Workington	42	13	12	17	53	60	51
Lincoln United	42	13	12	17	60	75	51
Gretna	42	12	12	18	72	82	48
Guiseley	42	11	15	16	37	50	48
Kendal Town	42	12	12	18	60	69	47
Farsley Celtic	42	12	11	19	53	71	47
Eastwood Town	42	13	8	21	40	63	47
Winsford United	42	13	11	18	61	70	44
Congleton Town	42	8	6	28	43	94	30

Trafford and Kendal Town both had 1 point deducted
Winsford United had 6 points deducted

2001-2002

Premier Division

Burton Albion	44	31	11	2	106	30	104
Vauxhall Motors	44	27	8	9	86	55	89
Lancaster City	44	23	9	12	80	57	78
Worksop Town	44	23	9	12	74	51	78
Emley	44	22	9	13	69	55	75
Accrington Stanley	44	21	9	14	89	64	72
Runcorn FC Halton	44	21	8	15	76	53	71
Barrow	44	19	10	15	75	59	67
Altrincham	44	19	9	16	66	58	66
Bradford Park Avenue	44	18	5	21	77	76	59
Droylsden	44	17	8	19	65	78	59
Blyth Spartans	44	14	16	14	59	62	58
Frickley Athletic	44	16	11	17	63	69	58
Gateshead	44	14	14	16	58	71	56
Whitby Town	44	15	8	21	61	76	53
Hucknall Town	44	14	9	21	50	68	51
Marine	44	11	17	16	62	71	50
Burscough	44	15	5	24	69	86	50
Gainsborough Trinity	44	13	10	21	61	76	49
Colwyn Bay	44	12	11	21	49	82	47
Bishop Auckland	44	12	8	24	46	68	44
Hyde United	44	10	10	24	61	87	40
Bamber Bridge	44	7	10	27	38	88	30

Frickley Athletic and Bamber Bridge both had 1 point deducted.

First Division

Harrogate Town	42	25	11	6	80	35	86
Ossett Town	42	21	13	8	73	44	76
Ashton United	42	21	12	9	90	63	75
Spennymoor United	42	22	6	14	75	73	72
Radcliffe Borough	42	20	8	14	73	51	68
Leek Town	42	20	8	14	67	51	68
Gretna	42	19	7	16	66	66	63
Eastwood Town	42	17	11	14	61	59	62
Rossendale United	42	17	10	15	69	58	61
Witton Albion	42	17	10	15	72	68	61
Guiseley	42	18	7	17	60	67	61
North Ferriby United	42	14	16	12	71	60	58
Chorley	42	16	9	17	59	57	57
Matlock Town	42	15	9	18	49	48	51
Trafford	42	14	9	19	64	80	51
Workington	42	12	12	18	51	57	48
Farsley Celtic	42	12	11	19	64	78	47
Belper Town	42	12	11	19	49	66	47
Lincoln United	42	11	14	17	62	80	47
Stocksbridge Park Steels	42	12	9	21	55	76	45
Kendal Town	42	9	9	24	52	76	36
Ossett Albion	42	8	8	26	43	92	32

Gretna had 1 point deducted.
Matlock Town had 3 points deducted.

2002-2003

Premier Division

Accrington Stanley	44	30	10	4	97	44	100
Barrow	44	24	12	8	84	52	84
Vauxhall Motors	44	22	10	12	81	46	76
Stalybridge Celtic	44	21	13	10	77	51	76
Worksop Town	44	21	9	14	82	67	72
Harrogate Town	44	21	8	15	75	63	71
Bradford Park Avenue	44	20	10	14	73	70	70
Hucknall Town	44	17	15	12	72	62	66
Droylsden	44	18	10	16	62	52	64
Whitby Town	44	17	12	15	80	69	63
Marine	44	17	10	17	63	60	61
Wakefield & Emley	44	14	18	12	46	49	60
Runcorn FC Halton	44	15	15	14	69	74	60
Altrincham	44	17	9	18	58	63	60
Gainsborough Trinity	44	16	11	17	67	66	59
Ashton United	44	15	13	16	71	79	58
Lancaster City	44	16	9	19	71	75	57
Burscough	44	14	9	21	44	51	51
Blyth Spartans	44	14	9	21	67	87	51
Frickley Athletic	44	13	8	23	45	78	47
Gateshead	44	10	11	23	60	81	41
Colwyn Bay	44	5	9	30	52	99	24
Hyde United	44	5	8	31	40	98	23

Division One

Alfreton Town	42	26	9	7	106	59	87
Spennymoor United	42	27	6	9	81	42	87
Radcliffe Borough	42	25	10	7	90	46	85
North Ferriby United	42	23	9	10	78	45	78
Chorley	42	21	10	11	80	51	73
Belper Town	42	20	13	9	53	42	73
Witton Albion	42	19	15	8	67	50	72
Matlock Town	42	20	10	12	67	48	70
Leek Town	42	20	9	13	63	46	69
Workington	42	19	10	13	73	60	67
Farsley Celtic	42	17	11	14	66	67	62
Kendal Town	42	18	7	17	68	58	61
Bamber Bridge	42	15	9	18	55	59	54
Guiseley	42	14	11	17	68	63	53
Bishop Auckland	42	13	10	19	58	83	49
Lincoln United	42	12	9	21	67	77	45
Stocksbridge PS	42	11	9	22	54	81	42
Rossendale United	42	12	5	25	58	88	41
Kidsgrove Athletic	42	9	11	22	49	71	38
Ossett Town	42	8	9	25	39	80	33
Eastwood Town	42	5	8	29	33	92	23
Trafford	42	5	6	31	34	99	21

2003-2004

Premier Division

Hucknall Town	44	29	8	7	83	38	95
Droylsden	44	26	8	10	96	64	86
Barrow	44	22	14	8	82	52	80
Alfreton Town	44	23	9	12	73	43	78
Harrogate Town	44	24	5	15	79	63	77
Southport	44	20	10	14	71	52	70
Worksop Town	44	19	13	12	69	50	70
Lancaster City	44	20	9	15	62	49	69
Vauxhall Motors	44	19	10	15	78	75	67
Gainsborough Trinity	44	17	13	14	70	52	64
Stalybridge Celtic	44	18	10	16	72	66	64
Altrincham	44	16	15	13	66	51	63
Runcorn FC Halton	44	16	13	15	67	63	61
Ashton United	44	17	8	19	59	79	59
Whitby Town	44	14	11	19	55	70	53
Marine	44	13	12	19	62	74	51
Bradford Park Avenue	44	12	14	18	48	62	50
Spennymoor United	44	14	6	24	55	93	48
Burscough	44	10	15	19	47	67	45
Radcliffe Borough	44	12	6	26	74	99	42
Blyth Spartans	44	10	10	24	54	74	40
Frickley Athletic	44	11	7	26	51	83	40
Wakefield & Emley	44	8	6	30	45	99	30

Division One

Hyde United	42	24	8	10	79	49	80
Matlock Town	42	23	7	12	78	51	76
Farsley Celtic	42	20	14	8	78	56	74
Lincoln United	42	20	11	11	73	53	71
Witton Albion	42	17	12	13	61	56	63
Gateshead	42	21	4	17	65	68	63
Workington	42	17	11	14	70	58	62
Leek Town	42	16	13	13	56	47	61
Guiseley	42	16	12	14	66	54	60
Bamber Bridge	42	16	12	14	64	53	60
Bridlington Town	42	16	10	16	70	68	58
Prescot Cables	42	16	10	16	63	65	58
Bishop Auckland	42	14	13	15	61	64	55
Ossett Town	42	15	10	17	62	73	52
Rossendale United	42	13	12	17	53	62	51
Colwyn Bay	42	14	9	19	56	82	51
North Ferriby United	42	13	11	18	64	70	50
Chorley	42	13	10	19	54	70	49
Stocksbridge Park Steels	42	12	12	18	57	69	48
Belper Town	42	9	15	18	44	58	42
Kendal Town	42	11	7	24	53	79	40
Kidsgrove Athletic	42	10	9	23	45	67	39

Gateshead had 4 points deducted. Ossett Town had 3 points deducted

2004-2005

Premier Division

Hyde United	42	25	13	4	80	43	88
Workington	42	26	7	9	73	30	85
Farsley Celtic	42	25	8	9	81	41	83
Whitby Town	42	23	11	8	65	49	80
Prescot Cables	42	21	8	13	63	54	71
Burscough	42	21	7	14	93	74	70
Leek Town	42	16	15	11	63	52	63
Witton Albion	42	15	17	10	56	44	62
Radcliffe Borough	42	16	14	12	60	60	62
Guiseley	42	16	13	13	70	64	61
Matlock Town	42	14	13	15	59	67	55
Blyth Spartans	42	13	13	16	53	55	52
Wakefield & Emley	42	14	10	18	60	67	52
Lincoln United	42	15	4	23	53	66	49
Marine	42	10	18	14	53	60	48
Ossett Town	42	11	13	18	53	62	46
Gateshead	42	11	12	19	61	84	45
Frickley Athletic	42	10	14	18	44	57	44
Bishop Auckland	42	11	7	24	51	74	40
Bridlington Town	42	7	14	21	43	66	35
Bamber Bridge	42	9	7	26	48	92	34
Spennymoor United	42	9	10	23	44	65	25

Spennymoor United had 12 points deducted.

Division One

North Ferriby United	42	25	8	9	83	49	83
Ilkeston Town	42	24	9	9	64	40	81
AFC Telford United	42	23	11	8	78	44	80
Willenhall Town	42	22	12	8	71	46	78
Kendal Town	42	21	8	13	89	69	71
Eastwood Town	42	20	9	13	73	54	69
Mossley	42	20	6	16	81	56	66
Brigg Town	42	15	19	8	59	46	64
Gresley Rovers	42	17	12	13	57	53	63
Kidsgrove Athletic	42	15	15	12	60	55	60
Woodley Sports	42	16	11	15	68	74	59
Ossett Albion	42	15	13	14	83	74	58
Colwyn Bay	42	14	13	15	54	62	55
Stocksbridge Park Steels	42	15	9	18	58	58	51
Shepshed Dynamo	42	13	11	18	53	75	50
Chorley	42	13	9	20	62	69	48
Belper Town	42	13	8	21	57	66	47
Spalding United	42	13	8	21	57	69	47
Clitheroe	42	12	10	20	47	57	46
Warrington Town	42	11	13	18	45	59	46
Rossendale United	42	10	10	22	64	87	40
Rocester	42	0	6	36	31	132	6

Stocksbridge Park Steels had 3 points deducted.

2005-2006 Premier Division

Blyth Spartans	42	26	11	5	79	32	89
Frickley Athletic	42	26	8	8	72	36	86
Marine	42	23	12	7	61	25	81
Farsley Celtic	42	23	10	9	84	34	79
North Ferriby United	42	21	10	11	77	54	73
Whitby Town	42	18	10	14	60	59	64
Burscough	42	19	6	17	64	64	63
Witton Albion	42	17	9	16	68	55	60
Matlock Town	42	16	11	15	60	55	59
AFC Telford United	42	14	17	11	54	52	59
Ossett Town	42	17	7	18	57	61	58
Leek Town	42	14	14	14	50	53	56
Prescot Cables	42	15	8	19	49	60	53
Guiseley	42	14	9	19	45	58	51
Ashton United	42	13	10	19	62	63	49
Ilkeston Town	42	12	13	17	48	51	49
Gateshead	42	12	10	20	52	77	46
Radcliffe Borough	42	12	8	22	54	62	44
Lincoln United	42	10	14	18	44	64	44
Wakefield Emley	42	11	9	22	38	69	42
Bradford Park Avenue	42	10	9	23	64	86	39
Runcorn FC Halton	42	6	11	25	36	108	29

Division One

Mossley	42	23	9	10	83	55	78
Fleetwood Town	42	22	10	10	72	48	76
Kendal Town	42	22	10	10	81	58	76
Woodley Sports	42	22	8	12	85	53	74
Gresley Rovers	42	20	10	12	79	64	70
Stocksbridge PS	42	17	16	9	66	43	67
Eastwood Town	42	16	14	12	66	58	62
Brigg Town	42	16	14	12	70	64	62
Belper Town	42	17	8	17	53	56	59
Shepshed Dynamo	42	15	13	14	57	56	58
Bridlington Town	42	16	10	16	61	68	58
Colwyn Bay	42	15	11	16	56	53	56
Bamber Bridge	42	13	15	14	65	59	54
Ossett Albion	42	15	9	18	54	64	54
Rossendale United	42	12	17	13	58	61	53
Clitheroe	42	15	8	19	54	73	53
Kidsgrove Athletic	42	14	9	19	66	69	51
Chorley	42	14	8	20	58	59	50
Warrington Town	42	11	15	16	62	74	48
Spalding United	42	10	15	17	49	70	45
Goole	42	11	11	20	55	85	43
Bishop Auckland	42	3	6	33	39	99	15

Goole had 1 point deducted.

2006-2007 Premier Division

Burscough	42	23	12	7	80	37	80
Witton Albion	42	24	8	10	90	48	80
AFC Telford United	42	21	15	6	72	40	78
Marine	42	22	8	12	70	53	74
Matlock Town	42	21	9	12	70	43	72
Guiseley	42	19	12	11	71	49	69
Hednesford Town	42	18	14	10	49	41	68
Fleetwood Town	42	19	10	13	71	60	67
Gateshead	42	17	14	11	75	57	65
Ossett Town	42	18	10	14	61	52	64
Whitby Town	42	18	6	18	63	78	60
Ilkeston Town	42	16	11	15	66	62	59
North Ferriby United	42	15	9	18	54	61	54
Prescot Cables	42	13	14	15	52	56	53
Lincoln United	42	12	15	15	40	58	51
Frickley Athletic	42	13	10	19	50	69	49
Leek Town	42	13	9	20	49	61	48
Ashton United	42	13	9	20	52	72	48
Kendal Town	42	12	11	19	59	79	47
Mossley	42	10	5	27	48	79	35
Radcliffe Borough	42	7	11	24	39	71	32
Grantham Town	42	3	8	31	39	94	17

Burscough had one point deducted.

Division One

Buxton	46	30	11	5	94	37	101
Cammell Laird	46	28	10	8	105	56	94
Eastwood Town	46	26	9	11	89	43	87
Bradford Park Avenue	46	24	10	12	77	47	82
Colwyn Bay	46	22	11	13	74	65	77
Stocksbridge Park Steels	46	22	10	14	82	49	76
Goole	46	21	9	16	80	84	72
Kidsgrove Athletic	46	21	7	18	91	80	70
Rossendale United	46	21	7	18	64	59	70
Woodley Sports	46	19	11	16	89	71	68
Ossett Albion	46	19	11	16	71	66	68
Harrogate Railway	46	21	5	20	72	78	68
Bamber Bridge	46	18	8	20	78	75	62
Alsager Town	46	18	7	21	72	75	61
Skelmersdale United	46	17	10	19	72	77	61
Clitheroe	46	18	6	22	78	75	60
Brigg Town	46	16	10	20	57	72	58
Gresley Rovers	46	16	7	23	59	75	55
Belper Town	46	17	4	25	58	86	55
Shepshed Dynamo	46	15	7	24	62	96	52
Wakefield	46	13	10	23	48	71	49
Warrington Town	46	13	8	25	64	84	47
Chorley	46	10	6	30	52	99	36
Bridlington Town	46	3	14	29	33	101	23

2007-2008

Premier Division

Fleetwood Town	40	28	7	5	81	39	91
Witton Albion	40	27	8	5	84	28	89
Gateshead	40	26	7	7	93	42	85
Eastwood Town	40	20	9	11	61	45	69
Buxton	40	20	8	12	60	50	68
Guiseley	40	19	10	11	65	43	67
Marine	40	19	4	17	70	65	61
Hednesford Town	40	15	8	17	62	65	53
Worksop Town	40	13	12	15	59	62	51
Ashton United	40	11	15	14	63	73	48
Kendal Town	40	12	11	17	61	70	47
Whitby Town	40	13	7	20	68	75	46
Prescot Cables	40	13	8	19	48	62	46
Frickley Athletic	40	11	13	16	50	68	46
North Ferriby United	40	13	7	20	53	76	46
Matlock Town	40	12	9	19	55	68	45
Ilkeston Town	40	10	14	16	64	72	44
Ossett Town	40	12	8	20	48	60	44
Leek Town	40	11	11	18	54	68	44
Stamford	40	11	10	19	59	86	43
Lincoln United	40	7	8	25	44	85	29

Prescot Cables had one point deducted.

Division One North

Bradford Park Avenue	42	25	7	10	91	43	82
FC United of Manchester	42	24	9	9	91	49	81
Skelmersdale United	42	23	9	10	94	46	78
Curzon Ashton	42	23	9	10	78	48	78
Bamber Bridge	42	22	8	12	70	54	74
Ossett Albion	42	20	10	12	77	65	70
Wakefield	42	19	7	16	58	49	64
Newcastle Blue Star	42	17	12	13	71	58	63
Rossendale United	42	16	11	15	66	74	59
Garforth Town	42	16	8	18	60	63	56
Lancaster City	42	15	9	18	54	70	54
Harrogate Railway	42	13	12	17	51	58	51
Clitheroe	42	13	11	18	63	77	50
Chorley	42	10	12	20	56	80	42
Mossley	42	12	6	24	60	100	42
Radcliffe Borough	42	9	11	22	53	75	38
Woodley Sports	42	7	13	22	38	65	33
Bridlington Town	42	8	8	26	42	99	32

Woodley Sports had one point deducted.

Division One South

Retford United	42	31	6	5	93	35	99
Cammell Laird	42	27	5	10	82	54	86
Nantwich Town	42	25	4	13	90	45	79
Sheffield	42	22	10	10	82	53	76
Stocksbridge Park Steels	42	21	9	12	72	61	72
Grantham Town	42	22	4	16	74	58	70
Colwyn Bay	42	19	8	15	86	65	65
Belper Town	42	17	13	12	73	64	64
Goole	42	18	10	14	77	69	64
Carlton Town	42	16	11	15	86	82	59
Gresley Rovers	42	18	5	19	53	69	59
Quorn	42	15	8	19	69	76	53
Warrington Town	42	13	8	21	51	78	47
Alsager Town	42	12	7	23	58	88	43
Shepshed Dynamo	42	10	8	24	44	75	38
Brigg Town	42	8	12	22	56	86	36
Kidsgrove Athletic	42	7	10	25	61	90	31
Spalding United	42	3	10	29	46	105	19

2008-2009

Premier Division

Eastwood Town	42	25	12	5	82	37	87
Ilkeston Town	42	23	13	6	59	34	82
Nantwich Town	42	22	10	10	83	41	76
Guiseley	42	22	10	10	98	60	76
Kendal Town	42	21	11	10	85	63	74
FC United of Manchester	42	21	9	12	82	58	72
Bradford Park Avenue	42	20	12	10	74	52	72
Hednesford Town	42	21	6	15	78	52	69
Ashton United	42	16	10	16	71	75	58
North Ferriby United	42	16	6	20	67	65	54
Frickley Athletic	42	13	15	14	50	58	54
Ossett Town	42	15	8	19	71	74	53
Marine	42	15	6	21	54	75	51
Buxton	42	13	10	19	56	58	49
Matlock Town	42	12	13	17	65	74	49
Boston United	42	12	13	17	38	52	49
Worksop Town	42	12	12	18	48	87	48
Cammell Laird	42	12	11	19	58	70	47
Whitby Town	42	12	10	20	58	71	46
Witton Albion	42	12	6	24	53	73	42
Leigh Genesis	42	11	7	24	42	88	40
Prescot Cables	42	5	12	25	52	107	27

Division One North

Durham City	40	25	12	3	98	41	87
Skelmersdale United	40	26	8	6	96	51	86
Newcastle Blue Star	40	21	10	9	93	54	73
Colwyn Bay	40	23	7	10	72	49	73
Curzon Ashton	40	20	8	12	66	44	68
Ossett Albion	40	19	9	12	76	61	66
Lancaster City	40	19	8	13	69	64	65
FC Halifax Town	40	17	12	11	71	52	63
Wakefield	40	16	8	16	65	62	56
Mossley	40	16	6	18	63	70	54
Bamber Bridge	40	16	5	19	69	78	53
Clitheroe	40	15	7	18	64	76	52
Woodley Sports	40	16	3	21	57	74	51
Chorley	40	13	8	19	56	66	47
Trafford	40	13	7	20	72	83	46
Garforth Town	40	13	5	22	77	99	44
Radcliffe Borough	40	12	6	22	51	66	42
Harrogate Railway	40	13	3	24	58	82	42
Warrington Town	40	11	8	21	50	73	41
Salford City	40	10	6	24	59	107	36
Rossendale United	40	8	10	22	53	83	34

Colwyn Bay had 3 points deducted.

Division One South

Retford United	38	24	9	5	88	34	81
Belper Town	38	24	9	5	79	41	81
Stocksbridge Park Steels	38	23	6	9	92	44	75
Carlton Town	38	20	10	8	83	50	70
Rushall Olympic	38	20	8	10	63	42	68
Glapwell	38	21	5	12	78	58	68
Stamford	38	15	16	7	65	51	61
Shepshed Dynamo	38	16	8	14	61	61	56
Leek Town	38	14	12	12	63	60	54
Lincoln United	38	14	9	15	58	65	51
Sheffield	38	14	8	16	67	69	50
Quorn	38	13	9	16	54	63	48
Grantham Town	38	12	11	15	49	65	47
Loughborough Dynamo	38	11	13	14	45	58	46
Kidsgrove Athletic	38	12	5	21	49	62	41
Willenhall Town	38	10	8	20	55	74	38
Spalding United	38	10	7	21	41	82	37
Goole	38	13	5	20	62	85	33
Gresley Rovers	38	6	7	25	41	78	25
Brigg Town	38	3	5	30	41	92	14

Goole had 11 points deducted.

2009-2010

Premier Division

Guiseley	38	25	4	9	73	41	79
Bradford Park Avenue	38	24	6	8	94	51	78
Boston United	38	23	8	7	90	34	77
North Ferriby United	38	22	9	7	70	38	75
Kendal Town	38	21	8	9	75	47	71
Retford United	38	18	11	9	73	46	65
Matlock Town	38	17	9	12	72	49	60
Buxton	38	16	12	10	66	43	60
Marine	38	17	6	15	60	55	57
Nantwich Town	38	16	6	16	64	69	54
Stocksbridge Park Steels	38	15	7	16	80	68	52
Ashton United	38	15	6	17	48	63	51
FC United of Manchester	38	13	8	17	62	65	47
Whitby Town	38	12	10	16	56	62	46
Frickley Athletic	38	12	9	17	50	66	45
Burscough	38	13	5	20	55	65	44
Hucknall Town	38	12	8	18	65	81	44
Worksop Town	38	7	9	22	45	68	30
Ossett Town	38	6	7	25	46	92	25
Durham City	38	2	0	36	27	168	0

Durham City had 6 points deducted.
King's Lynn folded and their record was expunged.
Newcastle Blue Star folded and resigned from the League before the start of the season.

2010-2011

Division One North

	P	W	D	L	F	A	Pts
FC Halifax Town	42	30	10	2	108	38	100
Lancaster City	42	31	3	8	95	45	96
Curzon Ashton	42	23	12	7	93	50	75
Colwyn Bay	42	23	6	13	77	57	75
Skelmersdale United	42	22	8	12	80	56	74
Leigh Genesis	42	21	8	13	81	51	71
Mossley	42	18	11	13	73	67	65
Clitheroe	42	18	8	16	72	66	62
Warrington Town	42	18	6	18	65	69	60
Radcliffe Borough	42	17	6	19	65	78	57
Salford City	42	16	8	18	63	74	56
Trafford	42	15	8	19	79	73	53
AFC Fylde	42	15	8	19	67	79	53
Bamber Bridge	42	14	10	18	58	67	52
Prescot Cables	42	13	11	18	51	68	50
Chorley	42	13	10	19	56	76	49
Harrogate Railway Athletic	42	15	7	20	58	79	49
Wakefield	42	12	12	18	49	58	48
Woodley Sports	42	10	15	17	53	67	45
Garforth Town	42	11	7	24	64	94	40
Ossett Albion	42	7	7	28	52	91	28
Rossendale United	42	6	7	29	38	94	25

Harrogate Railway Athletic had 3 points deducted.
Curzon Ashton had 6 points deducted, 3 for fielding an ineligible player and 3 for a financial irregularity. Initially 10 points were deducted for the financial irregularity, with 5 points suspended, but on appeal this was reduced to 6 points deducted with 3 suspended.

Premier Division

	P	W	D	L	F	A	Pts
FC Halifax Town	42	30	8	4	108	36	98
Colwyn Bay	42	24	7	11	67	56	79
Bradford Park Avenue	42	23	8	11	84	55	77
FC United of Manchester	42	24	4	14	76	53	76
North Ferriby United	42	22	7	13	78	51	73
Buxton	42	20	10	12	71	52	70
Kendal Town	42	21	5	16	80	77	68
Marine	42	20	7	15	74	64	67
Worksop Town	42	21	6	15	72	54	66
Chasetown	42	20	6	16	76	59	66
Matlock Town	42	20	6	16	74	59	66
Northwich Victoria	42	18	9	15	66	55	63
Stocksbridge Park Steels	42	17	6	19	75	75	57
Ashton United	42	16	5	21	57	62	53
Mickleover Sports	42	15	7	20	70	76	52
Whitby Town	42	14	9	19	58	77	51
Nantwich Town	42	13	7	22	68	90	46
Frickley Athletic	42	11	11	20	43	68	44
Burscough	42	12	7	23	56	73	43
Hucknall Town	42	11	10	21	57	80	43
Ossett Town	42	9	5	28	45	103	32
Retford United	42	5	2	35	31	111	17

Worksop Town had 3 points deducted.
Burscough were reprieved from relegation due to Ilkeston Town folding earlier in the season.

Division One South

	P	W	D	L	F	A	Pts
Mickleover Sports	42	28	5	9	93	51	89
Chasetown	42	24	10	8	78	42	82
Glapwell	42	23	12	7	73	42	81
Kidsgrove Athletic	42	22	12	8	93	50	78
Sheffield	42	21	10	11	75	51	73
Belper Town	42	21	8	13	83	55	71
Witton Albion	42	20	7	15	76	53	67
Leek Town	42	18	13	11	68	61	67
Carlton Town	42	19	9	14	74	68	66
Stamford	42	18	10	14	77	54	64
Grantham Town	42	17	11	14	62	56	62
Rushall Olympic	42	16	11	15	68	61	59
Market Drayton Town	42	16	5	21	71	81	53
Loughborough Dynamo	42	15	8	19	70	80	53
Brigg Town	42	15	7	20	60	77	52
Cammell Laird	42	13	11	18	51	66	50
Shepshed Dynamo	42	10	18	14	44	55	48
Goole	42	12	10	20	70	84	46
Lincoln United	42	13	5	24	57	67	44
Quorn	42	9	13	20	55	78	40
Spalding United	42	5	5	32	33	111	20Û
Willenhall Town	42	5	4	33	21	109	9

Willenhall Town had 10 points deducted for entering administration.

Division One North

	P	W	D	L	F	A	Pts
Chester	44	29	10	5	107	36	97
Skelmersdale United	44	30	7	7	117	48	97
Chorley	44	25	11	8	87	43	86
Curzon Ashton	44	25	10	9	85	49	85
AFC Fylde	44	24	9	11	91	59	81
Clitheroe	44	19	13	12	82	70	70
Bamber Bridge	44	20	10	14	70	60	70
Lancaster City	44	21	5	18	80	61	68
Warrington Town	44	18	16	10	70	50	67
Witton Albion	44	15	17	12	75	63	62
Woodley Sports	44	17	11	16	71	54	62
Salford City	44	17	11	16	68	73	62
Garforth Town	44	13	13	18	67	71	52
Trafford	44	15	7	22	73	92	52
Mossley	44	14	9	21	75	77	51
Wakefield	44	14	8	22	55	74	50
Durham City	44	13	10	21	75	92	48
Radcliffe Borough	44	12	12	20	60	89	48
Cammell Laird	44	13	8	23	66	94	47
Harrogate Railway Athletic	44	13	7	24	82	103	46
Prescot Cables	44	9	15	20	52	79	42
Ossett Albion	44	6	11	27	60	134	26
Leigh Genesis	44	5	8	31	39	112	23

Warrington Town and Ossett Albion both had 3 points deducted.
Durham City had 1 point deducted.

Division One South

Barwell	42	30	4	8	84	46	94
Newcastle Town	42	27	9	6	104	48	90
Rushall Olympic	42	26	3	13	78	45	81
Brigg Town	42	24	8	10	74	58	80
Grantham Town	42	23	10	9	69	48	79
Sutton Coldfield Town	42	23	6	13	89	60	75
Kidsgrove Athletic	42	23	6	13	88	59	75
Carlton Town	42	21	10	11	88	50	73
Glapwell	42	21	6	15	82	58	69
Romulus	42	20	7	15	71	65	67
Sheffield	42	15	10	17	73	86	55
Lincoln United	42	14	12	16	70	77	54
Goole	42	16	6	20	79	93	54
Belper Town	42	16	5	21	70	74	53
Quorn	42	11	14	17	57	61	47
Leek Town	42	14	5	23	64	74	47
Loughborough Dynamo	42	13	7	22	72	89	46
Market Drayton Town	42	13	5	24	67	91	44
Stamford	42	10	12	20	62	74	42
Rainworth Miners Welfare	42	11	7	24	53	85	40
Shepshed Dynamo	42	4	9	29	44	103	21
Spalding United	42	3	7	32	33	127	16

Glapwell resigned from the League at the end of the season.

Division One North

AFC Fylde	42	31	6	5	90	29	99
Curzon Ashton	42	28	11	3	91	44	95
Witton Albion	42	28	6	8	101	44	90
Farsley	42	25	6	11	86	48	81
Garforth Town	42	24	7	11	95	63	79
Lancaster City	42	24	5	13	80	48	77
Skelmersdale United	42	21	12	9	94	60	75
Woodley Sports	42	22	5	15	71	51	71
Durham City	42	20	2	20	81	80	62
Bamber Bridge	42	17	9	16	69	68	60
Warrington Town	42	17	9	16	69	71	60
Trafford	42	15	11	16	70	66	56
Salford City	42	14	10	18	69	71	52
Mossley	42	10	15	17	66	75	45
Radcliffe Borough	42	13	6	23	54	75	45
Prescot Cables	42	10	12	20	53	71	42
Ossett Town	42	11	9	22	41	84	42
Ossett Albion	42	11	6	25	59	95	39
Clitheroe	42	10	8	24	51	76	38
Wakefield	42	7	12	23	38	77	33
Harrogate Railway Athletic	42	8	7	27	54	115	31
Cammell Laird	42	8	4	30	34	103	28

Woodley Sports were relegated from the League at the end of the season due to ground grading and security of tenure issues. The club subsequently changed their name to Stockport Sports and joined the North West Counties Football League.
Durham City resigned from the League at the end of the season and joined the Northern League.

2011-2012

Premier Division

Chester	42	31	7	4	102	29	100
Northwich Victoria	42	26	8	8	73	43	83
Chorley	42	24	7	11	76	48	79
Bradford Park Avenue	42	24	6	12	77	49	78
Hednesford Town	42	21	10	11	67	49	73
FC United of Manchester	42	21	9	12	83	51	72
Marine	42	19	9	14	56	50	66
Rushall Olympic	42	17	10	15	52	51	61
North Ferriby United	42	16	10	16	56	70	58
Nantwich Town	42	15	13	14	65	61	57
Kendal Town	42	15	8	19	78	83	53
Ashton United	42	15	8	19	61	67	53
Buxton	42	15	8	19	64	77	53
Matlock Town	42	12	14	16	52	54	50
Worksop Town	42	13	10	19	56	76	49
Stafford Rangers	42	12	12	18	60	65	48
Whitby Town	42	12	11	19	57	80	47
Stocksbridge Park Steels	42	10	12	20	57	75	42
Frickley Athletic	42	10	12	20	48	69	42
Chasetown	42	10	11	21	50	75	41
Mickleover Sports	42	11	10	21	67	85	40
Burscough	42	5	11	26	54	104	26

Mickleover Sports had 3 points deducted for fielding an ineligible player.
Nantwich Town had 1 point deducted for fielding an ineligible player.
Northwich Victoria had 3 points deducted for fielding an ineligible player and were later expelled from the Northern Premier League after being found guilty of failing to comply with the League's financial rules.
On appeal this punishment was reduced to relegation from the League's Premier Division.

Division One South

Grantham Town	42	29	7	6	92	44	93
Carlton Town	42	26	5	11	101	52	83
Ilkeston	42	26	5	11	93	44	83
Sheffield	42	22	9	11	93	62	75
Leek Town	42	22	8	12	77	60	74
Belper Town	42	23	5	14	74	57	74
Stamford	42	20	8	14	77	75	68
Loughborough Dynamo	42	18	11	13	80	61	65
New Mills	42	17	12	13	79	76	63
Goole	42	18	8	16	72	78	62
Hucknall Town	42	16	9	17	54	61	57
Sutton Coldfield Town	42	16	7	19	72	63	55
Kidsgrove Athletic	42	13	16	13	62	59	55
Coalville Town	42	15	10	17	69	72	55
Newcastle Town	42	14	10	18	59	70	52
Market Drayton Town	42	11	15	16	61	84	48
Brigg Town	42	11	12	19	52	76	45
Lincoln United	42	10	13	19	65	85	43
Rainworth Miners Welfare	42	10	11	21	38	55	41
Romulus	42	7	15	20	56	85	36
Quorn	42	6	9	27	48	85	27
Shepshed Dynamo	42	5	10	27	45	115	25

Grantham Town had 1 point deducted for fielding an ineligible player.

2012-2013

Premier Division

North Ferriby United	42	28	9	5	96	43	93
Hednesford Town	42	28	9	5	91	47	93
FC United of Manchester	42	25	8	9	86	48	83
Witton Albion	42	24	8	10	85	57	80
AFC Fylde	42	23	6	13	93	51	75
Rushall Olympic	42	20	10	12	69	55	70
Buxton	42	18	13	11	72	56	67
Chorley	42	20	7	15	63	52	67
Worksop Town	42	20	6	16	91	68	66
Ashton United	42	15	14	13	71	66	59
Marine	42	16	11	15	61	61	59
Ilkeston	42	15	13	14	67	55	58
Whitby Town	42	16	9	17	68	72	57
Nantwich Town	42	15	8	19	63	76	53
Stafford Rangers	42	12	15	15	54	60	51
Blyth Spartans	42	15	6	21	70	87	51
Matlock Town	42	12	9	21	54	80	45
Frickley Athletic	42	10	9	23	58	88	39
Grantham Town	42	9	9	24	56	75	36
Stocksbridge Park Steels	42	9	9	24	67	106	36
Kendal Town	42	9	6	27	65	112	33
Eastwood Town	42	3	6	33	36	121	15

Division One North

Skelmersdale United	42	32	6	4	110	41	102
Cammell Laird	42	26	8	8	86	58	86
New Mills	42	26	7	9	107	69	85
Trafford	42	24	8	10	93	44	80
Mossley	42	24	8	10	83	48	80
Ramsbottom United	42	24	7	11	97	49	79
Curzon Ashton	42	22	7	13	98	67	73
Clitheroe	42	21	10	11	66	63	73
Bamber Bridge	42	21	7	14	86	58	70
Warrington Town	42	19	12	11	76	54	69
Burscough	42	14	17	11	81	64	59
Ossett Town	42	14	13	15	67	65	55
Lancaster City	42	15	8	19	70	73	50
Farsley	42	13	10	19	72	80	49
Radcliffe Borough	42	11	15	16	68	69	48
Salford City	42	11	13	18	65	79	46
Prescot Cables	42	12	10	20	51	67	46
Harrogate Railway Athletic	42	11	8	23	47	89	41
Wakefield	42	6	9	27	38	119	27
Ossett Albion	42	6	7	29	49	96	25
Goole AFC	42	5	8	29	44	89	23
Garforth Town	42	4	4	34	44	157	16

Lancaster City had 3 points deducted for fielding an ineligible player.

Division One South

King's Lynn Town	42	28	8	6	86	46	92
Coalville Town	42	25	11	6	108	44	86
Belper Town	42	23	13	6	95	42	82
Stamford	42	23	7	12	97	58	76
Chasetown	42	21	11	10	83	51	74
Sutton Coldfield Town	42	22	8	12	81	61	74
Halesowen Town	42	23	5	14	79	65	74
Northwich Victoria	42	19	10	13	88	58	67
Sheffield	42	18	9	15	85	82	63
Leek Town	42	15	14	13	72	60	59
Gresley	42	16	10	16	75	77	58
Carlton Town	42	16	8	18	67	68	56
Brigg Town	42	14	11	17	62	76	53
Rainworth Miners Welfare	42	14	9	19	59	75	51
Market Drayton Town	42	13	11	18	68	78	50
Loughborough Dynamo	42	13	10	19	75	75	49
Newcastle Town	42	11	13	18	45	58	46
Kidsgrove Athletic	42	12	7	23	75	89	43
Romulus	42	11	9	22	52	78	42
Lincoln United	42	9	9	24	64	102	36
Mickleover Sports	42	7	13	22	51	92	34
Hucknall Town	42	4	4	34	39	171	16

2013-2014

Premier Division

Chorley	46	29	10	7	107	39	97
FC United of Manchester	46	29	9	8	108	52	96
AFC Fylde	46	28	9	9	97	41	93
Worksop Town	46	27	7	12	120	87	88
Ashton United	46	24	8	14	92	62	80
Skelmersdale United	46	24	5	17	92	79	77
Rushall Olympic	46	21	12	13	79	65	75
Blyth Spartans	46	20	12	14	79	78	72
Whitby Town	46	18	16	12	82	64	70
Trafford	46	20	8	18	77	73	68
King's Lynn Town	46	20	8	18	76	77	68
Matlock Town	46	18	13	15	61	53	67
Buxton	46	16	14	16	63	60	62
Barwell	46	17	11	18	62	67	62
Grantham Town	46	17	10	19	77	78	61
Witton Albion	46	17	9	20	77	80	60
Ilkeston	46	17	8	21	81	77	59
Stamford	46	17	7	22	75	85	58
Nantwich Town	46	14	14	18	77	71	56
Marine	46	13	14	19	68	76	53
Frickley Athletic	46	12	13	21	62	80	49
Stafford Rangers	46	9	8	29	56	112	35
Stocksbridge Park Steels	46	5	8	33	60	130	23
Droylsden	46	2	3	41	40	182	9

Division One North

Curzon Ashton	42	31	6	5	92	36	99
Darlington 1883	42	28	6	8	101	37	90
Warrington Town	42	27	6	9	86	47	87
Bamber Bridge	42	26	5	11	81	45	83
Ramsbottom United	42	25	8	9	112	57	80
Lancaster City	42	24	8	10	75	52	80
Farsley	42	21	12	9	76	51	75
Ossett Town	42	19	8	15	66	63	65
Northwich Victoria	42	16	15	11	73	52	63
Kendal Town	42	17	5	20	83	84	56
Cammell Laird	42	15	9	18	65	64	54
Salford City	42	15	7	20	68	80	52
Harrogate Railway Athletic	42	14	6	22	52	66	48
Burscough	42	13	9	20	58	82	48
Mossley	42	13	8	21	73	90	47
New Mills	42	12	9	21	68	95	45
Clitheroe	42	12	7	23	55	81	43
Radcliffe Borough	42	12	7	23	57	93	43
Padiham	42	12	6	24	61	92	42
Prescot Cables	42	10	10	22	63	86	40
Ossett Albion	42	7	8	27	40	80	29
Wakefield	42	7	7	28	55	127	28

Ramsbottom United had 3 points deducted for fielding an ineligible player.
Cammell Laird resigned from the League at the end of the season.

Division One South

Halesowen Town	40	29	4	7	80	38	91
Coalville Town	40	27	8	5	101	35	89
Leek Town	40	28	4	8	85	35	88
Belper Town	40	24	9	7	98	50	81
Mickleover Sports	40	22	7	11	82	62	73
Sutton Coldfield Town	40	19	7	14	74	53	64
Scarborough Athletic	40	18	7	15	73	57	61
Newcastle Town	40	18	5	17	66	65	59
Gresley	40	17	5	18	66	67	56
Carlton Town	40	15	10	15	58	55	55
Romulus	40	16	7	17	66	64	55
Chasetown	40	14	10	16	52	59	52
Goole	40	15	6	19	60	75	51
Loughborough Dynamo	40	13	8	19	62	77	47
Rainworth Miners Welfare	40	12	10	18	52	72	46
Sheffield	40	12	8	20	69	80	44
Lincoln United	40	10	6	24	55	88	36
Brigg Town	40	9	8	23	49	94	35
Market Drayton Town	40	8	11	21	56	105	35
Bedworth United	40	9	7	24	48	83	34
Kidsgrove Athletic	40	7	9	24	41	80	30

Eastwood Town resigned from the League on 9th March 2014 and their playing record (Played 27, Won 2, Drawn 5, Lost 20) was expunged. Leek Town had 3 points deducted for fielding an ineligible player in a fixture against Eastwood Town. However, as Eastwood Town's record was expunged this has no effect on their points total in the above table.

Division One North

Salford City	42	30	5	7	92	42	95
Darlington 1883	42	28	7	7	99	37	91
Bamber Bridge	42	25	8	9	88	58	83
Northwich Victoria	42	25	7	10	75	39	82
Spennymoor Town	42	22	11	9	76	45	77
Scarborough Athletic	42	23	6	13	80	61	75
Mossley	42	23	6	13	79	63	75
Harrogate Railway Athletic	42	19	10	13	85	75	67
Warrington Town	42	19	8	15	65	55	65
Droylsden	42	20	3	19	98	84	63
Lancaster City	42	18	8	16	65	53	62
Farsley	42	18	7	17	73	64	61
Clitheroe	42	14	10	18	73	81	52
Brighouse Town	42	14	9	19	64	81	51
Burscough	42	12	12	18	62	73	48
Kendal Town	42	12	10	20	81	92	46
Ossett Albion	42	13	7	22	49	72	43
Ossett Town	42	12	6	24	48	89	42
Radcliffe Borough	42	8	11	23	49	91	35
Prescot Cables	42	7	12	23	45	84	33
New Mills	42	6	7	29	56	107	25
Padiham	42	6	6	30	50	112	24

Ossett Albion were deducted 3 points.

2014-2015

Premier Division

FC United of Manchester	46	26	14	6	78	37	92
Workington	46	27	9	10	63	39	90
Ashton United	46	24	12	10	75	54	84
Curzon Ashton	46	23	14	9	79	46	83
Ilkeston	46	22	15	9	79	56	81
Blyth Spartans	46	21	16	9	84	54	79
Skelmersdale United	46	21	10	15	58	48	73
Barwell	46	21	10	15	69	63	73
Rushall Olympic	46	21	9	16	76	64	72
Buxton	46	18	17	11	70	57	71
Halesowen Town	46	13	20	13	56	48	59
Grantham Town	46	15	14	17	64	72	59
Whitby Town	46	14	16	16	56	63	58
Matlock Town	46	15	11	20	57	60	56
Nantwich Town	46	16	7	23	61	76	55
Stourbridge	46	14	11	21	59	72	53
Ramsbottom United	46	15	8	23	66	80	53
King's Lynn Town	46	14	10	22	60	81	52
Frickley Athletic	46	12	14	20	60	73	50
Stamford	46	13	11	22	56	75	50
Marine	46	11	16	19	58	69	49
Witton Albion	46	14	7	25	58	86	49
Trafford	46	6	15	25	58	93	33
Belper Town	46	6	14	26	62	96	32

Division One South

Mickleover Sports	42	31	5	6	105	40	98
Leek Town	42	28	5	9	90	38	89
Newcastle Town	42	27	6	9	92	46	87
Sutton Coldfield Town	42	25	8	9	75	41	83
Gresley	42	25	6	11	96	51	81
Stafford Rangers	42	23	12	7	68	33	81
Spalding United	42	23	10	9	84	41	79
Tividale	42	20	11	11	65	43	71
Lincoln United	42	19	9	14	72	55	66
Coalville Town	42	19	4	19	76	71	61
Norton United	42	19	4	19	79	75	61
Romulus	42	18	7	17	69	65	61
Chasetown	42	14	9	19	60	64	51
Loughborough Dynamo	42	13	9	20	71	87	48
Sheffield	42	14	6	22	74	93	48
Goole	42	12	10	20	53	66	46
Stocksbridge Park Steels	42	10	11	21	53	84	41
Carlton Town	42	11	6	25	52	79	39
Market Drayton Town	42	11	4	27	66	109	37
Kidsgrove Athletic	42	9	9	24	48	96	36
Rainworth Miners Welfare	42	8	6	28	46	91	30
Brigg Town	42	3	3	36	26	153	12

Norton United folded at the end of the season.
Rainworth Miners Welfare and Brigg Town both resigned from the League at the end of the season and asked to be relegated to Step 5 of the National League System.

2015-2016

Premier Division

Darlington 1883	46	33	5	8	106	42	104
Blyth Spartans	46	32	3	11	89	41	99
Salford City	46	27	9	10	94	48	90
Ashton United	46	26	9	11	90	52	87
Workington	46	25	11	10	78	50	86
Stourbridge	46	25	9	12	90	63	84
Frickley Athletic	46	22	11	13	69	46	77
Nantwich Town	46	20	15	11	94	62	75
Barwell	46	23	4	19	82	66	73
Rushall Olympic	46	19	12	15	74	61	69
Buxton	46	21	4	21	71	74	67
Sutton Coldfield Town	46	17	11	18	59	66	62
Halesowen Town	46	17	11	18	53	63	62
Ilkeston	46	15	9	22	61	79	54
Marine	46	12	17	17	53	61	53
Skelmersdale United	46	14	11	21	66	82	53
Matlock Town	46	14	10	22	59	79	52
Grantham Town	46	13	12	21	51	85	51
Whitby Town	46	12	11	23	60	79	47
Mickleover Sports	46	11	13	22	50	74	46
Stamford	46	12	9	25	71	97	45
Hyde United	46	11	7	28	53	90	40
Colwyn Bay	46	10	8	28	51	95	38
Ramsbottom United	46	5	11	30	43	112	26

Division One North

Warrington Town	42	34	4	4	121	36	106
Spennymoor Town	42	27	10	5	113	35	91
Northwich Victoria	42	29	5	8	102	41	83
Glossop North End	42	24	9	9	78	41	81
Burscough	42	25	5	12	81	50	80
Lancaster City	42	18	15	9	74	57	69
Clitheroe	42	22	3	17	90	86	69
Trafford	42	19	8	15	78	51	65
Farsley Celtic	42	18	9	15	82	50	63
Ossett Albion	42	20	3	19	56	63	63
Witton Albion	42	18	7	17	85	72	61
Bamber Bridge	42	16	12	14	73	55	60
Mossley	42	18	6	18	80	76	60
Brighouse Town	42	17	8	17	75	72	59
Kendal Town	42	14	10	18	62	80	52
Prescot Cables	42	13	7	22	66	99	46
Ossett Town	42	12	7	23	51	94	43
Radcliffe Borough	42	11	7	24	54	75	40
Droylsden	42	11	6	25	68	139	39
Scarborough Athletic	42	10	8	24	40	64	38
Harrogate Railway Athletic	42	6	8	28	52	115	26
New Mills	42	0	3	39	26	156	3

Northwich Victoria had 9 points deducted for fielding an ineligible player

Division One South

Stafford Rangers	42	29	8	5	79	31	95
Shaw Lane Aquaforce	42	28	10	4	95	40	94
Coalville Town	42	25	10	7	81	46	85
Basford United	42	22	10	10	67	42	76
Lincoln United	42	21	11	10	70	46	74
Stocksbridge Park Steels	42	20	9	13	72	53	69
Chasetown	42	19	11	12	68	49	68
Leek Town	42	18	9	15	61	56	63
Rugby Town	42	17	9	16	73	68	60
Romulus	42	18	6	18	76	74	60
Market Drayton Town	42	16	10	16	65	65	58
Spalding United	42	14	14	14	52	54	56
Belper Town	42	15	9	18	66	65	54
Newcastle Town	42	15	8	19	65	68	53
Kidsgrove Athletic	42	12	14	16	81	78	50
Gresley	42	16	2	24	58	75	50
Sheffield	42	13	8	21	61	71	47
Carlton Town	42	14	5	23	60	72	47
Goole	42	10	8	24	51	87	38
Loughborough Dynamo	42	10	5	27	60	108	35
Daventry Town	42	10	3	29	43	112	33
Tividale	42	5	11	26	52	95	26

2016-2017

Premier Division

Blyth Spartans	46	31	8	7	114	44	101
Spennymoor Town	46	25	12	9	96	48	87
Stourbridge	46	25	10	11	84	51	85
Workington	46	26	5	15	73	56	83
Nantwich Town	46	23	12	11	86	59	81
Whitby Town	46	23	10	13	63	56	79
Buxton	46	22	12	12	81	54	78
Grantham Town	46	22	10	14	75	57	76
Matlock Town	46	22	9	15	68	58	75
Warrington Town	46	22	8	16	64	56	74
Ashton United	46	19	11	16	85	78	68
Rushall Olympic	46	18	10	18	60	60	64
Stafford Rangers	46	16	15	15	63	60	63
Barwell	46	16	14	16	58	53	62
Hednesford Town	46	18	7	21	68	65	61
Mickleover Sports	46	19	3	24	68	71	60
Coalville Town	46	15	10	21	71	79	55
Marine	46	14	13	19	62	74	55
Halesowen Town	46	13	12	21	46	70	51
Sutton Coldfield Town	46	12	11	23	49	79	47
Corby Town	46	12	10	24	49	72	46
Frickley Athletic	46	12	3	31	47	97	39
Ilkeston	46	7	6	33	31	86	27
Skelmersdale United	46	5	9	32	40	118	24

2017-2018

Division One North

	P	W	D	L	F	A	Pts
Lancaster City	42	27	4	11	73	41	85
Farsley Celtic	42	26	6	10	100	50	84
Scarborough Athletic	42	22	7	13	70	47	73
Ossett Town	42	22	7	13	69	49	73
Colne	42	22	7	13	74	50	72
Trafford	42	18	16	8	80	46	70
Clitheroe	42	20	10	12	74	54	70
Glossop North End	42	21	6	15	72	70	69
Brighouse Town	42	17	17	8	66	48	68
Hyde United	42	16	14	12	78	58	61
Bamber Bridge	42	16	7	19	59	58	54
Kendal Town	42	14	12	16	61	62	54
Droylsden	42	14	12	16	71	77	54
Ramsbottom United	42	16	9	17	64	81	53
Colwyn Bay	42	13	11	18	61	57	50
Prescot Cables	42	13	11	18	71	81	47
Mossley	42	14	4	24	67	87	46
Ossett Albion	42	13	6	23	47	78	45
Tadcaster Albion	42	11	11	20	57	70	44
Radcliffe Borough	42	12	8	22	59	82	44
Goole	42	9	9	24	39	83	36
Burscough	42	6	6	30	26	109	24

Colne had 1 point deducted.
Hyde United had 1 point deducted for fielding an ineligible player.
Ramsbottom United had 4 points deducted.
Prescot Cables had 3 points deducted.

Premier Division

	P	W	D	L	F	A	Pts
Altrincham	46	28	11	7	101	42	95
Ashton United	46	23	13	10	85	59	82
Warrington Town	46	23	13	10	72	49	82
Grantham Town	46	24	9	13	90	55	81
Farsley Celtic	46	23	11	12	87	69	80
Shaw Lane	46	25	7	14	79	62	79
Witton Albion	46	19	13	14	83	63	70
Rushall Olympic	46	19	9	18	73	79	66
Buxton	46	17	13	16	71	66	64
Barwell	46	17	13	16	65	67	64
Stourbridge	46	16	14	16	67	56	62
Workington	46	18	8	20	72	69	62
Mickleover Sports	46	16	13	17	68	60	61
Stafford Rangers	46	16	13	17	54	58	61
Matlock Town	46	18	6	22	69	75	60
Nantwich Town	46	16	9	21	62	72	57
Hednesford Town	46	15	12	19	60	79	57
Lancaster City	46	14	13	19	66	72	55
Marine	46	14	11	21	67	78	53
Coalville Town	46	15	7	24	70	92	52
Whitby Town	46	12	14	20	60	82	50
Stalybridge Celtic	46	14	6	26	57	90	48
Halesowen Town	46	13	10	23	48	76	45
Sutton Coldfield Town	46	10	6	30	52	108	35

Shaw Lane had 3 points deducted for fielding an ineligible player.
Halesowen Town had 4 points for fielding an ineligible player.
Sutton Coldfield Town had 1 point deducted for fielding an ineligible player.

Division One South

	P	W	D	L	F	A	Pts
Shaw Lane	42	32	6	4	104	36	102
Witton Albion	42	31	6	5	100	41	96
Spalding United	42	24	7	11	74	42	79
Stocksbridge Park Steels	42	22	7	13	67	50	73
AFC Rushden & Diamonds	42	20	11	11	73	52	71
Basford United	42	20	13	9	78	53	70
Newcastle Town	42	21	4	17	59	59	67
Lincoln United	42	19	8	15	67	61	65
Leek Town	42	18	10	14	63	63	64
Belper Town	42	15	13	14	55	55	58
Bedworth United	42	15	12	15	73	72	57
Kidsgrove Athletic	42	16	7	19	72	66	55
Romulus	42	14	9	19	65	75	51
Market Drayton Town	42	16	2	24	60	93	50
Sheffield	42	13	9	20	62	60	48
Stamford	42	13	9	20	62	80	48
Chasetown	42	13	8	21	64	75	47
Gresley	42	12	9	21	56	83	45
Carlton Town	42	10	12	20	48	68	42
Loughborough Dynamo	42	10	4	28	45	94	34
Rugby Town	42	8	6	28	44	77	30
Northwich Victoria	42	8	12	22	53	89	26

Witton Albion had 3 points deducted after fielding an ineligible player.
Basford United were had 3 points deducted after fielding an ineligible player.
Northwich Victoria had 10 points deducted after entering administration on 10th January 2017.

Division One North

	P	W	D	L	F	A	Pts
South Shields	42	32	7	3	112	37	103
Scarborough Athletic	42	30	5	7	101	42	95
Hyde United	42	27	11	4	90	35	92
Bamber Bridge	42	20	14	8	81	54	74
Prescot Cables	42	22	6	14	78	55	72
Trafford	42	17	15	10	61	50	66
Tadcaster Albion	42	17	11	14	67	46	62
Colne	42	18	8	16	68	61	62
Colwyn Bay	42	17	10	15	77	58	61
Atherton Collieries	42	15	13	14	50	55	58
Glossop North End	42	15	8	19	66	72	53
Clitheroe	42	15	6	21	69	79	51
Droylsden	42	13	11	18	67	77	50
Ramsbottom United	42	14	6	22	61	70	48
Ossett Albion	42	12	11	19	56	76	47
Ossett Town	42	14	5	23	55	77	47
Brighouse Town	42	14	4	24	59	93	46
Kendal Town	42	13	6	23	61	89	45
Mossley	42	11	11	20	57	81	44
Radcliffe Borough	42	12	8	22	51	89	44
Skelmersdale United	42	8	13	21	53	84	37
Goole	42	8	7	27	49	109	31

Ossett Albion and Ossett Town merged at the end of the season to become Ossett United.

Division One South

Basford United	42	31	7	4	101	42	100
Alvechurch	42	25	10	7	78	49	85
Frickley Athletic	42	26	7	9	117	61	82
Bedworth United	42	22	8	12	73	58	74
Chasetown	42	22	7	13	83	64	73
Stamford	42	19	14	9	66	34	71
Leek Town	42	20	8	14	80	50	68
Lincoln United	42	21	5	16	85	81	68
Corby Town	42	18	6	18	74	75	60
Cleethorpes Town	42	18	13	11	82	57	55
Stocksbridge Park Steels	42	13	14	15	75	66	53
Peterborough Sports	42	15	6	21	70	78	51
Spalding United	42	14	8	20	52	62	50
Loughborough Dynamo	42	13	10	19	61	78	49
Sheffield	42	10	15	17	66	85	45
Belper Town	42	12	9	21	46	90	45
Gresley	42	11	10	21	49	91	43
Kidsgrove Athletic	42	11	9	22	69	90	42
Carlton Town	42	10	11	21	66	76	41
Newcastle Town	42	10	9	23	49	73	39
Market Drayton Town	42	10	9	23	51	97	39
Romulus	42	8	11	23	57	94	35

Frickley Athletic had 3 points deducted for fielding an ineligible player.
Cleethorpes Town had 12 points deducted for fielding an ineligible player.

At the end of the season, the Northern Premier League realigned their two divisions at Step 4 so Division One (North) became Division One (West) whilst Division One (South) became Division One (East). This led to a number of clubs moving between the two divisions and several clubs from the Premier Division also transferred to the Southern League.

See page 134 for further details of these changes.

2018-2019

Premier Division

Farsley Celtic	40	28	6	6	82	40	90
South Shields	40	27	6	7	86	41	87
Warrington Town	40	25	9	6	69	33	84
Nantwich Town	40	19	12	9	70	59	69
Buxton	40	18	12	10	60	45	66
Gainsborough Trinity	40	19	8	13	53	41	65
Basford United	40	18	7	15	82	67	61
Scarborough Athletic	40	18	7	15	70	56	61
Witton Albion	40	16	10	14	45	41	58
Hyde United	40	15	8	17	58	53	53
Whitby Town	40	15	4	21	48	59	49
Lancaster City	40	12	13	15	42	61	49
Hednesford Town	40	13	9	18	51	63	48
Stafford Rangers	40	11	14	15	62	70	47
Matlock Town	40	12	8	20	58	79	44
Bamber Bridge	40	10	12	18	62	67	42
Stalybridge Celtic	40	11	9	20	46	62	42
Grantham Town	40	12	6	22	39	72	42
Mickleover Sports	40	10	11	19	37	61	41
Marine	40	10	10	20	39	54	40
Workington	40	8	5	27	38	73	29

North Ferriby United folded during the season and their record was expunged.

Division One West

Atherton Collieries	38	26	4	8	89	34	82
Radcliffe	38	23	6	9	73	34	75
Leek Town	38	22	8	8	78	34	74
Colne	38	22	7	9	71	44	73
Ramsbottom United	38	21	9	8	78	41	72
Runcorn Linnets	38	22	6	10	69	50	72
Prescot Cables	38	21	6	11	84	54	69
Mossley	38	19	8	11	66	51	65
Trafford	38	17	10	11	53	44	61
Kidsgrove Athletic	38	15	13	10	58	40	58
Colwyn Bay	38	15	7	16	73	66	52
Widnes	38	15	6	17	60	61	51
Chasetown	38	12	10	16	61	63	46
Droylsden	38	12	7	19	61	72	43
Newcastle Town	38	10	10	18	52	74	40
Market Drayton Town	38	11	7	20	55	94	40
Glossop North End	38	7	10	21	41	74	31
Clitheroe	38	7	7	24	45	88	28
Kendal Town	38	5	4	29	32	94	19
Skelmersdale United	38	2	7	29	24	111	13

Colwyn Bay resigned from the league at the end of the season to transfer to the Welsh Football Pyramid.

Division One East

Morpeth Town	38	28	4	6	90	33	88
Pontefract Collieries	38	23	7	8	91	54	76
Brighouse Town	38	21	8	9	74	43	71
Sheffield	38	21	6	11	81	63	69
Ossett United	38	18	13	7	65	37	67
Tadcaster Albion	38	20	6	12	71	47	66
Cleethorpes Town	38	18	10	10	90	62	64
Loughborough Dynamo	38	19	5	14	82	67	62
Belper Town	38	16	11	11	66	60	59
Marske United	38	16	10	12	63	47	58
Stamford	38	13	11	14	55	57	50
Frickley Athletic	38	13	9	16	54	60	48
Stocksbridge Park Steels	38	12	7	19	41	70	43
Lincoln United	38	12	7	19	53	83	43
AFC Mansfield	38	11	9	18	55	73	42
Pickering Town	38	8	11	19	45	72	35
Wisbech Town	38	6	13	19	43	70	31
Spalding United	38	6	13	19	38	67	31
Carlton Town	38	7	6	25	46	84	27
Gresley	38	7	4	27	37	91	25

AFC Mansfield were demoted after their ground failed grading regulations.

At the end of the season, the Northern Premier League once again realigned their two divisions at Step 4 so Division One (West) became Division One North-West and Division One (East) became Division One South-East.

2019-2020

Premier Division

South Shields	33	21	6	6	64	34	69
FC United of Manchester	32	16	9	7	73	51	57
Warrington Town	32	14	13	5	57	44	55
Basford United	32	16	7	9	49	39	55
Lancaster City	34	15	8	11	58	46	53
Nantwich Town	31	15	7	9	55	39	52
Whitby Town	31	14	8	9	54	42	50
Scarborough Athletic	35	14	8	13	44	47	50
Morpeth Town	27	14	6	7	48	37	48
Hyde United	33	12	7	14	55	55	43
Gainsborough Trinity	32	11	9	12	53	50	42
Stalybridge Celtic	33	12	6	15	42	50	42
Bamber Bridge	33	12	4	17	53	64	40
Witton Albion	31	10	9	12	40	43	39
Mickleover Sports	29	11	5	13	42	52	38
Radcliffe	32	11	5	16	34	50	38
Ashton United	29	10	7	12	40	45	36
Buxton	32	8	11	13	56	52	35
Grantham Town	32	7	9	16	38	71	30
Matlock Town	28	8	5	15	36	43	29
Atherton Collieries	26	8	4	14	36	49	28
Stafford Rangers	33	4	11	18	29	53	23

Ashton United had 1 point deducted for fielding an ineligible player.

Division One South-East

Leek Town	28	23	3	2	64	19	72
Stamford	29	22	4	3	74	27	70
Cleethorpes Town	29	17	6	6	67	40	57
Belper Town	26	14	7	5	44	29	49
Carlton Town	26	14	6	6	52	33	48
Stocksbridge Park Steels	30	13	8	9	49	45	47
Sutton Coldfield Town	28	13	5	10	45	34	44
Frickley Athletic	31	14	4	13	49	44	43
Ilkeston Town	32	12	7	13	52	50	43
Kidsgrove Athletic	27	11	6	10	42	31	39
Loughborough Dynamo	29	11	6	12	43	45	39
Worksop Town	32	12	2	18	41	55	38
Sheffield	27	10	7	10	49	47	37
Glossop North End	30	8	9	13	36	45	33
Chasetown	30	9	5	16	38	52	32
Spalding United	30	8	8	14	33	53	32
Newcastle Town	30	8	4	18	42	55	28
Lincoln United	29	8	3	18	30	60	27
Market Drayton Town	30	6	2	22	34	85	20
Wisbech Town	29	4	6	19	29	64	18

Frickley Athletic had 3 points deducted for fielding an ineligible player.

Division One North-West

Workington	31	22	5	4	77	25	71
Ramsbottom United	28	19	4	5	71	36	61
Marine	30	17	7	6	66	34	58
Pontefract Collieries	25	16	4	5	47	24	52
Marske United	26	15	6	5	50	25	51
Clitheroe	30	12	8	10	46	39	44
Mossley	30	12	6	12	37	49	41
Tadcaster Albion	27	11	7	9	40	30	40
Trafford	29	10	8	11	46	39	38
Runcorn Linnets	27	10	8	9	41	40	38
Brighouse Town	29	13	3	13	38	41	38
Widnes	31	9	10	12	47	49	37
Dunston UTS	28	9	8	11	41	45	35
Prescot Cables	30	8	9	13	32	41	33
Colne	25	7	9	9	31	31	30
Droylsden	30	7	6	17	28	75	27
City of Liverpool	27	9	5	13	32	45	26
Ossett United	28	5	7	16	38	57	22
Kendal Town	29	5	6	18	29	72	21
Pickering Town	30	4	4	22	37	77	16

Mossley had 1 opoint deducted for fielding an ineligible player.
Brighouse Town had 4 points deducted for fielding ineligible player(s) on two occasions.
City of Liverpool had 6 points deducted for fielding an ineligible player on more than one occasion.

STAFFORDSHIRE COUNTY SENIOR LEAGUE 2005-2020

The Gloucestershire Northern Senior League was founded in 1922 when 10 members of the North Gloucestershire League (formed 1907) joined together with 6 other clubs to form the new competition. The 10 clubs from the North Gloucestershire League were: Brimscombe, Chalford, Cheltenham Town, Dursley Town, Forest Green Rovers, Gloucester Y.M.C.A., Sharpness, Stonehouse, Woodchester and Wotton-under-Edge. Gloucester Y.M.C.A. had been in Division Two of the North Gloucestershire League while the other 9 had all been in Division One.

The other 6 founder members were: Dursley Rovers, Kingswood and Wickwar all from the Dursley & District League, King's Stanley from the Stroud & District League, Broadwell Amateurs whose previous league has not been found and Cinderford Town who had just been re-formed following several years of inactivity.

2005-06

Premier Division

Hanley Town	32	28	3	1	108	25	87
Ball Haye Green	32	18	7	7	57	32	61
Alsager Town Reserves	32	18	7	7	58	34	61
Newcastle Town Reserves	32	18	6	8	64	32	60
Foley	32	17	6	9	64	35	57
Goldenhill Wanderers	32	16	5	11	65	53	53
Eccleshall AFC	32	15	8	9	55	54	53
Hanford	32	16	1	15	63	56	49
Redgate Clayton	32	13	7	12	52	37	46
Abbey Hulton United	32	12	4	16	50	49	40
Florence Colliery	32	11	5	16	34	55	38
Fegg Hayes	32	9	5	18	45	77	32
Wolstanton United	32	7	10	15	36	72	31
Norton United Reserves	32	6	10	16	26	48	28
Stallington	32	7	4	21	36	71	25
Stone Dominoes Reserves	32	7	4	21	38	91	25
Rocester Reserves	32	6	4	22	28	58	22

Audley & District resigned during the season and their record was deleted when it stood as follows: 17   8   3   6   25   19   27
They re-formed and joined Division One for the 2006-07 season.
Ashbourne United joined from the West Midlands Regional League and Fegg Hayes disbanded.

Division One

Stafford Rangers Stripes	28	25	1	2	91	20	76
Congleton Vale	28	20	6	2	63	18	66
Wedgwood Sports & Social	28	15	6	7	75	43	51
Redgate Clayton Reserves	28	14	6	8	59	39	48
Foley Reserves	28	13	6	9	67	51	45
Featherstone Prison	28	14	2	12	76	78	44
Alsagers Bank	28	12	5	11	61	48	41
Hanley Town Reserves	28	11	7	10	70	52	40
Manor Inne	28	11	3	14	39	57	33
Ball Haye Green Reserves	28	9	5	14	54	64	32
Brocton Reserves	28	7	6	15	38	69	27
Holt JCB	28	6	5	17	31	70	23
Stone Old Alleynians	28	4	10	14	35	54	22
Newcastle Town Youth	28	5	6	17	40	89	21
Abbey Hulton United Reserves	28	6	2	20	30	77	20

Manor Inne had 3 points deducted.
Holditch Grandy's resigned during the season and their record was deleted when it stood as follows: 8   0   1   7   5   26   1
Wedgwood Sports & Social changed their name to Barlaston.
Ball Haye Green disbanded their reserve side.

Division Two

Chesterton	24	20	2	2	88	22	62
Biddulph Town	24	17	6	1	77	23	57
New Penny	24	15	9	0	81	28	54
Cheadle Town Old Boys	24	14	4	6	66	30	46
Ball Green Y & A	24	12	3	9	65	41	39
Hawkins Sports Youth	24	10	6	8	58	31	36
Stone Old Alleynians Reserves	24	11	3	10	62	48	36
Milton United	24	8	8	8	52	41	32
Chesterton Youth & Adult	24	6	8	10	49	52	26
Fegg Hayes Reserves	24	6	6	12	63	67	24
Holt JCB Reserves	24	5	3	16	28	64	18
Screwfix Direct	24	2	1	21	19	107	7
Tunstall Town	24	0	1	23	19	173	1

Lichfield Enots and Stretton Eagles both joined from the Burton & District F.A., Leek CSOB "A" joined from youth football, Real Macot joined from Sunday football and MS Akademik joined as a newly formed club. Stafford Rangers Under-21s, Stallington Reserves and Wolstanton United Reserves all joined as newly formed sides. Fegg Hayes Reserves disbanded.

2006-07

Premier Division

Wolstanton United	34	26	6	2	86	29	84
Hanley Town	34	26	4	4	91	34	82
Stafford Rangers Stripes	34	21	7	6	80	42	70
Ashbourne United	34	18	7	9	68	55	61
Alsager Town Reserves	34	17	7	10	82	55	58
Hanford	34	17	6	11	66	46	57
Norton United Reserves	34	16	4	14	55	54	52
Stallington	34	15	5	14	61	66	50
Ball Haye Green	34	14	7	13	69	59	49
Foley	34	12	8	14	67	56	44
Newcastle Town Reserves	34	11	9	14	60	66	42
Rocester Reserves	34	11	8	15	66	62	41
Redgate Clayton	34	11	8	15	59	60	41
Goldenhill Wanderers	34	9	10	15	76	91	37
Eccleshall AFC	34	10	5	19	54	65	35
Abbey Hulton United	34	9	3	22	49	88	30
Florence Colliery	34	4	8	22	33	80	20
Stone Dominoes Reserves	34	2	2	30	29	143	8

Hanford disbanded, Stafford Rangers disbanded their "Stripes" team and Stone Dominoes disbanded their reserve side. Florence Colliery changed their name to Florence.

Erratum

The following notes about the formation of the Staffordshire County Senior League were mistakenly omitted with notes about the Gloucestershire Northern Senior League left in their place:

STAFFORDSHIRE COUNTY SENIOR LEAGUE 2005-2020

The Staffordshire County Senior League was founded in 2005 by a merger of the Midland League (formed in 1984) and the Staffordshire County League (formed 1900). All 15 of the former Midland League clubs became members of the new league's Premier Division. They were Abbey Hulton United, Alsager Town Reserves, Audley & District, Ball Haye Green, Florence Colliery, Foley, Goldenhill Wanderers, Hanford, Hanley Town, Newcastle Town Reserves, Norton United Reserves, Redgate Clayton, Stallington, Stone Dominoes Reserves and Wolstanton United. These 15 were joined by Eccleshall AFC from the West Midlands Regional League and by Fegg Hayes and Rocester Reserves who were both promoted from the Staffordshire County League, thus creating an 18-club division.

13 of the 16 clubs who had been members of the Staffordshire County League Division One in 2004-05 became members of Division One of the new league – Abbey Hulton United Reserves, Alsagers Bank, Ball Haye Green Reserves, Brocton Reserves, Congleton Vale, Featherstone Prison, Foley Reserves, Hanley Town Reserves, Holt JCB, Manor Inne, Redgate Clayton Reserves, Stone Old Alleynians and Wedgwood Sports & Social.

The 3 missing clubs were Fegg Hayes and Rocester Reserves, who had been promoted to the new league's Premier Division, and Holditch Miners whose place was taken instead by Holditch Grandy's following a merger with Grandy's from Division Two of the Staffordshire County League. This division was made up to 16 clubs by the promotion of Newcastle Town Youth from Division Two of the Staffordshire County League and by the election of Stafford Rangers Stripes.

The remaining 4 clubs from Division Two of the Staffordshire County League – Biddulph Victoria Juniors (who changed their name to Biddulph Town), Chesterton Youth & Adult, New Penny and Tunstall Town – all joined Division Two of the new competition. This was made up to 12 clubs by the election of 6 new clubs – Cheadle Town Old Boys, Chesterton, Fegg Hayes Reserves, Hawkins Sports Youth, Holt JCB Reserves and Milton United – plus Ball Green Y & A, Screwfix Direct and Stone Old Alleynians Reserves. Penkridge Town had also been members of Division Two of the Staffordshire County League in 2004-05 but failed to complete the season and, in 2005-06, they joined the West Midlands Regional League.

Division One

Congleton Vale	32	25	1	6	87	29	76
Barlaston	32	24	1	7	85	30	73
Chesterton	32	21	5	6	83	47	68
Hanley Town Reserves	32	19	5	8	83	52	62
Alsagers Bank	32	19	1	12	75	48	58
New Penny	32	17	6	9	61	43	57
Redgate Clayton Reserves	32	15	10	7	57	48	55
Foley Reserves	32	15	4	13	65	53	49
Manor Inne	32	12	3	17	67	77	39
Holt JCB	32	10	4	18	65	70	34
Stone Old Alleynians	32	9	7	16	47	62	34
Featherstone Prison	32	10	3	19	61	86	33
Newcastle Town Youth	32	8	7	17	44	78	31
Audley & District	32	8	7	17	39	73	31
Abbey Hulton United Reserves	*32*	*10*	*1*	*21*	*49*	*87*	*31*
Biddulph Town	*32*	*7*	*8*	*17*	*59*	*76*	*29*
Brocton Reserves	32	6	1	25	37	105	19

Stone Old Alleynians moved to the West Midlands Regional League and Brocton disbanded their reserve side. Sandbach United joined from the Crewe & District League. New Penny changed their name to Northwood Town while Newcastle Town Youth became Newcastle Town 'A'.

Division One

Stretton Eagles	28	19	5	4	86	20	62
Sandbach United	28	20	2	6	77	30	62
Audley & District	28	18	5	5	71	44	59
Chesterton	28	16	5	7	57	41	53
Alsagers Bank	28	15	5	8	62	49	50
Redgate Clayton Reserves	28	15	3	10	66	47	48
Featherstone Prison	28	11	6	11	61	66	39
Lichfield Enots	28	11	5	12	51	49	38
Hanley Town Reserves	28	10	8	10	47	46	38
Northwood Town	28	10	7	11	36	45	37
Holt JCB	28	10	3	15	51	52	33
Hawkins Sports Youth	28	9	4	15	35	65	31
Manor Inne	28	5	5	18	37	73	20
Foley Reserves	*28*	*5*	*2*	*21*	*34*	*80*	*17*
Newcastle Town 'A'	28	2	3	23	29	93	9

Alsagers Bank disbanded. Congleton Athletic and Kidsgrove Carpets both joined from the Crewe & District League, Brereton Town joined from the West Midlands Regional League and Stafford Rangers Under-21s rejoined after one season's inactivity. Lichfield Enots disbanded and Newcastle Town disbanded their 'A' side. Hawkins Sports Youth changed their name to Hawkins Sports.

Division Two

Stretton Eagles	30	26	3	1	139	27	81
Hawkins Sports Youth	30	22	3	5	99	30	69
Lichfield Enots	30	22	2	6	97	30	68
Leek CSOB "A"	30	21	1	8	75	36	64
Wolstanton United Reserves	30	20	3	7	81	35	63
Cheadle Town Old Boys	30	15	7	8	58	34	52
Stafford Rangers Under-21s	30	14	5	11	77	44	47
Stallington Reserves	30	13	7	10	65	67	46
Ball Green Y & A	30	10	7	13	69	75	37
Holt JCB Reserves	30	11	1	18	50	66	34
Real Macot	30	8	7	15	44	70	31
Milton United	30	8	5	17	44	61	29
Stone Old Alleynians Reserves	30	7	6	17	56	66	27
Chesterton Youth & Adult	30	5	5	20	45	97	20
Screwfix Direct	30	5	3	22	36	116	18
Tunstall Town	30	0	1	29	8	189	1

MS Akademik resigned during the season and their record was deleted when it stood as follows: 16 1 0 15 19 84 3. Initial Spartans, Longton Harriers, Unity United and Waterhayes all joined as a newly formed clubs while Ball Haye Green Reserves and Florence Reserves both joined as a newly formed sides. Sandbach United Under-21s joined from youth football. Chesterton Youth & Adult disbanded while Leek CSOB disbanded their "A" side, Stafford Rangers disbanded their Under-21 side and Stallington and Holt JCB both disbanded their reserve sides. Screwfix Direct changed their name to Screwfix and Milton United changed their name to Barton United.

Division Two

Barton United	30	23	1	6	94	21	70
Longton Harriers	30	21	5	4	86	26	68
Ball Haye Green Reserves	30	21	5	4	100	41	68
Wolstanton United Reserves	30	20	5	5	70	36	65
Florence Reserves	30	19	1	10	86	59	58
Ball Green Y & A	30	16	4	10	93	68	52
Biddulph Town	30	14	5	11	98	70	47
Cheadle Town Old Boys	30	13	5	12	78	56	44
Abbey Hulton United Reserves	30	11	4	15	68	69	37
Waterhayes	30	10	5	15	65	70	35
Screwfix	30	9	5	16	73	93	32
Unity United	30	9	4	17	61	94	31
Real Macot	30	9	2	19	72	92	29
Sandbach United Under-21s	30	9	2	19	49	79	29
Stone Old Alleynians Reserves	30	6	5	19	54	74	23
Tunstall Town	30	1	0	29	12	211	3

Initial Spartans resigned during the season and their record was deleted when it stood as follows: 2 0 0 2 1 44 0. Unity United changed their name to Talbot Athletic, Real Macot changed their name to SFC and Sandbach United Under-21s became Sandbach United Under-19s. Biddulph Town and Screwfix both disbanded while Ball Haye Green disbanded their reserve side. Rugeley Rangers joined from youth football.

2007-08

Premier Division

Wolstanton United	32	25	2	5	95	24	77
Newcastle Town Reserves	32	19	7	6	81	43	64
Congleton Vale	32	19	7	6	55	33	64
Ball Haye Green	32	19	6	7	63	30	63
Hanley Town	32	18	7	7	61	41	61
Abbey Hulton United	32	15	7	10	67	40	52
Norton United Reserves	32	15	5	12	55	44	50
Foley	32	14	4	14	60	55	46
Redgate Clayton	32	13	5	14	58	60	44
Barlaston	32	12	4	16	36	56	40
Alsager Town Reserves	32	12	3	17	49	51	39
Rocester Reserves	32	11	3	18	55	69	36
Ashbourne United	*32*	*9*	*8*	*15*	*63*	*74*	*35*
Florence	32	10	5	17	42	71	35
Eccleshall AFC	32	10	4	18	40	65	34
Goldenhill Wanderers	32	8	2	22	45	92	26
Stallington	32	1	5	26	23	100	8

Stallington disbanded.

2008-09

Premier Division

Foley	34	23	5	6	84	34	74
Wolstanton United	34	22	7	5	95	33	73
Hanley Town	34	21	7	6	76	36	70
Stretton Eagles	34	20	10	4	64	28	70
Redgate Clayton	34	21	6	7	84	38	69
Congleton Vale	34	18	8	8	60	36	62
Ball Haye Green	34	18	4	12	82	43	58
Florence	34	16	7	11	56	37	55
Abbey Hulton United	34	15	7	12	58	59	52
Newcastle Town Reserves	34	11	11	12	50	45	44
Goldenhill Wanderers	34	11	4	19	51	67	37
Sandbach United	34	10	6	18	40	64	36
Eccleshall AFC	34	10	5	19	47	65	35
Norton United Reserves	34	10	5	19	43	70	35
Alsager Town Reserves	*34*	*8*	*7*	*19*	*40*	*79*	*31*
Barlaston	34	7	6	21	33	64	27
Audley & District	*34*	*5*	*4*	*25*	*33*	*118*	*19*
Rocester Reserves	34	3	5	26	33	113	14

Rocester disbanded their reserve side. Kidsgrove Athletic Reserves joined as a newly formed side.

Division One

Manor Inne	26	19	3	4	85	34	60
Holt JCB	26	17	3	6	64	41	54
Hanley Town Reserves	26	15	7	4	66	39	52
Barton United	26	13	7	6	60	38	46
Northwood Town	26	14	2	10	51	42	44
Chesterton	26	10	9	7	61	52	39
Congleton Athletic	26	10	7	9	53	58	37
Featherstone Prison	26	10	6	10	66	66	36
Kidsgrove Carpets	26	9	7	10	42	43	34
Redgate Clayton Reserves	26	8	6	12	48	44	30
Longton Harriers	26	6	8	12	38	57	26
Ashbourne United	26	5	6	15	48	77	21
Hawkins Sports	26	4	4	18	38	74	16
Stafford Rangers Under-21s	26	3	3	20	36	91	12

Brereton Town resigned during the season and their record was deleted when it stood as follows: 7 0 1 6 7 34 1
Featherstone Prison and Kidsgrove Carpets both disbanded and Stafford Rangers disbanded their Under-21 side. Keele University joined as a newly formed club and Stone Dominoes Reserves joined as a newly formed side. Ashbourne United merged with Ashbourne Town of the East Midlands Senior League to form Ashbourne who continued to play in Ashbourne United's place in Division One.

Division Two

Talbot Athletic	22	16	2	4	64	33	50
Wolstanton United Reserves	22	15	5	2	60	31	50
Cheadle Town Old Boys	22	15	4	3	80	27	49
Ball Green Y & A	22	12	6	4	74	39	42
Foley Reserves	22	12	4	6	67	32	40
Abbey Hulton United Reserves	22	10	3	9	65	30	33
Sandbach United Under-19s	22	9	3	10	60	46	30
Waterhayes	22	9	2	11	55	52	29
Stone Old Alleynians Reserves	22	9	1	12	46	47	28
Florence Reserves	22	6	4	12	37	51	22
Rugeley Rangers	22	2	0	20	36	90	6
Tunstall Town	22	0	0	22	7	173	0

SFC left during the season and their record at the time was deleted when it stood as follows: 10 5 2 3 37 25 17
Stretton Eagles Reserves joined from the Burton & District League, Cheadle South Moorlands United joined as a newly formed club while both Kidsgrove Athletic Youth and Keele University Reserves joined as newly formed sides. Ball Green Y. & A. changed their name to Norton Y. & A., Waterhayes changed their name to AFC Waterhayes and Sandbach United Under-19s became Sandbach United Reserves.

2009-10

Premier Division

Stretton Eagles	34	27	2	5	111	36	83
Kidsgrove Athletic Reserves	34	22	6	6	73	40	72
Wolstanton United	34	22	3	9	69	40	69
Hanley Town	34	21	3	10	78	47	66
Redgate Clayton	34	20	4	10	91	64	64
Newcastle Town Reserves	34	18	8	8	72	44	62
Ball Haye Green	34	17	6	11	72	43	57
Foley	34	15	7	12	46	45	49
Manor Inne	34	13	6	15	49	68	45
Abbey Hulton United	34	13	5	16	65	67	44
Norton United Reserves	34	11	8	15	59	58	41
Congleton Vale	34	11	8	15	44	61	41
Florence	34	10	9	15	37	45	39
Sandbach United	34	9	7	18	56	75	34
Barlaston	34	9	3	22	43	75	30
Goldenhill Wanderers	34	6	10	18	58	85	28
Holt JCB	34	5	5	24	38	84	20
Eccleshall AFC	34	5	4	25	29	113	19

Foley had 3 points deducted.
Stretton Eagles moved to the Midland Combination and Barlaston moved into Sunday football.

Division One

Barton United	28	21	2	5	72	27	65
Stone Dominoes Reserves	28	19	5	4	86	43	62
Cheadle Town Old Boys	28	19	4	5	67	30	61
Keele University	28	18	4	6	86	35	58
Chesterton	28	13	7	8	77	48	46
Congleton Athletic	28	12	8	8	53	52	44
Wolstanton United Reserves	28	13	3	12	70	43	42
Alsager Town Reserves	28	11	7	10	48	51	40
Longton Harriers	28	10	6	12	64	62	36
Ashbourne	28	10	4	14	46	66	34
Hanley Town Reserves	28	8	7	13	47	62	31
Northwood Town	28	8	4	16	58	89	28
Talbot Athletic	28	5	8	15	31	70	23
Redgate Clayton Reserves	28	5	4	19	38	76	19
Hawkins Sports	28	1	1	26	21	110	4

Division Two

Stretton Eagles Reserves	26	23	2	1	115	23	71
Audley & District	26	19	5	2	86	23	62
Florence Reserves	26	19	3	4	74	29	60
Abbey Hulton United Reserves	26	19	3	4	69	41	60
Stone Old Alleynians Reserves	26	13	2	11	67	53	41
Keele University Reserves	26	12	2	12	64	57	38
Foley Reserves	26	10	4	12	68	61	34
Norton Y & A	26	10	3	13	55	60	33
Cheadle South Moorlands United	26	9	5	12	51	56	32
Kidsgrove Athletic Youth	26	8	5	13	49	49	29
Sandbach United Reserves	26	8	3	15	74	67	27
Rugeley Rangers	26	6	3	17	37	78	21
AFC Waterhayes	26	5	2	19	47	67	17
Tunstall Town	26	0	0	26	16	208	0

Cheadle Town Old Boys Reserves, Talbot Athletic Reserves and Audley & District Reserves all joined as newly formed sides, Bradwell joined as a newly formed club, Lea Hall joined from youth football and MMU Cheshire joined from the Crewe & District League. AFC Waterhayes and Norton Y & A both left the league while Foley and Keele University both disbanded their reserve sides.

2010-11

Premier Division

Ball Haye Green	30	23	6	1	79	22	75
Hanley Town	30	23	2	5	90	31	71
Newcastle Town Reserves	30	22	4	4	90	35	70
Wolstanton United	30	18	6	6	85	45	60
Abbey Hulton United	30	17	6	7	64	38	57
Congleton Vale	30	14	8	8	56	43	50
Goldenhill Wanderers	30	14	4	12	61	61	46
Florence	30	13	4	13	51	51	43
Redgate Clayton	30	11	6	13	70	62	39
Eccleshall AFC	30	9	7	14	42	58	34
Stone Dominoes Reserves	30	10	3	17	38	51	33
Sandbach United	30	9	4	17	54	53	31
Kidsgrove Athletic Reserves	30	9	4	17	47	78	31
Norton United Reserves	30	7	5	18	50	75	26
Manor Inne	30	2	5	23	24	100	11
Foley	30	2	0	28	25	123	6

Sandbach United moved to the Cheshire League while Manor Inne and Goldenhill Wanderers both disbanded. Congleton Vale changed their name to Congleton Vale Rovers and Biddulph Town joined from the Midland Alliance having changed their name from Biddulph Victoria.

Division One

Audley & District	30	22	7	1	69	18	73
Barton United	30	21	6	3	83	30	69
Keele University	30	17	9	4	68	31	60
Stretton Eagles Reserves	30	18	2	10	62	42	56
Wolstanton United Reserves	30	15	8	7	50	38	53
Hanley Town Reserves	30	16	4	10	75	62	52
Cheadle Town Old Boys	30	13	9	8	84	48	48
Congleton Athletic	30	13	7	10	67	55	46
Redgate Clayton Reserves	30	12	4	14	57	62	40
Alsager Town Reserves	30	10	7	13	42	57	37
Ashbourne	30	9	3	18	56	73	30
Northwood Town	30	9	2	19	64	78	29
Chesterton	30	6	5	19	36	73	23
Talbot Athletic	30	5	7	18	45	78	22
Holt JCB	30	3	10	17	47	72	19
Longton Harriers	30	5	2	23	32	120	17

Barton United moved to the Midland Combination while Holt JCB and Northwood Town both disbanded. Talbot Athletic changed their name to Bradeley Town.

Division One

Hanley Town Reserves	30	22	5	3	96	35	71
Cheadle Town Old Boys	30	22	4	4	87	35	70
Wolstanton United Reserves	30	22	1	7	85	30	67
MMU Cheshire	30	18	5	7	87	49	59
Congleton Athletic	30	17	3	10	81	46	54
Redgate Clayton Reserves	30	17	0	13	75	51	51
Rugeley Rangers	30	15	4	11	76	64	49
Alsager Town Reserves	30	13	8	9	75	45	47
Lea Hall	30	14	3	13	66	82	45
Foley	30	14	2	14	73	65	44
Bradeley Town	30	11	3	16	61	74	36
Chesterton	30	9	5	16	68	65	32
Ashbourne	30	7	3	20	66	101	24
Sandbach United Reserves	30	6	4	20	49	94	22
Abbey Hulton United Reserves	30	6	3	21	41	104	21
Longton Harriers	30	0	1	29	33	179	1

Uttoxeter Town joined from Sunday football and Leek Town Reserves joined as a newly-formed side. Rugeley Rangers moved to the Midland Combination and Lea Hall disbanded. Cheadle Town Old Boys changed their name to Cheadle Town following promotion.

Division Two

MMU Cheshire	28	23	1	4	134	21	70
Lea Hall	28	22	3	3	120	35	69
Abbey Hulton United Reserves	28	20	3	5	81	41	63
Sandbach United Reserves	28	19	5	4	94	43	62
Rugeley Rangers	28	17	4	7	74	33	55
Audley & District Reserves	28	13	4	11	77	44	43
Hawkins Sports	28	14	0	14	63	62	42
Stone Old Alleynians Reserves	28	12	3	13	81	56	39
Cheadle South Moorlands United	28	11	3	14	57	46	36
Bradwell	28	11	3	14	66	70	36
Kidsgrove Athletic Youth	28	9	3	16	64	73	30
Florence Reserves	28	7	3	18	53	72	24
Cheadle Town Old Boys Reserves	28	6	3	19	53	97	21
Talbot Athletic Reserves	28	5	4	19	54	108	19
Tunstall Town	28	0	0	28	5	275	0

Whittington joined from youth football, AFC Milton, Hilton Harriers Athletic and Vodafone Stoke all joined as newly formed clubs and Congleton Vale Rovers Reserves, Norton United "A" and Stone Dominoes Youth all joined as newly formed sides. Florence and Talbot Athletic both disbanded their reserve sides.

Division Two

Audley & District Reserves	28	20	4	4	94	36	64
Vodafone Stoke	28	19	3	6	87	40	60
Cheadle South Moorlands United	28	18	5	5	94	34	59
Hilton Harriers Athletic	28	17	6	5	78	29	57
AFC Milton	28	19	4	5	112	41	55
Bradwell	28	17	3	8	107	56	54
Stone Old Alleynians Reserves	28	15	1	12	93	57	46
Kidsgrove Athletic Youth	28	14	2	12	101	62	44
Hawkins Sports	28	12	8	8	81	54	44
Norton United "A"	28	13	1	14	87	84	40
Cheadle Town Old Boys Reserves	28	11	3	14	74	78	36
Congleton Vale Rovers Reserves	28	6	0	22	48	118	18
Whittington	28	4	1	23	46	114	13
Stone Dominoes Youth	28	4	1	23	40	121	13
Tunstall Town	28	0	0	28	10	228	1

AFC Milton had 6 points deducted.
AFC Milton, Audley & District Reserves, Congleton Vale Rovers Reserves, Kidsgrove Athletic Youth, Stone Dominoes Youth, Stone Old Alleynians Reserves all left the league. Betley, Biddulph Town Reserves, FC Vibromax JCB, Florence Reserves, Hall Heath, Silverdale Athletic and Stapenhill Reserves all joined. Tunstall Town became OSSMA Blurton TT and Cheadle Town Old Boys Reserves changed their name to Cheadle Town Reserves.

2011-12

Premier Division

Hanley Town	30	23	3	4	80	27	72
Redgate Clayton	30	22	5	3	79	27	71
Wolstanton United	30	22	5	3	83	32	71
Biddulph Town	30	22	1	7	103	48	67
Abbey Hulton United	30	15	8	7	81	56	53
Audley & District	30	15	6	9	49	34	51
Kidsgrove Athletic Reserves	30	14	2	14	63	57	44
Eccleshall Reserves	30	10	6	14	66	76	36
Newcastle Town Reserves	30	10	5	15	41	54	35
Congleton Vale Rovers	30	10	4	16	43	58	34
Ball Haye Green	30	8	7	15	59	70	31
Florence	30	7	8	15	52	76	29
Stone Dominoes Reserves	30	8	4	18	37	78	28
Stretton Eagles Reserves	30	7	2	21	36	79	23
Norton United Reserves	30	5	6	19	46	103	21
Keele University	30	4	4	22	40	83	16

Congleton Vale Rovers moved to the Cheshire League.
Eccleshall AFC became Eccleshall Reserves.

2012-13

Premier Division

Hanley Town	30	24	5	1	101	29	77
Redgate Clayton	30	23	4	3	102	27	73
Audley & District	30	20	6	4	69	30	66
Abbey Hulton United	30	20	5	5	93	38	65
Cheadle Town	30	16	5	9	64	55	53
Ball Haye Green	30	16	4	10	74	53	52
Wolstanton United	30	17	2	11	70	53	50
Kidsgrove Athletic Reserves	30	15	4	11	79	49	49
Norton United Reserves	30	13	4	13	84	83	43
Keele University	30	10	3	17	51	70	33
Alsager Town Reserves	30	9	5	16	58	71	32
Newcastle Town Reserves	30	8	4	18	62	73	28
Eccleshall Reserves	30	7	5	18	52	106	26
Biddulph Town	30	6	3	21	45	93	21
Florence	30	3	3	24	39	107	12
Stretton Eagles Reserves	30	1	2	27	18	124	5

Stone Dominoes Reserves resigned during the season and their record was deleted.
Wolstanton United had 3 points deducted.
Biddulph Town and Stretton Eagles both disbanded and Hanley Town moved to the North-West Counties League.

Division One

Uttoxeter Town	32	29	2	1	148	32	89
Hilton Harriers Athletic	32	26	1	5	88	44	79
MMU Cheshire	32	24	4	4	86	38	76
Hanley Town Reserves	32	21	3	8	75	49	66
Wolstanton United Reserves	32	20	0	12	100	56	60
Leek Town Reserves	32	19	3	10	84	46	60
Ashbourne	32	18	4	10	89	61	58
Redgate Clayton Reserves	32	13	6	13	68	97	45
Congleton Athletic	32	13	2	17	64	68	41
Abbey Hulton United Reserves	32	10	7	15	58	71	37
Foley	32	9	7	16	59	70	34
Cheadle South Moorlands United	32	8	7	17	44	83	31
Bradwell	32	6	8	18	53	94	26
Chesterton	32	6	6	20	46	88	24
Vodafone Stoke	32	7	2	23	54	103	23
Bradeley Town	32	4	7	21	34	90	19
Sandbach United Reserves	32	3	3	26	48	108	12

Bradeley Town, Chesterton, Vodafone Stoke and Wolstanton United Reserves all left the league. Brereton Social and Knypersley Victoria both joined as newly re-formed clubs and Milton United also joined.

Division One

MMU Cheshire	32	26	4	2	97	38	82
Stapenhill Reserves	32	23	4	5	91	40	73
Bradwell	32	19	6	7	80	51	63
Knypersley Victoria	32	18	6	8	78	51	60
Brereton Social	32	18	6	8	70	45	60
Silverdale Athletic	32	17	3	12	76	56	54
Ashbourne	32	15	5	12	70	59	50
Cheadle South Moorlands United	32	14	5	13	58	57	47
Congleton Athletic	32	13	4	15	56	59	43
Betley	32	11	5	16	66	71	38
Redgate Clayton Reserves	32	10	7	15	62	76	37
Milton United	32	10	5	17	51	73	35
Foley	32	9	6	17	40	59	33
Hall Heath	32	7	8	17	76	106	29
Abbey Hulton United Reserves	32	7	6	19	46	65	27
Norton United "A"	32	7	2	23	60	106	23
Sandbach United Reserves	32	4	6	22	47	112	18

Bradwell, Congleton Athletic, Hall Heath, Sandbach United Reserves and Stapenhill Reserves all left the league.
Leek CSOB joined from the North-West Counties League.

Division Two

Silverdale Athletic	24	19	3	2	85	31	60
Hall Heath	24	17	2	5	117	54	53
Florence Reserves	24	14	4	6	77	50	46
Stapenhill Reserves	24	14	3	7	79	50	45
Biddulph Town Reserves	24	15	0	9	72	53	45
Betley	24	13	3	8	67	36	42
Norton United "A"	24	12	4	8	77	47	40
Hawkins Sports	24	10	5	9	52	63	35
FC Vibromax JCB	24	10	2	12	75	69	32
Cheadle Town Reserves	24	8	3	13	53	52	27
Longton Harriers	24	4	2	18	32	91	14
Whittington	24	3	2	19	38	99	11
OSSMA Blurton TT	24	0	1	23	22	151	1

Biddulph Town Reserves, FC Vibromax JCB and Florence Reserves all left the league. Betley Reserves, Featherstone Prison, Hilton Harriers Athletic Reserves, Leek CSOB Reserves, Longton Adderley Green, Milton United Reserves, Staffordshire LA, Stone Old Alleynians Reserves and Uttoxeter Town Reserves all joined. Longton Harriers changed their name to Longton.

Division Two

Featherstone Prison	26	20	3	3	97	32	63
Uttoxeter Town Reserves	26	20	2	4	66	28	62
Hawkins Sports	26	18	6	2	87	35	60
Longton Adderley Green	26	18	2	6	106	43	56
Stone Old Alleynians Reserves	26	14	2	10	74	61	44
Whittington	26	13	3	10	87	46	42
Leek CSOB Reserves	26	12	5	9	52	45	41
Milton United Reserves	26	11	4	11	40	45	37
Cheadle Town Reserves	26	10	2	14	45	67	32
Longton	26	8	0	18	40	82	24
Hilton Harriers Athletic Reserves	26	7	2	17	52	75	23
Betley Reserves	26	6	2	18	46	90	20
Staffordshire LA	26	6	2	18	38	82	20
OSSMA Blurton TT	26	1	1	24	24	123	4

Longton, Longton Adderley Green and Milton United Reserves all left the league.

Division Two was split into two sections, North and South.

Betley Reserves, Leek CSOB Reserves, OSSMA Blurton TT and Staffordshire LA were placed in the North Section and were joined by 7 new members – AFC Alsager, Alsagers Bank, Congleton Rovers, Eastwood Hanley, Florence Reserves, Knypersley Victoria Reserves and Market Drayton Tigers.

Cheadle Town Reserves, Hilton Harriers Athletic Reserves, Stone Old Alleynians Reserves and Whittington were placed in the South Section and were joined by 6 new members – Brereton Social Under-21s, Cannock United, Hawkins Sports Reserves, Real Medina (from the Burton & District League), Walsall Phoenix (from the Birmingham A.F.A.) and Wolverhampton Sporting Community Under-21.

2013-14

Premier Division

Wolstanton United	32	24	5	3	101	23	77
Uttoxeter Town	32	23	5	4	112	40	74
Ball Haye Green	32	16	11	5	70	40	59
Redgate Clayton	32	17	4	11	75	54	55
Norton United Reserves	32	15	9	8	59	57	54
Audley & District	32	13	11	8	54	36	50
Abbey Hulton United	32	14	5	13	68	64	47
Kidsgrove Athletic Reserves	32	13	5	14	49	61	44
Newcastle Town Reserves	32	12	6	14	51	63	42
Cheadle Town	32	11	8	13	52	52	41
Hilton Harriers Athletic	32	10	6	16	66	83	36
Leek Town Reserves	32	10	4	18	55	88	34
Eccleshall Reserves	32	9	7	16	58	93	34
Hanley Town Reserves	32	8	8	16	53	66	32
Florence	32	8	7	17	59	81	31
Keele University	*32*	*7*	*4*	*21*	*49*	*92*	*25*
Alsager Town Reserves	32	4	11	17	56	94	23

Hanley Town Reserves became AFC Hanley Town and Leek Town Reserves became AFC Leek Town. Uttoxeter Town moved to the Midland League.

2014-15

Premier Division

Wolstanton United	32	30	1	1	132	33	91
Redgate Clayton	32	26	1	5	114	34	79
Abbey Hulton United	32	25	2	5	127	40	77
Audley & District	32	18	7	7	74	34	61
Hilton Harriers Athletic	32	17	6	9	81	61	57
Florence	32	14	8	10	81	56	50
MMU Cheshire	*32*	*15*	*5*	*12*	*87*	*71*	*50*
Norton United Reserves	32	15	3	14	88	77	48
Eccleshall Reserves	32	13	7	12	80	59	46
Ball Haye Green	32	12	7	13	76	90	43
AFC Hanley Town	32	11	5	16	57	68	38
Newcastle Town Reserves	32	9	8	15	60	84	35
Cheadle Town	32	9	5	18	43	73	32
Alsager Town Reserves	32	7	4	21	45	106	25
AFC Leek Town	32	5	4	23	49	111	19
Kidsgrove Athletic Reserves	32	4	4	24	31	117	16
Brereton Social	32	2	3	27	34	145	9

Newcastle Town Reserves and Brereton Social both left the league and Norton United disbanded. Uttoxeter Town joined from the Midland League. AFC Hanley Town became Hanley Town Reserves and AFC Leek Town became Leek Town Reserves.

Division One

Leek CSOB	**28**	**24**	**1**	**3**	**102**	**29**	**73**
Cheadle South Moorlands United	**28**	**19**	**6**	**3**	**61**	**28**	**63**
Silverdale Athletic	**28**	**18**	**6**	**4**	**83**	**32**	**60**
Knypersley Victoria	**28**	**17**	**6**	**5**	**83**	**42**	**57**
Uttoxeter Town Reserves	28	17	3	8	68	53	54
Ashbourne	28	13	5	10	63	46	44
Keele University	28	10	8	10	53	51	38
Redgate Clayton Reserves	28	9	8	11	59	73	35
Milton United	28	10	2	16	60	83	32
Abbey Hulton United Reserves	28	8	4	16	48	71	28
Hawkins Sports	28	9	0	19	59	79	27
Foley	28	7	5	16	48	82	26
Norton United "A"	28	6	5	17	49	82	23
Featherstone Prison	28	6	2	20	36	81	20
Betley	28	5	3	20	40	80	18

Featherstone Prison and Uttoxeter Town Reserves both left the league and Norton United "A" disbanded. Stone Dominoes joined after two years of inactivity and Foley became Foley Meir.

Division Two (North)

Market Drayton Tigers	**20**	**15**	**4**	**1**	**65**	**32**	**49**
Staffordshire LA	**20**	**12**	**5**	**3**	**59**	**37**	**41**
Florence Reserves	20	12	4	4	56	35	40
Leek CSOB Reserves	20	9	4	7	38	31	31
Alsagers Bank	20	8	5	7	48	42	29
Knypersley Victoria Reserves	20	8	1	11	35	41	25
Eastwood Hanley	20	6	6	8	58	53	24
AFC Alsager	20	6	4	10	42	49	22
Congleton Rovers	20	6	0	14	36	54	18
OSSMA Blurton TT	20	5	2	13	40	72	17
Betley Reserves	20	4	3	13	22	53	15

Alsagers Bank, Florence Reserves and Knypersley Victoria Reserves all left the league. Audley & District Reserves, Chesterton, Goldenhill Wanderers, Hardman Development Centre, Keele University Reserves and Norton Athletic all joined.

Division Two (South)

Whittington	**18**	**13**	**3**	**2**	**74**	**28**	**42**
Wolverhampton S.C. Under-21	**18**	**13**	**1**	**4**	**63**	**35**	**40**
Cheadle Town Reserves	**18**	**13**	**0**	**5**	**48**	**27**	**39**
Stone Old Alleynians Reserves	18	11	2	5	52	38	35
Walsall Phoenix	**18**	**7**	**2**	**9**	**33**	**38**	**23**
Brereton Social Under-21s	18	5	4	9	36	45	19
Real Medina	18	6	1	11	40	63	19
Hawkins Sports Reserves	18	4	4	10	31	36	16
Hilton Harriers Athletic Reserves	18	4	2	12	31	58	14
Cannock United	18	4	1	13	28	68	13

Hawkins Sports Reserves and Real Medina both left the league. Acorn Albion, Barton United Reserves, Eastfield, Penkridge, Shenstone Pathfinder Reserves, Walsall Phoenix Under-21s and Whittington Reserves all joined.

2015-16

Premier Division

Leek CSOB	32	26	5	1	90	19	83
Wolstanton United	32	22	3	7	93	33	69
Redgate Clayton	32	22	3	7	79	39	69
Florence	32	19	7	6	75	40	64
Hilton Harriers Athletic	32	18	2	12	57	47	56
Uttoxeter Town	32	17	4	11	71	43	55
Silverdale Athletic	31	14	9	8	62	41	51
Abbey Hulton United	31	15	3	13	58	48	48
Knypersley Victoria	32	14	6	12	63	73	48
Cheadle Town	32	11	8	13	38	35	41
Ball Haye Green	32	11	5	16	65	62	38
Hanley Town Reserves	32	10	8	14	55	57	38
Audley & District	*32*	*7*	*8*	*17*	*29*	*41*	*29*
Cheadle South Moorlands United	31	6	7	18	29	69	25
Alsager Town Reserves	32	5	7	20	33	77	22
Eccleshall Reserves	32	5	6	21	33	71	21
Leek Town Reserves	31	2	1	28	20	135	7

Kidsgrove Athletic Reserves resigned during the season and their record was deleted. Two games remained unplayed. Uttoxeter Town moved to the Midland League and Leek Town Reserves also left the league. Newcastle Town Reserves joined.

Division One

Redgate Clayton Reserves	26	20	2	4	68	25	62
Ashbourne	**24**	**17**	**2**	**5**	**77**	**25**	**53**
Walsall Phoenix	**26**	**14**	**8**	**4**	**66**	**41**	**50**
Stone Dominoes	26	15	4	7	79	35	49
MMU Cheshire	26	14	6	6	56	43	48
Keele University	26	11	9	6	72	46	42
Market Drayton Tigers	25	10	7	8	59	62	37
Milton United	26	10	6	10	57	51	36
Wolverhampton S.C. Under-21	24	9	1	14	44	59	28
Cheadle Town Reserves	26	6	6	14	40	74	24
Foley Meir	26	5	6	15	46	80	21
Staffordshire LA	26	5	4	17	45	86	19
Hawkins Sports	23	3	5	15	36	83	14
Abbey Hulton United Reserves	26	3	6	17	47	82	15

Betley resigned during the season and their record was deleted. Whittington also resigned during the season, their record was deleted and they replaced their reserves in Division Two (South) in 2016-17. Four games remained unplayed.

Division Two (North)

Eastwood Hanley	20	18	1	1	68	15	55
Audley & District Reserves	20	13	2	5	61	34	41
Leek CSOB Reserves	20	12	2	6	48	28	38
Norton Athletic	20	10	4	6	62	49	34
Goldenhill Wanderers	20	10	2	8	52	33	32
Hardman Development Centre	20	9	1	10	44	41	28
AFC Alsager	20	8	3	9	49	65	27
Keele University Reserves	20	6	2	12	46	57	20
Congleton Rovers	20	5	3	12	52	57	18
Chesterton	20	5	3	12	31	58	18
OSSMA Blurton TT	20	2	1	17	25	101	7

Betley Reserves resigned during the season and their record was deleted.
Foley Meir Reserves, Milton United Reserves and Staffordshire Moorlands all joined.

Division Two (South)

Penkridge	20	16	1	3	77	29	49
Shenstone Pathfinder Reserves	20	15	3	2	83	24	48
Brereton Social Under-21s	20	14	1	5	76	18	43
Stone Old Alleynians Reserves	20	11	2	7	48	29	35
Cannock United	20	9	5	6	37	41	32
Hilton Harriers Athletic Reserves	20	8	4	8	44	34	28
Whittington Reserves	20	7	3	10	37	53	24
Walsall Phoenix Under-21s	20	6	0	14	34	62	18
Barton United Reserves	20	4	6	10	26	58	18
Acorn Albion	20	3	5	12	23	54	14
Eastfield	20	1	2	17	15	98	5

Whittington Reserves were replaced by their first team and Brereton Social Under-21s became the club's first team. Barton United Reserves and Eastfield both left the league.
Red Star Alma joined from the West Midlands Regional League.

2016-17

Premier Division

Abbey Hulton United	30	23	2	5	91	32	71
Wolstanton United	30	21	2	7	79	37	65
Silverdale Athletic	30	16	9	5	79	38	57
Leek CSOB	30	17	5	8	57	36	56
Redgate Clayton	30	16	7	7	78	42	55
Ball Haye Green	30	16	4	10	83	62	52
Newcastle Town Reserves	30	13	7	10	67	54	46
Ashbourne	30	12	6	12	56	53	42
Florence	30	11	8	11	58	57	41
Hilton Harriers Athletic	30	10	9	11	57	59	39
Hanley Town Reserves	30	9	11	10	44	52	38
Walsall Phoenix	30	10	4	16	56	71	34
Cheadle Town	30	9	5	16	43	63	32
Knypersley Victoria	30	8	3	19	54	109	27
Eccleshall Reserves	30	3	4	23	36	109	13
Alsager Town Reserves	30	2	2	26	37	101	8

Cheadle South Moorlands United resigned during the season and their record was deleted.
Abbey Hulton United moved to the North-West Counties League, Hilton Harriers Athletic moved to the Central Midlands League and Eccleshall Reserves also left.

Division One

Foley Meir	26	20	2	4	83	33	62
Stone Dominoes	26	19	3	4	81	33	60
Eastwood Hanley	26	16	5	5	74	41	53
MMU Cheshire	26	16	2	8	84	32	50
Penkridge	26	16	0	10	93	58	48
Keele University	26	13	3	10	79	52	42
Market Drayton Tigers	26	12	6	8	64	59	42
Milton United	26	11	2	13	72	55	35
Audley & District	26	10	5	11	60	59	35
Redgate Clayton Reserves	26	10	3	13	55	62	33
Wolverhampton S.C. Under-21	26	8	1	17	44	72	25
Abbey Hulton United Reserves	26	4	7	15	32	87	19
Staffordshire LA	26	4	2	20	37	153	14
Cheadle Town Reserves	26	2	1	23	28	90	7

Hawkins Sports resigned during the season and their record was deleted.
Stone Dominoes were promoted to the North-West Counties League and their reserves took the club's promotion place in the Premier Division.
MMU Cheshire, Staffordshire LA and Wolverhampton S.C. Under-21 all left the league.

Division Two (North)

OSSMA Blurton TT	24	22	1	1	130	36	67
Foley Meir Reserves	24	20	0	4	72	29	60
Leek CSOB Reserves	24	15	3	6	71	39	48
Chesterton	24	11	3	10	58	55	36
Goldenhill Wanderers	24	10	5	9	66	52	35
AFC Alsager	24	11	2	11	60	62	35
Norton Athletic	24	8	6	10	58	56	30
Staffordshire Moorlands	24	9	2	13	46	58	29
Hardman Development Centre	24	8	4	12	51	58	28
Milton United Reserves	24	8	1	15	31	81	25
Audley & District Reserves	24	6	3	15	29	62	21
Keele University Reserves	24	5	3	16	38	76	18
Congleton Rovers	24	4	5	15	41	87	17

Congleton Rovers, Hardman Development Centre, Milton United Reserves and Norton Athletic all left the league.

Division Two (South)

Shenstone Pathfinder Reserves	21	18	1	2	77	13	55
Brereton Social	21	16	3	2	53	19	51
Walsall Phoenix Under-21s	21	8	5	8	54	50	29
Cannock United	21	8	4	9	40	52	28
Acorn Albion	21	7	5	9	39	39	26
Red Star Alma	21	7	2	12	28	49	23
Whittington	21	4	2	15	29	62	14
Hilton Harriers Athletic Reserves	21	4	2	15	24	60	14

Stone Old Alleynians Reserves resigned during the season and their record was deleted.
Shenstone Pathfinder's first team had resigned from the West Midlands Regional League during the season and so their promoted reserve side became their first team.
Walsall Phoenix Under-21s became Walsall Phoenix Reserves.

The two regional sections of Division Two combined to form a single division.

AFC Fenton, Featherstone and NDFC joined the new combined division.

2017-18

Premier Division

Wolstanton United	30	25	4	1	105	41	79
Foley Meir	30	21	5	4	118	49	68
Silverdale Athletic	30	21	3	6	94	39	66
Leek CSOB	30	18	5	7	79	48	59
Eastwood Hanley	30	14	7	9	64	45	49
Redgate Clayton	30	14	5	11	76	73	47
Alsager Town Reserves	30	13	5	12	52	48	44
Ball Haye Green	*30*	*14*	*2*	*14*	*84*	*76*	*44*
Newcastle Town Reserves	30	10	6	14	64	70	36
Ashbourne	30	10	6	14	59	66	36
Stone Dominoes Reserves	30	10	4	16	55	79	34
Walsall Phoenix	30	10	2	18	79	88	32
Cheadle Town	30	9	4	17	55	82	31
Hanley Town Reserves	30	6	8	16	46	72	26
Knypersley Victoria	30	6	3	21	67	117	21
Florence	30	4	1	25	56	160	13

Knypersley Victoria, Newcastle Town Reserves and Stone Dominoes Reserves all left the league. Stafford Town joined from the Midland League.

Division One

OSSMA Blurton TT	**26**	**22**	**4**	**0**	**83**	**19**	**70**
Brereton Social	**26**	**18**	**4**	**4**	**64**	**27**	**58**
Shenstone Pathfinder	26	18	1	7	79	33	55
Penkridge	26	12	5	9	62	52	41
Market Drayton Tigers	26	11	7	8	47	37	40
Foley Meir Reserves	26	12	3	11	44	53	39
Abbey Hulton United Reserves	26	12	3	11	51	37	39
Audley & District	26	10	6	10	41	41	36
Leek CSOB Reserves	26	9	3	14	51	61	30
Redgate Clayton Reserves	26	10	3	13	52	50	33
Milton United	26	6	6	14	38	51	24
Keele University	26	6	3	17	33	63	21
Walsall Phoenix Reserves	26	6	1	19	45	89	19
Cheadle Town Reserves	*26*	*4*	*3*	*19*	*24*	*101*	*15*

Penkridge left the league and Norton Wanderers joined. OSSMA Blurton TT reverted to their original name of Tunstall Town.

Division Two

Whittington	**26**	**17**	**5**	**4**	**86**	**40**	**56**
Goldenhill Wanderers	26	17	2	7	74	38	53
Red Star Alma	**26**	**17**	**1**	**8**	**80**	**55**	**52**
Staffordshire Moorlands	**26**	**14**	**4**	**8**	**93**	**58**	**46**
AFC Alsager	26	14	3	9	76	57	45
Acorn Albion	26	13	1	12	60	60	40
NDFC	26	11	4	11	64	68	37
Hilton Harriers Athletic Reserves	26	11	3	12	46	51	36
Cannock United	26	9	4	13	61	73	31
Keele University Reserves	26	9	4	13	58	74	31
Featherstone	26	8	5	13	52	73	29
Chesterton	26	6	7	13	70	89	25
Audley & District Reserves	26	5	6	15	41	69	21
AFC Fenton	26	5	3	18	44	100	18

AFC Fenton, Goldenhill Wanderers and NDFC all left the league. Newport Town Reserves joined from the Shropshire Premier League and Coven Athletic, Eastwood Hanley Reserves, Hawkins Sports and Lichfield City Casuals all also joined.

2018-19

Premier Division

Silverdale Athletic	28	22	2	4	125	30	68
Leek CSOB	28	20	5	3	103	32	65
Tunstall Town	28	16	7	5	77	41	55
Foley Meir	28	17	3	8	99	42	54
Stafford Town	28	16	2	10	93	48	50
Alsager Town Reserves	28	13	7	8	64	32	46
Redgate Clayton	28	13	6	9	71	52	45
Wolstanton United	28	11	7	10	70	40	40
Brereton Social	28	11	4	13	75	53	37
Eastwood Hanley	28	10	6	12	76	55	36
Cheadle Town	28	10	1	17	42	65	31
Hanley Town Reserves	28	9	2	17	54	68	29
Ashbourne	28	7	3	18	49	72	24
Walsall Phoenix	28	5	5	18	48	83	20
Florence	28	0	0	28	12	345	0

Stafford Town moved to the Midland League while Florence and Tunstall Town also left the league.
Note: Florence's record is not a misprint. They really did concede 345 goals in 28 games, an average of 12.3 goals per game. Their biggest defeat was 25-0 away to Brereton Social and they conceded more than 20 goals in 3 other games and 19 goals twice. They did manage to hold Cheadle Town to 3-2 in a home game, their best result!

Division One

Audley & District	**28**	**21**	**5**	**2**	**91**	**37**	**68**
Abbey Hulton United Reserves	**28**	**18**	**4**	**6**	**81**	**41**	**58**
Shenstone Pathfinder	28	16	6	6	85	40	54
Leek CSOB Reserves	28	16	5	7	76	46	53
Foley Meir Reserves	28	15	6	7	65	44	51
Market Drayton Tigers	28	14	6	8	76	48	48
Redgate Clayton Reserves	28	14	3	11	71	57	45
Whittington	28	11	6	11	59	62	39
Milton United	28	11	5	12	72	71	38
Norton Wanderers	28	10	6	12	42	52	36
Keele University	28	10	0	18	61	68	30
Staffordshire Moorlands	28	6	8	14	62	79	26
Walsall Phoenix Reserves	*28*	*6*	*2*	*20*	*49*	*84*	*20*
Red Star Alma	28	4	3	21	42	119	15
Ball Haye Green	28	4	3	21	40	124	15

Foley Meir Reserves, Norton Wanderers, Red Star Alma and Staffordshire Moorlands all left the league. City of Stoke joined.

Division Two

AFC Alsager	**26**	**19**	**4**	**3**	**89**	**29**	**61**
Hawkins Sports	**26**	**16**	**4**	**6**	**62**	**39**	**52**
Lichfield City Casuals	**26**	**16**	**3**	**7**	**92**	**46**	**51**
Chesterton	**26**	**16**	**3**	**7**	**79**	**47**	**51**
Hilton Harriers Athletic Reserves	26	14	5	7	53	50	47
Newport Town Reserves	26	15	1	10	75	62	46
Coven Athletic	26	15	1	10	75	67	46
Acorn Albion	26	10	3	13	56	63	33
Cannock United	26	8	4	14	44	66	28
Eastwood Hanley Reserves	26	8	4	14	40	67	28
Featherstone	26	8	5	13	55	62	26
Audley & District Reserves	26	6	5	15	26	50	23
Cheadle Town Reserves	26	7	2	17	40	71	23
Keele University Reserves	26	2	0	24	21	88	6

Featherstone had 3 points deducted.
Acorn Albion, Coven Athletic, Featherstone, Keele University Reserves and Newport Town Reserves all left the league. Ball Haye Green Reserves, Madeley White Star, Staffordshire Victoria and Wyrley Titans all joined. Eastwood Hanley Reserves became Eastwood Hanley Development.

2019-20

Tables include results up to and including 14th March 2020 when the
season was abandoned due to the Covid-19 pandemic.

Premier Division

Leek CSOB	15	13	0	2	39	14	39
Alsager Town Reserves	19	12	3	4	38	18	39
Brereton Social	22	11	5	6	57	47	38
Redgate Clayton	18	10	2	6	48	27	32
Foley Meir	12	9	1	2	36	18	28
Walsall Phoenix	19	9	0	10	40	44	27
Audley & District	18	8	2	8	33	33	26
Wolstanton United	16	7	4	5	34	28	25
Hanley Town Reserves	14	7	1	6	31	28	22
Silverdale Athletic	15	5	5	5	31	22	20
Ashbourne	15	4	4	7	25	29	16
Abbey Hulton United Reserves	16	4	0	12	22	40	12
Cheadle Town	19	1	5	13	19	54	8
Eastwood Hanley	20	0	6	14	25	76	6

Division One

AFC Alsager	20	19	0	1	71	22	57
Ball Haye Green	17	13	0	4	48	19	39
Shenstone Pathfinder	16	9	3	4	39	22	36
Milton United	17	8	4	5	45	36	28
Market Drayton Tigers	14	9	0	5	34	23	27
Lichfield City Casuals	15	8	1	6	51	42	25
Whittington	17	6	0	11	31	37	18
Chesterton	15	5	2	8	25	35	17
Leek CSOB Reserves	17	6	2	9	38	49	17
Redgate Clayton Reserves	15	4	2	9	31	32	14
City of Stoke	16	4	2	10	35	56	14
Keele University	18	4	2	12	32	76	14
Hawkins Sports	17	2	2	13	26	57	8

Shenstone Pathfinder had 6 points added.
Leek CSOB Reserves had 3 points deducted.

Division Two

Walsall Phoenix Reserves	15	11	1	3	41	23	34
Madeley White Star	11	8	1	2	43	12	28
Eastwood Hanley Development	11	7	2	2	34	23	23
Audley & District Reserves	14	7	2	5	32	25	23
Ball Haye Green Reserves	12	6	2	4	25	25	23
Hilton Harriers Athletic Reserves	12	4	4	4	27	22	16
Cheadle Town Reserves	13	2	5	6	25	32	14
Cannock United	11	4	0	7	17	35	12
Staffordshire Victoria	11	1	2	8	24	45	5
Wyrley Titans	12	1	1	10	20	46	4

Madeley White Star, Ball Haye Green Reserves and Cheadle Town Reserves
all had 3 points added.